700 Places to
Volunteer
Before You Die

A Traveler's Guide

Nola Lee Kelsey

ISBN: 978-0-9825494-8-3
LCCN: 2010921227

Published by Dog's Eye View Media
Edited by Barbara Hautanen
Cover design by Nola Lee Kelsey

Printed in the U.S.A.

Cover photographs:

Reclining Buddha, Monkey, lady with Elephant , Macaw, Lao Children, Man at Zion NP by Nola lee Kelsey

Tiger, Hiking Boots (back cover) courtesy of Alan K. Anderson at Reflected Sun: http://www.reflectedsun.com

Disclaimer: Most project descriptions contained in this title were submitted by the organizations themselves and should be considered subject to change. They are not recommendations, but illustrations of the vast variety of volunteer opportunities available. Always check recent references and ask questions before signing up for a volunteer project. Prior to booking travel check a country/region's current political situation, visa regulations and travel requirements. Both countries and project hosts may have specific requirements not mentioned in this book.

www.TheVoluntaryTraveler.com

Dedicated to those who live for their dreams
and dream of doing good

Table of Contents

Project Listings by Location

Index of Volunteer Listings by Project Type   I

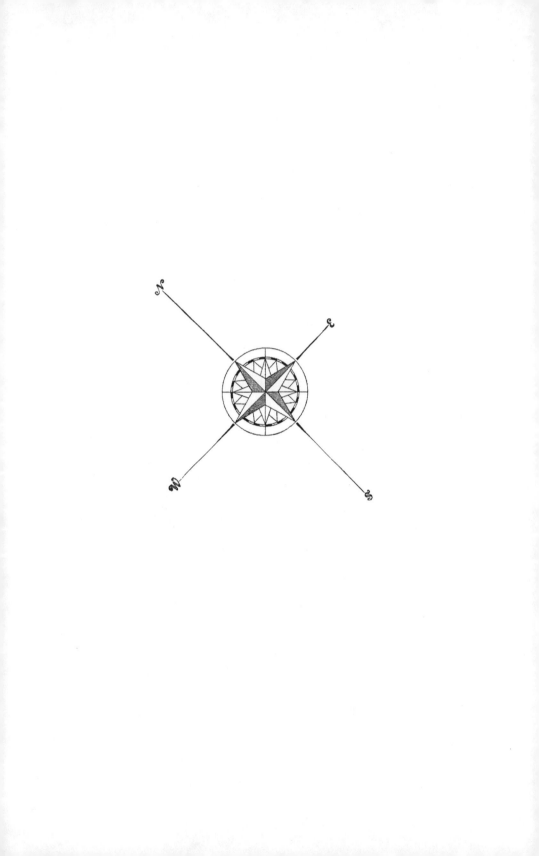

Introduction
Getting Started

"The World is a book, and those who do not travel
read only a page."

~ St. Augustine

An introduction to this title is an introduction to a world of
immense diversity and to finding your own personal style of
volunteerism within that world.

Inside these pages you will not be instructed on how to
arrange for a travel visa or ways to properly fold your underwear
in order to achieve maximum suitcase efficiency. There is an
ample supply of books, service providers and lecturers out there
better suited to help you with such issues. These pages are
already packed full and are very focused - focused on
opportunity.

The goal here is to entice, excite and even overwhelm your
senses. For the world of philanthropic-based travel is virtually
limitless. The potential is too exciting to spend time on the more
basic aspects of travel. A new definition for 'adventure' is at your
door. Step to the threshold. Begin your journey.

✦ ✦ ✦

That you are reading this book shows you have questions,
and rightfully so. You likely know you can work at an orphanage

as a volunteer, but exactly what does that truly entail? You may have heard you can live out that long suppressed 'Jane Goodall' fantasy, but can you really? Everyone knows you get those warm fuzzy, do-good feelings from volunteering, but what exactly do you do on these trips?

In short, you can do almost anything! Each teaching job has its own nuances, each animal rescue its own needs. Diversity in volunteerism stretches beyond a basic location or 'type' of work. A project's opportunities are born from a comingling of needs, cultural aspects, habitat, history – new or established – and so on.

To say voluntourism offers something for everyone would be an understatement. Consider the diversity reflected in just the titles of the 758+ (700 simply sounded better) opportunities described in this book:

- *Saving Albania's Ottoman Architecture*
- *Media TV Project in Mongolia*
- *Survey Endangered Gorillas and Chimpanzees*
- *Help Build the First Eco-Village in Burkina Faso*
- *Teaching Tennis for Blind Children*
- *Refuge for Trafficked Women and Girls*
- *Hunan Providence Teaching Year*
- *Integrated Orphanage Care, Teaching and Health – Cambodia*
- *Ecotourism Development in Nazareth*
- *Creating Affordable Housing – United States*
- *English Education Program for Children of the City Dump – Guatemala*
- *Whales and Tourism – Iceland*
- *Scotland Conservation Work Weeks*
- *Youth Fair Collaboration – Honduras*
- *Ionian Dolphin Project: Delphi's Dolphins – Greece*
- *Equine Aid to Underprivileged Working Animals*
- *Alternative Education Project in a Mayan Village*

- *Mapping Change in California's Mountains*
- *Integrated Eco-Cultural Resource Management Project in Sri Lanka*
- *Teach, Learn-Organic Farming & Sustainable Living*
- *M*A*S*H* Save Dogs and Cats - Fifty at a Time!*
- *White Wilderness: Winter Wolf and Lynx Tracking – Slovakia*

You can even send your 11 to 17 year old off on their own educational service adventure, while you camp under an Outback sky monitoring hairy-nosed wombats or while you use your business savvy to help a women's art cooperative in South America bring their products to a global market.

Each of the project details in this book are keys to unlocking over 700 doors. Peek inside. Find the opportunity that beckons to you and step through. This will be your first step down the road best traveled, a road that journeys much further than any of the typical tourism trappings, winding deep into your heart and enveloping your soul.

☩　☩　☩

As with all roads there will be bumps along the way. Often with "voluntourism" those bumps come in the form of other peoples' voices or judgments. They may say, "Don't pay to volunteer." or "Don't trust a small organization with no formal program." "Don't use some big organization that coordinates formal programs." "Volunteering as part of a tour is not real volunteering" "Volunteering as part of a tour is a great way to introduce kids or yourself to voluntary travel." It is human nature to have opinions – often on subjects we know little about. So consider the source and then decide for yourself where to begin.

Prior to the pages containing project listings, there are several chapters designed to help you make your selection of a project a little easier. Advice is provided from a diverse mix of experts in the industry. (Yes, volunteer travel is an industry.)

Their input and suggestions are tools for you to use in the forming your own educated approach to volunteer travel, thus finding your own personal "voluntary style".

+ + +

Additional sources of information are also available. Readers are invited to ask questions and receive up-to-date news online, through the *Volunteer Before You Die Network*™. The final chapter of this book provides further details for those wishing to learn more about these resources. However, in the end, you will know in your heart when you find the program that suits you best. Good project matches call out to your passions, take hold of your imagination and demand to be experienced.

+ + +

Don't go forth and conquer the world. Go forth and embrace the world fully as an equal among all living things.

You Want Me to Pay to do What?

Getting Started

When first presented, the concept of paying to do volunteer work frequently rubs people the wrong way. I was no exception. All through college I scooped poop, cleaned wounds and built enclosures (mostly held together by my own dried blood) as a 25+ hour per week volunteer. The only costs to me were those of the occasional rabies shot and tetanus booster, or so I thought. Later, as a 'real' wildlife keeper, foolish people paid me money to do what I loved. Given that lofty accomplishment, how could anyone now ask me to give up both my vacation time and my money to contribute such fabulously honed talents? The audacity!

Time changes all things, especially perspective and attitude. Recently I read a blog comment from a young man proclaiming, "Sorry to say it, but all projects where you pay money to volunteer are a scam." His ignorance rubbed me the wrong way. By scratching just below the surface a case for paid voluntourism can easily be made. Consider the following points, only then will you have the tools necessary to make an educated decision as to whether or not paid volunteer travel opportunities are right for you.

First recognize that you are not paying to work. Responsible volunteer travel providers "provide". Go figure. They supply services to you and should also benefit the projects you work on. To varying degrees, often dependent on cost, you as the traveler can expect any of the following services.

- ✓ Project information and/or training prior to your trip
- ✓ Assistance with making travel arrangements
- ✓ Airport pick-up, transfers and other logistics taken care of for you
- ✓ Side trips, escorts, translators and other assistance acclimating you to the region where you are volunteering
- ✓ Prearranged accommodations and meals may be provided
- ✓ Emergency assistance
- ✓ An onsite representative familiar with the work, the country and how to resolve issues that may arise
- ✓ Defined expectations

In other words you are freed up to share your skills, learn from the project hosts and experience the culture without sweating the innumerable logistical hassles of self-travel. Will problems still arise from time to time? Sure! Such things are a part of travel. Nonetheless, fewer hassles and a good safety net are never a bad thing to have. In addition the best philanthropic travel providers also benefit the non-governmental organizations (NGOs), nonprofits, research teams, projects, etc. which they work with by 'providing' them help in many of the following ways:

- ✓ Providers can locate (provide) qualified, prescreened/pre-trained assistance to charities and causes without the recipient of the volunteers having to administer their own volunteer recruitment program.

✓ An intermediary is available to deal with volunteer emergencies and problematic volunteers. (Yes, they do exist.)

✓ Not all charities are prepared to deal with the housing, feeding, transport and other logistical issues that come with having a formal volunteer program. Yet, they desperately need more helping hands. Intermediaries, such as voluntourism operators bridge this gap.

✓ Frequently organizations providing volunteers also make monetary contributions, donate supplies and assist the programs in other ways. Always ask a potential provider the exact ways they contribute to the programs they represent and/or the communities they work within.

These are just a few illustrations of how both travelers and charitable operations benefit from the use of a good volunteer travel coordinator program. Paying to volunteer does not seem quite as bad when you look at the realities of what providers do. And don't forget they have their own administrative costs to cover, including:

✓ Paying salaries of staff (I'd much rather help support jobs for someone who coordinates trips to help orphanages than to see all my money support some Wall Street banker's Christmas bonus)

✓ Locating and inspecting responsible projects for volunteers, often all over the world, and weeding out those that may indeed be scams themselves.

✓ Advertising/recruiting/screening volunteers and providing them with pre-trip assistance, training and information. Good marketing takes money and a unique skill set small third world charities don't always have the resources to perfect.

✓ Websites, and taxes, and office equipment – oh my!

As you see good quality organizations connecting people to projects desperately needing volunteers provide legitimate services. Often they do so at a minimum of expense and can be an invaluable tool in making sure your travel experience is both positive and productive.

Keep in mind volunteering is like a short marriage. One way or another you pay. Should you choose to go it alone, washing up on some distant shore looking for a volunteer project - that approach works for some types of travelers. Everyone has their own voluntary style. I confess, I've taken this approach many times. However, it was not free! I still needed accommodations. I still had to find places to eat and to tackle the challenges of foreign transportation. Many lessons were learned the hard (and often expensive) way. Nonetheless, that was my personal voluntary style at the time.

For the most part, it still is my approach, especially when volunteering is just one facet of a more extensive journey. Yet, as I get a little bit older, I find no shame in wanting to focus purely on the projects which I long to volunteer with; concentrating specifically on the animals, the children, the primary work at hand. Leaving lesser arrangements to someone else from time to time can be a blessing. I suspect this new forming love of singular focus and ease will grow with the passing years. In fact, the very thought of approaching a project with a poop-scoop in one hand and no worries in the other makes me grin just a little bit bigger as I contemplate my next volunteer adventure.

What Makes a Good Volunteer?
Getting Started

> "Don't ever question the value of volunteers. Noah's Ark was built by volunteers; the Titanic was built by professionals."
>
> ~ Unknown

Is volunteering right for everyone? Honestly, no. However, when approached with some thought, volunteering is right for almost every traveler. Consider that it is the nature of the traveler to have an unyielding thirst for visiting new places and a craving for new experiences. Volunteering heightens these sensations 100 fold, because the experience is real. Reality, not tour buses, adds a quantifiable quality to your journey.

Of course, we can't all be Mother Teresa. We do not need to be. Those who only know me by reputation as a serial volunteer and writer could presume me to be delicate and gentle. I assure you, those who know me in person don't often make that connection. But, most everyone will agree they likely never wanted to witness a 90 year old Mother Teresa push-boarding a sea lion into a squash cage, nor do I have any business working with children. My voluntary style, or niche as it were, is best practiced on projects where more colorful English language phrases will not be readily absorbed by the locals - then passed from one generation to the next around the slums of Calcutta. I recognize this shortfall. Luckily voluntourism offers something for everybody.

There will always be an inevitable few who show up to walk sanctuary dogs wearing white pants and high-heeled shoes or those who comment that they wish the refugee camp was located in a better neighborhood. Fortunately, these folks are in the minority. Better still, as hard as it is to believe, there is actually hope for them too.

Even those travelers who initially appear to be better off left back on the shallow end of the cruise ship's pool do harbor the potential to be fantastic volunteers. The secret is to find the program best suited to their voluntary style. Ms. White Pants may not find her glory as a dog walker, but she may be perfect for coordinating a fashion show/fundraiser for that very same shelter. Matching talents to projects is one of the biggest keys to being a good volunteer, and thus, to having a positive experience.

A large part of achieving a good match comes from understanding what is expected of you. What do organizations needing volunteers hope to see you bring to the table when you arrive at a project? I surveyed volunteer travel providers and asked just one question: *"What makes a good volunteer?"* Their answers were surprisingly similar. The following responses best summarize the industry replies.

✦ ✦ ✦

David Minich
Director of Global Volunteer Engagement
Habitat for Humanity International: www.Habitat.org

A good volunteer understands the organization's goals and is willing to continually learn more. They are curious, committed, flexible, and passionate. Dedicated volunteers work in all capacities – as builders, educators, advocates, fundraisers—to move the mission forward.

✦ ✦ ✦

Dayne Davey
Co-Director
EDGE of AFRICA: www.EdgeOfAfrica.com

Our volunteers come from all over the world, with varying backgrounds, histories, goals and ideas. This is what makes each individual so important to our projects. Every person has the ability to contribute unique aspects of themselves to their chosen project and time and time again we have seen our volunteers flourish with their ideas when applied to specific goals.

The best attribute a volunteer can have is enthusiasm! A good volunteer will want to get stuck in, learn about (and not criticize) new cultures, understand the African environment and people, as well as our own short and long term goals within each project- but most of all, have the confidence to know that, wherever your skills lie, you have the potential to become an excellent volunteer and make a difference to the people and environment of South Africa!

✦ ✦ ✦

Jonathan Gilben
Director
GoEco: www.GoEco.org

A good volunteer is someone who is open-minded enough to experience a new culture and way of life. Patience is an important virtue on a volunteer project and a strong motivation to do the tasks at hand. A volunteer should know what he/she wants to do, yet be able to cope with the unexpected.

Expect to be surprised and if you come with the right attitude you might just have the experience of a lifetime.

✦ ✦ ✦

Jill Robinson
Project Assistant
Greenheart Travel: www.CCI-Exchange.com

A good volunteer is many things; the obvious being compassionate, open-minded and hard-working, but often times it is having a sense of humor that makes all the difference. The environment and culture where many projects are located can be physically and emotionally taxing, and living conditions are probably not going to be five-star accommodations. Cold showers might be uncomfortable, but chalking this up to one more character-building experience can help a volunteer stay motivated and positive, especially when a kind word or smile can be the most important contribution in the day.

✦ ✦ ✦

Kalene Craddock
Volunteer Manager
Best Friends Animal Society: www.BestFriends.org

Volunteers come from all walks of life and different backgrounds. People tend to volunteer for a particular cause because they are passionate about it and because they believe they can also benefit from the experience. But no matter who the person, their background, and the reasons they volunteer, we, as the organizations, all look for the same things in our volunteers:

Passion: Do what you love and have passion for the cause
Compassion: Having empathy for those you are helping with a desire to help and give back
Enthusiasm/Energy: A positive, upbeat attitude is a MUST (no 'negative Nellie's' wanted)
Commitment: It shows your passion for the cause
Dependability: Willing to devote time to your cause; remember, organizations depend on you
Patience: With those you work with and work for (help)
Communication: Be able to relate to those you work with and work for, following directions, listen to other and share your ideas

+ + +

Greg Scruggs
Vice-President and Volunteer Coordinator-U.S.A.
Two Brothers Foundation: www.2Bros.org

A good volunteer does not arrive with preconceived notions, but can roll with the punches and adapt to the particular circumstances of location, culture, and organizational strength of the place where he/she is volunteering. At the same time, one of my parents' favorite pearls of wisdom definitely applies:

"Did you leave it in better shape than when you arrived?"

+ + +

As you can see, whatever the type of project, whatever organization you are working for, it is your positive attitude, your spirit, that is fundamental to a fantastic volunteer experience. By arriving with an open-mind, a determination to work hard and an honest smile, the ability to be a good, even a great, volunteer is within you. Find a project that suits your niche and set your spirit free.

Considerations in Selecting a Project
Getting Started

"We travel, some of us forever, to seek other states, other lives, other souls."

– Anaïs Nin

Now that you know what traits organizations hosting volunteers desire in their participants, the next step in matching yourself to an adventure will be determining what you yourself want in, and from, a project. Yes. I said "you" and "want".

This is not as selfish as it sounds. Everyone has different ideologies, and even physical needs which determine what experiences in life are best tailored to them. Like projects, no two volunteers are the same. It is important you be honest with yourself about what you need from the experience of volunteering. What are your mental expectations and physical limitations?

Just one example of expectations would be that some travelers are happy knowing a percentage of the fees they pay to volunteer will go to help 'global' building projects. Others may expect (or assume) it is all invested in the exact community where they volunteer. Check with your provider in advance, so you are not disillusioned mid-trip.

Physical needs reach beyond just admitting to yourself you'll likely have a heart attack scaling the mountain to reach a hilltribe school, or that you prefer hotels over camping. Considerations such as climate, even introverted tendencies, or conversely, not being able to handle isolation need to be allowed for.

Your needs may also evolve from project to project. For example, while volunteering on your honeymoon, honeyteering (seriously) is a fantastic way to start a new life together, I believe I speak for everyone when I ask that you don't plan to share a dormitory with your fellow travelers. Locking (or worse still, not locking) others out while you indulge in conjugal recreations will not endear you to anyone on your team. Please, look for a project that offers private accommodations. After a few years you may evolve to a point where even separate dormitories (or continents) will be an acceptable option for you.

Ultimately, selfishness is more likely to come from not considering your own wants and needs. When you don't think first, you, your fellow travelers and your host organization all pay the price. Negative feelings can snowball. So remember, if you can't stand the heat, stay out of the tropics!

✦ ✦ ✦

To start you asking questions of yourself that will pinpoint your personal voluntary style, I surveyed the best of adventurers; folks who are travel writers, serial volunteers or both. The question this time: *What do you feel is the most important thing for a traveler to look for when selecting an organization to volunteer with?*

Derek Turner
Travel Writer/Photographer/Volunteer Vagabond
www.TheWorldBySea.com

Trying to find the right organization to volunteer with is sort of like finding your soul mate through an online dating service. You can scroll through pages and pages of perfect potential, where every clever name is matched to a pretty picture with perfect lighting and a mysterious blur around the edges. Everyone seems to enjoy long walks on the beach, hanging out with friends, and can either dress up for a night on the town, or dress down for a casual, relaxing night at home. Then finally, after all the anticipation and bloated daydreams, you learn on your first date that the self-proclaimed supermodel is actually 20 years older than the glamour shot that first caught your eye. And instead of the "deep conversation" and "active lifestyle" he or she claimed to enjoy, the person talks in incomplete sentences and is probably only active in chat rooms.

So how DO you find your soul mate??? Well the truth is; you may not... and you may not need to. A lot of organizations will have strong points, but it's going to be hard to find the "perfect" match. What's important is that you find an organization that's compatible. Here are few tips that might be useful in your search for love and/or volunteer projects:

Know yourself: What is it that inspires and drives you? There are millions of needs out there; you might as well meet one that's close to your heart. It's hard to find your soul mate, especially if you don't know what's most important to you.

Know your partner: Dig a little bit. Ask a lot of questions before you take the next step. It's easy to get swept up in the profile pictures and pretty words, but to really know someone you need to ask questions. Ask about the overall goals of the organization and the specific goals of the project you would be a part of. Ask about their expectations. While you may want to help an orphanage in a third world country, that could mean anything from teaching kids to digging a hole to throw trash into. Both are good and helpful, just make sure your expectations match theirs.

Who's supporting who: It's not wrong to want to be with someone who is financially stable. The same goes with volunteer organizations. Often times a "volunteer" project comes with a healthy price tag. Again, that's not necessarily bad, but if I'm going to pay money to make a difference- I want to make sure my money is making a difference too.

+ + +

Joyce Major
Volunteer/Writer/Speaker
www.InexpensiveGlobalVolunteering.com
www.SmilingAtTheWorld.com

Going to a foreign country to do volunteer work for a week or a month is both a challenging and rewarding endeavor. You arrive, look around to see what needs to be done and then scatter as much good as you can in a short time before heading home chock-full of memories and with a heart full of joy from volunteering. With many questions coming up about the details of your voluntourism vacation, you may forget the most important thing...YOU!

Successfully choosing your project will be easier if you recognize what makes your heart sing and your spirit soar. What is it that you want to feel when the project is over? A sense of accomplishment for something tangible you helped create? The memory of a child's face lighting up when you come into the room? A new found passion to focus your energy on when you return home? What do you want to learn about yourself and this new culture? As a volunteer, you will be fitting your tiny puzzle piece into their large puzzle and it would be good if you first had a sense of your own priorities.

Once you have zeroed in on the details of your personal quest, I suggest volunteering with grassroots organizations that reflect your mission. Work with the founders of wildlife sanctuaries like Lek at The Elephant Nature Park in Thailand or Carol at Roo Gully Sanctuary in Australia. Travel to Languages El Nahual in Guatemala to meet Jaime, who started a school for poor children. Grassroots organizations are not catering to volunteers as a business but rather truly need your help. You'll soon be pitching in feeling like one of the family. If successful, your journey as a volunteer will end with you having received more than you could ever give.

✦　✦　✦

Barb Hautanen
Editor: Dog's Eye View Media/Serial Animal Volunteer
www.DogsEyeViewMedia.com

'Details' are the most important thing to look for in order to make your volunteer adventure a positive experience. Below I will list some important items to consider.

Location: Where do you want to go?
Rural area versus city life. I have been on projects where some volunteers were going crazy because the only thing to do at night was read a book wearing a head lamp under a mosquito net. If you want some night life, restaurants, shops, Internet, then don't choose a project in the jungle.

Climate: Tropical, temperate or cool?
When just the 'thought' of high heat & humidity makes you melt , then it is best to not choose a place located by the equator. Conversely, if you hate the cold you won't enjoy tracking snow leopards, even if you love them.

Accommodations: Do you crave privacy?
If so, sharing a room with six others and sleeping in bunk beds will make you unhappy. Many projects provide homestays so you can really get to know the local people. Just realize your hosts take their role very seriously and may want to include you in everything the family does. At my homestay, I was the afternoon entertainment for the neighbors. Since I was the only mazungu (white person) for miles, my host family would allow local kids to come in and watch me as I drank tea.

Food: Carnivore, omnivore or vegetarian?
If you are a meat lover, you might not enjoy the vegetarian
diet served at many animal rescue projects. Also, find out if
the project requires the volunteers to cook their own meals.
I am embarrassed to admit that this is a consideration for
me. I hate to cook. When volunteer cooking unexpectedly
occurred on a project, I offered to be the clean up person &
dishwasher. Not surprisingly, no one fought with me for that
position & I was loved by all the volunteers ;-)

Type of work: Do your expectations match the job?
You may choose an animal program thinking you will have
'hands on' contact with the elephants, orangutans or
whatever. But, you could end up surprised to learn that your
duties are building enclosures, planting/harvesting food for
the animals, maintenance/clean-up work at the rescue
center, etc. Or, you may want to 'save the whales', but if you
get seasick--not good. If you desire to join a healthcare
project, you have to consider that third world clinics,
hospitals, and patients can be very different from back
home. It is heartbreaking to see people ill or die from
diseases that are easily curable where you live.

Costs involved with the project: What's not included?
Prospective volunteers may just look at the program price &
think that they can afford it. But, you need to look beyond
the basics. Here are some other costs to consider: visas (can
be $10 to over $100), immunizations (some are quite
costly), you may need to stay overnight at a hotel en route to
your destination, some countries charge entrance & exit fees
and if you plan to do touring on your days off you will need
extra cash. If a project requires you to do your own cooking,
you will have to purchase food when you arrive. Then there
are personal extras--Internet fees, buying snacks, going out
for a meal or drinks, etc.

Learn more about the project: What's the inside scoop? The information given by the volunteer organization may say one thing, but in reality it could be a different story. This is where the Internet can help you. Enter the name of your possible future project and see what comes up. You can find information on such sites as Lonely Planet, VolunteerBeforeYouDie.com and similar travel pages. Or maybe some media organization has written about the project you want to join on. If you are a member of Facebook, type in the name of the group you are interested in and then join it. These pages are often full of photos, personal accounts and sometimes even videos of volunteer work at the place you are thinking about. If you have questions, you can post them on the site and get a reply from someone who has 'been there, done that'.

I hope these tidbits of information will help you have a wonderful volunteer experience. The only problem with having a great time volunteering is you can get addicted to it and end up being a 'serial volunteer' like I am!

✦ ✦ ✦

Jane Stanfield
Author of *Mapping Your Volunteer Vacation*
www.JaneStanfieldWISH.com

International volunteering is so exciting to contemplate, but before you go be sure to do your "heart" research. The best experiences happen when both you and the organization have the same outlook about the worth of the project and the value it gives to the local community.

Having a true and deep interest in the project and a willingness to do whatever it takes to get the job done is key to the quality of your experience. When you are excited and eager to get out of bed (at whatever hour you are needed) to do your volunteer work, you are in for an amazing experience. After all, who cares if you are woken up at 5:15 am by wild baboons dancing on the roof of your dorm when an infant baboon clings to you for comfort and you need to bottle feed him at 7:00 am! Where else could you have this type of experience other than on an international volunteer trip?

When you find the right project you return home filled with the wonder of the experience and the drive to volunteer again and again. With proper time spent on research you can find an organization that offers you volunteer work that fits your interest, time and budget, but more importantly, your heart!

✦ ✦ ✦

Joshua Berman
Travel Writer
www.JoshuaBerman.net

The first thing I want to know about my host organization is: How are they are connected to the local community? Who are their neighborhood affiliations and what is their role and reputation? Some of these things are difficult to assess from home, but these are questions you can ask directly to the organization before committing to anything. Having ties to a long-standing local group and/or community leader is crucial. Swooping into a completely new and foreign environment as a volunteer is much smoother when your organization is part of a strong network of active families in your host village.

If you are paying a fee or tuition to volunteer, ask questions about where your money goes and how much, if any, of your fee is being donated to a local project, fund, or NGO. Also, how much experience, if any, do your host organization and group leaders have working in the host community where you are going? More experience is better, but then again, someone always has to be the first group at a new site and there are unexpected advantages to being in a guinea pig group.

Finally, find out about language issues: Are you expected to study the language before you go? Will there be translators present in your organization or among your group leaders? Obviously, the more language you can acquire before you go (even just a few words and phrases) will facilitate making the personal connections with host country nationals, which is one of the main reasons most people decide to volunteer in the first place. Ask your organization about resources for learning the language.

✍**Editor's note:** Joshua Berman is a Returned Peace Corps Volunteer, trip leader, Spanish teacher and travel writer. He is the author of Moon Belize, Moon Nicaragua, and Living Abroad in Nicaragua. His blog, "The Tranquilo Traveler, is a celebration of voluntourism, slow travel, and other interesting ways to see the world.

+ + +

How does that old saying go? "To thine own self be true." Shakespeare must have been a volunteer. Knowing yourself and asking questions of a project host that focus on your needs and expectations will match you to the right philanthropic opportunity more precisely than any glitzy advertisement or website ever could. When selecting a project, search your heart AND use you head. Then you will be ready to truly make a difference, to discover a new way of travel, to elevate yourself while lifting up others and to truly (as the other saying goes) be the change you want to see in the world.

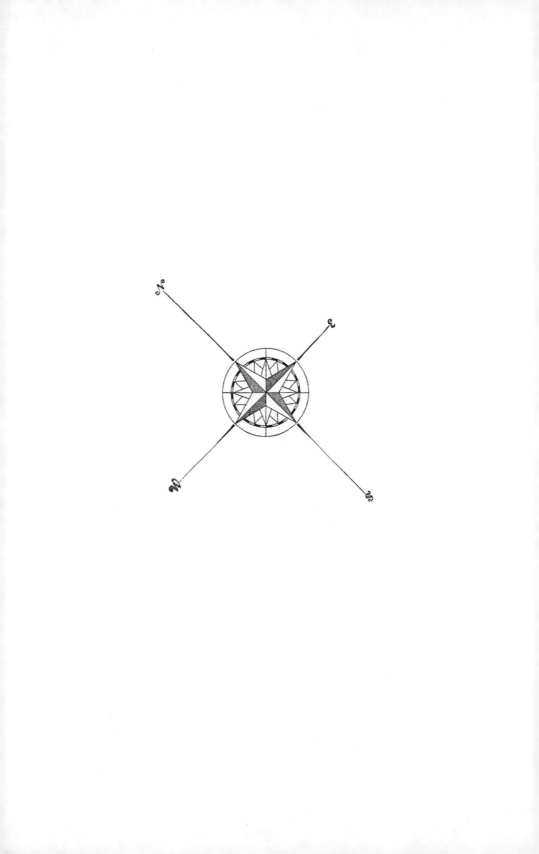

The Guide's Guide
Getting Started

"It is not down in any map; true places never are."
~Herman Melville

In the creation of this guidebook over a thousand organizations offering volunteer opportunities to travelers were contacted for information. The responses are fresh. Most of the project details were created by the NGOs, individual project representatives or organizations coordinating volunteer travel programs themselves. They were not harvested from old data found lying around the dusty basement of the World Wide Web.

As indicated in the table of contents, the listings are organized by region and then alphabetized, usually by country if not prominent destination (e.g. separate listing exist for both Israel and the Palestinian Territories). The types of projects detailed are diverse.

There are books for those who have only one specific interest, such as publications geared toward travelers wanting to volunteer at an archeological site. However it is the nature of travelers to want to, even need to, discover new things. Even if you have a feel for the type of volunteer work you are mostly interested in, running your eyes across other listings will reveal a wealth of new possibilities. The journey you had in mind when you purchased this book may be quite different from where you wind up going. Opportunities along with new twists on old concepts about voluntourism abound. Your journey begins here and now.

+ + +

Organization: The specific organization whose details are listed. This may be the charity itself or it may be a travel operator hosting/supplying volunteers for the project. For example, there are a number of organizations bringing in volunteers to work on sea turtle projects in Costa Rica. They may differ by project location, type of work undertaken, the level of accommodations, etc. Some may provide additional tours before or after your volunteer experience. Projects vary by any number of factors.

Location: This is the project's primary work location, not necessarily where the main office is based.

Cost: Prices are given in U.S. Dollars. Fee free and low budget projects have been placed at the beginning of each region's listings, making them easier to find. The cost should be considered a starting point and also subject to change. Nonetheless, it is a good indicator of whether a volunteer opportunity falls within your particular budget constraints.

Duration: Many volunteer projects have set durations. A summer camp for at risk youth may need volunteer counselors to stay for the entire five weeks of the camp. Teaching projects may last a semester or a year. Other opportunities such as a wildlife rescue may require a minimum stay of two weeks, but no maximum (beyond what the country's visa requirements allow). A set duration insures that the investment a project makes in training you is worth their time. On the flip side, some facilities, such as an orphanage or even dog rescues, may be grateful just to have folks stop in for half a day, be it to play with the kids or socialize the pups.

Age: In most cases volunteer projects are for those 18 years and older. Some, right or wrong, have maximum age limits. There are also a nice selection of projects available which are suitable for families. Some organizations even specialize in 'give-back' travel and service tours designed specifically for teens, high school classes and the like. To readily locate these specialized opportunities see this book's *Index of Volunteer Listings by Project Type.*

Contact: Contacts for organizations are usually listed as an email address, although some have provided phone numbers as well. Please be respectful of an organizations time. Read all the project details and visit their website prior to asking for further information.

Learn more: Once you find a project that intrigues you, the best place to gather further details will almost always be a website. Be careful though. Once you visit their site, you will often find that an organization offering one opportunity that gives you a rush of excitement tends to offer many projects that speak to you. This is how serial volunteers are first conceived. Thus far, there is no cure for this condition.

Special skills: Many volunteer opportunities are open to everyone. Some train you as part of the experience. Other times organizations are in great need of people with very specific skills, such as doctors, veterinary nurses, builders, people with experience in marketing or fair trade, etc. If you see a project you desperately want to work on and your skills do not match the description, it never hurts to contact the organization. Talk to them. You may be able to show them how your unique experience is related and beneficial. Exchanging knowledge and ideas is one of the most rewarding parts of the volunteer process.

Details: This is where readers can get a better feel for the specific project and often for the host organization itself.

✦ ✦ ✦

As with all things in life the usual disclaimers should be kept in mind. Information in the book may change. Volunteer organizations grow. They close. They alter their focus. Please always check recent references and, of course, practice safe travel.

Beyond common sense there are several additional tools now at your disposal. In the final chapter of this book, The Volunteer Before You Die Network, a support system for volunteers is laid out. Readers of *700 Places to Volunteer Before You Die* and *The Voluntary Traveler: Adventures from the Road Best Traveled* can network with other like-minded adventurers, sharing information, tips, experiences and more. Join the conversation.

South America
Volunteer Opportunities

"Only with a burning patience can we conquer the splendid City which will give light, justice and dignity to all mankind. In this way the song will not have been sung in vain."

~ Pablo Neruda

Argentina

Support Communities Affected by Mining

Organization: Asociación MAPU/Assembly of Self-Organized Neighbours against Mining of Esquel
Location: Esquel, Patagonia
Cost: $550 includes MAPU membership and 1 month's accommodation
Duration: 1+ month **Age:** 18
Contact: info@patagoniavolunteer.org
Learn more: www.patagoniavolunteer.org
Special skills: Intermediate level of Spanish plus English, German, French or Italian as mother tongue
Details: MAPU Association is currently cooperating with the Assembly of Self-Organized Neighbours against Mining of Esquel on the national and international awareness campaign regarding the issue of communities affected by mining. The goal is to raise awareness about the environmental, social and economic dangers of metal mining exploitation, as well as to expose the ways in which foreign governments, financial entities, the international mining-lobby, etc. promote the plundering of developing countries. The activities related

to this volunteering placement include: edition and translation of texts, coordination and follow-up of virtual volunteers, searching and processing information, developing presentations, writing reports and press releases, contacting other communities affected by mining, assisting in the organization and coordination of activities (talks, assemblies, meetings), raising awareness about this issue, participating in meetings, assemblies, etc.

Community Radio Operator

Organization: Asociación MAPU/Kalweche FM 909
Location: Esquel, Patagonia
Cost: $550 includes MAPU membership and 1 month's accommodation
Duration: 1+ month **Age:** 18
Contact: info@patagoniavolunteer.org
Learn more: www.patagoniavolunteer.org
Special skills: Studies or experience as a radio technician/operator
Details: One of the Education and Culture projects promoted by MAPU Association is the organization of an FM community radio station in the city of Esquel, where MAPU is based in Patagonia. As a volunteer in the Community Radio Operator program, you will be responsible for controlling the broadcast equipment, carrying out broadcasting activities, mixing sounds and other tasks related to the functioning of the community radio station. Also, according to your experience, you will be able to help with setting up the studio, organize the production equipment, control the acoustic balance of the studio, etc.

Tutoring Children and Teenagers

Organization: Asociación MAPU/Asociación Barrial
Location: Esquel, Patagonia
Cost: $550 includes MAPU membership and 1 month's accommodation
Duration: 2+ months, flexible maximum **Age:** 18
Contact: info@patagoniavolunteer.org
Learn more: www.patagoniavolunteer.org
Special skills: Studies and/or experience in the field of education and the treatment of children and/or teenagers.
Details: The Barrio Badén organization provides social support to children, teenagers and adults of the Baden neighbourhood in the Patagonian city of Esquel. Children of different ages participate in free activities during the morning and then have breakfast and lunch at the project site. During the afternoon several workshops are offered to both children and adults, such as: cooking, sewing, handcrafts, computer literacy, etc. Your responsibility will be to tutor children and teenagers

through workshops and non-formal educational activities on the organization's premises. Activities will be organized according to your experience, preference and the interests of the participants. Some of the possible options are: music workshops, sports, games and outdoor activities, radio and communication workshop, computer literacy classes and handcrafts workshops.

Collaboration on Solidarity Website Development

Organization: Asociación MAPU
Location: Esquel, Patagonia
Cost: $550 includes MAPU membership and 1 month's accommodation
Duration: 1+ month **Age:** 18
Contact: info@patagoniavolunteer.org
Learn more: www.patagoniavolunteer.org
Special skills: Some knowledge of web development
Details: The Solidarity Websites project is one of the regional development projects that MAPU Association offers. Solidarity websites are intended for non-profit organizations and groups in Patagonia who benefit from having a web presence to facilitate their activities and achieve their objectives. Some of the solidarity websites that MAPU Association has developed are: www.noalamina.org, www.santarosarecuperada.com.ar, www.asociacion-piuke.org.ar, www.mapuzungunchubut.com.ar. With your skills you can be a part of bringing a small community into the World Wide Web, helping to lay the groundwork for their future.

Outdoor Activities and Education

Organization: Asociación MAPU/The Club Andino Cholila
Location: Cholila, Patagonia
Cost: $550 includes MAPU membership and 1 month's accommodation
Duration: 1+ month **Age:** 18
Contact: info@patagoniavolunteer.org
Learn more: www.patagoniavolunteer.org
Special skills: Intermediate level of Spanish, decent physical shape
Details: Volunteer in specialized areas of this one program.
1) Environmental Education: creating trail/topography maps of the region, designing a brochure, recording the songs of singing birds, putting together a brochure about native species, drawing/designing a constellation sky map, running environmental education workshops and outdoor activities for kids and teenagers, etc. 2) Maintenance and Recovery of the Region: removing trash from the shores of the nearby

31

river and lake; cutting away bushes and roots to eliminate a certain species of "Rose Hip"; clearing and marking new hiking trails; etc. 3) Organic Farming: creating an herb garden, gardening, harvesting and picking fruits/vegetables, etc. 4) Construction: gathering and placing stones, gravel and sand for construction purposes; completing masonry and carpentry projects; etc. Other Activities: gathering firewood for heating; making and dispersing yellow-jacket traps; installing water filters; exploring; cooking; etc.

Assisting People with Disabilities

Organization: Asociación MAPU/The Centre for Work Integration
Location: Esquel, Patagonia
Cost: $550 includes MAPU membership and 1 month's accommodation
Duration: 2+ months   **Age:** 18
Contact: info@patagoniavolunteer.org
Learn more: www.patagoniavolunteer.org
Special skills: Studies or experience in working with people with disabilities and the ability to work and communicate with people with diverse levels of mental/physical disability.
Details: This volunteer position involves assisting with the daily tasks of The Centre for Work Integration helping teachers and other personnel. Volunteers work Monday to Friday either in the mornings or the afternoons.

Eco Volunteering and Project Puma

Organization: El Eden Flora and Fauna
Location: Villa Rumipal, Cordoba, Argentina.
Cost: $600 per month includes accommodations, meals & private bathroom
Duration: 1+ month   **Age:** 18 (less with parental authorization)
Contact: marianacarrascosa@yahoo.com.ar - phone: 0054 351 154085198.
Learn more: www.eledenflorayfauna.org
Special skills: Love for animals, care for nature
Details: El Eden Flora and Fauna is 25 hectares with 350 animals representing about 40 different species, most living free. Volunteers do feeding, cleaning, breeding, build/repair, horse riding, veterinary help, learn about flora and fauna and have real and meaningful contact with animals.

Helping Hands

Organization: Academia Buenos Aires
Location: Buenos Aires, Argentina

Cost: None (if volunteer takes 4 weeks of Spanish lessons with the organization at $200 per week) **Duration:** 1+ Months **Age:** 18
Contact: info@academiabuenosaires.com
Learn more: www.academiabuenosaires.com
Special skills: An intermediate level of Spanish
Details: This project offers a variety of activities and offers you the possibility to help where it is needed in 3 different neighborhoods of Buenos Aires (La Boca, Villa Soldati and Parque Patricios). Volunteers can help in a community centre that benefits the people in the neighborhood, running a soup kitchen and offering computer and English lessons and educational reinforcement for the kids. At a daycare center the children of the neighborhood need school support and people who care about their continuous education. This also includes recreational activities. Another project is helping children that are HIV positive (between 6 and 16 years old). Volunteers help the coordinators of the home to organize the different activities such as: music, English, computation, school support, sports or chess.

Stay Together

Organization: Academia Buenos Aires
Location: Buenos Aires
Cost: None (if volunteer takes 4 weeks of Spanish lessons with the organization at $200 per week)
Duration: 1+ month **Age:** 18
Contact: info@academiabuenosaires.com
Learn more: www.academiabuenosaires.com
Special skills: An intermediate level of Spanish
Details: This project has its focus on improving the standard of living of the low and medium income families – such as housing, security, education and pollution. Help is needed in different parts of Buenos Aires. Through a neighborhood association they fight for self empowerment, so that the community itself can take the initiative to solve the problems they confront. There is also a children daycare centre offering school support, music, dance, cooking, yoga, English, arts, soccer and sports, computer classes and workshops. For adults they offer English lessons and a literacy program.

Caring Angels

Organization: Academia Buenos Aires
Location: Buenos Aires
Cost: None (if volunteer takes 4 weeks of Spanish lessons with the organization at $200 per week) **Duration:** 1+ month **Age:** 18
Contact: info@academiabuenosaires.com
Learn more: www.academiabuenosaires.com
Special skills: An intermediate level of Spanish

Details: Volunteers are needed in three homes for orphans or children, whose parents cannot care for them. Some of the children are HIV positive; others experienced mistreatment and neglect, family violence or sexual abuse. The children are between 6 months and 18 years old (but mostly under the age of 10), live on site and go to school half a day. Volunteers who have experience in working with children are particularly needed!

Black Howler Monkey Rehabilitation

Organization: Refugio Monos de Caraya
Location: La Cumbre (near Cordoba)
Cost: $730 for 3 weeks, $875 for 1 month, $1,170 2 months...

Duration: 3 weeks to 3 month or possibly longer **Age:** 18
Contact: carayaproject@yahoo.com.ar
Learn more: www.volunteer-with-howler-monkeys.org
Special skills: Love of animals, patience, some Spanish
Details: Volunteers help in the daily running of the center: prepare food for monkeys, clean enclosures, and assist with medical treatments. Good food and very basic accommodations are provided. The centre is located in a very remote area.

Soup Kitchen Volunteerism

Organization: Experiential Learning International
Location: Buenos Aires
Cost: $945+ **Duration:** 4+ weeks **Age:** 18
Contact: info@eliabroad.org **Learn more:** www.eliabroad.org
Special skills: Intermediate Spanish Language Skills
Details: According to some Argentine organizations, around 100 people in Argentina die every day due to malnourishment or hunger related disease. Thousands of people in Buenos Aires depend on soup kitchens as a daily source of food. The kitchens welcome volunteers to assist with preparing and serving meals as well as cleaning up and interacting with the people who come in for meals. Volunteers are also welcome to help with other projects such as clothing donation drives, youth programs and distribution of food baskets and medical supplies.

Helping Non-Profits Succeed in Beautiful Cordoba

Organization: Fundación AFOS
Location: Cordoba, Argentina at the base of breath-taking "Sierras".
Cost: $490+ includes pick up, lodging, orientation, certificate & more
Duration: 2 to 52 weeks **Age:** 18

Contact: afos@fundacionafos.org.ar
Learn more: www.fundacionafos.org.ar
Special skills: Intermediate Spanish - reinforcing classes can be arranged
Details: Fundación AFOS is a non-profit whose mission is to assist the consolidation and growth of other small and midsized nonprofits in the city of Córdoba, Argentina. Its main objective is to generate initiatives, projects and tools for these organizations to carry out their daily tasks and achieve their long-term goals. For each project, Fundación AFOS combines their experience and resources with the help of foreign volunteers who contribute their time, energy and know-how to support our mission. Thus, volunteer participation is key as the talent and knowledge they bring to our organizations reinforce the quality and effectiveness of the programs. Volunteer opportunities are diverse, ranging anywhere from helping children in poor settings to assisting in strategic planning and marketing.

Animal Conservation
Organization: uVolunteer
Location: Cordoba, Calamuchita Valley
Cost: $1,230 for the first month; $125 each additional week
Duration: 1+ month **Age:** 18
Contact: info@uvolunteer.org **Learn more:** www.uvolunteer.org
Special skills: Intermediate Spanish
Details: While volunteering in Argentina, you will be working with the local community to protect and conserve endangered animals, wildlife and their surrounding environment. There are a growing number of animals so volunteers are needed to help watch over the conservation effort. The main goal of this project is the conservation of certain endangered species in Córdoba. This project is based in a private park, where volunteers will assist in the care and conservation of the environment and wildlife. Not enough local volunteers are available to provide proper oversight on the growing numbers of animals; thus they need the help of international volunteers. Three meals will be provided daily and you will stay with a local Argentinean family.

Women's Rights Center
Organization: uVolunteer
Location: Cordoba, the heart of Argentina
Cost: $1,230 for the first month; $125 each additional week
Duration: 1+ months **Age:** 18
Contact: info@uvolunteer.org **Learn more:** www.uvolunteer.org
Special skills: Intermediate Spanish

Details: The goal of this project is to educate the local community about women's rights and to promote the empowerment of women. Volunteers will be working in a women's center that strives for a more just and peaceful Argentina. Volunteers will be motivating the women of Córdoba to practice their rights. Through various activities, volunteers will educate women about the prevention of, and assistance for, domestic violence, personal development and health, as well as other social issues.

Teaching English in Cordoba

Organization: uVolunteer
Location: Cordoba, the heart of Argentina
Cost: $1,230 for the first month; $125 for each additional week
Duration: 1+ month **Age:** 18
Contact: info@uvolunteer.org **Learn more:** www.uvolunteer.org
Special skills: Intermediate Spanish
Details: Teaching English projects in Argentina help develop the local community by sending volunteers to teach English language skills to children. This private, non-profit organization aims to improve the quality of life in an important area in Córdoba. They started as a small open library located in a poor area on the east side of Córdoba city. Since then, the organization has been very successful in improving the living conditions of the local population, from a cultural, social and economic perspective. The government of Córdoba established a cultural center in the city, and together, they have the capacity to organize different kinds of cultural and educational events.

Other organizations offering projects in Argentina:
Center for Cultural Interchange: www.cci-exchange.com
Connect 123: www.connect-123.com
Fundación Banco de Alimentos (food bank Foundation):
   www.volunteersouthamerica.net
i-to-i: www.i-to-i.com
GeoVisions: www.geovisions.org
GIC Argentina: www.gicarg.org
Patagonia School: www.patagoniaschool.com
Projects Abroad: www.projects-abroad.org
Service Civil International: www.sci-ivs.org
Voluntario Global: www.voluntarioglobal.org.ar
Volunteer Latin America: www.volunteerlatinamerica.com
Worldwide Opportunities on Organic Farms: www.wwoof.org

Bolivia

Proyecto Horizonte: Uspha Uspha

Organization: Proyecto Horizonte
Location: Cochabamba
Cost: None **Duration:** 1+ month **Age:** 18
Contact: info@uspha-uspha.com
Learn more: www.uspha-uspha.com
Special skills: Intermediate Spanish
Details: Proyecto Horizonte is a NGO providing development services to the community of Mineros San Juan, Cochabamba. In just a little over five years, the organization has progressed to a full-fledged community development organization, providing education for community members of all ages, healthcare, infrastructure, community enrichment and awareness activities and economic development services like microfinance and microenterprise support. Approximately 70 teachers and staff work to ensure the education and well-being of more than 600 children, a number that is continually increasing. As a volunteer you are more than welcome to use your own abilities and profession in any of their various workfields.

Child Minding Center

Organization: Luz Del Mundo
Location: Santa Cruz de la Sierra, Bolivia
Cost: None
Duration: Volunteers usually stay 1 to 2 months, but anyone is welcome
Contact: volunteerldm@gmail.com
Learn more: www.volunteersouthamerica.net
Special skills: Basic knowledge of Spanish
Details: Luz del Mundo is located in a neighborhood of Santa Cruz de la Sierra - the largest city in Bolivia. About 40 kids come to the center 4 times a week, for 3-4 hours in the morning. (They go to school in the afternoon.) Volunteers play with the kids, teach them English, computers and other subjects. There's no curriculum, and you are encouraged to be creative! Sometimes the children need help with their homework and Gabriela, the director, might need your assistance to help to run the place. Any other activities initiated by the volunteers are very welcome. There are usually 3-5 volunteers on site. You'll need to arrange your own meals and accommodations. The total cost of living in Santa Cruz is around US $400 per person per month.

Hostal Volunteer in Beautiful Samaipata

Organization: Andoriña Hostal, Arte & Cultura, Samaipata - Bolivia
Location: Subtropical town of Samaipata is at an altitude of 1,650 m.
Cost: None   **Duration:** 6+ weeks (five afternoons-evenings a week)
Contact: noilenna@hotmail.com
Learn more: www.andorinasamaipata.com
Special skills: Speak at least basic Spanish, be motivated and have social and cultural interests
Details: This volunteer work is as a hostel volunteer. You are needed five days a week with two days free, working hours mostly from 13.00 onwards. But, they are flexible and if you wish to take a hike, tour or go elsewhere it can be arranged. Working at Andoriña mainly requires being available for telephone calls, receiving visitors, preparing small meals like pancakes, juices, coffees, etc. You will also be giving visitors information or sometimes opening the door for night visitors. They have balconies, hammocks, and a private room for you, plus breakfast and use of the kitchen is included. You should speak English and a reasonable amount of Spanish.

Non-Profit Tourism in the Bolivian Highlands

Organization: Condortrekkers
Location: Sucre, Bolivia
Cost: Volunteers pay for their first hike which costs around $50 to $75 and this is refundable after 2 months of service.
Duration: 1+ month, open for as long as you like   **Age:** 18
Contact: condortrekkers@gmail.com
Learn more: www.condortrekkers.org
Special skills: Fit and healthy people able to lead mountain hikes. Spanish, first aid and tourism experience are an advantage
Details: Lead hikes through the magnificent Andes Mountain Range and by doing so you will raise funds to support social projects in the local area. Work with underprivileged youths and experience life in rural villages. There is also the opportunity to be involved in side projects, such as reforestation, composting and to introduce your own ideas.

Teach, Learn-Organic Farming & Sustainable Living

Organization: Andoriña Hostal, Arte & Cultura, Samaipata
Location: Small cloud forest farming community of Chorolque
Cost: $10 per day, of which 75% goes straight to the community and attending family, includes a good bed, meals, etc., children 6+ pay half of the cost
Duration: 1+ week of six mornings around 4 hours

Age: No restrictions, parents with children are welcome
Contact: noilenna@hotmail.com
Learn more: www.andorinasamaipata.com
Special skills: Speaking reasonable Spanish, prefer organic farming
Details: This project is in the first phase of creating an example for other communities in sustainable living and farming. You will be hosted by a local family who themselves also still have a lot to learn – so volunteers have an opportunity to learn, teach and interact. You'll work with the earth, plants, fruit and forest trees, animals, help with small construction projects, clean ponds and invent new solutions for all kind of problems. This is a very beautiful area, quiet and convenient to local transport (35 minutes uphill by truck) every Sunday afternoon or Monday morning. Private transport can be arranged for $10-$15. You are free in the afternoons and evenings to relax, walk, read, meditate...

Wild Animal Care and Rehabilitation Project

Organization: Inti Wara Yassi
Location: 3 locations
Cost: $178 - $200 for first 2 weeks then $7-$9 a day after that
Duration: 2+ week   **Age:** 18
Contact: info@intiwarayassi.org
Learn more: www.intiwarayassi.org
Special skills: You do not need to have previous experience; all you need is a big heart and the desire to work hard to save the animals.

Details: If you volunteer with Inti Wara Yassi be prepared for some hard but extremely rewarding work. Your time will be spent predominantly with one animal so that it will become accustomed to you. This helps to keep them relaxed and happy and give them the best life possible. Work for everyone starts at around 7 a.m. and finishes late in the afternoon or sometimes goes on into the evening. Volunteers are required to stay for a minimum of 15 days, this is to protect and reassure the animals. Volunteers who wish to be responsible for a specific animal will need further training and therefore are required to stay for a month (usually more for cat species).

Bring Happiness to Disabled Kids

Organization: Reach Bolivia
Location: La Paz, Bolivia
Cost: $250 -$700   **Duration:** 2 weeks to 6 months   **Age:** 18
Contact: contact@reachbolivia.com
Learn more: www.reachbolivia.com

Details: Visit Bolivia and help a group of disabled kids who attend a special class to be able to be in school with other children. You will work as an assistance teacher for this special classroom, creating fun activities, exercising, dancing and helping to develop their self confidence. The school is located in a very poor area of La Paz (close to El Alto), and the kids normally do not have access to special education centers making this school their only opportunity to receive the education they need. You will work 4 to 8 hours a day 5 days a week and you can arrange other activities with the rest of the school.

Art to Heal for Burn Children

Organization: Reach Bolivia
Location: La Paz, Bolivia
Cost: $250 -$700   **Duration:** 2 weeks to 6 months   **Age:** 18
Contact: contact@reachbolivia.com
Learn more: www.reachbolivia.com
Details: Art is known to be a powerful healing method, therefore, volunteers are invited to work with burned children who are hospitalized as they pass their days laying in bed. Help them became resilient through art. It does not matter if you are not an artist! It does not even matter if you are not very talented! Painting, acting, laughing will make it all worthwhile. This volunteer position can change not only the child's life, but the parents as well, teaching them how to interact with their children again. This position is from Monday to Friday 4 hours a day.

Caring for the Little Ones

Organization: Reach Bolivia
Location: La Paz, Bolivia
Cost: $250 -$700   **Duration:** 2 weeks to 6 months   **Age:** 18
Contact: contact@reachbolivia.com
Learn more: www.reachbolivia.com
Details: Here is a chance to work in a Bolivian orphanage with children from 0 to 8 years old who live in houses of 10 kids along with a Mamita who takes care of them all. Volunteers give her a hand and give children the love and happiness they need for their development. You will play with the kids, help the Mamita around the house, create special activities for each house, help the kids with their homework and teach them some English as well. It has been proven that after a long period with a volunteer kids of 2 years start talking and they seem happier, so volunteer and plant a seed. This position is from Monday to Friday 4 hours a day. Lower fees may be available.

Orphanage with Unique Arts Program

Organization: Creative Corners; The Global Arts Project
Location: La Paz City
Cost: 1 month $935, 2 months $1130, additional months $315
Duration: 1+ month   **Age:** 20
Contact: enquiries@creative-corners.com
Learn more: www.creative-corners.com
Details: This project for orphaned, abused and abandoned children is part of a state-run temporary home and cares for around 75 children between the ages of 6 and 12. A unique creativity program was started at this home in 1992 which has been regularly staffed by volunteers who have their own workshop where they conduct artistic activities with small groups of children in the afternoons. Each child gets to do the activity once during the week and the activity changes or develops on a weekly basis. The focus of the volunteer program is to provide the emotional support and love that the children desperately lack and give them the opportunity to express themselves through creative and artistic work thus strengthening their self-esteem.

Helping Children with Speech and Hearing Impairments

Organization: Creative Corners; The Global Arts Project
Location: La Paz City
Cost: 1 month $935, 2 months $1,130, additional months $315
Age: 20
Contact: enquiries@creative-corners.com
Learn more: www.creative-corners.com
Details: This project works as an afternoon school for children with speech and hearing impairments. There are few provisions for the deaf community in Bolivia and this school provides a much valued resource. As a state run school it lacks sufficient funds, staff and resources. The children at this project would greatly welcome creative opportunities in the classroom such as art which is the perfect medium for expression. There is plenty of room for outdoor activities, mural painting, workshops in puppetry, mime, painting, circus skills, drama, collage, mural painting, games and other creative activities. You may work as a classroom assistant or run your own class workshops.

Creative Education

Organization: Creative Corners; The Global Arts Project
Location: La Paz City
Cost: 1 month $ 935, 2 months $1,130, additional months $315
Age: 20
Ccontact: enquiries@creative-corners.com

Learn more: www.creative-corners.com
Details: This volunteer project uses creative education to reach out to the children of La Paz including street children, shoe shine boys, children of stall sellers and children who have dropped out of school. There are 3 parts to the project: "Formation of Socio-Cultural Animators" where you'll work with Bolivian teachers to experience activities where you learn how art and play interact. "Ludoteques" involve structured sessions in parks, plazas and libraries where children get back into learning through creative play. "Creativity and Free Expression Workshops" are similar, but set in less central areas around the city. The project relies on Bolivian volunteers to act as the leaders of the street workshops so innovative volunteers are always needed to support and assist in the many areas of creative play.

Children with Physical and Learning Disabilities
Organization: Creative Corners; The Global Arts Project
Location: La Paz City
Cost: 1 month $ 935, 2 months $1130, additional months $315
Age: 20
Contact: enquiries@creative-corners.com
Learn more: www.creative-corners.com
Details: These special centers for children with physical and learning disabilities are located about 10 minutes south from the center of La Paz. In Bolivia these communities are often forgotten and the children here really love creative activities and are always waiting for their next creative friend to come along! Will it be you? Activities could include: organize party activities and games, run arts and crafts workshops, run fundraising activities, redecorate the home, paint a mural, organize excursions and more.

Work with Youth in a Detention Center
Organization: Creative Corners; The Global Arts Project
Location: La Paz City
Cost: 1 month $935, 2 months $1130, additional months $315
Age: 20
Contact: enquiries@creative-corners.com
Learn more: www.creative-corners.com
Details: Many youth in Bolivia who are deprived of their family environment for various reasons choose to live on the streets rather than being placed in institutions. They may have been abandoned or driven from their homes by poverty or violence. Generally between ages 10-19, they develop sometimes illegal survival strategies and band together in groups or gangs (pandillas). Their lives render them vulnerable to inhalant, drug and alcohol abuse which often drives them into prostitution and violent behavior leading them to spending time in

a juvenile detention center. The youth at these projects greatly welcome creative opportunities, activities ,and learning new skills such as computers, photography or clothes design. There is plenty of room here for working with kids who are very keen for your company and support.

Street Kids' Music Project

Organization: Volunteer Bolivia
Location: Cochabamba
Cost: $1,500 to $3,000
Duration: 3+ months   **Age:** 21
Contact: info@volunteerbolivia.org
Learn more: www.volunteerbolivia.org
Special skills: Musical background and Spanish speaking
Details: This volunteer position is with a non-profit organization that helps youth who are working and/or living on the streets of Cochabamba, Bolivia. The project works to empower children by teaching them creative activities such as artisan crafts, and performing and visual arts as healthy alternatives for avoiding drugs and delinquency, while also improving their economic well-being. They are a youth-led and managed organization. Participating youth are street and working kids who are supporting themselves or contributing to the support of their families. They are primarily from indigenous communities and outlying areas of the city. The program helps participants improve their living and economic conditions in order to realize a better future for themselves and their families.

Women's Weaving Cooperative Project

Organization: Volunteer Bolivia
Location: The town of Independencia nestled in an isolated valley of the Cordillera Oriental of the Andes about 7 hours form Cochabamba
Cost: $1,500 to $3,000   **Duration:** 3+ months   **Age:** 21
Contact: info@volunteerbolivia.org
Learn more: www.volunteerbolivia.org
Special skills: Spanish speaking; experience living in rural Latin America
Details: The goal of the project is designed to revive cultural expression through traditional weavings and find markets for the woven products to supplement rural incomes in a dependable manner. Weaving is an activity the women can do at home and work around their other chores. In 2007 a workshop was developed for training women in the use of natural dyes. That first workshop has evolved into

a series of five workshops available to any women's organization. Volunteer possibilities include assisting in the expansion of product line and marketing.

Coaching Sports and Physical Education

Organization: uVolunteer
Location: Santa Cruz
Cost: $865 for the first 2 weeks; $120 each additional week
Duration: 2+ weeks   **Age:** 18
Contact: info@uvolunteer.org
Learn more: www.uvolunteer.org
Special skills: Intermediate Spanish

Details: While volunteering on this project you will organize sports activities, games and competitions to get the children of Bolivia actively engaged in physical activities. The main goal of this project is promoting sports and fitness amongst Bolivian youth. Most of the children that you will be working with come from an orphanage and lack a sufficient support system. The sports project is a way for these children to become involved in healthy activities and stay away from the crime and drugs that plague certain neighborhoods in Santa Cruz.

Animal Conservation in Santa Cruz

Organization: uVolunteer
Location: Santa Cruz
Cost: $865 for the first 2 weeks; $120 each additional week
Duration: 2+ weeks   **Age:** 18
Contact: info@uvolunteer.org   **Learn more:** www.uvolunteer.org
Special skills: Intermediate Spanish
Details: This project is based in a zoo located in Santa Cruz. Its main purpose is the protection and conservation of wild fauna and to run studies and investigations in order to increase the life expectancy of wild animals. The zoo opened its doors to the public in 1979 and is now one of the leading zoos in South America. As a non-governmental and privately funded project, the zoo lacks readily available financial resources and depends upon private donors and aid in order to maintain its operations. The zoo mainly represents Bolivian fauna (reptiles, birds and mammals), as well as animals from other parts of South America. It is largely dependent on volunteers for upkeep of the facility and caring for the animals.

Media and Art Projects

Organization: uVolunteer
Location: Santa Cruz, Bolivia

Cost: $865 for the first 2 weeks; $120 each additional week
Duration: 2+ weeks **Age:** 18
Contact: info@uvolunteer.org **Learn more:** www.uvolunteer.org
Special skills: Intermediate Spanish
Details: Depending on your background and interests, you might be placed in either a museum or the institute for audiovisual learning. *Museum:* The aim of the project is to increase awareness and appreciation of art amongst the people of Bolivia. Working on this project means you will help organize and set up art exhibitions, as well as design promotional material such as invitations, online promotion ads. *Institute for Audiovisual Learning and Video Editing:* The objective of this project is to develop specialists in audiovisual techniques. You will help out the teacher in the classroom and your tasks could range from supervising classes to helping the students with their projects. If you are confident, you may also be asked to lead classes on your own.

Other organizations offering projects in Bolivia:

Amanecer (street kids in Cochabamba): www.amanecer-bolivia.org
Casa Do Caminho Child Centres (At risk youth):
  www.casadocaminhobrasil.org
Curamericas Global: www.curamericas.org
DELPIA foundation (indigenous persons/often need construction,
  agriculture and biologists) www.fundacion-delpia.org
Ecoteer: www.ecoteer.com
Foundation for Sustainability Development (professional
  placements): www.fsdinternational.org
Global Crossroads: www.globalcrossroad.com
Lead Adventure: lead-adventures.com
Projects Abroad: www.projects-abroad.org
Reach Bolivia: www.reachbolivia.com
Volunteering Solutions: www.volunteeringsolutions.com

Brazil

Working in a Favela (Squatter Community) in Rio

Organization: Instituto Dois Irmãos / Two Brothers Foundation
Location: Rocinha, Rio de Janeiro
Cost: None **Duration:** 3+ months preferred **Age:** 18
Contact: greg2bros@gmail.com
Learn more: www.2bros.org
Details: The Instituto Dois Irmãos is a school, community center,

reading room and information center all-in-one, located in the favela of Rocinha in Rio de Janeiro. The Instituto is supported financially by its sister non-profit, the Two Brothers Foundation, based in the U.S. Volunteers at the Instituto help it offer a full range of English classes for children and adults, other language classes, art/dance/photography classes, computer training, organized sports, cultural excursions, and anything else a volunteer would like to contribute. They are open-minded with regards to programming, so please bring your own skills to the table!

Casa do Caminho

Organization: Kids Worldwide
Location: Casa do Caminho on the outskirts of Tingua Rainforest
Cost: None
Duration: 6+ months, 1 to 2 year long-term placements are preferred.
Age: 21
Contact: casadocaminho@kidsworldwide.org
Learn more: www.casadocaminhobrasil.org
Special skills: Comfortable in Portuguese (Spanish speakers can learn quickly) or expertise in areas such as special needs education, psychologist, organic farming, electrician etc.
Details: Casa do Caminho has existed for 25 years and cares for approximately 40 children and teenagers. Casa do Caminho offers shelter and education to give these children an opportunity for a better future. Children come to Casa do Caminho via the governmental Youth Welfare Office. They need volunteers who can help with organic farming, a Sports and Community Center, becoming a godparent to a child, computer education (ICT) and/or sex education. The center is divided into three houses (one for children up to 12 in the countryside, and 2 houses for teenage girls and boys respectively situated in Xerém – the closest town). Xerem is a country town with cobblestone streets in the county of Duque de Caxias, an hour from Rio de Janeiro.

Brazilian Rainforest Conservation Center

Organization: Iracambi
Location: Serra do Brigadeiro, in the Atlantic Forest area of Minas Gerais
Cost: $700 per month   **Duration:** 1 to 6 months   **Age:** 18
Contact: volunteers@iracambi.com
Learn more: www.iracambi.com
Details: Iracambi's mission is to work with the community to make conservation of the rainforest more attractive than its destruction. Located in the Serra do Brigadeiro, in the highly endangered Atlantic Forest area of Minas Gerais, where most of the forest is privately owned by smallholders, we face the same challenges as our neighbors: how can

we make a sustainable living while conserving our globally important biodiversity? They are looking for volunteers to help with reforestation projects, clearing trails, ecotourism, environmental education, marketing, GIS (geographical information systems), IT support, web design and fundraising.

Arts, Sports and Dance Projects in Favellas

Organization: Kaya Responsible Travel
Location: Bahia's seaside capital – Salvador
Cost: $1,325+ **Duration:** 2 to 26 weeks **Age:** 18-80
Contact: info@kayavolunteer.com
Learn more: www.KayaVolunteer.com
Special skills: No special skills required, but mountains of enthusiasm, patience and resourcefulness are a must
Details: This wonderful project uses art, sports and dance including samba, graffiti, percussion lines, Community Theater, soccer, circus training, and capoeira to transform the lives of children and adults who

 live in favellas (shanty towns). Through these activities, this project educates and installs values to keep children out of the drug trade and help people develop microenterprises with their skills. It is a chance to bring talents to the forefront of the community. These programs help to prevent children from thieving, getting involved in drugs and gang violence. Volunteers can get involved in an array of activities, including setting up street soccer tournaments and street dance lessons culminating in performances for the community and providing positive role models for those without.

Community Building Projects in Salvador

Organization: Kaya Responsible Travel
Location: Bahia's seaside capital - Salvador
Cost: $1,325+ **Duration:** 2 to 26 weeks **Age:** 18-80
Contact: info@kayavolunteer.com
Learn more: www.KayaVolunteer.com
Special skills: A moderate level of fitness to conduct manual labor is essential. Any additional construction skills are invaluable as a bonus.
Details: Work to improve the living conditions of children and families in poverty. This program supervises the construction of classrooms, libraries, communal water wells, homes, housing improvements, and new sanitation systems. Volunteers also help families to develop sustainable income-generating programs. All year round they are involved in various building projects which really need the assistance of volunteers to keep them going. The influx of enthusiastic volunteers is essential as budgets are always tight and

there is little money available beyond material costs and equipment. Those with specific construction skills are particularly encouraged to assist in their specialist area.

HIV & AIDS Prevention

Organization: Kaya Responsible Travel
Location: Bahia's seaside capital - Salvador
Cost: $1,325+ **Duration:** 2 to 26 weeks **Age:** 18-80
Contact: info@kayavolunteer.com
Learn more: www.KayaVolunteer.com
Special skills: A background in medicine, public health or health science is required for this project
Details: The HIV/AIDS problem in the impoverished state of Bahia continues to grow. Kaya projects aim to lead community programs to raise awareness, educate and provide preventative measures in the form of psychotherapy, hospital visits and contraception. Their projects aim to create a space not only for policy action but also for the growing responsibility of others confronting the crisis. Young people are well placed to deliver programs because rural youth relate to them, but they also know that volunteers need training, guidance and support to fulfill their potential. Depending on your skills, qualifications and the location of your placement, you may be providing counseling, collaborating in education and prevention programs, assisting with medical and psychological care, supporting in administration and helping in antiretroviral treatment programs.

Community Development in Piracicaba

Organization: World Endeavors
Location: Piracicaba, Brazil
Cost: $1,308+ **Duration:** 2 to 12 weeks **Age:** 18
Contact: inquiry@worldendeavors.com
Learn more: www.worldendeavors.com
Details: Learn Portuguese while working on community development projects in the Brazilian city of Piracicaba. You will work with a local organization to build homes for low-income families or to improve facilities for local schools and orphanages. Stay with a local host family, who will provide breakfast and dinner, and take advantage of the opportunity to truly immerse yourself in Brazilian culture. For placements of four weeks or longer, a week of Portuguese language classes are included (prior language knowledge is not required).

Orphanage Assistance Programs

Organization: World Endeavors
Location: Multiple locations available

Cost: $1,308+ **Duration:** 2 to 12 weeks **Age:** 18
Contact: inquiry@worldendeavors.com
Learn more: www.worldendeavors.com
Details: Volunteer with impoverished children in local Brazilian orphanages and children's homes. Volunteers provide warmth and support for the children and teach English, with an emphasis on activities such as health education, games, and art projects. Participants stay with host families and are provided with two meals per day. For placement of four weeks or longer, one week of Portuguese language classes is included (prior Portuguese knowledge is not required).

Health Care and Health Education

Organization: World Endeavors
Location: Brazil
Cost: $1,308+ **Duration:** 2 to 12 weeks **Age:** 18
Contact: inquiry@worldendeavors.com
Learn more: www.worldendeavors.com
Details: Volunteer at a community health clinic or hospital, assisting in general care duties. Volunteers are also needed to provide support for patients at a children's hospital, and to work on health education campaigns. Volunteers with and without healthcare experience are welcome. Participants work five to six hours each day, Monday through Friday, between 7 am and 5 pm and stay with local host families who provide breakfast and dinner. Portuguese knowledge is recommended, but not required; participants with placements of four weeks or longer receive language classes.

Lost World: Studying Jaguars, Pumas and their Prey

Organization: Biosphere Expeditions
Location: Brazil's Atlantic rainforest near Curitiba, Brazil
Cost: $1,870 **Duration:** 2 week (or multiple expeditions) **Age:** 18
Contact: info@biosphere-expeditions.org
Learn more: www.biosphere-expeditions.org
Special skills: Open to all who care enough to become actively involved in conservation
Details: This conservation volunteer expedition will take you to the Atlantic rainforest of Brazil to study jaguars and pumas. You will share this jungle expedition experience with a small international team, alongside the scientist and expedition leader. You will assist local conservation efforts by initiating research in this unstudied area of forest and gathering key information vital for the protection of this highly endangered habitat and its resident species. You will

be walking on jungle paths or taking river canoes into densely forested mountains and lowland mangrove wetlands looking for tracks, kills, scats and the animals themselves, plus setting camera traps for them. You will also be interviewing local people.

Waterfalls and Wetland

Organization: Hands Up Holidays
Location: Campinas - Brazil
Cost: $3,000 per person, based on sharing a room
Duration: 4 days volunteering/12 day trip
Age: 18 years unless accompanied by an adult
Contact: info@handsupholidays.com
Learn more: www.handsupholidays.com
Special skills: None required, but mechanical, cooking and teaching English as a second language ("ESL") skills desirable, as is Portuguese language.
Details: Delve deep into the Brazilian culture as you assist an organization devoted to transforming the lives of the street kids of Campinas. The focus is on giving these children a safe, secure and happy childhood and so allowing them to evolve into dignified, fulfilled adults. Learning about the fascinating cultural mix and meeting wonderful people is fantastic, but your Brazil immersion would not be complete without samba dancing and cooking lessons. Also, marvel at the majestic Iguacu Falls and the diverse wildlife in the Pantanal. Here, seasonal rains ensure that this marshland plays host to a huge array of flora and fauna. Join a trained naturalist as you go in search of the elusive jaguar, puma, tapir and giant anteater.

Sustainable Agriculture & Community Projects

Organization: Academic Treks
Location: The heart of the Amazon
Cost: $4,980
Duration: 35+ hours of volunteerism as part of a 23-day service and cultural immersion program   **Age:** Teens finishing grades 9-12
Contact: info@academictreks.com; 919-256-8200 or 888-833-1908
Learn more: www.academictreks.com
Details: Students on Academic Treks Adventure Brazil program work on various projects which contribute to the sustainable development of the Xixuau-Xiparina Reserve in the heart of the Amazon. Projects range from assisting local women with jewelry and handicraft making to practicing permaculture and assisting with sustainable agricultural practices. From the carnival city of Rio to colonial Salvador to the remote corners of the Amazon rainforest, this 23 day college-accredited program will leave you with a lasting impression of Brazil's ecological treasures and kind people. Teens will learn about sustainable

development, study basic Portuguese and do service work alongside the Brazilian people in magnificent wilderness settings.

Natural Natal

Organization: Hands Up Holidays
Location: Araruna – North-East Brazil
Cost: $4,900 per person, based on sharing a room
Duration: 4 days volunteering/14 day trip
Age: 16 with an adult
Contact: info@handsupholidays.com
Learn more: www.handsupholidays.com
Special skills: None required but engineering, horticultural and teaching English as a second language skills desirable, as is Portuguese language.
Details: Participate in a blend of people, history and nature. Get an in-depth understanding of the wonderful people of Brazil's Natal Province. Enjoy a daylong project that improves the lives of the Natal city community by providing disabled access facilities. Later in your stay, involve yourself in a variety of projects in Araruna: assist with construction projects, help with honey extraction and put your 'green thumbs' to work as you assist with reforestation. Aside from your volunteering, Natal province promises many other fantastic experiences: explore the coast by 4WD buggy, delve into old colonial cities and discover the UNESCO World Heritage town of Olinda. For nature lovers, visit the Manatee (Dugong) research centre and the Charles Darwin Ecological refuge.

Other organizations offering projects in Brazil:

AEC-TEA Association (located in Capim Grosso, Bahia):
   www.aec-tea.org
Amazon-Africa Aid (health & education): www.amazonafrica.org
Family Health International: www.fhi.org
Global Leadership Adventures (for high school students):
   www.experiencegla.com
Global Visions International: www.gviusa.com or www.gvi.co.uk
i-to-i: www.i-to-i.com
Monte Azul (long term – provide meals & accommodations):
   www.monteazul.org.br
Peace Village Foundation: www.peacevillages.org

Chile

Patagonia Sur Year

Organization: WorldTeach
Location: Futaleufú or Palena in
southernmost Chile
Cost: None. Fully Funded – by Patagonia
Sur Foundation
Duration: One Year (late February thru
December) **Age:** 18-74

Contact: info@worldteach.org **Learn more:** www.worldteach.org
Special skills: Native English Speaker, Bachelor's Degree
Details: As a volunteer English teacher in Futaleufú or Palena, your
full-time teaching schedule will have great variety. You will collaborate
with a Chilean English teacher in several of his or her classes ranging
from kindergarten to tenth grade. An opportunity to lead your own
English workshops with students who choose to participate may also be
available. A rural school placement will be assigned as well, where you
will visit and teach at least once a week. Finally, there will be one or two
evening adult courses based on the New Interchange series that you
will be responsible for. Although you will be teaching diverse age
groups, most classes will be beginner to intermediate. You will have
support, from the WorldTeach Chile Field Director, based in Santiago,
and the Patagonia Sur Program Coordinator, based in Coihaique. You
will live with a Chilean host family (or other pensión-style housing).

Chile DuocUC Year

Organization: WorldTeach
Location: Urban areas of Santiago, Valparaiso, Vina del Mar or
Conception
Cost: $3,590 – subsidized by the DuocUC
Duration: One Year (Departure in early February) **Age:** 18-74
Contact: info@worldteach.org **Learn more:** www.worldteach.org
Special skills: Native English Speaker, Bachelor's degree
Details: WorldTeach volunteers working with Duoc Pontificia
Universidad Católica (DuocUC) teach English to post-secondary and
adult students in technical/professional institutes similar to adult
technical or trade schools in the US. With small classes (a maximum of
18 students) volunteers will have the opportunity to make a significant
impact on the students they teach. WorldTeach volunteers are also
expected to engage in programs or projects outside of their assigned
classes. You may choose to participate in or lead extracurricular
activities or hold additional English classes, depending on your time,

your interests and talents and local needs. Volunteers will live with host families relatively near their teaching sites. Host families will be compensated monthly, through funding provided by WorldTeach from DuocUC, to cover the costs they incur supporting a volunteer in their home.

Chile Ministry of Education Year

Organization: WorldTeach
Location: Chile- Bío-Bío, Araucanía and Los Ríos Regions
Cost: $4,190 – in cooperation with Ministry of Education of Chile
Duration: 1 Year (Departure in early February) **Age:** 21-45
Contact: info@worldteach.org **Learn more:** www.worldteach.org
Special skills: Native English Speaker (or use English in their everyday language), Bachelor's degree, experience working with children/teaching, Basic Spanish proficiency and/or be willing to Ministry of Education on-line Spanish course prior to departure.
Details: As a volunteer, you will be teaching English to public and semi-public school students. While most placements will involve teaching students in grades five through twelve, it is possible that some volunteers may teach younger students as well, especially in more rural placements. Since motivating students and creating opportunities for practicing English is a key goal of the program, volunteers will devote the rest of their full-time commitment to extracurricular activities both at their schools and in their communities. Volunteers will live with host families selected by the Ministry of Education, relatively near their school campuses. Host families provide an important entry into the community and a unique cultural learning opportunity. The Ministry of Education provides In-country training and support.

Chile Ministry of Education Semester

Organization: WorldTeach
Location: Chile
Cost: $3,690 – in cooperation with the Ministry of Education of Chile
Duration: One Semester (mid-July thru mid December) **Age:** 21-45
Contact: info@worldteach.org **Learn more:** www.worldteach.org
Special skills: Native English Speaker (or use English in their everyday language), Bachelor's degree, experience working with children/teaching, basic Spanish proficiency and/or be willing to complete the Ministry of Education online Spanish course prior to departure.
Details: As a volunteer, you will be teaching English to public and semi-public school students. While most placements will involve teaching students in grades five through twelve, it is possible that some volunteers may teach younger students as well, especially in more rural placements. Since motivating students and creating opportunities for

practicing English is a key goal of the program, volunteers will devote the rest of their full-time commitment to extracurricular activities both at their schools and in their communities. Volunteers will live with host families (selected by the Ministry of Education) who live relatively near their school campuses. Host families provide an important entry into the community and a unique cultural learning opportunity. The Ministry of Education provides in-country training and support.

Wild Patagonia - Future Patagonia National Park

Organization: inside/out Humanitourism™ Adventures
Location: Southern Patagonia, Chile
Cost: $2,000+
Duration: 1 week + 1 week of locally guided active adventures
Age: No age minimum, determined on an individual basis
Contact: info@theinsideandout.com
Learn more: www.theinsideandout.com
Details: This will be an unforgettable adventure experience for the rough and rugged, with physical labor outdoors to facilitate the creation of a future national park in a remote region of Chile. You will be helping to create a wildlife corridor in this unbridled area. The rewards will be incredibly spectacular rugged scenery, exploration of one of the only remaining truly wild areas in the world and fantastic distinctively Patagonian adventures. Inside/Out trips are designed around opportunities to do humanitarian volunteer work on meaningful international projects and are combined with sustainable eco-adventure travel in the local area of the project and people. Their trips are designed to create longer-term relationships between communities and travelers.

Easter Island (Rapa Nui) Culture

Organization: Earthwatch Institute
Location: Rendezvous: Hanga Roa, Easter Island, Chile
Cost: $4,050+ **Duration:** 14 days **Age:** 18
Contact: info@earthwatch.org **Learn more:** www.earthwatch.org

Details: Earthwatch volunteers explore and uncover the evolution of agriculture and the consequences of environmental degradation. You'll work in a uniquely beautiful landscape amid the warm sea breezes on the island's western and northern coasts searching for prehistoric dwellings, earth ovens, gardens, livestock enclosures and agricultural fields. Under the gaze of the giant stone *Moai*, you'll conduct surface surveys of house sites and dig test pits in gardens to document the evolution of farming. The artifacts you find will throw light on the lives of Rapa Nui's original inhabitants, their culture and its ultimate fate. In your recreational time, wander through nearby petroglyphs, caves and ceremonial centers to capture your imagination. Take a horseback ride along the island's rocky headlands or a swim at a secluded beach.

Other organizations offering projects in Chile:

A Broader View (humanitarian): www.abroaderview.org
Center for Cultural Interchange/Greenheart: www.cci-exchange.com
Chol-Cjol Foundation (fair trade/economic development)
  www.cholchol.org
Eco Yoga Farms: ecological-farms.blogspot.com
Ecoteer: www.ecoteer.com
Gap Chile: www.gap-chile.com
Habitat for Humanity: www.habitat.org
One World Nursery (bilingual preschool): www.oneworldnursery.cl
Save the Wild Chinchillas (conservation): www.wildchinchillas.org
South American Connections: www.samconnects.com
United Planet: www.unitedplanet.org
Volunteer Chile/Bruce Chile: volunteerchile.com

Columbia

Teaching 9th Graders Computer & Communication Skills

Organization: Voces de Mompox
Location: Mompox, Colombia
Cost: None **Duration:** Open-ended **Age:** 21
Contact: writingjulie@gmail.com
Special skills: Blog and website building; story writing; photography; videography
Details: At Voces de Mompox you will work with 9th grade students, sharing your talents as a writer, photographer and/or videographer. The goal of this project is to teach kids usable skills while providing them with the opportunity to tell their own stories, ultimately learning how to upload these to a blog/website and share them with the world. Volunteers do bear the costs of transportation to/from/within Colombia as well as lodging, though some lodging opportunities may be available via the program in the future. The  town of Mompox is quite isolated, so this placement is not appropriate

for someone who needs/prefers urban areas, but is perfect for those wanting to experience the small-town Columbia while helping children expand their view of the world and their role in it.

Columbia Teaching Year

Organization: WorldTeach
Location: Columbia- on Isla Baru isthmus
Cost: $1,000 – subsidized by partner organizations
Duration: One Year (Departure in early January) **Age:** 18-74
Contact: info@worldteach.org **Learn more:** www.worldteach.org
Special skills: Native English Speaker, Bachelor's Degree
Details: Volunteers will primarily provide instruction to students in grades 4-11 (the Colombian equivalent of grades 5-12 in the U.S.), and each volunteer will specialize in designated grades. Class size will consist of approximately 20 students. Volunteers are usually responsible for teaching 20-25 hours a week, in addition to allotting time for planning lessons, developing new language instruction materials, and coordinating some activities, such as providing introductory English instruction to younger students at the schools. Volunteers will teach at two schools on Isla Baru. One is a charter school by the non-profit Fundacion Mario Santo Domingo (also a large landowner on the island). Adjacent to the charter school is a local public school. All volunteers will live in teacher housing at the charter school. The approximately 30 Colombian teachers who work at the school also reside on campus. The pupils themselves are all day students, returning home in the afternoons.

Fostering Leadership in Street Youth

Organization: The Humanity Exchange
Location: Medellin, Colombia
Cost: $1,600 for 1 month, $2,200 for 2 months, $2,550 for 3 months, $3,050 for 4 months
Duration: 1 to 4 months. The longer you stay, the greater the impact (for both you and the host community). **Age:** 18
Contact: director@thehumanityexchange.org
Learn more: www.thehumanityexchange.org
Details: Street youth in Medellin face a very real risk of getting into gangs and the drug trade. The Humanity Exchange partners work directly with such youth to provide meaningful alternatives. You will be part of an exceptional team working on the front lines of urban poverty and community development. Through your role, you will help youth to become leaders in their community. Volunteers mentor children and youth, tutor children in various academic subjects, help to run after-school programs for the children and coordinate special activities such as excursions and community visits. Comprehensive pre-departure

support, fundraising guide, food, lodging, airport pick-up and drop-off, and an Exchange Manager who is available 24/7 are all included in this program. The Humanity Exchange can also arrange Spanish classes, help you plan onward travel, and coordinate with your college or university so can obtain course credit.

Our Children, Our Future

Organization: The Humanity Exchange
Location: Medellin, Colombia
Cost: $1,600 for 1 month, $2,200 for 2 months, $2,550 for 3 months, $3,050 for 4 months
Duration: 1 to 4 months. The longer you stay, the greater the impact (for both you and the host community). **Age:** 18
Contact: director@thehumanityexchange.org
Learn more: www.thehumanityexchange.org
Details: Nearly 10% of Colombia's population has been displaced due to the many years of armed conflict, one in three Colombians have been negatively affected by the armed conflict, and there is great wealth disparity, leaving much of the country in poverty. This has created a

dire situation for Colombia's orphaned children. Volunteers are needed to work with orphans by dressing and feeding children, tutoring children in various academic subjects, assisting staff in the nursery school and mentoring children. Comprehensive pre-departure support, fundraising guide, food, lodging, airport pick-up and drop-off, and an Exchange Manager who is available 24/7 are all included in this program. The Humanity Exchange can also arrange Spanish classes, help you plan onward travel, and coordinate with your college or university so can obtain course credit.

Colors of Colombia

Organization: Hands Up Holidays
Location: Santa Marta - Colombia
Cost: $3,500 per person, based on sharing a room
Duration: 4 days volunteering/14 day trip
Age: 16 years unless accompanied by an adult
Contact: info@handsupholidays.com
Learn more: www.handsupholidays.com
Special skills: None required, but accounting, marketing, hospitality, teaching English as a second language ("ESL") or IT skills are desirable.
Details: Prepare to have your perceptions about Colombia shattered! It is truly a wonderful country, with immense diversity, proud, welcoming people, stunning colonial buildings in Bogota and

Cartegena, and many areas where you can make a positive impact through volunteering. You can help ensure that a new eco-tourism initiative is sustainable by training the staff in professionalism, English and hospitality skills. The community where you are assisting is comprised of former coca leaf growers (used to make cocaine) who have left this activity to pursue tourism as a source of income for them and their families. You'll also experience Bogota, the Salt Cathedral, the house where Simon Bolivar died, the rugged beauty of Tayrona National Park and the spectacularly beautiful Cartagena.

Other organizations offering projects in Columbia:

CFH International (economic development, post-disaster service...):
  www.chfinternational.org
Fundacion ProAves (birds & conservation): www.proaves.org
Fundación Omacha (wildlife): omacha.org
Let's Go Volunteer: www.letsgovolunteer.com
Peace Brigades International: www.peacebrigades.org.uk
United Planet: www.unitedplanet.org
Volunteer Columbia (under-privileged children in Cartagena)
  www.volunteercolombia.org

Ecuador

Resident Appropriate Technology Design/Development

Organization: Sacred Suenos
Location: 2-3 hour hike up a mountainside from the village of Vilcabamba
Cost: $120 per month   **Duration**: 3+ months   **Age:** 18
Contact: sacredsuenos@wildmail.com
Learn more: www.sacredsuenos.com
Special skills: Some engineering background would be preferred. Reasonable practical skills, or a willingness to learn them, respecting the type of activity to be attempted are required.
Details: While most mornings will be spent working alongside the Regenerative Rural Workers, the rest of the time will be spent researching and developing techniques and technologies that can be reproduced by Andean farmers and can offer a sustainable solution to a difficult problem. Projects include, but are not limited to the following: Value added food processing; Manual and Ram water pumps; Water storage; Shelter; Pasture management; Reforestation Earthworks; Micropower; and Bicycle powered appliances.

Regenerative Rural Work

Organization: Sacred Suenos
Location: 2-3 hour hike up a mountainside from the village of Vilcabamba
Cost: $150 per month **Duration**: Indefinite **Age:** 18
Contact: sacredsuenos@wildmail.com
Learn more: www.sacredsuenos.com
Special skills: Willingness to live in a community setting and work hard.
Details: Volunteers will participate in the daily activities of a small farm and Permaculture demonstration site striving to be self sufficient. This includes gardening, care of animals, natural building, tree planting, trail maintenance, food preparation and anything else that might come up.

Ecuador Teacher Year

Organization: WorldTeach
Location: Ecuador – mostly in urban areas, a few placements in rural
Cost: $4,990 **Duration:** One Year (Departures in early February and mid-August) **Age:** 18-74
Contact: info@worldteach.org **Learn more:** www.worldteach.org
Special skills: Native English speaker, Bachelor's Degree
Details: Depending on the placement, volunteers are usually responsible for teaching 20-25 hours a week, in addition to allotting time for planning lessons, holding regular office hours, developing new language instruction materials, and coordinating some activities, such as setting up and running an English club for students or other teachers. Class size varies widely as do the type of students and their level of English. Volunteers may teach university students, faculty and staff, and/or open-enrollment classes for members of the local community. They usually live with host families. Most host families will have electricity and running water, though hot water is inconsistent at best. Placements in Ecuador are based on the best match between the needs of the host institution and the personal qualifications of the volunteers.

Help Run an Award Winning Ecolodge

Organization: Black Sheep Inn, Ecolodge, Ecuador
Location: Chugchilán, Cotopaxi, Ecuador in the high rural Andes
Cost: $150 for first 2-week trial period
Duration: 2+ months minimum **Age:** 25
Contact: blacksheepinn@yahoo.com
Learn more: www.blacksheepinn.com

Details: Black Sheep Inn aims to provide a comfortable, educational experience for guests, teaching about the local area, local customs and permaculture, while contributing to and improving the local community and the natural environment. Volunteers help to run the lodge & work closely with guests. The goal is to be a leader in environmental stability and ecotourism. There are several micro-climates and attractions all within hiking distance including: Laguna Quilotoa, a volcanic crater-lake, Rio Toachi Canyon, Iliniza Ecological Reserve, with huge tracts of Cloud Forest and high Andean Paramó alpine grasslands. Black Sheep Inn offers affordable lodging in the

heart of the rural Ecuadorian Andes. Truly off the beaten path, guests enjoy horseback riding, mountain biking and day hiking. Enjoy spectacular views, delicious vegetarian cooking, home baked deserts, wood-fired sauna and hot-tub, zipline cable swing, yoga studio, solar-powered waterslide, Frisbee golf course, family fun and adventure.

𝍐 **Editors Note:** Black Sheep Inn is listed among the "Top 10 Ecolodges in the World" by Outside Magazine (2008). It has also taken a myriad of other awards by various organizations. Their Eco-Permaculture Features include: solar panels, adobe construction, composting toilets, recycling, roof-water collectors, gray-water systems, organic gardens, community education and aid work, reforestation, erosion control and more. This is a chance to see and learn about this type of facility firsthand while increasing you knowledge on eco-lodge management.

Arutam Rainforest Reserve

Organization: FUNDECOIPA
Location: Arutam Community, Pastaza Province
Cost: $75 per week **Duration:** 2+ weeks **Age:** 15-60
Contact: info@fundecoipa.com **Learn more:** www.fundecoipa.com
Special skills: Spanish is an advantage, but not a requirement
Details: This volunteer placement provides a fantastic opportunity to experience the Amazon, its flora and fauna, while learning about the language and culture of indigenous communities. Volunteers can participate in a series of ongoing projects that include teaching in local schools, traditional farming, construction, trail creation, reforestation, building tourist infrastructure, nursery work, medicinal garden and other community activities. This project was initiated by the villagers of Arutam to serve as a platform for addressing the social, cultural and economical difficulties faced by its members and neighboring communities. The aim of the project is to create community

development in the indigenous communities of Pastaza based on sustainable use of the biological resources and cultural norms.

Work in a Hostel and a School

Organization: Hostel Llullu Llama
Location: Isinlivi, a small village in the Andes of Ecuador
Cost: $320 for 4 weeks includes food and stay at Hostel Llullu Llama. Stay 2 month and you get food plus stay for free.
Duration: 4+ weeks **Age:** 18
Contact: info@llullullama.com **Learn more:** www.llullullama.com
Special skills: It will make your project more fun if you speak some Spanish.
Details: Llullu Llama hostel will be the base of your volunteer project. Besides helping run the hostel volunteers help at the local schools (primary or secondary), teaching English and reading books to the children, both in the village and from the surrounding communities. You will work 5 days a week. On your free days you can hike around the region, visit the local markets or travel around Ecuador.

Small Indigenous Community Volunteering

Organization: Hostal Llullu Llama
Location: Malinguapamba, a small community in the Andes of Ecuador
Cost: $320 for 4 weeks includes food and stay at Hostel Llullu Llama. Stay 2 month and you get food plus stay for free.
Duration: 4+ weeks **Age:** 18
Contact: info@llullullama.com **Learn more:** www.llullullama.com
Special skills: It will make your project more fun if you speak some Spanish.
Details: Immerse yourself in Ecuador and help by teaching at the primary or secondary school of Malinguapamba. You can teach English or other subjects like math, computers, geography, etc. It is also possible that you help out with other activities in the community like planting seeds, reforestation, or any other things they might need your assistance with. During your time in the community you will stay with the family of the president of the community. You will work 5 days a week. On the weekends you are free and you can hike around the beautiful region. Please keep in mind that it will take you some time to get used to the way of working and living in a small indigenous community. Also there is no phone or Internet in the community – perfect for going 'off-grid' and reconnecting with a simpler, peaceful way of life.

Rebuilding Homes in the Amazon Jungle

Organization: Ecuador Volunteer Foundation
Location: Puyo in the Amazon Jungle
Cost: $360 per month   **Duration:** 1 month
Age: 18, or 16 with parental consent
Contact: info@ecuadorvolunteer.org
Learn more: www.ecuadorvolunteer.org
Details: This project gives you the opportunity to work with an indigenous community in the Amazon jungle of Ecuador. Your work benefits the neediest families in the community, rebuilding and extending their homes. In addition, the volunteers involved in this project may also immerse themselves deeply into the culture, getting to know the customs and lifestyles of the indigenous Shuar and other ethnic groups which are typical of the Ecuadorian Amazon. The volunteers will participate in activities such as planning the construction, purchasing tools and materials, organizing mingas (work groups) for the withdrawal of other materials and building rooms, kitchens, drop ceilings and more. The volunteer will receive training from the community and from the coordinators of the project for the planning and accomplishment of this work.

Farm Facilitator Internship

Organization: Sacred Suenos
Location: 2-3 hour hike up a mountainside from the village of Vilcabamba, Ecuador.
Cost: $300, plus $100 for the Introduction to Regenerative Andean Design
Duration: 3 months, with options to extend   **Age:** 18
Contact: sacredsuenos@wildmail.com
Learn more: www.sacredsuenos.com
Special skills: A passion for the project is essential for this leadership position. Prior managerial or organizational skills are preferred. Anyone without a significant background in Permaculture principals must participate in an Introduction to Regenerative Andean Design course which will be held during the week prior to the internship, which will take place during the second week of September or the second week of January.
Details: Interns work alongside the Regenerative Rural Worker volunteers, but on top of this, they will: list and prioritize all the tasks necessary for the maintenance and reasonable development of the farm; organize, train and direct the volunteers to accomplish these tasks; manage supplies and resources; be in charge of keeping the

kitchen and tool rooms sufficiently supplied to support all the residents and their projects; and participate in general farm meetings. Interns will meet with one or more directors on a regular basis to discuss projects and tasks, as well as any other issues that may come up.

Caring for Poor Children

Organization: Ecuador Volunteer Foundation
Location: Quito
Cost: $450 per month with host family/$150 per month in volunteer house **Duration:** 1+ month **Age:** 18
Contact: info@ecuadorvolunteer.org
Learn more: www.ecuadorvolunteer.org
Special skills: Love and patience with children
Details: The objective of this project is to help underprivileged children and their parents who cannot always afford a good education for their children. EVF needs volunteers to help take care of the children and to support community mothers in their daily tasks, including play activities, emotional and motor development. The volunteers will work with children from 2 to 5 years old from families that suffer from an excessive amount of violence or poverty.

Teaching English to Youth

Organization: Ecuador Volunteer Foundation
Location: Quito
Cost: $450 per month with host family/$150 per month in volunteer house **Duration:** 1 month **Age:** 18
Contact: info@ecuadorvolunteer.org
Learn more: www.ecuadorvolunteer.org
Special skills: Prefer people with TEFL knowledge
Details: The project has various objectives. One is to improve the level of academic English for children between 5 to 12 years of age, who attend the program. Volunteers will help directly by guiding and strengthening the children's learning. The schools currently have an average of 30 children per class. Each class is divided into three different groups for the academic year. However, there is only one English teacher per school (two in total), hence the need for volunteers to assist with English instruction is great.

Caring for Children and Adults with Special Needs

Organization: Ecuador Volunteer Foundation
Location: Quito
Cost: $450 per month with host family/$150 per month in volunteer house **Duration:** 1 month **Age:** 18
Contact: info@ecuadorvolunteer.org

Learn more: www.ecuadorvolunteer.org
Special skills: Love and patience with children and adults
Details: This project's mission is to give love, health, empowerment, education, recreation, work and spiritual discipleship to children, teens and youth with disabilities or at risk. They come from families with limited economic resources and seek independence and integration into society. The volunteers will support activities such as classroom assistance, homework help, encouragement to complete the plans of the school, recreation, entertainment, music, sports, help with feeding the children, cleaning, linen change, mental stimulation and more.

Garden, Reforestation and Environmental Education

Organization: Ecuador Volunteer Foundation
Location: Mindo, Northwest Ecuador
Cost: $280 per month **Duration:** 1 month
Age: 18, 16 with parental consent
Contact: info@ecuadorvolunteer.org
Learn more: www.ecuadorvolunteer.org
Details: This project seeks to reforest desolate areas with plants and trees from the primary forest with the hope that birds and wildlife will return to the region and repopulate the area. The town of Mindo depends on ecotourism and supports this project, not only to improve the environment, but also to improve the standard of living. The main volunteer activities for this project are collection of seeds and plants in the primary forest, maintenance of seedbeds, construction of new seedbeds, planting seeds, maintaining the garden, organizing excursions so the children can learn about the environment and ecology, preparation of materials for the children with recycled items (paper, cardboard, bottles) and teaching them to make cards from recycled paper, decorations, puppets and other items.

Tracking Andean Bears in Ecuador

Organization: Andean Bear Foundation / Espiritu del Bosque
Location: A tiny village within a cloud forest clearing in the Intag Region of Northern Ecuador
Cost: $600 for 4 weeks including accommodation and food
Duration: 2 to 12 weeks per volunteer **Age:** 19
Contact: bearsecuador@yahoo.co.uk – quote reference DEVMAsst
Learn more: www.andeanbear.org
Special skills: Good level of fitness required to walk at altitude in the Andes Mountains
Details: How fantastic is this? Volunteers will help collect radio telemetry data for a ground-breaking project investigating the ranges and habits of the

Andean bear in the mountains, cloud forests and páramo (treeless plateau). Andean bears are timid, solitary creatures rarely seen by humans and are classed as "vulnerable" due to habitat loss and illegal killings by farmers. Your work will extend the world's understanding of these bears´ ecology and behavior in the hope of saving them from extinction by creating a land management plan to avoid human-bear conflict in agricultural areas. This is a fantastic opportunity for biology students or those wanting a career in conservation biology or mammal monitoring to gain practical field experience. Volunteers must be patient, adaptable, healthy and fit enough to walk at altitude in variable weather conditions.

Teaching Rural Schools for the Andean Bear Project
Organization: Andean Bear Foundation / Espiritu del Bosque
Location: A tiny village within a cloud forest clearing in the Intag Region of Northern Ecuador
Cost: $560 for 4 weeks including accommodation and food
Duration: 4 to 24 weeks per volunteer **Age:** 24
Contact: bearsecuador@yahoo.co.uk
Learn more: www.andeanbear.org
Special skills: Spanish language – at least basic level; teaching qualification & experience
Details: Experienced primary teachers are needed in the Andes Mountains in Northern Ecuador in an area of beautiful cloud forests which are home to the Andean Bear. The project is looking for teachers who can design and teach course modules which can also be implemented in the future by less-experienced volunteers. Your volunteer work will strengthen relations between the local community and the Andean Bear Conservation Project. The primary schools want help in teaching English and computing. If you're Spanish is good enough you can also teach other subjects. Andean Bear Foundation wants you to include environmental education in your classes and you can also make an impact by encouraging better nutrition and dental health. The one college in the area also welcomes assistance.

Teachers´ Assistants for the Andean Bear Project
Organization: Andean Bear Foundation / Espiritu del Bosque
Location: A tiny village within a cloud forest clearing in the Intag Region of Northern Ecuador
Cost: $560 for 4 weeks including accommodation and food
Duration: 4 to 12 weeks per volunteer **Age:** 19
Contact: bearsecuador@yahoo.co.uk, quote reference DEVMAsst
Learn more: www.andeanbear.org
Special skills: A basic level of Spanish

Details: You'll assist the local teachers or qualified volunteer teachers with environmental education as well as other subjects such as English, computers, sports and art in the Andes Mountains in Northern Ecuador in an area of beautiful cloud forests which are home to the Andean Bear. The one college in the area welcomes assistance in teaching computer skills and English to older students. Your volunteer work will strengthen relations between the local community and the Andean Bear Conservation Project and encourage the next generation to conserve the cloud forest and the wildlife it supports. This is a great opportunity for those wanting to go into teaching or environmental education as a career to gain some experience.

Community Ecotourism and Conservation

Organization: Santa Lucia Cooperative
Location: Santa Lucia Cloudforest Reserve, 2.5 hours NW of Quito, Ecuador by road plus an hour's uphill hike.
Cost: $105 per week **Duration:** 2+ weeks
Age: 18, some opportunities for families with children exist.
Contact: info@santaluciaecuador.com
Learn more: www.santaluciaecuador.com
Special skills: None required. Spanish helpful but not essential
Details: Santa Lucia is a community-owned and community-run organization which owns a primary cloud forest reserve and lodge. In the Choco region, a biodiversity hotspot, the reserve is home to the endangered Spectacled Bear, Puma and 390 species of birds. They need volunteers to support their ecotourism project which provides a sustainable income for members, allowing them to protect and conserve the forest. Volunteers are needed to support this work: trail maintenance, organic gardening and agroforestry - sugar, coffee and bananas. Accommodations are in a lodge in the heart of the forest on a mountain peak with spectacular views. This is a great opportunity to learn more about and contribute to community conservation and sustainable tourism, work alongside long people and improve your Spanish.

Community Under-Fives Nursery

Organization: Santa Lucia Cooperative
Location: Small rural town of Nanegal, 2 hours NW of Quito
Cost: $105 per week **Duration:** 2+ weeks
Age: 18, some opportunities for families with children exist.
Contact: info@santaluciaecuador.com
Learn more: www.santaluciaecuador.com

Special skills: Enjoy being with children, Spanish helpful but not essential

Details: Centro de Desarrollo de Infantil is run by the local community and Fundacion Mariana de Jesus. They provide a stimulating environment & nutritious meals. Santa Lucia seeks volunteers to support this project. If you are committed to the Rights of the Child and enjoy being with children, join them and help with the Centre's activities, care of the children and also practical projects such as constructing play equipment. Longer term volunteers can also teach English to older children/adults. Accommodation is one mile away in a volunteer house set in a pretty countryside. Enjoy a great opportunity to get involved in a typical rural Ecuadorian community, make a difference to children in need and improve your Spanish.

Wild Animal Rescue and Conservation

Organization: Santa Martha Wild Animal Rescue Centre
Location: Outside Quito
Cost: $120+ weekly contribution to the rescue
Duration: 2+ weeks   **Age:** 18
Contact: santamartha@mail.com
Learn more: www.santamartharescue.org
Special skills: Conversational English or Spanish speaking, all types of life and /or animal skills needed.

Details: Santa Martha Rescue Centre is located one hour south of Quito, in the "Avenue of Volcanoes". It was founded by Johnny and Brenda Córdova who still live on site with their family. Ecuador is one of the most bio diverse countries in the world and it is possible to buy a huge variety of animals ranging from large cats to monkeys, crocodiles and parrots. It is illegal to keep wild animals as pets though, so they are often confiscated by the police. Many so-called "rescue centres" unfortunately function as a zoo and they continue to maltreat the animals. The Santa Martha -El Arca- Yanacocha alliance works closely with the Environmental Police and the Environmental Ministry to rescue, rehabilitate and release these animals back into their natural habitat and to, by providing a good example, influence other zoo/rescue centres to become true refuges to wild animals.

✍**Editor's Note:** According to their staff, the centre's work could not be done without the help of volunteers. Their sheer existence depends on the participation of enthusiastic animal lovers from all over the world. Santa Martha needs help all year round who can participate in general animal care (cleaning, feeding, assisting the vet), construction and maintenance, fundraising and promotion, public education (including teaching English), arts and design (improving the appearance of the project areas, designing posters etc), etc.

Amazon Reserve Project

Organization: Global Volunteer Network
Location: Amazon (Amazonia)
Cost: $527 for 2 weeks **Duration:** 2 to 24 weeks **Age:** 18
Contact: info@volunteer.org.nz **Learn more:**
www.volunteer.org.nz
Special skills: A basic level of Spanish is required for all reserves.
Volunteers can choose to attend a 2 week Spanish course in Quito prior
to volunteering.
Details: The Amazon Biological Station was founded in 1986, creating
a conservation, investigation and education center to host scientists
and students interested in preserving tropical rainforest. This band of
wet forest is one of the most biologically diverse areas in the world.
More than fifty species of mammals inhabit the reserve, including large
cats like pumas and jaguars, demonstrating how well the area has been
preserved. Volunteer activity in Amazon Biological Station includes
reforestation, experimental silviculture of tropical trees, development
and maintenance of the reserve's botanical garden and plant
conservation center and much more.

Galapagos: San Cristobal Reserve

Organization: Global Volunteer Network
Location: In the highlands of San Cristobal Island, in the Galapagos
chain, on a 200 hectare site where there is still native vegetation.
Cost: $527 for 2 weeks **Duration:** 2 to 24 weeks **Age:** 18
Contact: info@volunteer.org.nz **Learn more:**
www.volunteer.org.nz
Special skills: A basic level of Spanish is required for all reserves.
Volunteers can choose to attend a 2 week Spanish course in Quito prior
to volunteering.
Details: As a volunteer in San Cristobal Reserve, you will work on both
habitat restoration and agricultural components. In addition Station
staff will lead volunteers on various destination hikes throughout the
reserve and nearby locations to explain the ecological and human
dynamic of the legendary Galapagos Islands. Activities include clearing
land of invasive plant species in the wildlife corridor established on the
Reserve, digging and planting new gardens, recognizing and collecting

seeds from native plants, identifying and tagging native plants, making fertilizer, construction of volunteer housing, and repair and maintenance of the Reserve's water supply. Volunteers work around 5-7 hours each day.

La Hesperia Reserve Project

Organization: Global Volunteer Network
Location: La Hesperia is located in the western range of the Andes at an altitude of 1100 - 2040 meters above sea level.
Cost: $527 for 2 weeks **Duration:** 2 to 24 weeks **Age:** 18
Contact: info@volunteer.org.nz **Learn more:** www.volunteer.org.nz
Special skills: A basic level of Spanish is required for all reserves. Volunteers can choose to attend a 2 week Spanish course in Quito prior to volunteering.
Details: La Hesperia is an extremely important area for conservation of biodiversity and the protection of local watersheds. Currently, almost 300 bird species have been identified at La Hesperia, of which ten are endemic to the region and seven are vulnerable or in danger of extinction. At La Hesperia Biological Station & Reserve, there are three different programs designed for the volunteers: (A) Conservation in the Cloud Forest (B) On the Way to Sustainability (C) Social Development. Volunteers are encouraged to focus their time in the activities that best suits their interests. The programs are flexible so you may concentrate on one area or work in a combination of the projects offered.

Bilsa Biological Reserve

Organization: Global Volunteer Network
Location: The reserve is located in one of the world's most important biodiversity hotspots, and is a rare area of pristine forest in the region.
Cost: $527 for 2 weeks **Duration:** 2 to 24 weeks **Age:** 18
Contact: info@volunteer.org.nz **Learn more:** www.volunteer.org.nz
Special skills: A basic level of Spanish is required for all reserves. Volunteers can choose to attend a 2 week Spanish course in Quito prior to volunteering.
Details: Among all the reserves, Bilsa is the most remote and is also the reserve where you will encounter the most wildlife; more than 15 troops of Howler Monkeys inhabit the reserve, while there are also many different bird and plant species. Through an in-depth botanical inventory being conducted by Ecuador's National Herbarium, over 2,000 different plant species have been documented. For almost four years scientists have been conducting research at Bilsa. The scientists spend about 17-20 days a month at the reserve and during that period it is possible for volunteers to assist and learn from them. Volunteer

activities in this reserve include reforestation and station maintenance, nature hikes, etc.

Congal Biological Reserve

Organization: Global Volunteer Network
Location: The Western Ecuador Choco-Darien bio geographical region.
Cost: $527 for 2 weeks **Duration:** 2 to 24 weeks **Age:** 18
Contact: info@volunteer.org.nz **Learn more:**
www.volunteer.org.nz
Special skills: A basic level of Spanish is required for all reserves. Volunteers can choose to attend a 2 week Spanish course in Quito prior to volunteering.
Details: The purpose of the Station in Congal Reserve is to develop projects in the fields of conservation, aquaculture, farming and forestry. These projects are intended to be implemented in local communities to provide sources of income and to reduce the pressure on already overexploited and threatened natural resources. Volunteer activities in Congal Reserve include mangrove and tropical forest restoration, station maintenance and development, sustainable aquaculture ponds, clean-ups and recycling, agro forestry, local initiatives and community social development.

Lalo Loor Biological Reserve

Organization: Global Volunteer Network
Location: The Lalo Loor Dry Forest Biological Station is located in the Northern Manabi Province on Ecuador's coast, from the beach inland.
Cost: $527 for 2 weeks **Duration:** 2 to 24 weeks **Age:** 18
Contact: info@volunteer.org.nz **Learn more:**
www.volunteer.org.nz
Special skills: A basic level of Spanish is required for all reserves. Volunteers can choose to attend a 2 week Spanish course in Quito prior to volunteering.
Details: The goal of Lalo Loor reserve is to work towards the preservation and conservation of the unique transitional dry forest ecosystem found in the area. First, and foremost, by protecting existing forests and restoring degraded areas within and outside the reserve. As the reserve develops, we will have a number of conservation projects focused on the restoration of the natural ecosystems, environmental education, and income generation. Volunteer activities in Lalo Loor Reserve include reforestation and agroforestry, trail maintenance, reserve infrastructure, teaching opportunities and forest hiking.

School Support Program

Organization: International Volunteer HQ
Location: Placements in Quito, the capital city of Ecuador
Cost: $230 for 1 week to $2,300 for 6 months, includes food and accommodations
Duration: 1 week to 6 months   **Age:** 18
Contact: volunteer@volunteerhq.org
Learn more: www.volunteerhq.org
Special skills: Spanish is required for this program (Basic to Conversational)

Details: Quito, the capital of Ecuador is nestled high in the Andes and considered by many to be one of the most beautiful cities in South America. Despite this aesthetic beauty, there is a great need for volunteers to assist with the development of this city and its communities. The Ecuador School Support Program (only available September-July) involves teaching children at summer school and during the school year in a broad range of subjects. This program can encompass, but is not limited to – teaching and planning activities for classroom such as art, music, painting, math, English, reading-writing and plays (Drama). A reasonable level of Spanish is required for this program (basic to conversational) as you must be able to communicate with the children.

Street Children Work

Organization: International Volunteer HQ
Location: Placements in Quito, the capital city of Ecuador
Cost: $230 for 1 week to $2,300 for 6 months, includes food and accommodations
Duration: 1 week to 6 months   **Age:** 18
Contact: volunteer@volunteerhq.org
Learn more: www.volunteerhq.org
Special skills: Volunteers need a basic level of Spanish to participate effectively on this program.
Details: School is simply not an option for many children in Ecuador as they work the streets with their parents to help stay alive. Every day of the year these children work the streets of Quito with their parents, selling goods and performing to make a living. The Street Children Program in Ecuador focuses on giving these children some enjoyment in their lives. This program is popular with the children and their families as it gives them opportunities and perspectives on life they would never have otherwise been provided with. Work consists of teaching basic school lessons, playing with the children, providing

medical support and introducing them to activities (such as painting) that they would never otherwise have a chance to do.

Summer Volunteer Program

Organization: The Tandana Foundation
Location: The Andean villages outside of Otavalo
Cost: $1,850   **Duration:** 6 weeks   **Age:** 18
Contact: tandanafoundation@gmail.com
Learn more: www.tandanafoundation.org
Special skills: Conversational Spanish
Details: Volunteer in an indigenous community in the mountains of Ecuador. Live with a host family and experience local culture firsthand. Share your energy and skills with the community, working in either education or health. Offer vacation English or math classes for high school students and friends or assist nurses and doctors in a rural health center. Participate in community work days to improve the village water system, community center or facilities. Meet traditional healers, indigenous leaders, students, and families. Hike to alpine lakes, waterfalls and sacred sites with your new friends. You should have the ability to hold a basic conversation in Spanish and a desire to make new friends and learn about Otavaleno culture.

Hospital in Ambato

Organization: Greenheart Travel
Location: Ambato, about 2.5 hours south of Quito, the capital city of Ecuador.
Cost: $1,290 for 4 weeks   **Duration**: 2 to 12 weeks   **Age:** 18
Contact: info@greenhearttravel.org
Learn more: www.cci-exchange.com
Special skills: Experience and/or education in medicine is required; exceptions may be made on a case by case basis for those interested in exploring a career in medicine, but who have limited experience. An intermediate level of Spanish is required. Spanish lessons are available in Quito prior to the volunteer project for an additional fee. Volunteers must submit a full resume with application for this project.
Details: As one of the few hospitals in the area, the doctors, staff, and volunteers work hard to attend to the hundreds of patients that line the waiting room every day. With many services specializing in mother and infant care, it is not uncommon to have a ward filled with newborns and recovering mothers. The hospital also has a large clinic that tends to the daily needs of the sick and injured. Help is needed in all hospital departments. Depending upon your level of Spanish and previous experience, volunteers could help with intake and general patient exams or assisting with minor surgeries and emergency room traumas.

Host family accommodations and all meals are included in the program.

Organic Farming Project

Organization: Greenheart Travel
Location: The organic farms are located in Tabacundo, a small town on the way north to Ibarra from Quito.
Cost: $1,290 for 4 weeks **Duration**: 2 to 12 weeks **Age:** 18
Contact: info@greenhearttravel.org
Learn more: www.cci-exchange.com
Special skills: Volunteers must enjoy working outdoors and must be interested in farming. Experience and/or education in biology, ecology or environmental studies is helpful but not required. Basic Spanish is necessary. Spanish lessons are available prior to the volunteer project in Quito for an additional fee.
Details: Growing organic fruits and vegetables is very important to these two family-owned farms. These farmers are also part of the Centro de Acopio, located a few miles down the road in the center of Tabacundo, sending their extra fresh produce and grains to sell to the community at affordable prices. All volunteers will be working on the farms helping with the day to day responsibilities of planting, cultivating, fertilizing, and tending to animals. They will also learn about the organic growing process, as well as sell goods at the Centro de Acopio. In addition, volunteers have the chance to get involved in any current community education campaigns. Host family accommodations and all meals are included in the program.

Animal Rescue Center

Organization: Greenheart Travel
Location: 15 minutes outside of Ibarra, a large town about 2.5 hours north of Quito.
Cost: $1,290 for 4 weeks **Duration**: 2 to 12 weeks **Age:** 18
Contact: info@greenhearttravel.org
Learn more: www.cci-exchange.com
Special skills: Volunteers must enjoy working outdoors and must be interested in working with the animals. Experience and/or education in biology, ecology or environmental studies is helpful but not required. Basic Spanish is helpful. Spanish lessons are available in Quito prior to the volunteer project for an additional fee.
Details: The rescue center is home to many exotic animals that are endangered or have been rescued from trafficking situations, especially at the borders and in the Amazon. The staff tries to educate the community

73

on the dangers of animal trafficking and how that can lead to possible extinction. Volunteers will be working directly with the animals as well as with the groups of weekly visitors. Duties include feeding the animals, building and cleaning cages, planting trees and flowers, constructing toys and exhibits, acting as a guide for English speaking tourists that come to tour the Rescue Center, and working with the other staff and volunteers on a variety of projects that are needed. Host family accommodation and all meals are included in the program.

Orphanage & Development Center for Infants/Toddlers

Organization: Greenheart Travel.
Location: 20 minutes by bus from downtown Cuenca
Cost: $1,290 for 4 weeks   **Duration**: 2 to 12   **Age:** 16
Contact: info@greenhearttravel.org
Learn more: www.cci-exchange.com
Special skills: Volunteers must be prepared to work with babies and small children. Experience or education in early childhood development, teaching and/or childcare is helpful, but not required. An intermediate level of Spanish is necessary. Spanish lessons are available in Quito prior to the volunteer project for an additional fee
Details: Serving infants and toddlers ages newborn to 4 years old, the orphanage focuses on early childhood development. From providing basic child care and nourishment for infants to working with toddlers by helping them to walk, the orphanage is committed to giving these children a healthy start in life. Volunteers are needed to assist with feeding, changing, and general care of infants, working with toddlers teaching them school basics like counting and word pronunciation, organizing small recreational activities for free time, and providing any support needed to the staff. Host family accommodations and all meals are included in the program.

Tortoise Project on the Galapagos Islands

Organization: Greenheart Travel
Location: On the Island of Isabela in the Galapagos, about 200 miles off the coast of Ecuador in the Pacific Ocean.
Cost: $1,530 for 4 weeks   **Duration**: 2 to 12 weeks   **Age:** 16
Contact: info@greenhearttravel.org
Learn more: www.cci-exchange.com
Special skills: Volunteers must enjoy working outdoors and must be interested in working with the animals. Basic Spanish is helpful.
Details: The center for the famous endangered tortoises of the Galapagos is quite a unique experience. It is only here that you will be able to take such a hands-on approach when working with these tortoises. Located on Isabela, the most diverse of all the Galapagos Islands, you are constantly immersed in the natural beauty of your

surroundings. From its many active volcanoes to its beautiful beaches, there is always something to enjoy. Focused on preserving this particular species of tortoise, the breeding center is dedicated to monitoring their health, aiding in new births, providing a healthy living environment, and securing their release back in to the wild. Host family accommodations and meals are included in your program.

ELI Community Development

Organization: Experiential Learning International
Cost: Starting at $985   **Duration:** 2+ weeks   **Age:** 18
Contact: info@eliabroad.org   **Learn more:** www.eliabroad.org
Special skills: Intermediate Spanish language skills
Details: The economic crisis of the late 1990s affected almost everyone in Ecuador. Today approximately 40% of Ecuadorians still live below the poverty line. ELI works with several governmental and non-governmental organizations in Ecuador devoted to giving small communities the tools they need to pull themselves from poverty. Possible projects include helping with infrastructure development, educational programs, capacity building, and microloan programs. Volunteers will work directly with these organizations and community members.

Ecuadorian Street Children Assistance

Organization: World Endeavors
Location: Guayaquil, Ecuador
Cost: $1,308+ **Duration:** 2 to 12 weeks **Age:** 18
Contact: inquiry@worldendeavors.com
Learn more: www.worldendeavors.com
Details: Make a difference in the lives of local Ecuadorian street children. Participants assist with projects such as English language teaching, homework help, and general emotional support. Volunteers work five to six hours a day, five days a week, and have the opportunity on the weekends to explore Guayaquil and the Pacific coast. Housing is provided in homestays, giving volunteers a great way to improve their Spanish and learn Ecuadorian culture. Two weeks of Spanish language training is included with placements of four weeks or longer.

Teaching Children in Guayaquil

Organization: World Endeavors
Location: Guayaquil, Ecuador
Cost: $1,308+ **Duration:** 2 to 12 weeks **Age:** 18
Contact: inquiry@worldendeavors.com
Learn more: www.worldendeavors.com

75

Details: Provide English teaching instruction to children in underfunded schools. Though English education is required in Ecuador, there is frequently a lack of qualified teachers. Native or fluent English speakers shadow local teachers as an orientation for teaching independently in classes of children ages 5-12. Volunteers have the opportunity to live with host families and to truly immerse themselves in the local culture. Two weeks of Spanish language training is included with placements of four weeks or longer.

Special Education Program

Organization: World Endeavors
Location: Guayaquil, Ecuador
Cost: $1,308+   **Duration:** 2 to 12 weeks   **Age:** 18
Contact: inquiry@worldendeavors.com
Learn more: www.worldendeavors.com
Details: Assist social workers and staff in a local school for children with disabilities. Volunteers teach, provide basic care, organize events and outings, and help children with special projects. Past projects include teaching children how to plant and care for a vegetable garden. Along with their placement, volunteers have an opportunity to explore Guayaquil and the beautiful Pacific coast. Volunteers stay with local host families; all breakfasts are included. Two weeks of Spanish language training is included with placements of four weeks or longer.

Deaf Education Program in Guayaquil

Organization: World Endeavors
Location: Guayaquil
Cost: $1,308+   **Duration:** 2 to 12 weeks   **Age:** 18
Contact: inquiry@worldendeavors.com
Learn more: www.worldendeavors.com
Details: Make connections with young deaf students in Ecuador. Volunteers assist classroom teachers, participate one-on-one with students, and help lead activities. Learn Ecuadorian sign language and gain a unique cultural experience. Along with their placement, volunteers have an opportunity to explore Guayaquil and the Pacific coast. Stay with local families for a truly immersive experience; all breakfasts are included. Two weeks of Spanish language training is included with placements of four weeks or longer.

Amazon Conservation

Organization: Greenforce
Location: Between the Andes and the Amazon
Cost: $1,900+   **Duration:** 2+ weeks   **Age:** 17
Contact: info@greenforce.org   **Learn more:** www.greenforce.org

Details: The biology station is located at the thin band of tropical forest that connects the Andes Mountains with the Amazon. The station is part of 2,000 hectares of reserves and forest in which volunteers contribute directly to its progress and success. Assist with important scientific and ecological research; turn left and explore the Andes, turn right and enter the Amazon rainforest. Enjoy the remoteness of the station by canoeing to neighboring tribes and experience the indigenous cultures of the communities there. Visit the home of a local shaman and witness rituals and customs like never before. Contrast these cultural endeavors with the adventure of exhilarating whitewater rafting or a night hiking through the rainforest as you listen to the cacophony of sounds as the woods come alive.

Island Conservation

Organization: Kaya Responsible Travel
Location: Living in the busy coastal city of Guayaquil and working on a nearby island.
Cost: $1,270+ **Duration:** 2 to 26 weeks **Age:** 18-80
Contact: info@kayavolunteer.com
Learn more: www.KayaVolunteer.com
Special skills: A moderate level of fitness to conduct manual labour is essential. Any additional construction skills are an invaluable bonus.
Details: Restore the neglected Santay Island and help it become a protected ecological paradise and wildlife sanctuary. This project is supported by volunteers working for responsible development of the island, firstly as a protected ecosystem and second as an eco-tourism attraction. It needs people willing to do hands-on conservation work, but also needs those with special skills such as education, promotion, marketing, web and brochure design. There are many facets to this project and a wide range of skills and interests are needed. Volunteers are expected to take an active role in the field trips to the island, assist with assigned duties which may include working on habitat development, and participating in the estuary program educating children on the environment.

Sustainable Building Projects

Organization: Kaya Responsible Travel
Location: The busy coastal city of Guayaquil
Cost: $1,270+ **Duration:** 2 to 26 weeks **Age:** 18-80
Contact: info@kayavolunteer.com
Learn more: www.KayaVolunteer.com
Specials: No specific skills required, but an interest in environmental conservation is important. Those with computer, marketing or business skills are very helpful with the ecotourism aspect of the project.

Details: Work to improve the living conditions of children and families in poverty. This program supervises the construction of classrooms, libraries, communal water wells, homes, housing improvements, and new sanitation systems. Volunteers also help families to develop sustainable income-generating programs. All year round they are involved in various building projects which really need the assistance of volunteers to keep them going. The influx of enthusiastic volunteers is essential as budgets are always tight and there is little money available beyond material costs and equipment. Those with specific construction skills are particularly encouraged to assist in their specialty area.

Volunteer Abroad and Learn to Surf

Organization: Eco Surf Volunteers
Location: Ecuador
Cost: $1,395 **Duration:** 10 days **Age:** 18-35
Contact: info@ecosurfvolunteers.org
Learn more: www.ecosurfvolunteers.org
Special skills: Hard worker and a positive attitude
Details: Enjoy the beautiful beaches and the warm tropical ocean of an historic Ecuadorian fishing village while the friendliest of locals invite you into their lives. Eco Surf is a volunteer abroad program, a cultural immersion program and an international surf camp all rolled into one! Volunteer with their English Through Art program that teaches local children English in a creative and engaging atmosphere, while local surfers teach you to surf on their favorite nearby waves. Learn to Salsa dance, enjoy a beach party bonfire, meet indigenous tribes and explore a wildlife sanctuary - all with Eco Surf Volunteers.

VISIONS Ecuador & Galapagos for Teens or Groups

Organization: VISIONS Service Adventures
Location: Ecuador & Galapagos
Cost: $5,000+ **Duration:** 4 weeks, and customized programs
Age: Teens, customized programs for all ages
Contact: info@VisionsServiceAdventures.com

Learn more: www.VisionsServiceAdventures.com
Special skills: A minimum requirement of two years of high school Spanish
Details: "Mitad del Mundo" (middle of the earth) offers Spanish language and indigenous culture immersion on the Galapagos Islands and in a mainland Andean community. This program combines group living and a home-stay experience. One week of the program unfolds on the Galapagos and for three weeks participants live in a mainland Andean village. Projects mix construction, agriculture/farming, and ecological and environmental work. Participants actively explore a "megadiverse" World Heritage Site (the Galapagos) and the diverse beauty and culture of Ecuador's Andean highlands. Recreation includes snorkeling, wildlife viewing, and hiking; treks to waterfalls and lakes; visits to marketplaces and thermal baths; and learning about folkloric music, arts, and dancing.

Work at the Maquipucuna Ecological Reserve for Teens

Organization: Academic Treks
Location: Quito, Cuenca, Tosagua and the Andes
Cost: $5,580
Duration: 40+ hours of volunteerism as part of 30-day language and cultural immersion program   **Age:** Teens finishing grades 10-12
Contact: info@academictreks.com; 919-256-8200 or 888-833-1908
Learn more: www.academictreks.com
Special skills: Two years high school Spanish
Details: On Academic Treks Spanish language and cultural immersion program in Ecuador, students work with the Maquipucuna Ecological Reserve, helping with organic gardening projects, trail maintenance, local cottage industry efforts and educating local youth about conservation and sustainable development practices. Working alongside local volunteers and conservationists, they practice their Spanish and develop meaningful friendships. Students are engaged in service work for most of the day for one week of the program. During the rest of this 30-day adventure, they can expect to experience the spectacular Andes Mountains, Incan culture, gracious people and historic colonial towns on an unforgettable journey.

Customized Group Service Project in Ecuador

Organization: The Tandana Foundation
Location: Otavalo
Cost: Varies, depending on the project
Duration: Variable, depending on the group's needs
Age: 12+ welcome with adult chaperones
Contact: tandanafoundation@gmail.com
Learn more: www.tandanafoundation.org

79

Details: Let your group make a difference in the lives of rural Ecuadorians while becoming part of the community you serve. Stay with host families or in a community building, eat local foods with your hosts, help villagers replace inadequate drinking water pipes or paint their community center, harvest corn and use its flour to bake bread, hike to sacred places while hearing legends about their importance, and play games with schoolchildren. Whether you have a class, school group, church group, or set of friends--any group that wants a new experience and a chance to make friends by helping out-- Tandana Foundation can coordinate a service project and a unique learning experience for your groups.

Health Care Volunteer Vacation

Organization: The Tandana Foundation
Location: Quichinche, in the Andean valleys near Otavalo, Ecuador
Cost: $1,350 for 1 week, $2,200 for 2 weeks **Duration:** 1 to 2 weeks
Age: 12+ welcome with parent, most participants are 18-85
Contact: tandanafoundation@gmail.com
Learn more: www.tandanafoundation.org
Special skills: Tandana needs both licensed health care providers and other volunteers with no special skills
Details: Experience life in the highlands of Ecuador while sharing your valuable skills with villagers by joining this volunteer vacation in service of others. Be part of a team that provides medical care for rural community members. After a lunch provided by the community, view  breathtaking scenery by walking to the Peguche waterall or the legendary Lechero tree, or visit local craftspeople, such as Miguel Andrango, master weaver. A delicious dinner and time to socialize with this great group of travelers in comfortable Las Palmeras Inn will cap off your day. Short, but so much deeper than a tour, this opportunity is unique in its ability to connect you with people on another part of the planet.

Other organizations offering projects in Ecuador:

Fundacion Arte del Mundo: www.artedelmundoecuador.com
Child and Family Health International: www.cfhi.org
Cielo Azul (indigenous people & disadvantaged children):
  www. cieloazul.ch
Colibris Women's Artisian Cooperative: www.colibrisecuador.org
Eco Volunteer UP Foundation: www.volunteer-latinamerica.com
Global Visions International: www.gviusa.com or www.gvi.co.uk
Lifewater International: www.lifewater.org
Comuna de Rhiannon (solar, permaculture, yoga, holistic):
  www.rhiannon-community.org

Reptile and Amphibian Ecological International:
  reptilesandamphibians.org
Sacred Suenos (permaculture): www.sacredsuenos.com/who.html
Volunteers for Economic Growth Alliance: www.vegaalliance.org
Yanapuma Foundation (community development):
  www.yanapuma.org

Guyana

Guyana Teaching Year

Organization: WorldTeach
Location: Guyana – mostly rural placements, but a few urban
Cost: $2,000 – subsidized by Ministry of Education of Guyana
Duration: One Year (Departure in early August) **Age:** 18-74
Contact: info@worldteach.org **Learn more:** www.worldteach.org
Special skills: Native English Speaker, Bachelor's Degree
Details: Volunteers have been requested to teach chemistry, physics,
biology, and mathematics. Volunteers will be placed at schools located
in the deep riverain/hinterland and in the southern savannah
region. Both regions are relatively undeveloped and have few trained
teachers, and both serve primarily Amerindians populations.
Volunteers may also teach at schools in larger towns in the riverain
area. These schools serve students from all six of Guyana's main ethnic
groups. They are larger and have more trained teachers on staff than
schools in more rural areas. Volunteers might also serve in larger high
schools in coastal cities such as Georgetown, Guyana's
capital. Volunteers will live in teacher housing near their schools
provided by the Ministry of education. You will be given contacts of
individuals and families who serve as a support network at their site,
although you will find many Guyanese eager to be your friend.

Other organizations offering projects in Guyana:

Florida Association for Volunteer Action in the Caribbean and the
  America's: www.favaca.org
Habitat for Humanity International: www.habitat.org
Operation Renewed Hope Christ (medical & disaster relief):
  www.operationrenewedhope.org
World Hope International: www.worldhope.org
Youth Challenge Australia: www.youthchallenge.org.au

Paraguay

Paraguarí, Paraguay - Health
Organization: Amigos de las Américas
Location: Paraguarí in southern Paraguay
Cost: $4,000+ **Duration:** 8 weeks **Age:** 16 by Sept. 1st
Contact: info@amigoslink.org **Learn more:** www.amigoslink.org
Details: Volunteers will facilitate educational activities 3 times a week
with youth age 5-12. Topics include nutrition, cultural exchange,
physical education and dental hygiene. Special emphasis will be placed
on environmental health issues. Help is also needed running a 2 week
long day camp for children during the Paraguayan winter break.

Global Village Trip to Paraguay
Organization: Habitat for Humanity
Location: Seven different project locations.
Cost: $1,140–$1,300 (10 days); $1,450–1,600 (15 days)
Duration: 10 or 15 days
Age: 18, 14 with a legal guardian or as part of an established group.
Contact: gv@habitat.org, 1-800-HABITAT (422-4828), ext. 7530
Learn more: www.habitat.org
Special skills: Global Village teams are open to all with a willingness
to work hard, learn new skills and explore a new culture. Many trips
require strenuous manual labor, so all participants should be in good
health.
Details: Paraguay is the third poorest country in South America, and
 few government-funded housing subsidy
programs exist in Paraguay. At 2.6 percent, the
population growth in Paraguay is one of the
highest in Latin America, creating an
immediate need and high demand for adequate
housing. Paraguay has 400,000 families without a decent house, and at
least 10,000 more houses are needed each year. (Felipe Cabrera, leader
of Coordinadora Intergremial de Organizaciones Populares/Popular
Association Network leader.) Habitat for Humanity was established in
Paraguay in 1998. Since then HFH Paraguay has built more than 900
houses, providing decent housing for more than 4,500 people. Each
Habitat for Humanity housing project is unique and adapts to the
needs of the families and the communities where Habitat Paraguay
builds.

Other organizations offering projects in Paraguay:

ACDI/VOCA (agriculture, finance, community development):
www.acdivoca.org
Amigos de las Américas: www.amigoslink.org
Fauna Paraguay: www.faunaparaguay.com
Habitat for Humanity International: www.habitat.org
Kiva Fellows Program: www.kiva.org
Para La Tierra (conservation): www.paralatierra.org
Volunteers for Economic Growth Alliance: www.vegaalliance.org

Peru

Teaching English to the Disadvantaged

Organization: Espaanglisch Language School
Location: Coastal city of Trujillo, Peru
Cost: None **Duration:** 1+ months **Age:** 18
Contact: davidmercedes@espaanglisch.com
Learn more: www.espaanglisch.com
Details: Espaanglisch is a small organization that needs volunteer
English language teachers to work with disadvantaged children and
adults. English is a very important skill for a Peruvian to have. The
school helps out those who otherwise wouldn't have access to English
language education. They look for volunteers that know how to work
hard and relax even harder! You will work an average of a few hours a
day, and are otherwise encouraged to get out there and soak up the
Peruvian culture... whether that be through Spanish, salsa, the cuisine
or just having a chat with a local fisherman! It is especially important
that a volunteer be creative and confident, not afraid to work
independently. There is no charge to volunteer, simply cover your own
living costs.

Mundo de Niños Home for Ex-Street Children

Organization: Otra Cosa Network
Location: The fishing/seaside/surfing resort of Huanchaco, 12 km
from Trujillo in Northern Peru.
Cost: Service fee approx US$115 payable on arrival in local currency.
You pay your own accommodation and food. The options of a low cost
volunteer house at US$150/month with kitchen, fridge, cooker, etc or
family homestays are also options.

Duration: A minimum stay of 6 weeks is required although more is preferred by the institution and its kids. Then, you can really get to know the kids and they know you.
Age: 18 with some relevant experience with children or 21+ without
Contact: otracosavoluntario@gmail.com
Learn more: www.otracosa.org
Special skills: A minimum of an intermediate command of Spanish on arrival. Some experience or affection for working with children
Details: Mundo de Niños is a project set up in 2001 designed to help get children off the streets and into the loving, secure, home lifestyle they deserve. Given their background, working with these children can be a challenge, but giving them the chance to rehabilitate their lives makes Mundo de Niños a hugely rewarding project. Instilling the norms and values of life as a family group, as well as offering psychological and educational support and basic hygiene care, the team is a multi-disciplined support network that gives the children a chance to work towards a better future. Any artistic or sports-related skills are a great advantage to organizing activities. However anyone who is a competent, motivated team player with a genuine interest in helping and working with children is very welcome here.

Children with Down's Syndrome (& other disabilities)

Organization: Proyecto Yannick
Location: Celendín (Cajamarca), Perú
Cost: $30, or family stay with 3 meals a day: $250 a month
Duration: 1+ month   **Age:** 18
Contact: py@celendinperu.com
Learn more: www.celendinperu.com
Special skills: They prefer people who have experience in working with disabled children, for example physiotherapists or special education teachers. It helps if you speak at least some basic Spanish.
Details: Disabled children in this poor part of Peru aren't part of society. A lot of parents feel ashamed and hide their children. By empowering them with information, teaching them how to do exercises and providing help with their education, they can participate better in daily life. This region is beautiful and hardly known by tourists! It is still authentic, with traditional weekly markets, pre-Inca-ruins, Guinea pigs running through the kitchens, etc. You will get to know the real Perú.

Protection of Llamas and Vicuña

Organization: A Pas de Loup
Location: Southern province of Arequipa
Cost: $8 per day for meals

Duration: 1+ months   **Age:** 18 to 77
Contact: info@apasdeloup.org
Learn more: www.apasdeloup.org
Special skills: Have very good knowledge of Spanish and have
already participated in a mission with
Ecovolontariat A Pas de Loup.
Details: À Pas de Loup is an independent
nonprofit organization, staffed mainly by
volunteers, that aims to make people aware of
the importance of safeguarding the environment.
The mission is part of a contracted partnership
between three structures: A Pas de Loup, the
Ministry of the Environment and the Peruvian
National Reserve Salinas y Aguada Blanca. The onsite team consisting
of a director, 16 guards and 34 volunteers, is responsible for overseeing
the reserve, the establishment of scientific research and advocacy with
the local population.

St Toribio School for Special Needs Children

Organization: Otra Cosa Network
Location: Florecia de Mora shanty town in Trujillo, Northern Peru,
near the fishing/seaside/surfing resort of Huanchaco.
Cost: Approx $115 payable on arrival in local currency. You pay your
own accommodations and food. Options of a low cost ($150 per month)
volunteer house or a family home stay exist, or choose your own hostel.
Duration: At least 6 weeks around 4 hours per morning
Age: 18 with relevant experience with children or 21+ without
Contact: otracosavoluntario@gmail.com
Learn more: www.otracosa.org
Special skills: A basic to intermediate command of Spanish on arrival
and it is advisable you have some experience or affection for working
with children.
Details: The placement is a hands-on job with disabled children.
Santo Toribio is a special needs school for children from disadvantaged
backgrounds, based in a poor area of Trujillo. Adopting a unique
approach to the children's education, it offers them the chance to learn
valuable practical skills through hands-on workshops in baking, shoe
making, jewelery making and woodcraft, as well as basic numerical
skills, reading and writing. Equipping the children with this important
creative expertise boosts their self-esteem as they transcend the poor
life chances they once had and sets them in step for a successful and
happy future. Santo Toribio promotes a positive, supportive and loving
environment in which the children are encouraged to become
independent, productive and happy individuals. All that is required of

you is to arrive at work with a smile, a positive attitude and a genuine willingness to help.

Reconstruction of Pisco

Organization: Pisco Sin Fronteras
Location: Pisco
Cost: $5 per day **Duration:** Unknown **Age:** 18
Contact: piscosinfronteras@hotmail.com
Learn more: www.piscosinfronteras.org

Special Skills: Construction, Carpentry, Plumbing, Electricty, teaching English, a big heart and the willingness to get things done.
Detail: Eighty percent of the city of Pisco was destroyed by an earthquake, leaving most of the inhabitants without homes and killing over 600 people, It's been three years since the disaster and in places it looks like it just happened. Aid from the state has not been as anyone had expected. Please be part of the reconstruction of this beautiful city and change people's lives. Volunteers make a difference. You really don't need certain skills. You will learn from both other experienced volunteers and the local community. This is a great way to get to know the culture of Peru.

Fighting Poverty with Education

Organization: Asociacion Incawasi
Location: Cajamarca, Peru
Cost: $300 per month **Duration:** 2+ months **Age:** 20
Contact: incawasi.peru@gmail.com
Learn more: www.incawasi.org.pe
Details: Help break the chain of poverty and social inequality in Andean Peru. Incawasi is a non-profit organization which since 2005 has worked to provide educational and nutritional support to children from poor backgrounds in the city of Cajamarca, in the north of Peru. Children visit the center everyday for a warm meal as well as to attend workshops and activities, organized by a team of international and local volunteers. Asociacion Incawasi also works to ensure their right to an education and healthcare, and provide them with the means to build a better future. Volunteers actively participate in the development of their creative, behavioral and intellectual skills, and are more than welcome to participate in all other aspects of the organization's work (fund-raising, communication, website, etc.) Meals and accommodations are included in the center itself for a total immersion in the local culture and language.

Teach English, Transform Huaycan!

Organization: Light and Leadership Initiative
Location: Huaycan, just outside of Lima
Cost: $75 per week or $300 per month
Duration: 1 day to 1 year   **Age:** 18
Contact: Lara@lightandleadership.org
Learn more: www.lightandleadership.org
Special skills: Native English speaker
Details: The Light and Leadership Initiative is an entirely volunteer run organization, so they need you in order to continue their impact! The organization is looking for volunteers who believe in education and are excited to teach in Huaycan, a shantytown outside of Lima. The English program is Light and Leadership's largest program and positively impacts several different areas of Huaycan. You will work directly with kids and adults to help shape their future and transform their community. It's about more than just teaching English—it's about community transformation! Internships, short-term stays and long-term stays are all available.

Teach French to Eager Kids

Organization: Light and Leadership Initiative
Location: Huaycan, just outside of Lima
Cost: $75 per week or $300 per month
Duration: 1 day to 1 year   **Age:** 18
Contact: Lara@lightandleadership.org
Learn more: www.lightandleadership.org
Special skills: Native French speaker
Details: Entirely run by volunteers, The Light and Leadership Initiative needs you to continue their impact! Volunteers who believe in education and are excited about making a difference are needed to teach French in Huaycan, a shantytown outside of Lima. Work with kids who are eager to learn French to advance their studies in high school, university or culinary arts school. Plus you gain valuable Spanish language practice, make lasting friendships, and discover the positive impact you'll have through education. Internships, short-term stays and long-term stays are all available.

Kids Discover Education Through Art

Organization: Light and Leadership Initiative
Location: Huaycan, just outside of Lima
Cost: $75 per week or $300 per month
Duration: 1 day to 1 year   **Age:** 18
Contact: Lara@lightandleadership.org
Learn more: www.lightandleadership.org

Special skills: Basic Spanish skills
Details: The Light and Leadership Initiative is an entirely volunteer run organization, so they need you to continue our impact! They are looking for volunteers who believe in education and are excited to teach in Huaycan, a shantytown outside of Lima. Their art program is always in need of dedicated and inspired teachers to promote education through art. The art program is Light and Leaderships most popular program. Gain insight into Peruvian culture, practice and develop your Spanish, and discover the positive impact you'll have through education. Internships, short-term stays and long-term stays are all available.

Teaching English to Primary Grade Children

Organization: Supporting Kids In Peru (SKIP)
Location: El Porvenir, outside of Trujillo
Cost: $125 - $350 per month depending on length of stay
Duration: 1+ month **Age:** 18
Contact: volunteering@skipperu.org
Learn more: www.skipperu.org
Special skills: Prior experience working with children and an energetic personality.
Details: SKIP aims to support the community of El Porvenir in a multi-faceted approach: high quality education for youth and economic assistance for entire families are the pillars of their program. Early education is a vital part of community development; SKIP is looking for enthusiastic volunteers willing to teach English to primary school children. Certification in English teaching is not required. SKIP's English teaching coordinator will be able to provide you with guidance and advice. You will plan lessons as a team with other volunteers from around the world, but you will be teaching classes by yourself or co-teaching with one other person. This is a fantastic opportunity for anyone looking to gain experience teaching or who enjoys spending time with children. It's a fun but challenging job benefiting countless people.

Work with Nursery Children

Organization: Supporting Kids In Peru (SKIP)
Location: El Porvenir, outside of Trujillo, Peru
Cost: $125 - $350 per month depending on length of stay
Duration: 1+ month **Age:** 18
Contact: volunteering@skipperu.org
Learn more: www.skipperu.org
Special skills: Background in education for young children

Details: SKIP aims to support the community of El Porvenir in a multi-faceted approach. As SKIP's approach to family care is very holistic, they have a nursery program that includes educational  workshops with the parents. This has been very effective in educating parents on issues such as child development, which improves their understanding of what young children need during their formative years. Volunteers working with the nursery will write the curriculum for these meetings, thus an ability to organize and plan effectively will be essential. SKIP is running this project on a small budget, so innovative and creative thinkers able to come up with inexpensive activities are needed. Any background in child psychology or social work would be invaluable, as well. Spanish level can be very low.

Help to Develop the Economy of El Porvenir

Organization: Supporting Kids In Peru (SKIP)
Location: El Porvenir, outside of Trujillo, Peru
Cost: $125 - $350 per month depending on length of stay
Duration: 1+ month **Age:** 18
Contact: volunteering@skipperu.org
Learn more: www.skipperu.org
Special skills: Background in business and/or economic development
Details: SKIP is looking for enthusiastic and innovative thinkers to help with their Economic Development (EcoDev) Program. Volunteers involved in the EcoDev department will get to know all aspects of the program; namely the microcredit project, the business and productive workshops as well as the marketing and distribution of products the SKIP mothers manufacture within these workshops. Volunteers will be appointed to projects that best suit their skills and interests and in which their help is most needed. The more time one is able to commit, the more they will gain from the volunteer experience. A more advanced level of Spanish is desirable as well as this will mean the volunteer is better able to communicate with the families and understand their situation and how they benefit from the program.

Social Work in Developing Communities

Organization: Supporting Kids In Peru (SKIP)
Location: El Porvenir, outside of Trujillo, Peru
Cost: $125 - $350 per month depending on length of stay
Duration: 1+ month **Age:** 18
Contact: volunteering@skipperu.org
Learn more: www.skipperu.org
Special skills: Background in social work, high level of Spanish

Details: SKIP is looking for qualified social workers who can utilize past experience from study and practice to benefit families in El Porvenir. SKIP is also looking for student social workers and those who have an interest in the profession. SKIP works with about 150 families in total, and social workers carry out visits to each family at least twice per year. The purpose of these visits is to talk about how things are going for the family, both financially and emotionally and to try to solve problems through various methods of support. Staff will also meet with families who come to the office on occasion. Additionally, the Social Work team is responsible for assessing new applicants, running educational group sessions with parents and teaching workshops for teens.

Teaching Primary Grade School

Organization: Supporting Kids In Peru (SKIP)
Location: El Porvenir, outside of Trujillo
Cost: $125 - $350 per month depending on length of stay
Duration: 1+ month   **Age:** 18
Contact: volunteering@skipperu.org
Learn more: www.skipperu.org
Special skills: Background in teaching primary level children, high level of Spanish
Details: Because the public school system in Peru is severely lacking, SKIP has developed a project to supplement primary school lessons in class by offering additional lessons. They also offer help with homework. They are looking for volunteers who are interested in staying long term (3+ months preferable) and can help in the development and implementation of this project. A high level of Spanish is necessary as this will be the teaching language. You will be teaching the children in the afternoons and on Saturday mornings. Attempts are made to use interactive teaching methods that enable the children to learn concepts in a fun environment – something lacking in their school experience in general.

Self-Sustainable Conservation Project

Organization: Rumi Wilco Ecolodge and Nature Reserve
Location: Vilcabamba
Cost: $5 per day ($3 if camping)
Duration: 1 week to 3 months   **Age:** 18
Contact: rumiwilco@yahoo.com
Learn more: www.rumiwilco.com
Details: Rumi Wilco is a small, but quite appealing protected area adjacent to a village's centre. Notable among its forest members is the legendary Wilco tree (*Anadenanthera colubrina*) whose association

with Native American peoples dates back many thousands of years. Their distribution within Ecuador is restricted almost entirely to the Vilcabamba valley and its environs. Volunteer work at Rumi includes trail maintenance; riverbank repair and reinforcement; reforesting with native tree species; organic gardening; basic carpentry; coffee picking/processing; fruit gathering & making marmalades. If scientifically trained: species' identification (especially mammals, reptiles), ecological research and other.

Incawasi - Peru

Organization: Kids Worldwide
Location: Cajamarca, a beautiful colonial city in Peru's northern highlands
Cost: $300 per month includes a donation to fund the project plus volunteer's accommodation and meals from Monday to Friday.
Duration: 2 weeks minimum, 2 month+ preferred
Age: 18, kids welcome with a parent after prior consultation.
Contact: incawsi@kidsworldwide.org
Learn more: www.incawasi.org.pe
Special skills: Conversational level of Spanish and preferably some background in working/volunteering with children.
Details: Incawasi is a non-profit organization whose objective is to improve the educational, social and nutritional situation of children from disadvantaged areas in the city of Cajamarca, Peru. They currently work with forty children between the ages of 7 and 16. These children come from overcrowded, extremely poor and mainly female-headed households located in the rural and marginal urban areas of Cajamarca. Volunteers provide food, classes and medical attention to children who would otherwise be on the streets. The main goal is to enable those children whose families cannot offer them an opportunity to attend school. Incawasi helps with the provision of school materials, small scholarships and educational support. It also fosters good relations within the community, offering consultancy and support to the families.

Small Animals Spay and Neuter Project

Organization: Asociacion Humanitaria San Fransisco de Asis
Location: Colan, Northern Peru
Cost: $20 per day   **Duration:** Varies
Contact: rosagordon2003@hotmail.com
Learn more: www.ahsfa.org
Special skills: Veterinarians, vet techs and vet students
Details: AHSFA has been running for 8 yrs. They are situated on the North West coast of Peru on a wonderful stretch of beach, sunsets fishing boats and the sound of the sea to lull volunteers to sleep. This is

a small dedicated group striving to improve animal and community life in the nearby rural villages in northern Peru. There is much need for volunteers to help these animals. Asociacion Humanitaria San Fransisco de Asis has been awarded for their "outstanding commitment and achievement". In 2001 they spayed and neutered 18 animals. By mid-2009 they raised enough funding through "Fundacion Brigitte Bardot" and donors, and had enough volunteers to altered 500 animals. Talk to them about volunteering and hear the pride they take in their work.

Equine Aid to Underprivileged Working Animals

Organization: Asociacion Humanitaria San Francisco de Asis
Special Skills: Equine Vet especially Equine Dentistry Vet, Farrier
Location: Colan, Northern Peru
Cost: $20.00 per day **Duration:** Varies
Contact: rosagordon2003@hotmail.com
Learn more: www.ahsfa.org
Details: Situated on the North West coast of Peru on a wonderful stretch of sundrenched beach, sunsets, fishing boats and the sound of the sea to lull you to sleep. This is a small dedicated group striving to improve animal and community life in the nearby rural villages in northern Peru. This project has a special need for equine dentistry work as well as for a farrier. For horse-savvy volunteers seeking a fulfilling experience, this could be the unique opportunity that allows you to make a difference in your own life and in the lives of some very special animals desperately in need of your help.

Healthcare in Mountain Communities

Organization: The Mountain Fund
Location: Varies by project
Cost: $200+ **Duration:** 2+ weeks **Age:** 18
Contact: jenn@mountainfund.org
Learn more: www.mountainfund.org
Special skills: Spanish speaking is helpful, but not mandatory
Details: Volunteers are needed for medical clinics and orphanages. The Mountain Fund works hand in hand with local community leaders to identify solvable problems in the community and take action to do those things that can be done now. Their goal is to create healthy, vibrant mountain communities where people have access to healthcare, education and economic opportunity in an environment where human rights are valued and respected. These goals must be undertaken with respect and preservation of underlying cultural practices and norms. In mountain communities the suffering caused by poverty can be overwhelming. The needs far outstrip the local resources. The

Mountain Fund's approach is to discover those things that can be done today, with very little funding and by local protagonists dedicated to their own communities.

The Mountain School

Organization: Tinkuy Peru
Location: Huancayo
Cost: $560 for one month **Duration:** 1+ weeks **Age:** 17
Contact: Leonciotinoco@hotmail.com
Learn more: www.tinkuyperu.com
Details: The Mountain School is a grassroots program founded in 2005. They teach not only English, but crafts, mathematics, geography and health issues as well as other skills that promote growth and development among underprivileged children. Many of these students would not receive any formal education without the help of volunteers like you. For example, the school currently provides educational opportunities for special needs children, an opportunity that the local government fails to provide them. Your weekly payment covers accommodations and 3 meals a day Monday through Sunday. On the weekend, you will have the opportunity to partake in a diverse range of guided trips. For instance, the glacier in Huaytapallana that surely ranks alongside the most stunning natural attractions in the world.

Huancayo Community Education

Organization: Tinkuy Peru
Location: Huancayo, Peru.
Cost: $560 for one month **Duration:** 1+ week **Age:** 17
Contact: Leonciotinoco@hotmail.com
Learn more: www.tinkuyperu.com
Details: A major problem in Huancayo is the state of the local environment. Streets littered with rubbish and dangerously low levels of sanitation are commonplace. Volunteers will have the opportunity to visit houses in the local community in order to educate people in the very basics of general cleanliness. The difference you can make through education, to environmental preservation, and the reduction of children's susceptibility to avoidable illnesses is incomprehensible. Your weekly payment covers accommodations and 3 meals a day Monday through Sunday. On the weekend, you will have the opportunity to partake in a diverse range of guided trips for a modest fee. For instance, the glacier in Huaytapallana, surely rank alongside some of the most beautiful natural attractions in the world.

Torre Torre

Organization: Tinkuy Peru
Location: Huancayo
Cost: $560 for one month **Duration:** 1+ week **Age:** 17
Contact: Leonciotinoco@hotmail.com
Learn more: www.tinkuyperu.com
Special skills: Experience in construction, marketing or business would be invaluable, but is not required
Details: Located in one of the poorest regions of Huancayo the captivating natural beauty of "Torre Torre" (a labyrinth of hiking trails among a beautiful vista of natural sandstone pillars) seems somewhat out of place given its impoverished surroundings. But with your help there is hope that these unfortunate surroundings will gradually become a thing of the past. The ultimate aim of this project is to bring tourism, and the prosperity that accompanies it to the area. Given that Huancayo is the closest major city to Lima with good transport links and also boasts an impressive array of tourist attractions, this is certainly realizable. However, due to the direction of government resources and the general perception of the city as a Mecca for commerce and little else, it has struggled to create a big tourist market. As such, substantial work needs to be carried out to put Torre Torre on the map. The most pressing concerns for the project involve the construction of access paths and the promotion of Torre Torre. As such, any experience in construction, marketing or business would be invaluable to the program.

Amazon Rainforest Wildlife Rehab & Relocation

Organization: Center for Rehabilitation and Conservation for Wild Animals
Location: Near Puerto Maldonado
Cost: $25 per day includes meals and accommodations
Duration: 2+ weeks **Age:** 18
Contact: ediaz@amazonshelter.org
Learn more: www.amazonshelter.org

Details: Delve into the lush Amazonian Rainforest and travel with a purpose. The non-profit C.R.C.A.S. was born out of a need to fight against the illegal traffic of wild animal species. Their mission is *"to contribute to the education of people so they can understand, respect and conserve Nature"*. The shelter needs versatile volunteers who are proactive and ready to do whatever needs done: cleaning, improving or building enclosures, taking care of animals, acting as guides, repairing tools, computer work, lab studies, keeping daily notes about the animals, interacting with people from local communities, environmental education, etc. With such a variety of work this could be a perfect project for couples or small groups with different of skill sets.

CEP Shanty Town School

Organization: Otra Cosa Network
Location: Ramon Castilla shanty town in Trujillo. This is a short commute from Otra Cosa Network's base in the nearby resort of Huanchaco.
Cost: Service fee approx US$115 (for 2010). They offer the options of a low cost volunteer house at around US$150 per month with kitchen, fridge, cooker etc, family homestays or you can choose your own hostel.
Duration: 4 weeks, work is mornings only, around 4 to 5 hours per day
Age: 18 with relevant experience, or 19+
Contact: otracosavoluntario@gmail.com
Learn more: www.otracosa.org
Special skills: Basic Spanish on arrival. This placement is a hands-on job with children. You need some experience or affection for work with children.
Details: The 'Corporation de Educacion Popular' (C.E.P.) is a unique schooling project built by of the population of one of Trujillo's shanty towns, Ramon Castilla. The parents took action because the Peruvian state could not offer them anything better. Currently, they have over 250 students from 3 to 10 years old. Kids get free education, school materials and the poorest get a free meal a day while at school. Volunteers can assist in a number of areas. The school requires assistant teachers who can help give more attention to the children. They also need volunteers who can lead projects in English, art, theatre, sporting activities and other workshops. Anyone with a flexible and open minded personality and affection for children is welcome.

St Toribio School for Special Needs Children

Organization: Otra Cosa Network
Location: Florecia de Mora shanty town in Trujillo, Northern Peru.
Cost: Service fee approx US$115 (for 2010). They offer the options of a low cost volunteer house at around US$150 per month with kitchen, fridge, cooker etc, family homestays or you can choose your own hostel.
Duration: 4 weeks, work is mornings only, around 4 to 5 hours per day
Age: 18 with relevant experience or 19+
Contact: otracosavoluntario@gmail.com
Learn more: www.otracosa.org
Special skills: Basic Spanish on arrival. This placement is a hands-on job with children. You need some experience or affection for working with children.

95

Details: Santo Toribio is a special needs school for children from disadvantaged backgrounds, based in a poor area of Trujillo. Adopting a unique approach to the children's education, it offers them the chance to learn valuable practical skills through workshops in baking, shoe making, jewelry making and woodcraft, as well as basic numerical skills, reading and writing. Equipping the children with this important creative expertise boosts their self-esteem as they transcend the poor life chances they once had and sets them in step for a happy and successful future. Santo Toribio promotes a positive, supportive and loving environment in which the children are encouraged to become independent, productive and happy individuals. All that is required of you is to come to work with a smile, a positive attitude and a genuine willingness to help.

Sicches Organic Farm

Organization: Otra Cosa Network
Location: The villages of Sicchespampa and San Marcos, in the Cloud Forest of Northern Peru
Cost: Service fee approx US$115 (for 2010). You live with the farm families. They provide free basic accommodation and basic food. You can provide some extra food.
Duration: The demands here are seasonal so check with Otra Cosa Network **Age:** 19
Contact: otracosavoluntario@gmail.com
Learn more: www.otracosa.org
Special skills: An intermediate command of Spanish ability to work with organic coffee farmers, of special interest to volunteers with a desire to work in and learn about organic agriculture, fair trade and small scale farm organization.
Details: In this project you work with the family farmers who cultivate organic coffee and sugar. The farmers are organized in an association called CEPICAFE. They work together on each other's fields and are inviting volunteers to come and help the group out. This project is not for everyone. This can be hard physical work up the mountain in the sun. It's living in basic conditions and is isolated from Westerners, telephones and Internet (nearest town with a phone is a 2 hour walk down the mountain) so you can feel isolated. However, if you want to be away from it all with the locals and don't mind some hard physical labor, this can be very rewarding to be in this beautiful location, living and working as part of a local family.

Abandoned Dogs' Home

Organization: Otra Cosa Network
Location: 10 minutes outside of Huanchaco.
Cost: $115 **Duration:** 2 to16 weeks **Age:** 19, 18 with relevant experience
Contact: otracosavoluntario@gmail.com
Learn more: www.otracosa.org
Special skills: A basic level of Spanish, a genuine interest in and love for animals and a willingness to help.
Details: The conditions at the Abandoned Dogs' Home are very basic. Can you handle working in a very primitive environment with sick,  disabled and maybe dirty animals? In other words, they really need you! Most of the work will be based at the shelter. Working hours will be negotiable, but dependent on when you are needed you'll be at the shelter 4-5 times a week. There is also the opportunity to be involved when they go for their outreach activities in different neighborhoods. This project has just started taking volunteers, so you should be a hardier, animal-savvy traveler, comfortable in primitive conditions and not expect a formalized volunteer program.

Domestic Worker Education

Organization: Experiential Learning International
Special Skills: Intermediate Spanish Language Skills
Location: Lima
Cost: Starting at $885 **Duration:** 2+ weeks **Age:** 18
Contact: info@eliabroad.org **Learn more:** www.eliabroad.org
Details: Over the last century, Peru has been experiencing a massive rural to urban migration. Many of the workers pouring into Lima are domestic workers hoping to make their fortune and support their families. Many domestic service workers find themselves in abusive situations. Volunteers work with an education center that offers adult education, training, advocacy programs, and assistance with job placement. This organization serves to empower newly arrived domestic workers and encourages everyone to support each other, make friends, and create a support system for themselves. Volunteers can assist with teaching classes and workshops. Possible topics include English, Spanish, child development, cooking, arts and crafts, family planning, and other subjects.

Teaching English in Urubamba

Organization: Nexos Voluntarios (NeVo)
Location: Urubamba (1 Hour from Cusco)

Cost: $1,750+ (includes housing) **Duration:** 8+ weeks **Age:** 18
Contact: coordinator@nexosvoluntarios.org
Learn more: www.nexosvoluntarios.org
Special skills: Intermediate level of Spanish
Details: Urubamba is located in the Sacred Valley, surrounded by the significant ruins of the Inca Empire. This Peruvian town is eagerly seeking volunteers to teach English to children in pre-Kindergarten, primary and high school. Nexos Voluntarios works closely with three different schools in the community where English is either not being taught, or not being taught effectively. English is a potential tool in empowering the community to improve its quality of life. Help be responsible for the success of this project and expand your own skills during this rewarding experience.

Supporting the Artisans in the Sacred Valley

Organization: Nexos Voluntarios (NeVo)
Cost: $1,750+ (includes housing) **Duration:** 8+ weeks **Age:** 18
Contact: coordinator@nexosvoluntarios.org
Learn more: www.nexosvoluntarios.org
Location: Urubamba (1 Hour from Cusco)
Special skills: Intermediate level of Spanish
Details: Cusco is the center of the Incan Empire and it receives thousands of visitors a year heading to Machu Picchu. Urubamba is a transit hub for regional buses. Here, many artisans have discovered a good market in which to improve and sell their products. However, the number of markets and increased competition has reduced the profits of the artisans. They are looking for volunteers who are students or experts in the following areas: business administration, accounting, global development, international commerce and art & design. With the volunteers' help the goals are to develop: a business plan for the association, additional sales channels in order to increase revenue, a marketing campaign to promote the market, training sessions in basic business tools and improving the design of their products. Help prepare the artisans to be self-sufficient in one of our most rewarding projects.

Reproductive Health Campaign

Organization: Nexos Voluntarios (NeVo)
Location: Urubamba, Peru (1 Hour from Cusco)
Cost: $1750+ (includes housing) **Duration**: 8+ weeks **Age:** 18
Contact: coordinator@nexosvoluntarios.org
Learn more: www.nexosvoluntarios.org
Special skills: Intermediate level of Spanish
Details: Located in the Sacred Valley surrounded by the ruins of the Inca Empire, the birthrate is more than double what it is in Lima. Many

of the Peruvians lacking information and access to reproductive health services are adolescents. This leads to a high rate of adolescent pregnancy in addition to the problems that adult Peruvian women face from protecting themselves from sexually transmitted diseases. Supported by the United Nations Population Fund, this project is based on the implementation of reproductive health classes in several high schools that will strive to inform adolescents about the consequences and facts of sexual activity so that they can better control their futures. If you are a student or expert in the field of human rights, social development, public health, medicine or education, they want your enthusiasm and desire to promote social equality for the development of this community.

Human Rights Campaign Against Racism in Peru

Organization: Nexos Voluntarios (NeVo)
Location: Urubamba, Peru (1 Hour from Cusco)
Cost: $1,750+ (includes housing) **Duration:** 8+ weeks **Age:** 18
Contact: coordinator@nexosvoluntarios.org
Learn more: www.nexosvoluntarios.org
Special skills: Intermediate level of Spanish
Details: Racism and racial discrimination have a long history in Peru. With the support of specialists in this area, NeVo is leading a campaign against racism within and across the various socio-economic groups from Lima and Urubamba-Cusco. This project seeks to create awareness of discriminatory practices by collaborating with children, families, schools, and government agencies to advocate policy changes in local government. Volunteers are responsible for the success of the campaign by carrying out educational sessions about discrimination in school, the development of a research plan to evaluate the practicality of the anti-discrimination law and analyze how it can be enforced and formulating a strategy for legally punishing those who violate the anti-discrimination law. Help bring public consciousness of racism and discrimination in order to bring equality to Peru.

Community Development- Helping Media Luna

Organization: Nexos Voluntarios (NeVo)
Location: Media Luna near the district of Urubamba, in the province of Cusco
Cost: $1,750+ (includes housing) **Duration:** 8+ weeks **Age:** 18
Contact: coordinator@nexosvoluntarios.org
Learn more: www.nexosvoluntarios.org
Special skills: Intermediate level of Spanish
Details: With a total population of 600 people, Media Luna has electricity and running water but lacks many of the necessary components to rise develop out of poverty. It needs adequate:

infrastructure, educational level for its population, health services and public health capacities to promote good health and a culture promoting equity among men and women particularly in the role of reproductive health and labor rights and economic activity that is profitable and sustainable. NeVo proposed a diagnosis of the key areas of development in order to analyze the current situation in regard to each of the different fields, defining the major problems and possible solutions. This project has volunteers as its foundation; they are responsible for its success and continued existence, and they provide the physical and intellectual energy that make it an effective project.

Saving the Environment in the Sacred Valley of the Incas

Organization: Nexos Voluntarios (NeVo)
Location: Urubamba, Peru (1 hour from Cusco)
Cost: $1,750+ (includes housing)   **Duration:** 8+ weeks   **Age:** 18
Contact: coordinator@nexosvoluntarios.org
Learn more: www.nexosvoluntarios.org
Special skills: Intermediate level of Spanish
Details: Peru has an immense natural beauty with coasts, mountainous regions and tropical forests; however, important environmental issues are not being addressed. They include: deforestation, desertification, soil erosion, air pollution in urban centers, pollution of rivers and coastal waters from municipal and mining wastes, and the depletion of fisheries. As awareness of these problems grows, there has been a rise in movements to protect the environment, as well as Peru's indigenous people. NeVo has teamed up with EcoValles, a non-profit organization promoting environmental protection in the Sacred Valley and combating the destruction of Peru's breathtaking natural environment. Volunteers who are interested in ecology, environmental science, ecological tourism or public health are an integral and indispensable part of this project.

Community Development-Helping Shismay

Organization: Nexos Voluntarios (NeVo)
Location: San Sebastian de Shismay, Peru (17 km from Huanuco)
Cost: $1,750+ (includes housing)   **Duration:** 8+ weeks   **Age:** 18
Contact: coordinator@nexosvoluntarios.org
Learn more: www.nexosvoluntarios.org
Special skills: Intermediate level of Spanish
Details: The Community of San Sebastian de Shismay is located 17 km away from the city of Huanuco, located on a lovely mountain with gorgeous scenery. It is an ideal place to learn more about the Andean culture and to help the people living in extreme poverty. In spite of the

current peacefulness and beauty of the place, Shismay carries a sad history, related to politics, social abandonment and poverty. However, the willingness to grow out of poverty is something visitors perceive in its inhabitants, as is a drive for better education and health care services. This project has volunteers as its foundation; they are responsible for its success and continued existence, and they provide the physical and intellectual energy that make it an effective project.

Orphanage Work in Lima

Organization: International Volunteer HQ
Location: They have a great variety of placements available in Lima.
Cost: $220 for 1 week to $2,220 for 6 months, includes food & accommodations **Duration:** 1 week to 6 months **Age:** 18
Contact: volunteer@volunteerhq.org
Learn more: www.volunteerhq.org
Details: Developing and third world countries tend to have a large number of orphaned children and orphanages due to the general  poverty and poor conditions in which many families live. Peru is no exception to this and there is a real need for helpers and volunteers willing to work in these orphanages and help with the education and development of the children. Work at the orphanage varies but can involve cooking, cleaning, playing with children, entertaining children, assisting with feeding programs, caring for children and babies and teaching. Volunteers on the orphanage program need only basic to no Spanish, but must be prepared to take a Spanish language course offered by local staff.

Teaching English in Lima

Organization: International Volunteer HQ
Location: We have a great variety of placements available in Lima.
Cost: $220 for 1 week to $2,220 for 6 months, includes food and accommodations
Duration: 1 week to 6 months **Age:** 18
Contact: volunteer@volunteerhq.org
Learn more: www.volunteerhq.org
Special skills: Volunteers will need a basic level of Spanish
Details: English is widely recognized as the 'universal language' and with Peruvians naturally being Spanish speakers, there is a real demand from local people to be taught English by fluent foreigners. Work is mainly in schools and directed towards children but there is also a lot of demand from community groups and adult groups. Volunteers are placed in community schools, public schools or orphanage schools. Many of the people volunteers teach know only very

basic English, therefore at least a basic level of Spanish will be an advantage on this program. Naturally a volunteer's Spanish will improve over the course of their volunteering, but it is highly recommended that the volunteer take advantage of the Spanish lessons offered by the program's staff in Peru.

Girls Shelter Education

Organization: uVolunteer
Location: Cuzco, the Inca City located in the Southern Sierras
Cost: $900 for the first month; $120 each additional week
Duration: 1+ month **Age:** 18
Contact: info@uvolunteer.org **Learn more:** www.uvolunteer.org
Special skills: Basic Spanish
Details: The purpose of this project is to provide community development assistance to the Shelter for Girls in Cuzco. While onsite, volunteers will provide training to the girls in computers, English, and other areas of education through workshops. Volunteers will also act as role models and a support system to the girls. This shelter is a house for girls who have suffered violence in their homes, sexual abuse, are abandoned by their family or are orphans. It provides a place for the girls to stay, eat and feel protected. Donate your time and change lives!

Animal and Environmental Conservation

Organization: uVolunteer
Location: Cuzco, the Inca City located in the Southern Sierras
Cost: $900 for the first month; $120 each additional week
Duration: 1+ month **Age:** 18
Contact: info@uvolunteer.org **Learn more:** www.uvolunteer.org
Special skills: Basic Spanish
Details: While volunteering in Peru, you will help preserve various species of flora and fauna at risk for extinction, and protect the threatened ecosystems, wetlands and migratory birds. This project provides animal and environmental conservation via the efforts of volunteers and local community members. You will assist in activities that focus on sustainability. It is vital to have volunteers so the program can continue developing.

Teaching Sports and Physical Education

Organization: uVolunteer
Location: Urubamba, the heart of the sacred valley of the Andes Mountains
Cost: $900 for the first month; $120 each additional week
Duration: 1+ month   **Age:** 18
Contact: info@uvolunteer.org   **Learn more:** www.uvolunteer.org
Special skills: Basic Spanish
Details: This program is ideal for volunteers who want to teach physical education, but are also interested in becoming involved in a program of community development. This project is specifically designed to give volunteers, who have a background and/or passion in sports education, the unique opportunity to help construct and run a program for a low-resourced community in Peru. Your role is to get children from the community involved in physical education through various activities and workshops. There may not always be resources and supplies available so it is necessary to get help from volunteers like you who have a proactive attitude with a positive and creative mind.

Cusco Arts Haven

Organization: Creative Corners; The Global Arts Project
Location: Cusco City
Cost: 1 month $960, 2 months $1200, additional months $405
Duration: 2+ weeks   **Age:** 20
Contact: enquiries@creative-corners.com
Learn more: www.creative-corners.com
Details: Volunteers will work with a non-profit organization based in the heart of Cusco that acts as a haven for children & adolescents who are at risk and live in extreme poverty. Most attend the state schools where there is a lack of creative education. This project wishes to nurture and develop the creative skills of children. It is open throughout the day and is run by a staff of volunteer teachers and social workers. Children are given the opportunity to voluntarily drop in and participate in a variety of creative classes and workshops; learning valuable skills which include carpentry, handicrafts, shoe repair, cooking, music, arts and English. Children also come by for homework support from volunteers and local staff.

Medical Placement in Cusco

Organization: International Volunteer HQ
Location: Placements in Cusco and surrounding valleys
Cost: $250 for 1 week to $2,800 for 6 months, includes food and accommodations   **Duration:** 1 week to 6 months   **Age:** 18
Contact: volunteer@volunteerhq.org

Learn more: www.volunteerhq.org
Special skills: Volunteers can be pre-med or qualified in a relevant medical field
Details: Clinics and hospitals for low income families in Cusco tend to be underfunded and understaffed. As a result, volunteers can play an important role in assisting local nurses and doctors, while also learning about the healthcare system in Peru. It is important that healthcare volunteers have realistic expectations with regard to the activities that they will get involved in, as this is determined by a volunteer's previous training and experience. Cusco Medical Clinic is a possible placement; this clinic receives 150-200 patients a day and the majority are children from low-income backgrounds. This clinic is run by a combination of local doctors and nurses and its objective is to provide low income families with quality service for basic healthcare and specifically for child healthcare.

Childcare Work in Cusco

Organization: International Volunteer HQ
Location: Placements in Cusco and surrounding valleys
Cost: $250 for 1 week to $2,800 for 6 months, includes food & accommodations **Duration:** 1 week to 6 months **Age:** 18
Contact: volunteer@volunteerhq.org
Learn more: www.volunteerhq.org
Details: The aim of this childcare program is to provide individual attention and assistance to children from difficult backgrounds. Many children at the projects do not receive the level of affection and education that they deserve. Therefore, volunteers play an important role in working alongside local staff to improve the educational, emotional, and hygiene conditions of the children. Volunteers will work in orphanages, community centers, daycare centers, schools and kindergartens. Work varies, but generally consists of providing individual attention, sharing affection with children, playing with children, organizing games and activities, educating children regarding hygiene and assisting with homework.

Jungle Conservation Around Cusco

Organization: International Volunteer HQ
Location: Placements in the Amazon valleys surrounding Cusco
Cost: $285 for 1 week to US$3,730 for 6 months, includes food and accommodation **Duration:** 1 week to 6 months **Age:** 18
Contact: volunteer@volunteerhq.org
Learn more: www.volunteerhq.org
Details: The objective of this project is ecological restoration - the process of re-establishing an ecosystem that has been degenerated, damaged or destroyed. The project has a number of different phases so

each individual volunteer will form part of a much bigger picture. Volunteers will work in local jungles and ecological reserves located in valleys surrounding Cusco. Volunteer work varies depending on the time of year. Generally, volunteers help with the planting and monitoring of orchids and the removal of non-native bamboo. Volunteers also assist with creating an inventory of animals such as the "Gallito De Las Rocas" (a typical Peruvian bird) and monkeys. During rainy days, there is the option of helping with crafts and artwork at the lodge or helping at the local school.

Sacred Valley Arts Orphanage

Organization: Creative Corners; The Global Arts Project
Location: Llamay in the Sacred Valley
Cost: 1 month $1450, 2 months $2099, additional months $800
Duration: 2+ weeks **Age:** 20
Contact: enquiries@creative-corners.com
Learn more: www.creative-corners.com
Details: This childrens' home is set in truly magical surroundings inside a beautiful old hacienda in the Sacred Valley near historic Machu Pichu. It provides a special environment where 30 orphans prosper through education, cultural & performing arts, permaculture, spiritual development & social and vocational programs. With their own greenhouse, chickens, colorful murals and backdrop view of the Andes Mountains and the surrounding valley this is a project for someone who really wants to get away from it all. The home is looking for creative volunteers to assist their work in a truly unique environment that aims to provide positive long-term benefits to the regions social and environmental problems.

Peru Medical Center Volunteer Program

Organization: Greenheart Travel
Location: A southern district of Lima called Chorrillos. Once a beach resort, the town has a very relaxed and festive atmosphere.
Cost: $1,550 for 4 weeks, includes host family accommodations, two meals daily six days a week, plus medical insurance coverage
Duration: 2 to 12 weeks **Age:** 18
Contact: info@greenhearttravel.org
Learn more: www.cci-exchange.com
Special skills: Intermediate Spanish skills. Experience or education medicine is preferred. Medical students and professionals are encouraged to apply.
Details: The medical center is located in a beautiful coastal area and

serves approximately 40 patients daily. The center aims to provide quality health care to all residents of the community regardless of their ability to pay. Volunteers assist the medical staff in providing primary care and health information to patients, and in some cases, may accompany staff on house calls. Volunteers are encouraged to share the knowledge and expertise they have gained in their studies with the staff of the center through workshops or talks, and are also welcome to teach English to staff members.

Peruvian Elementary School Volunteer Program

Organization: Greenheart Travel
Location: A southern district of Lima called San Juan de Miraflores, the area is poor and underdeveloped, and only recently acquired running water. Some homes continue to be without indoor plumbing and some are without electricity.
Cost: $1,550 for 4 weeks includes host family accommodations, two meals daily six days a week, plus medical insurance coverage
Duration: 2 to 12 weeks   **Age:** 18
Contact: info@greenhearttravel.org
Learn more: www.cci-exchange.com
Special skills: Intermediate Spanish skills are required. Experience or education in counseling and/or teaching is helpful, but not required.
Details: This public school in a poor and underdeveloped area of Lima lacks many tools and resources. The school serves students in grades K through 12, and since 2005, volunteers have helped to set up a library, recreation area and a computer lab, as well as assist teachers in providing quality education. Volunteers will work directly with the students by acting as teaching assistants wherever they are most needed. Volunteers may also organize games, recreational activities, arts and handicrafts, and sports activities such as soccer and volleyball. You are also encouraged to be creative and to bring any of your own personal skills to work with the students.

Surf and Volunteer in Peru

Organization: WAVES for Development
Location: Lobitos, Peru
Cost: $400, plus $250 weekly program fee
Duration: 2+ weeks   **Age:** 18
Contact: info@wavesfordevelopment.org
Learn more: www.wavesfordevelopment.org
Details: WAVES for Development believes that surf travel should benefit the people and communities where it happens. You can help the youth and community members of the small fishing town of Lobitos in Northern Peru while volunteering on your next surf vacation. With food, lodging and surfboards included, you will have time to catch

waves, lead a community project, take Spanish classes and even get certified in Emergency First Response. The program starts and ends in the Northern Peru town of Talara. Stay in the house of a local family and meet people from all over the world. Past volunteer community projects include: beach clean ups, surf contests, environmental education curriculum, surfboard repair shack design and construction, and documentary film projects - the possibilities are many!

Shelter for Boys Volunteer Program

Organization: Greenheart Travel
Location: Cuzco (or Cusco) in the southern Andes of Peru
Cost: $1,700 for 4 weeks includes host family accommodations, two meals daily six days a week, plus medical insurance coverage
Duration: 2 to 12 weeks **Age:** 18
Contact: info@greenhearttravel.org
Learn more: www.cci-exchange.com
Special skills: Intermediate Spanish skills are required. Experience or education in counseling, and/or teaching is helpful, but not required.
Details: Located in beautiful and historic Cuzco, this shelter provides care to orphaned boys and those who have been victims of abuse and neglect. The shelter provides for the basic needs of the children, including medical and psychological care administered by

professionals. Volunteers will work as assistants wherever they are most needed, play with the children and help to care for them. They will also help the boys to get ready for school, prepare meals, and organize arts and recreational activities. You are also encouraged to be creative and to bring any of your own personal skills to work with the students. Included in the program are host family accommodations, two meals a day six days a week and medical insurance coverage. Spanish lessons are available for an additional fee prior to beginning the project.

Daycare Volunteer Program

Organization: Greenheart Travel
Location: Cuzco (or Cusco) in the southern Andes of Peru
Cost: $1,700 for 4 weeks includes host family accommodations, two meals daily six days a week, plus medical insurance coverage
Duration: 2 to 12 weeks **Age:** 18
Contact: info@greenhearttravel.org
Learn more: www.cci-exchange.com
Special skills: Intermediate Spanish skills are required. Experience or education in counseling and/or teaching is helpful, but not required. Volunteers must love children and enjoy working with them.
Details: This day care center is located in a busy market area of Cuzco

and serves 30 children ages 2 to 5. The day care center is a public institution and lacks many of the modern facilities and resources, and volunteers will work as assistants to the caregivers wherever they are most needed, playing with the children and helping to care for them. Volunteers are also encouraged to be creative and to bring any of their own personal skills to work with the students. The schedule is Monday through Friday from 8 am to 1 pm. Included in the program are host family accommodations, two meals daily six days a week and medical insurance. Spanish lessons are available for an additional fee prior to beginning the project.

Home for Teenage Mothers

Organization: Experiential Learning International
Special Skills: High Intermediate Spanish Language Skills
Location: Cusco
Cost: $885+ **Duration:** 2+ weeks **Age:** 18
Contact: info@eliabroad.org **Learn more:** www.eliabroad.org
Special skills: Highly proficient in Spanish and volunteers must love children and enjoy working with them.
Details: Statistically, 1 in 4 Peruvian mothers are under the age of 18. Many of these young mothers are the victims of sexual abuse and have been abandoned by their families. ELI works with an organization in Cusco devoted to providing shelter for young mothers while educating them and giving them the life skills they need to provide the best care possible for their children. All the mothers complete their secondary education and receive vocational training as well as training on child health issues, the importance of hygiene, and other child development topics.

Peru Childcare Project

Organization: Global Volunteer Network
Location: Volunteers will primarily be based in Cusco - the historical capital of the Inca Empire, but may also participate in projects in Arequipa.
Cost: $472 for 1 week **Duration:** 1 to 24 weeks **Age:** 18
Contact: info@volunteer.org.nz
Learn more: www.volunteer.org.nz/peru
Details: On childcare placements volunteers assist the children with their homework, organize educational activities and provide the children with love and attention. There are many different childcare placements available in Cusco, including: working at orphanages, homes for abused children, daycares for babies, community centers and working with street children at shelters. There is also the possibility to work at a boarding school for deaf children and at a school for children and young adults with Down syndrome. If you have an area which you

are particularly interested in please let them know, although it will depend on availability as to which project you will be placed.

Peru Teaching English Project

Organization: Global Volunteer Network
Location: Volunteers will primarily be based in Cusco - the historical capital of the Inca Empire, but may also participate in projects in Arequipa.
Cost: $472 for 1 week **Duration:** 1 to 24 weeks **Age:** 18
Contact: info@volunteer.org.nz
Learn more: www.volunteer.org.nz/peru
Details: At teaching English placements volunteers assist the full time teachers with speaking, listening, writing, reading, grammar and vocabulary lessons. Volunteers may also be asked to help with specific learners in terms of their pronunciation and for one-on-one tutoring.

Peru Construction Project

Organization: Global Volunteer Network
Location: In Oropesa, near Cusco
Cost: $472 for 1 week **Duration:** 1 to 24 weeks **Age:** 18
Contact: info@volunteer.org.nz
Learn more: www.volunteer.org.nz/peru
Details: At construction projects volunteers assist with construction and/or renovation usually at a childcare facility. Construction projects change all the time, but our partner organization is currently helping to build a new orphanage in Oropesa, near Cusco. Tasks on the program may include: renovation, manual labor, painting, decorating and carpentry.
Volunteers will assist with cement mixing, sand sifting, cutting wood and transporting building materials. The building projects are to help the community improve their schools and community centers.

Peru Healthcare Project

Organization: Global Volunteer Network
Location: In Oropesa, near Cusco
Cost: $472 for 1 week **Duration:** 1 week to24 weeks **Age:** 18
Contact: info@volunteer.org.nz
Learn more: www.volunteer.org.nz/peru
Special skills: At least intermediate Spanish
Details: There are two options for this program. The first is to work at a clinic for mentally and physically disabled children. This project does not require any qualifications or experience. It is in a clinical setting,

but volunteers essentially help look after the children, organize activities and help at meal times. There are options at this project to assist in physiotherapy and to shadow a doctor as well. The second option is to work at a clinic for low-income families. This project is for medical students, qualified nurses or doctors. Notarized documentation of your medical school, nursing school, or other medical credentials will be required.

Conservation/Wildlife Project

Organization: Global Volunteer Network
Location: Cusco and Sacred Valley
Cost: $472 for 1 week **Duration:** 1 to 24 weeks **Age:** 18
Contact: info@volunteer.org.nz
Learn more: www.volunteer.org.nz/peru
Details: There are two options for this program. The first is to volunteer at a zoo in Cusco, assisting with cleaning and feeding. This is a small zoo which also houses injured animals. These are taken in and rehabilitated to go back into the wild. The second option is to work at Manu National Park in the jungle region of Peru in the Sacred Valley. At the jungle project, volunteers may assist in orchid planting, bamboo removal, teaching at the local school, and creating an inventory of species. Please note that for the Jungle Project volunteers will complete one week of Spanish lessons in Cusco before heading to Sacred Valley for the remainder of their stay.

Andean Culture Immersion Project

Organization: Global Volunteer Network
Location: Sacred Valley
Cost: $472 for 1 week **Duration:** 1 to 24 weeks **Age:** 18
Contact: info@volunteer.org.nz **Learn more:** www.volunteer.org.nz
Special skills: Intermediate Spanish
Details: At the Andean project, volunteers live with a host family in the mountains in the Sacred Valley. You will assist the family with agriculture and textiles practices. You will also provide some workshops to members of the local community, for example teaching English or reading and writing. Please note that for this program volunteers will complete one week of Spanish lessons in Cusco before heading to their host family in the Sacred Valley for the remainder of their stay.

Summer International Health Fellowship

Organization: Foundation for International Medical Relief of Children
Location: Huancayo, Peru
Cost: $3,082 **Duration:** 4 weeks (June and July sessions) **Age:** 18
Contact: missions@fimrc.org
Learn more: www.fimrc.org/fellowship
Special Skills: This program is specially focused for students interested in health professions.
Details: Gain intensive daily clinical experience while becoming immersed in an underserved community! Fellows will be based in a public hospital, performing rotations alongside Peruvian medical students. During their stay, Fellows will learn about the Peruvian medical system in substantial depth by forming relationships with staff and patients. The program provides not only a valuable experience for resumes or medical school applications, but will expand participants' knowledge and perspectives on healthcare. Opportunities also exist to interact with patients on a daily basis and scrub in for surgeries. Fellows will make a difference by implementing preventative health campaigns in close collaboration with field staff. Fellows will travel to community centers in the city, as well as rural towns in the Peruvian highlands to promote community health initiatives.

Service Work and Andean Discovery

Organization: VISIONS Service Adventures
Location: Urubamba
Cost: $3,900+ **Duration:** 3 or 4 weeks, and customized programs
Age: Teens, customized programs for all ages
Contact: info@VisionsServiceAdventures.com
Learn more: www.VisionsServiceAdventures.com
Special skills: A minimum requirement of two years of high school Spanish
Details: VISIONS Peru combines service work in a southeastern Andean village with discovery of ancient Inca and colonial Spanish cultures. Participants live in a highland community while accomplishing adobe construction projects, environmental work and volunteering in local schools. Students explore Peru's majestic landscapes by hiking and traveling to centuries old marketplaces and resplendent historic sites, including Machu Picchu. Groups learn local customs and sometimes participate in cultural traditions. They work with and meet Andean farmers, educators, politicians, musicians, and artisans. VISIONS programs for teens blend ambitious service, cultural immersion, and adventure. Know the people whose lives you impact, and return home a more confident global citizen with genuine appreciation for our multi-cultural world.

Incas & Amazons

Organization: Hands Up Holidays
Location: Cuzco
Cost: $3,150 per person, based on sharing a room
Duration: 4 days volunteering/15 day trip
Age: 16 years unless accompanied by an adult
Contact: info@handsupholidays.com
Learn more: www.handsupholidays.com
Special skills: None required, but teaching English as a second language (ESL), gardening, medical or building skills are desirable
Details: This intriguing adventure in Peru was designed to capture your imagination. Explore ancient ruins, marvel at architectural feats, enjoy phenomenal scenery and gain intimate knowledge of these amazing people and their culture. Spend four remarkable days in a village near Cuzco where you teach, build, paint or garden. Furthermore, if you have medical skills, these can be put to great use. After getting acclimatized to the high altitude while volunteering, you get to do the world famous Inca Trail trek, culminating with sunrise through the Sun Gate to arrive at Machu Picchu. Your adventure ends with a trip to the Amazon jungle, where you have the chance to see jaguar, puma, tapir, giant otter and toucan.

Community Development Projects in Peru

Organization: Academic Treks
Location: The hills of the Cordillera Negra
Cost: $4,980
Duration: 55+ hours of volunteerism as part of a 23-day service and cultural immersion program **Age:** Teens finishing grades 9-12
Contact: info@academictreks.com; 919-256-8200 or 888-833-1908
Learn more: www.academictreks.com
Details: On this community service and cultural immersion adventure, students work on service projects in partnership with Peace Corps volunteers in indigenous communities tucked into the hills of the Cordillera Negra. The projects are designed to improve the communities' quality of life and infrastructure. Students also teach English, assist in organic agricultural projects and educate locals about nutrition and preventive health measures. All work is done alongside local community members. When not working on service projects, students hike an ancient Incan trail to Machu Picchu, explore villages and study Spanish.

Other organizations offering projects in Peru:

Awaiting Angels: www.awaitingangels.org
Cross-Cultural Solutions: www.crossculturalsolutions.org
FairMail (teach photography to underprivileged teens producing
  cards to earn money): www.fairmail.info
Fauna Forever: www.faunaforever.org
Institute For Field Research Expeditions: www.ifrevolunteers.org
International Volunteer HQ: www.volunteerhq.org
Kids Alive International: www.kidsalive.org
La Casa De Mayten: www.volunteersouthamerica.net
Máximum Level: www.maximonivel.com
People and Places: travel-peopleandplaces.co.uk
Peru's Challenge ("Highly Recommended" in the 'Best Volunteer
  Organization' category by Virgin Holidays Responsible Tourism
  Awards 2009): www.peruschallenge.com
VolunTraveler (placement agency helping small organizations in Peru
  get noticed and find voluntary hands) www.voluntraveler.com

Uruguay

Promoción de Derechos Humanos (Human Rights)

Organization: Academia Uruguay
Location: Montevideo, Uruguay
Cost: Free if volunteer takes 3+ weeks of Spanish lessons with the
organization **Duration:** 1+ months **Age:** 16
Contact: info@academiauruguay.com
Learn more: academiauruguay.com
Special skills: An intermediate level of Spanish
Details: This project promotes the work of individuals or other
organizations that are in the human rights' field, striving to strengthen
democracy and enabling equal opportunities for everyone. They need
people to help them create, organize and develop new projects. Some of
the activities that are coming will include: an exhibition of photographs
of the time of the Latin American dictatorships in the 70s, workshops
about democracy and human rights and their plans to expand their
actions to the interior of the country. This program is especially
enriching for people interested in social movements, activism and who
would like to learn about the recent history of Latin America and
Uruguay.

Laughing Against All Odds

Organization: Academia Uruguay
Location: Montevideo
Cost: Free if volunteer takes 3+ weeks of Spanish lessons with the organization **Duration:** 2+ months **Age:** 18
Contact: info@academiauruguay.com
Learn more: academiauruguay.com
Special skills: An intermediate level of Spanish, experience working with children and a high degree of emotional strength to face tough situations
Details: The premise of this project is that laughter and joy do heal. Each day a group of volunteers goes to a children's hospital to cheer up hospitalized kids. They use all sort of 'tricks' to make the kids feel better and help them have a faster recovery. The group has a special room in the hospital where they organize costume catwalks, hand puppet plays, paint, play board games, etc. When kids aren't able to leave their room, clowns and jugglers visit them making their day brighter. Everything is carried out by volunteers, so any help and ability you can contribute is of great help.

Future Building

Organization: Academia Uruguay
Location: Around different neighborhoods in Montevideo
Cost: Free with 3+ weeks of Spanish lessons
Duration: 2 days (one weekend) **Age:** 18
Contact: info@academiauruguay.com
Learn more: academiauruguay.com
Special skills: An intermediate level of Spanish
Details: This project aims to improve the standard of life of those who live in the most impoverished areas of Montevideo by building a very simple wooden home for a family that has been living in a ramshackle house. Homes are assembled with any material available (cardboard, wood, metal, leaves, etc) and not comfortable enough to protect residence from winter, rain or humidity. After the project has attended the most urgent needs in the settlement they will also build a community center that would be run by the neighborhood. Volunteers may also offer counseling on how to address problems such as contacting the authorities to get electricity or a fresh water supply for the neighborhood.

Other organizations offering projects in Uruguay:
Karumbé (sea turtle & marine biodiversity): www.karumbe.org
Volunteers for Economic Growth Alliance: www.vegaalliance.org

Venezuela

Youth Care, Community and Conservation
Organization: Fundacion Aldeas de Pas
Location: Santa Elena de Uairen
Cost: $260 per week
Duration: 1 week to 1 year   **Age:** 8 (with parent) up to 100
Contact: mail@peacevillages.org
Learn more: www.peacevillages.org
Details: The Peace Villages Foundation (PVF) is a sustainable grassroots NGO based in Santa Elena de Uairen, Venezuela, near the borders with Brazil and Guyana in South America. PVF is independent from political, religious or business interests. The Peace Villages Foundation is exclusively financed and operated by volunteers. Share the values of peace, justice and tolerance, fundamentally focusing on the preservation of indigenous cultures and the empowerment of young people while valuing local knowledge and working with cultural sensitivity. You will assist local people in carrying out objectives they deem important. Volunteer opportunities are truly the microcosm of a world where people join together giving priority to improving life for humanity and promoting a Culture of Peace.

✍**Editor's Note:** Peace village offers a diverse range of volunteer opportunities for families available at one site. If you are traveling with kids and looking for a program that introduces them to give-back travel, then visit the Peace Village website to learn more and watch their video on family projects.

Other organizations offering projects in Venezuela:
Adventure Heart: www.adventureheart.com
Ecoteer: www.ecoteer.com
Florida Association for Volunteer Action in the Caribbean and the America's: www.favaca.org
Habitat for Humanity International: www.habitat.org
International YMCA: www.internationalymca.org
Volunteers for Economic Growth Alliance: www.vegaalliance.org
Volunteers for Peace: www.vfp.org

North America
Volunteer Opportunities

"Perhaps travel cannot prevent bigotry, but by demonstrating that all peoples cry, laugh, eat, worry, and die, it can introduce the idea that if we try and understand each other, we may even become friends."

~ Maya Angelou

Antigua and Barbuda

Organizations offering projects in Antigua and Barbuda:
Florida Association for Volunteer Action in the Caribbean and the America's: www.favaca.org
Habitat for Humanity International: www.habitat.org

Bahamas

Animal Shelter and Veterinary Clinic
Organization: The Bahamas Humane Society
Location: The island of New Providence, Grand Bahama, Eleuthera, Exuma and Abaco.
Cost: None   **Duration:** 1+ days   **Age:** 18
Contact: petinspector@gmail.com or bhscruelty@gmail.com
Learn more: www.bahamashumanesociety.com

Special skills: Any person who loves animals and enjoys working around them and with other people.

Details: The Bahamas Humane Society was founded in 1924 and is the oldest charity in the Bahamas. They provide a 24 hour emergency ambulance service, free spay and neuter clinic, veterinary clinic, adoption program, educational program, cruelty investigation, boarding kennels and an inspectorate division. BHHS has lobbied for changes in many of the Bahamas' animal related laws and lobbied for better conditions for surrey horses. In addition, they hold free spay/neuter clinics on islands that have no veterinarians or animal welfare groups. People who are willing to get themselves dirty while cleaning, feeding, bathing and walking animals or those who like to do maintenance, painting, cleaning windows or sweeping down cobwebs are valuable volunteers. Also, persons who have fundraising or public relations experience like folding bills or copying files are also welcome.

Marine Conservation & Learn to Dive in the Bahamas

Organization: Greenforce
Location: The Bahamas
Cost: $1,900+   **Duration:** 2 to 10 weeks   **Age:** 17
Contact: info@greenforce.org   **Learn more:** www.greenforce.org
Details: Greenforce has the privilege of working closely with the Bahamas National Trust collecting data to help create managed marine parks. On the project volunteers help protect Andros Island (home to the world's third largest barrier reef) from unplanned tourism. Volunteers complete PADI Open Water, Advanced and Emergency First Response dive training and then undertake marine conservation scientific training before they begin to carry out Monday to Friday survey dives. Saturday is fun dive day, with a deep dive or photography dive followed by beach games. Volunteers also work with a local school on a marine conservation awareness programme, to help young Bahamians understand the importance of the marine environment.

Wild Dolphin Research

Organization: The Wild Dolphin Project
Location: Bahamas
Cost: $2,495   **Duration:** 10 days (May - early September)   **Age:** 16
Contact: info@wilddolphinproject.org
Learn more: www.wilddolphinproject.org
Special Skills: Good swimmer/snorkeler
Details: This is your chance to help with amazing long-term research on wild Atlantic spotted and bottlenose dolphins. As a participant with The Wild Dolphin Project, you will help with research tasks such as dolphin watch and data entry. You will be able to snorkel with wild

dolphins as well as snorkel on interesting underwater reefs and shipwrecks. Learn all about these amazing, intelligent creatures and help with the continued research as you learn more about their lives, 'In their world, on their terms'. All meals and accommodations are included for the duration of the trip aboard a 62' catamaran (live aboard).

Bahamian Reef Survey

Organization: Earthwatch Institute
Location: Rendezvous at San Salvador Island, Bahamas
Cost: $2250 - $2450+ **Duration:** 8 days **Age:** 18
Contact: info@earthwatch.org **Learn more:** www.earthwatch.org
Details: Volunteers will snorkel through the crystal clear waters around a remote Bahamian island to survey endangered coral reefs, document the threats to their health and help test techniques that might restore them. You will learn to conduct ecological field measurements: surveying hard corals and other reef animals and plants, mapping transect sites and taking reef measurements and testing water chemistry. On land, you'll map corals and monitor beach profile data for changes. Volunteers help refine methods for repairing and even rebuilding reefs that have been damaged by bleaching, storms, run-off, and systemic threats (global warming). In the evenings, you'll transcribe the day's data and enjoy films and lectures. In your recreational time, you can scuba dive, go caving, take nature hikes or just enjoy the beautiful surroundings.

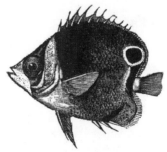

Other organizations offering projects in the Bahamas:

Cape Eleuthera Institute (environmental): www.ceibahamas.org
*Bahamas Habitat (Christian, dental, pilots, community
    development...): www.bahamashabitat.org/wordpress*
*Bimini Biological Field Station (Shark lab, biology):
    www6.miami.edu/sharklab*
Blue Planet Divers: www.blueplanetdivers.org
Concordia: www.concordia-iye.org.uk

Belize

Furry Felines for Fuzzy Feelings

Organization: PAW (Protect Animal Welfare) Cat Sanctuary and Humane Society
Location: Caye Caulker
Cost: None   **Duration:** ½ day or more
Contact: pawanimalsanctuarybelize@yahoo.com
Learn more: www.pawanimalsanctuarybelize.com
Special skills: The desire to do more.
Details: Why not make your next vacation a worthy cause and help the animals at PAW? For a small program fee & 5 hours of volunteer work you will be provided with accommodations in their Jaguar Beach Cabana in the sleepy fishing village of Caye Caulker (pronounced Key Korker). They also welcome day to day volunteers if you are planning on vacationing on Caye Caulker and would like to stop by to spend some time with the animals or

helping with all the chores. Volunteers are needed to assist with animal care duties, public relation, fundraising, designing and implementing humane education programs and more.

✍**Editor's note:** Four years ago PAW's Founder, Madi Collins left her corporate life in the United States and returned to her childhood home of Belize. She arrived with her three cats. Madi was immediately distraught by the cruelty and conditions that local animals were subjected to. PAW grew from her combination of patience, raw tenacity, business-savvy and past volunteer experience at animal shelters in New York, proving one person can bring about a better world for hundreds of animals.

Prevention of Child Abuse Program

Organization: Kaya Responsible Travel
Location: The busy market town of San Ignacio in Belize's tropical hills
Cost: $1,270+   **Duration:** 2 to 26 **weeks**   **Age:** 18-80
Contact: info@kayavolunteer.com
Learn more: www.KayaVolunteer.com
Special skills: Confidence speaking and presenting in groups
Details: This project was founded in response to the increasing evidence of child maltreatment and other difficult circumstances impacting the Belizean family, such as child abuse, adolescent pregnancy, school dropouts, crime and violence, and juvenile

delinquency. In an effort to ensure the rights of our children, the project instituted a comprehensive program that integrates school-based and community-based child abuse prevention and intervention strategies. Volunteers will work with a leading nongovernmental organization in advocating for the rights of children and families in Belize. In this program, volunteers help to promote the project's mission to break the generational cycle of child abuse and neglect.

Environmental and Cultural Preservation

Organization: Kaya Responsible Travel
Location: The busy market town of San Ignacio in Belize's tropical hills
Cost: $1,270+ **Duration:** 2 to 26 weeks **Age:** 18-80
Contact: info@kayavolunteer.com
Learn more: www.KayaVolunteer.com
Special skills: Good communication skills a must. Any background in environmental, sustainable practice, research or education is useful
Details: The natural beauty of Belize is unique and in danger of disappearing unless the proper steps are taken. Environmental and cultural appreciation is important to promote, and educating the community is essential to preserving this rich culture and diverse environment. Volunteers are needed to bring their knowledge, enthusiasm and drive to the project. Volunteers participate in a number of programs promoting cultural and environmental preservation, including research, education in the schools, and working with local community partners to foster environmental conservation and pride in this unique Mayan culture.

Family planning and HIV Education

Organization: Kaya Responsible Travel
Location: The busy market town of San Ignacio in Belize's tropical hills
Cost: $1,270+ **Duration:** 2 to 26 weeks **Age:** 18-80
Contact: info@kayavolunteer.com
Learn more: www.KayaVolunteer.com
Special skills: None, but knowledge of HIV/AIDS, pre/post natal care, youth education and Spanish language skills are all useful
Details: The HIV/AIDS rate in Belize is the highest in Central America. Educating youth is vital to ensure the health of younger generations. Additionally, there is a growing epidemic of teenage pregnancy. It is crucial to educate and empower young women about the choices they have. Volunteers can prepare reproductive and sexual

health educational materials. They conduct educational sessions in primary schools, secondary schools and youth workshops in community centers for teenagers. There is also a chance for them to get involved in the production of educational radio shows and drama productions. Volunteers can also get involved in prenatal and postnatal care workshops and parenting lessons.

Summer Camp for Disadvantaged Kids

Organization: Kaya Responsible Travel
Location: The busy market town of San Ignacio in Belize's tropical hills
Cost: $1,270+ **Duration:** 2 to 26 weeks **Age:** 18 - 80
Contact: info@kayavolunteer.com
Learn more: www.KayaVolunteer.com
Special skills: A love for working with children, patience and enthusiasm are a must
Details: Summer camp provides a rare opportunity for disadvantaged and at-risk kids to play sports, create arts and crafts, and participate in other educational and teambuilding activities. Volunteers are needed to

supervise the children, organize activities and bring their energy. Volunteers will develop programs for summer camp and coordinate activities with the children ages 7-12. Volunteers will lead games, sports, and arts and crafts sessions as camp counselors and role models. It is important that volunteers are very patient and have time to listen and talk to the children.

Other organizations offering projects in Belize:

Barton Creek Outpost: www.bartoncreekoutpost.com
Belize Audubon Society: www.belizeaudubon.org
Global Visions International: www.gviusa.com or www.gvi.co.uk
Maya Mountain Research Farm: www.mmrfbz.org
SeaAid: www.seaaid.org
Transitions Abroad: www.transitionsabroad.com

Bonaire (see Netherlands Antilles)

British Virgin Islands (United Kingdom)

VISIONS Island Passages

Organization: VISIONS Service Adventures
Location: Virgin Gorda
Cost: $3,000+ **Duration:** 3 weeks, and customized programs
Age: 11-13, or customized programs for all ages
Contact: info@VisionsServiceAdventures.com
Learn more: www.VisionsServiceAdventures.com
Details: Island Passages is a special program for 11-13 year olds who want to get an early start on ambitious community service work. In Virgin Gorda, VISIONS groups work on community projects in collaboration with the Ministry of Health and Welfare, National Parks Trust, Red Cross and Disaster Relief Services. Construction is the focus—housing from the ground up, public buildings, structures and trails for the National Parks Trust. VISIONS also works with public school summer programs, the elderly and subsistence farmers. The classic Caribbean beaches and coves are perfect for snorkeling and scuba diving. VISIONS challenges every part of the participant—the mind, muscles and heart. The coed programs for teens blend community service, cross-cultural immersion and adventurous exploration in impoverished communities.

VISIONS British Virgin Islands

Organization: VISIONS Service Adventures
Location: Tortola
Cost: $3,500+ **Duration:** 3 or 4 weeks, and customized programs
Age: Teens, customized programs for all ages
Contact: info@VisionsServiceAdventures.com
Learn more: www.VisionsServiceAdventures.com
Details: In the Caribbean Virgin Islands, VISIONS groups work on community projects in collaboration with the Ministry of Health and Welfare, National Parks Trust, Red Cross, and Disaster Relief Services. Construction is the focus—housing from the ground up, public buildings, structures, and trails for the National Parks Trust. VISIONS also works with public school summer programs, the elderly and subsistence farmers. The classic Caribbean beaches and coves are perfect for snorkeling and scuba diving. VISIONS programs for teens blend ambitious service, cultural immersion and adventure. Teens get to know the people whose lives they impact and return home a more confident global citizen with genuine appreciation for our multicultural world.

123

Other organizations offering projects in British Virgin Islands:

Adventist Volunteer Service: www.adventistvolunteers.org
Lifeworks International (service adventures for teens):
   www.lifeworks-international.com
Reef Check: reefcheck.org
Virgin Islands National Park: www.virgin.islands.national-park.com

Canada

Landmark Wall - Strawbale Interpretive Wall

Organization: Cochrane Ecological Institute
Location: Alberta
Cost: $10 per day with shared accommodations
Duration: 1+ month **Age:** 20
Contact: cei@nucleus.com **Learn more:** www.ceinst.org
Special skills: Not required, but being good at photography, art and/or research is appreciated
Details: Building the Landmark Wall which will be a work of art 400m long by 2.5 m high of straw-bale construction (straw bales covered in cement). Set within the wall will be "portals", large tempered glass windows through which visitors can view the free ranging buffalo, elk, deer, moose and coyotes of the CEI...or, if they happen to be rehabilitating them, bears, skunks, badgers. Between the portals are large expanses of cement. They have set some examples of rocks, fossils, bones, in the cement of the wall and will have bird houses, solitary bee habitats, bat hibernacula. Cement is the canvas. Volunteers will also paint replicas of rock art and indent examples of petroglyphs all copied from existing examples both local and international.

Handbook and Film Creation

Organization: Cochrane Ecological Institute
Location: Alberta
Cost: $10 per day with shared accommodations
Duration: 1+ month **Age:** 20
Contact: cei@nucleus.com **Learn more:** www.ceinst.org
Details: Volunteers are needed to film the building of a Landmark Wall which will be a work of art 400m long by 2.5 m high made of

straw bale construction (straw bales covered in cement), also the designing of bird houses, solitary bee habitats, bat hibernacula, etc. which will be set into the wall. Your skills are also needed in researching and designing the educational materials to go with the overall project.

Gardening Where Mammoths and Cave Bears Trod

Organization: Cochrane Ecological Institute
Location: Alberta
Cost: $10 per day with shared accommodations
Duration: 1+ month **Age:** 20
Contact: cei@nucleus.com **Learn more:** www.ceinst.org
Special skills: Volunteer should enjoy gardening and landscaping
Details: CEI has been researching plant species that were alive in Alberta during the Cenozoic Era and are alive now. For educational purposes (and just plain fun) CEI intends to plant a garden where mammoths and cave bears trod with these plant species. Mammoths and cave bears are now extinct, but some of the grasses they fed upon or walked over are still here. This project needs volunteers who like gardening, researching plant collections and developing educational programmes about the gardens. You will need to enjoy hoeing, weeding and landscaping.

Social Initiative: Enlarging Happy Trails Pet Resort

Organization: Cochrane Ecological Institute
Location: Alberta
Cost: $10 per day with shared accommodations
Duration: 1+ month **Age:** 20
Contact: cei@nucleus.com **Learn more:** www.ceinst.org
Special skills: Should like dogs and cats, construction skills are helpful
Details: The programmes of the CEI could not be undertaken without funding from the proceeds of the CEI's social initiative Happy Tails Pet Resort. If they can enlarge the kennel slightly they'll make more money and will be able to do more conservation work. Therefore, the intention of the CEI to enlarge the existing Happy Tails facility by building 10 more runs, a storage enclosure and a small chalet. During this time, CEI will expect that volunteers will participate in the construction work. In doing so, you will learn how buildings are built, something that is useful for everyone to know!

Building a Sustainable Green House

Organization: Cochrane Ecological Institute

Location: Alberta
Cost: $10 per day with shared accommodations
Duration: 1+ month   **Age:** 20
Contact: cei@nucleus.com   **Learn more:** www.ceinst.org

Special skills: Must enjoy construction and research into alternative heating and water use
Details: CEI has the glass set aside for this environmentally sustainable green house construction project. They hope to construct a building which will demonstrate that it is possible to be self-sufficient in growing your own vegetables and a building that is warm enough to enable Ginkgo trees (once native to Alberta) to survive. This is a very educational program.

Habitat Evaluation for Wildlife Reintroduction

Organization: Cochrane Ecological Institute
Location: Alberta
Cost: $10 per day with shared accommodations
Duration: 1+ month   **Age:** 20
Contact: cei@nucleus.com   **Learn more:** www.ceinst.org
Special skills: Clean driver's license
Details: The successful release of orphaned and injured wildlife back into the wild is dependent upon two points. Point one is that they are healthy, fit and ready for release. Point two is that there is suitable habitat available for their release where they won't come into conflict with people. For Point two you need suitable habitat (example: you cannot release pika and badgers in the same habitat), knowledge of present and future land use, suitable forage, knowledge of prey availability, predator pressure, land ownership, land owner support for reintroduction and government jurisdiction. Little or no research has been undertaken for point two. This project strives to remedy that lack knowledge.

Climate Change at the Arctic's Edge

Organization: Earthwatch Institute
Location: Rendezvous at Churchill, MB, Canada
Cost: $2,950+   **Duration:** 11 days   **Age:** 18
Contact: info@earthwatch.org   **Learn more:** www.earthwatch.org
Details: In this inimitable Arctic landscape, you'll study climate change at sites ranging from the tundra into the forest by monitoring changes affecting the gases stored in these peat-rich ecosystems. Summer and fall teams will use ground-penetrating radar, microclimate dataloggers and soil coring to measure the permafrost's

organic carbon levels. You'll also live-trap small mammals, evaluate growth rings in trees and shrubs through sampling, and monitor plant development. February teams will experience the Arctic's edge in its most dramatic season. Traveling by *gamutik* (sled) towed by snowmobiles, you'll classify ice crystals, and measure snowpack thickness, density, and temperature. You can also learn how to build an igloo and sleep in it comfortably, even when the temperature outside is -30 or -40 degrees Celsius.

Other organizations offering projects in Canada

Canadian Alliance for Development Initiatives and Projects: www.cadip.org
Churchill Northern Studies Centre (environmental): www.churchillscience.ca
Frontiers Foundation (Northern aboriginal, teaching, library, housing): frontiersfoundation.ca
Global Citizens Network: www.globalcitizens.org
Red Leaf Student (high school) Programs (Canada-based, animals, eco, children...): red-leaf.com
The International Internship & Volunteer Network: www.iivnetwork.com
Environment Canada: www.ec.gc.ca/volunteers-benevoles

Costa Rica

Domestic Animal Rescue and Education
Organization: Asociación El Arca de Noe
Cost: None **Duration:** 1 week **Age:** 18
Email: arcadenoe.pa@gmail.com
Learn more: www.acradenoecr.com

Details: This desperately underfinanced sanctuary has a need for Spanish speaking volunteers to help with socializing animals, health checkups (a good learning experience for veterinary students), facility maintenance and animal care. They have dogs, horses, a pig, farm birds and more. Volunteers also may help with a spay/neuter campaign and the education of local school children. Contact Arca de Noe in advance to discuss what volunteer work is needed and what you can do.

✍**Editor's note:** Asociación El Arca de Noe (Noah's Ark) could provide a bed and meals for two people, but keep in mind that the money to do so comes out of the pocket of the president. Please pay your own expenses and pack your own food to take out to the sanctuary each day.

Costa Rica Teaching Year

Organization: WorldTeach
Location: Various rural communities
Cost: $4,990 **Duration:** One Year (Departure in early January)
Age: Any with bachelor's degree
Contact: info@worldteach.org **Learn more:** www.worldteach.org
Special skills: Native English speaker, Bachelor's degree
Details: Upon completion of orientation, volunteers begin their teaching assignments. Volunteers serve as English teachers at public primary schools throughout the country. Responsibilities will include teaching classes (usually for first through sixth grades), attending monthly meetings with a regional supervisor and developing lesson plans and assessments. You may also be asked to co-teach with a Costa Rican counterpart, organize adult classes, form English clubs in host communities, and otherwise help with your community's particular educational needs. Housing is with local Costa Rican families who receive compensation for providing volunteers with food and lodging. The host families are chosen by the WorldTeach Field Staff and take part because they enjoy the cultural exchange of hosting a volunteer. Many families host for several years. Being part of a family gives you a place in the community and a great opportunity to learn about the culture and enhance your Spanish.

Costa Rican National Parks and Wildlife

Organization: Asociacion de Voluntarios (ASVO)
Location: Parks, reserves and communities
Cost: $14 per day with food, accommodations and coordination
Duration: 30+ days, 2 months for special projects.

Age: 18, children under 18 must be accompanied by an adult
Contact: info@asvocr.org, lmatarrita@asvocr.org
Learn more: www.asvocr.org
Special skills: Volunteers should be in good physical condition and able to tolerate the tropical climate.
Details: ASVO is the Costa Rican organisation responsible for volunteer programmes in their National Parks and Reserves. Volunteers are needed for research, construction and maintenance work. English teaching, tourist assistance and interpretation are also important activities where volunteers are needed. Volunteers can also participate in sea turtle conservation projects on the Caribbean or Pacific coasts. Special qualifications are necessary for some research projects.

Reception at The Children's Eternal Rainforest

Organization: La Asociación Conservacionista de Monteverde (ACM)
Location: Children's Eternal Rainforest Cerro Plano (2km from Santa Elena and Monteverde),
Cost: $16-18 a day for accommodation with all meals
Duration: Preferably at least a month, half time   **Age:** 18
Contact: info@acmcr.org   **Learn more:** www.acmcr.org
Special skills: Spoken Spanish and English, working with the public Handling cash (colones), some food handling
Details: The Children's Eternal Rainforest is the largest private reserve in Costa Rica and has been funded largely by school fundraisers around the world. You can contribute to keeping the reserve going by running the reception area in their new shop/booking centre. The job involves: answering inquiries about the protected areas and the services available, selling products in the shop (books, clothes, cds/dvds), backup for the cafe (coffee, cold drinks, cakes), etc.

Materials Production Assistant

Organization: La Asociación Conservacionista de Monteverde (ACM)
Location: Children's Eternal Rainforest, San Gerardo and Pocosol Field Stations and Cerro Plano office
Cost: $16-18 a day for accommodation with all meals
Duration: At least a month full time   **Age:** 18
Contact: info@acmcr.org   **Learn more:** www.acmcr.org
Special skills: GPS, map making, interpretation, biological field skills (identification of points of interest). Reasonably high fitness level
Details: The Children's Eternal Rainforest is the largest private reserve in Costa Rica and has been funded largely by school fundraisers around the world. San Gerardo Field Station is an important source of income for the running of the reserve. You are able to help bring visitors to the reserve by creating maps and field guides for the trails

around San Gerardo and Pocosol field stations. The field stations are a considerable walk from the nearest transportation, are off-grid and have no hot water.

Environmental Educator

Organization: La Asociación Conservacionista de Monteverde (ACM)
Location: Bajo del Tigre, Monteverde, 5 minute walk from public bus
Cost: $16-18 a day for accommodation with all meals
Duration: 1+ months, half-time **Age:** 18
Contact: info@acmcr.org **Learn more:** www.acmcr.org
Special skills: Curriculum design, developing teaching materials, teaching Spanish
Details: The next generation is critical to the maintenance of private reserves in Monteverde. As part work for the Children's Eternal Rainforest you will help inspire youth to protect these important conservation areas. The work involves developing environmental education programs and materials for teaching elementary school age children. It is based in an environmental education classroom at the reserve with internet access. The Children's Eternal Rainforest is the largest private reserve in Costa Rica and has been funded largely by school fundraisers around the world.

Leatherback Turtle Conservation

Organization: Rainforest Concern/The Endangered Wildlife Trust
Location: Pacuare Reserve
Cost: $150 per week. Price includes meals and accommodations.
Duration: 1+week from mid March to the end of September
Age: 18, children under 18 must be accompanied by an adult
Contact: Carlos Fernandez : carlos57fer@yahoo.com, +506 224 8568 or info@rainforestconcern.org
Learn more: www.turtleprotection.org
Special skills: Just a keen interest in conservation required
Details: Volunteers are needed at the Pacuare Reserve in Costa Rice to help protect endangered Leatherback turtles, the largest of the sea turtles. Volunteers participate in every aspect of the project. The project offer an exciting opportunity to be involved in the work and help protect these amazing turtles which are listed as critically endangered species. Volunteers will help with beach cleaning, making pathways and building trails, helping with the wildlife inventories and assisting with projects carried out by the researchers. During the day the volunteer will search for nest excavations. To protect the turtles and their nests from poachers, the beaches are patrolled every night from early March to late September.

Wildlife Rescue Center Work

Organization: Rainsong Wildlife Sanctuary
Location: Cabuya, Costa Rica
Cost: $20 per weekly, plus lodging ($6 day or free under certain conditions). Meals (not provided)
Duration: Open **Age:** Any
Contact: rainsongwildlifesanctuary@gmail.com
Learn more: www.rainsongsanctuary.com
Details: Volunteers at Rainsong are involved with the caretaking of the animals and birds in the rescue center, reforestation projects, conservation education in local schools and the ongoing peaceful resolution of many conservation issues in this lil' piece of paradise!

Sea Turtle Conservation

Organization: Association Salvemos las Tortugas de Parismina
Location: Barra de Parismina, Costa Rica
Cost: Inscription fee $30 then $20 to 25 per person per night, accommodations and meals included
Duration: 3 days to several months
Age: No limit, children welcome with parent
Contact: parisminaturtles@gmail.com
Learn more: www.parisminaturtles.org
Special skills: Physically able to walk on the beach, good night vision
Details: Join a truly community-based sea turtle conservation project! ASTOP needs volunteers from March through September to accompany local guides on 4-hour night patrols, searching for nesting females and collecting /relocating eggs to protected areas, safeguarding them from poachers. Since there is an ongoing scientific investigation, turtles are measured, checked for diseases and tagged. Volunteers also guard the hatchery day and night, make nest baskets, keep pests (crabs, dogs) out of the hatchery, clean the beach of debris, release hatchlings and participate in nest exhumations. Other daytime activities include: helping in our recycling center, teaching English or doing arts and crafts with the village children. Volunteers are essential and well accepted in the village as they provide the only funding for this grass roots project.

Campus Volunteer at an Environmental School

Organization: The Cloud Forest School / Centro de Educación Creativa
Location: Monteverde, Costa Rica (rural)
Cost: $25 a day includes room, board and services
Duration: 3+ weeks, during school year only **Age**: 18
Contact: opportunities@cloudforestschool.org

Learn more: www.cloudforestschool.org
Special skills: Love of the outdoors and desire to work with children
Details: Volunteers keep the CFS both beautiful and functional. A volunteer's day may include working on the reforestation project, caring for plants in the greenhouse or gardens, maintaining trails, painting buildings, or assisting in environmental education classes. Past volunteers with special skills have helped to network our computers, taught music lessons, yoga classes, made brochures and films for our school or painted beautiful murals on our campus. All applicants must be at least 18 years old and have graduated from high school. They provide homestays with local school families as well as extensive orientation, trips, tours and Spanish classes. Volunteering guests mostly work with the Land Manager, who is Costa Rican, and has worked with volunteers of all Spanish-speaking abilities for a number of years.

Trail Building and Maintenance

Organization: La Asociación Conservacionista de Monteverde (ACM)
Location: Children's Eternal Rainforest
Cost: $32 per day full board (at field station) or $16-18/day (in town)
Duration: 1+ months, half-time   **Age:** 18
Contact: info@acmcr.org   **Learn more:** www.acmcr.org
Special skills: Carpentry, trail building, good fitness
Details: The Children's Eternal Rainforest is the largest private reserve in Costa Rica and has been funded largely by school fundraisers around the world. Visitation is an important source of income for the running of the reserve. Help bring visitors to the reserve by assisting with the maintenance of signage, tracks, fences, handrails, benches, lookouts and buildings in the reserve. Field stations are a considerable walk from nearest transport and are off-grid and have no hot water.

Rainforest Field Biologists

Organization: La Asociación Conservacionista de Monteverde (ACM)
Location: Children's Eternal Rainforest, Cerro Plano (2 km from Santa Elena and Monteverde)
Cost: $32 per day full board
Duration: 3+ months for each species group. For non-resident species, surveys at different times of year may be necessary   **Age:** 18
Contact: info@acmcr.org   **Learn more:** www.acmcr.org
Special skills: Species identification, conducting field surveys
Details: The Children's Eternal Rainforest is the largest private reserve in Costa Rica and has been funded largely by school fundraisers around the world. Help maintain the area's conservation value by monitoring the status of key species within the reserve. The work involves conducting field surveys of birds, mammals and amphibians in

the reserve. The conditions include off-trail hiking in cloud forest and rainforest habitat in wet conditions, often far from the nearest road, plus camping and carrying all requirements except water.

Sanctuary Sloths, Smiles and More Sloths

Organization: Sloth Sanctuary of Cost Rica
Location: Aviarios
Cost: $30 per day full board   **Age:** 18
Contact: slothsanctuary@gmail.com
Learn more: www.slothrescue.org
Special skills: Volunteers need to be healthy, in good physical condition, adaptable, self-starters, have a flexible attitude toward work and a good disposition. They also a have special need for those experienced in veterinary/pet care, biology, information technology, marketing, landscaping, graphic design, grant writing, fund raising and cooking – for the boss!
Details This unique animal rescue center cares for over 100 endangered sloths and the numbers continue to increase. Many are orphans, abandoned by starving mothers due to deforestation or whose mothers were killed, either by accident or poisoned by agrochemicals. Or sometimes babies fall from a tree and mothers are simply too afraid to descend to the ground to retrieve them because of their natural fear of predators, humans and dogs. Adult sloths arrive with life-threatening injuries from power lines, encounters with cars, dogs, even cruel humans. Baby sloths are quite delicate and very high maintenance. A dedicated staff of full time employees cares for the

animals, but volunteers are needed to help provide the sloths with the extra loving care they require in order to survive and thrive. Volunteers play a vital role in helping to care for the sloths (adults and babies), learning about their ways and educating others. Additionally volunteers play an active role in helping to maintain the jungle trails and the sanctuary grounds, guiding tours, helping with cage cleaning and maintenance, preparation of sloth meals and lending a hand to staff veterinarians and other specialists and researchers.

Energy Systems Technician

Organization: La Asociación Conservacionista de Monteverde (ACM)
Location: San Gerardo Field Station, Children's Eternal Rainforest
Cost: $32 per day full board   **Age:** 18
Contact: info@acmcr.org   **Learn more:** www.acmcr.org

Special skills: Energy system design, appropriate technology or fundraising
Details: San Gerardo field station is an important source of income for the running of the reserve/Children's Eternal Rainforest. Currently, lighting is powered by generator and fuel has to be brought in by quad bike. There is no refrigeration, drying facilities or hot water, but there is a partially built hydro station. This project involves designing, implementing and running off-grid energy systems for San Gerardo Field Station and writing grant applications. San Gerardo is a one and a half hour walk from nearest transport.

Childcare Work in Costa Rica

Organization: International Volunteer HQ
Location: Placements available in San Jose and surrounding areas
Cost: $250 for 1 week to $3,350 for 6 months, includes food and accommodations
Duration: 1 week to 6 months   **Age:** 18
Contact: volunteer@volunteerhq.org
Learn more: www.volunteerhq.org
Details: Costa Rica is becoming an affluent country. This has caused citizens from neighboring countries (such as Nicaragua) to immigrate into Costa Rica, causing an increase in unemployment, homelessness and poverty. The childcare program provides individual attention and assistance to children from difficult backgrounds. Many children do not receive the level of affection and education they deserve. Volunteers play an important role in working alongside local staff to improve the educational, emotional and hygiene conditions of the children. Volunteers work in orphanages, community centers, daycare centers, schools, soup kitchens and kindergartens. Work varies but consists of providing individual attention, sharing affection and playing with children, organizing games and activities, educating children regarding hygiene and assisting with homework.

Construction and Renovation

Organization: International Volunteer HQ
Location: Placements available in San Jose and surrounding areas
Cost: $250 for 1 week to $3,350 for 6 months, includes food and accommodation
Duration: 1 week to 6 months   **Age:** 18 years and over
Contact: volunteer@volunteerhq.org
Learn more: www.volunteerhq.org
Details: One of the ways to provide support to the different projects we work with is through International Volunteer HQ's construction and renovation projects. Many sites are underfunded and rundown, and are in need of renovation work. Volunteers usually work alongside a local

construction worker who provides them with direction and motivation. Volunteers work on a variety of buildings such as schools, orphanages, community centers and clinics. Volunteer work varies, but generally consists of renovating buildings, repainting community centers and building required infrastructure such as orphanages and landscape gardening. You are not required to have experience with construction work, but a good energy level, a reasonable level of fitness and good dedication will go a long way to ensuring you get the most out of your volunteer experience.

Sea Turtle Conservation Program

Organization: Asociacion Widecast (Latin American Program).
Location: Caribbean Side
Cost: $40 per day   **Duration:** 7+ days from February to October.
Age: 18, 16 with a parents
Contact: volunteers@latinamericnaseaturtles.org, claudio@widecast.org (506)22613814 (506) 88182543
Learn more: www.latinamericanseaturtles.org or www.widecast.org
Details: Volunteers are encouraged to join the team at any point during the season. For eighteen years, this project has welcomed students, travelers and professionals from countries around the world who have an interest in hands-on conservation and data collection work with an endangered species. Widecast is committed to an integrated, regional capacity that ensures the recovery and sustainable management of depleted sea turtle populations. Through volunteering you gain work experience, develop leadership skills, and learn new things about yourself. You will meet interesting people, be part of a team and be appreciated for your service. Volunteering is a unique way to have fun while doing something meaningful for endangered sea turtles. You might even discover a new career!

Turtle Conservation in Costa Rica

Organization: International Volunteer HQ
Location: Projects on the Pacific Coast and Caribbean Coast
Cost: $285 for 1 week to $4,280 for 6 months, includes food and accommodation
Duration: 1 week to 6 months   **Age:** 18
Contact: volunteer@volunteerhq.org
Learn more: www.volunteerhq.org
Details: At the turtle conservation project, volunteers assist a Costa Rican biologist with their work at the beach. Volunteers help with studies and protection work of the sea turtles and with the sustainable egg harvesting programs. You will live in one of three beach locations where International Volunteer HQ offers the Turtle Conservation program in Costa Rica. You must be prepared to work hard. Living

conditions are quite basic and volunteers work day and night shifts. Activities can vary at different times of the year but general work includes: beach patrols, building greenhouses to keep eggs away from predators, beach cleaning, counting and tagging sea turtles, locating nesting females and working with local staff to harvest eggs.

Teaching English in Low Income Schools

Organization: uVolunteer
Location: San Ramon, Central Valley of Costa Rica
Cost: $1,005 for the first month, $120 each additional week
Duration: 1+ month **Age:** 18
Contact: info@uvolunteer.org **Learn more:** www.uvolunteer.org
Special skills: Basic Spanish
Details: Many schools in Costa Rica lack a solid English department. This project helps the community develop by sending volunteers to teach English to children and adults. You will assist the teacher with the practical uses of the English language, such as current vocabulary, proper pronunciation, conversational skills and new creative classroom activities. If you're experienced and confident you will have the chance to be the sole teacher in the classroom. uVolunteer provides 2 meals a day and you can choose to stay in either a dormitory or with a Costa Rican family.

Beach Town Community Arts Project

Organization: Creative Corners; The Global Arts Project
Location: Puerto Viejo, Caribbean Coast
Cost: 1 month $1,215, 2 months $1,775, additional months $645
Duration: 1+ months **Age:** 20
Contact: enquiries@creative-corners.com
Learn more: www.creative-corners.com
Details: This volunteer opportunity is located in the stunning Puerto Viejo de Limon, a wonderful beach town on the Caribbean side of Costa Rica that holds many surprises. Currently, the south Caribbean is undergoing rapid development and tourism is increasingly taking over the lives of the people. This project illustrates the importance of establishing creative activities for the local children in their spare time to deter them from the problems that rapid tourism sometimes brings

– such as involvement in drugs or alcohol. The aim is to create alternative leisure activities for the village children of the village by offering creative workshops and arts activities where they can develop their creative abilities and imagination through diverse activities.

Cloud Forest School

Organization: Creative Corners; The Global Arts Project
Location: Monteverde and the Cloud Forrest
Cost: 1 month $ 1,380, 2 months $2,090, additional months $795
Duration: 1 to 3 months   **Age:** 18
Contact: enquiries@creative-corners.com
Learn more: www.creative-corners.com
Details: The Cloud Forest School, locally known as the Centro de Educación Creativa, is a bilingual school located in the tropical cloud forest of Monteverde, Costa Rica. This independent school offers creative, experiential education to 220 students with an emphasis on integrating environmental education into all aspects of the school. Over half of the students receive significant scholarships since their families' incomes are often less than $500 per month. The campus is located on 106 acres of cloud forest and has garden plots maintained by each grad. On trails that wind through the forest, classes embark on journeys of exploration and discovery. There are few school settings where children so completely integrate experience, observation and formal learning into their lives.

Teacher's Assistant Intern at an Environmental School

Organization: The Cloud Forest School / Centro de Educación Creativa
Location: Monteverde, Costa Rica (rural)
Cost: $2,250 (fall), $2,350 (spring) includes room, board, and services
Duration: 3 months, during school year only   **Age**: 18
Contact: opportunities@cloudforestschool.org
Learn more: www.cloudforestschool.org
Special skills: Love of the outdoors, desire to work with children
Details: Interns assist full-time with a lead classroom teacher in a grade level or subject area of their choice. Depending on the intern's interests and the lead teacher's needs, interns may lead activities or whole units, work in small groups or one-on-one with special needs students and support their lead teacher with preparations, activities, classroom management and teaching responsibilities. In addition, past interns have also taken responsibility for after school clubs and programs, special events and assemblies. CFS will provide homestays with local school families as well as extensive orientation, trips, tours and Spanish classes. Although the majority of academic instruction is

in English, a working knowledge of Spanish (or the desire to learn!) is helpful.

Migratory and Resident Bird Monitoring Program

Organization: Canadian Organization for Tropical Education and Rainforest Conservation (COTERC)
Location: Caño Palma Biological Station
Cost: $250 per week
Duration: Open **Age:** 18
Contact: info@coterc.org
Learn more: www.coterc.org
Details: Roughly 350 bird species are found inhabiting the forests, lagoons, canals and

beaches surrounding Caño Palma Biological Station. One-third are North American migrant species dependent upon these habitats during the northern winter. Monitoring has been ongoing since 1991, resulting in an improved understanding of population status and trends of both migrant and resident tropical bird species. Project goals include: 1) Maintaining a long-term monitoring program to study migrant and resident birds 2) Providing training and research opportunities to biologists 3) Developing a long-term database for research and conservation purposes

Resident Bird Survey

Organization: Canadian Organization for Tropical Education and Rainforest Conservation (COTERC)
Location: Caño Palma Biological Station
Cost: $250 per week **Duration:** Open **Age:** 18
Contact: info@coterc.org **Learn more:** www.coterc.org
Details: Tropical birds comprise a large portion of the world's total biological diversity, yet knowledge of their reproductive behavior and ecology in this ecosystem is poorly understood. This survey provides data on nesting behavior, ecology and habitat use. Goals include: 1) Improving the knowledge of resident bird ecology and population dynamics 2) Increasing awareness of tropical birds and conservation among local people 3) Documenting location, species, clutch size, hatching and fledging success rates 4) Providing research opportunities that share information with national and international biologists.

Marine Turtle Monitoring & Community Conservation

Organization: Canadian Organization for Tropical Education and Rainforest Conservation (COTERC)
Location: Caño Palma Biological Station. Costa Rica

Cost: $250 per week **Duration:** 2 weeks or more **Age:** 18
Contact: info@coterc.org **Learn more:** www.coterc.org
Special skills: 1 week training provided. Need to be fit for hard daily walks on beach required.
Details: This program, which occurs on an unprotected and previously unstudied beach, responds to an urgent need for the protection of marine turtles whose conservation status is endangered or critically endangered. Nesting turtles and their freshly laid eggs face an increasing threat from poaching and coastal development. Goals include: 1) Improved understanding of Leatherback, Green, Loggerhead and Hawksbill turtles 2) Documenting marine turtle nesting patterns 3) Increasing awareness and improve conservation education among local residents and businesses 4) Continued decreasing of the rate of poaching and human disturbance 5) Sharing monitoring results and conservation success stories with governments and conservation organizations.

Large Mammal Monitoring Program

Organization: Canadian Organization for Tropical Education and Rainforest Conservation (COTERC)
Location: Caño Palma Biological Station, Costa Rica
Cost: $250 per week **Duration:** Open **Age:** 18
Contact: info@coterc.org **Learn more:** www.coterc.org
Special skills: Must be physically fit as terrain is difficult and may be flooded.
Details: Terrestrial and arboreal mammals play an important role in rainforest maintenance and regeneration. Yet, many mammal species are endangered due to habitat loss and hunting, and are sensitive to poorly managed ecotourism and habitat disturbance related to human activities. Understanding the species of mammals present, their population size, and the habitat they utilize is critical for conservation management decision making. Program goals include: 1) Increasing the knowledge of mammal richness, ecology and population trends 2) Enhancing the knowledge and appreciation of local wildlife diversity, and promote social and environmental benefits of wildlife conservation 3) Provide research opportunities, and share information with national and international biologists

Volunteer in an Orphanage/Children's Home

Organization: uVolunteer
Location: San Ramon, Central Valley of Costa Rica
Cost: $765 for 2 weeks; $120 each additional week
Duration: 2+ weeks **Age:** 18
Contact: info@uvolunteer.org **Learn more:** www.uvolunteer.org

Details: During your project in Costa Rica, you will be assisting the staff at a children's home/ orphanage by helping underprivileged children develop academically and emotionally. There is always a shortage of staff in the children's homes so it's very difficult for them to attend to all of the children. Your job as a volunteer is to provide academic support to the children, particularly in the subject of English. Volunteers may develop games based on English vocabulary, or other recreational activities that the children can learn and enjoy. Volunteers

on this project need to be creative and self-motivating, and also enjoy working with children. The children benefit from volunteers who model proper behavior and provide kind words of encouragement.

Marine and Sea Turtle Conservation

Organization: uVolunteer
Location: On the Pacific or Caribbean coasts of Costa Rica
Cost: $765 for the first 2 weeks; $126 each additional week; uVolunteer provides three meals daily.
Duration: 2+ weeks **Age:** 18
Contact: info@uvolunteer.org **Learn more:** www.uvolunteer.org
Special skills: No prior knowledge or experience is necessary.
Details: During your uVolunteer Turtle Conservation project in Costa Rica, you will be helping an endangered species of turtles flourish by protecting the nests from all predators. The main objective of this project is to protect the turtle nests from human poachers, animal predators, and more recently from the erosion of the beach. Turtle Conservation Projects are a great way to get hands-on experience in marine and sea turtle conservation. Volunteers applying should enjoy manual work, handling wildlife and working unusual hours; as turtle nesting occurs during the night.

At-Risk Children's Programs

Organization: Experiential Learning International
Location: Heredia
Cost: Starting at $905 **Duration:** 2+ weeks **Age:** 18
Contact: info@eliabroad.org **Learn more:** www.eliabroad.org
Special skills: Intermediate Spanish Language Skills
Details: These programs target at-risk children living in impoverished areas or unsafe conditions. Volunteers can assist teaching English and other subjects in classrooms in primary and middle schools in poorer neighborhoods, assist with after school programs, and help run day camps for the children during school vacations. Some activities may include teaching English, dancing, drawing, organizing arts and crafts,

helping with homework, and teaching social skills. By working with children at risk, volunteers have the chance to use their skills and energy to encourage the children to become good citizens and productive members of society.

Olive Ridley & Leatherback Sea Turtle Programs

Organization: Global Volunteer Network
Location: Various locations along Costa Rica's Pacific and Caribbean Coasts.
Cost: $914 for 2 weeks   **Duration:** 2 to 12 weeks   **Age:** 18–60
Contact: info@volunteer.org.nz   **Learn more:** www.volunteer.org.nz
Details: Volunteers will work with Leatherback turtles between January and July and Olive Ridley Turtles between August and December. These programs will give you the chance to make an important contribution to the preservation of these species. This includes assisting NGOs and local communities who carry out conservation work. You will also gain first-hand knowledge about Costa Rica's biodiversity and its culture. In addition, they also offer non-turtle projects for longer-term volunteers who may participate in more than one project during their time in the program. These include working with eco-cooperatives, at national parks and teaching English in local schools.

Costa Rica Teaching Summer

Organization: WorldTeach
Location: Small towns in rural areas
Cost: $3,990   **Duration:** 2 months (early June-August)   **Age:** 18-74
Contact: info@worldteach.org   **Learn more:** www.worldteach.org
Special skills: Fluent in English
Details: WorldTeach volunteers in Costa Rica teach English at public secondary schools under the auspices of the Ministry of Education. Teaching placements are in small towns in rural areas throughout the country. The schools are part of the Liceo Rural program, which constructs schools in rural areas where few if any teachers are available. Students learn English mostly via videos during the school year, and WorldTeach summer volunteers provide a "real life" experience for the students. Most volunteers will work with 7th through 9th grade students, though the students may range widely in age. Housing and meals provided with a host family.

Coffee and Community Project

Organization: Greenheart Travel
Location: A rural village near the town of Buenos Aires in the Puntarenas province
Cost: $2,050 for 4 weeks; Host family accommodations and three meals per day included
Duration: 2 to 12 weeks   **Age**: 18
Contact: info@greenhearttravel.org

Learn more: www.cci-exchange.com
Special skills: An intermediate level of Spanish
Details: Created in 2002, this project was developed to improve the quality of life for small organic coffee farmers and their families. By focusing on organic production, ecological and community tourism and development of new products to bring to market, the project is providing long-term sustainable methods for generating income. The project also teaches environmental education to the farmers and promotes measures to protect, conserve and recover the natural resources of the area. Volunteers will be assisting with organic horticulture, especially working with the organic coffee production. Other duties include helping with the maintenance of trails, planting, general environmental conservation activities and leading workshop sessions.

Women's Empowerment and Development Project

Organization: Greenheart Travel
Location: The northern lowlands near the Nicaraguan border
Cost: $2,050 for 4 weeks; Host family accommodations and three meals per day included
Duration: 2 to 12 weeks   **Age:** 18
Contact: info@greenhearttravel.org
Learn more: www.cci-exchange.com
Special skills: An intermediate level of Spanish
Details: In this small rural community located near the Nicaraguan border, poverty is high. There are very few opportunities for women and help is needed to work directly with them in their quest for personal and professional development. Volunteers will assist with formulating strategic plans, computer training, project management, micro-enterprise training, outreach campaigns linking the group to other women in the area, and most importantly, helping to build the self-esteem and confidence of each woman.

Eco-Reserve and Animal Rescue Center

Organization: Greenheart Travel
Location: A rural town in San Carlos province
Cost: $2,050 for 4 weeks; Host family accommodations and three meals per day included.
Duration: 2 to 12 weeks   **Age:** 16
Contact: info@greenhearttravel.org
Learn more: www.cci-exchange.com
Special skills: A beginner to intermediate level of Spanish is required. Spanish classes are available before or during your project for an additional fee. Volunteers must be prepared to work outdoors and engage in hands-on conservation work.
Details: Based at a private ecological reserve in the rainforests of northern Costa Rica, this project cares for rescued animals, as well as work in ongoing conservation projects. In addition, a women's cooperative makes products from recycled materials and banana paper to learn skills that help generate a small income and increase self-esteem and self-sufficiency. Volunteers are needed to help in the Animal Rescue Center building cages, feeding and observing animals and administering general care. Volunteers will also help with a variety of conservation projects on the reserve including planting trees, digging ponds and gardening. There is also the option to teach English in the local school or help the women's group.

Center for Abused Children

Organization: Greenheart Travel
Location: In the town of Turrialba in the Cartago province
Cost: $2,050 for 4 weeks; Host family accommodations and three meals per day included.
Duration: 2 to 12 weeks   **Age:** 18
Contact: info@greenhearttravel.org
Learn more: www.cci-exchange.com
Special skills: An intermediate level of Spanish
Details: This community based organization gives children that are suffering from physical or psychological abuse a temporary place to live while the parent(s) undergo counseling or treatment. The center focuses on giving them necessary interim counseling as well as providing them with an atmosphere of love and support. Volunteers will work directly with the children in the center by organizing games, recreational activities, arts and handicrafts, acting classes and academic tutoring sessions. Volunteers are also encouraged to be creative and to bring any of their own personal skills to work with the children. New workshops or ideas are always helpful!

Sustainable Tourism through Environmental Education

Organization: Greenheart Travel
Location: The rural town of Los Planes, near Corcovado National Park
Cost: $2,050 for 4 weeks; Host family accommodations and three meals per day included.
Duration: 2 to12 weeks   **Age:** 18
Contact: info@greenhearttravel.org
Learn more: www.cci-exchange.com
Special skills: An intermediate level of Spanish
Details: This organization was founded by a group of women living in the community of Los Planes. The women wanted to become self-sufficient while also living in harmony with nature. Today the organization has 12 acres of protected forest and their own eco-lodge. By leading environmental education programs for the community and engaging in sustainable tourism, the women have been working hard to conserve the natural resources. Volunteers are needed to help with trail maintenance and signage, assisting visitors and general duties at the eco-lodge, teaching English, leading group workshops on customer service, helping with cooking classes, and occasionally tutoring in the local school.

Bambu Indigenous Reserve

Organization: Tropical Adventures
Location: Bambu
Cost: $995 per week, $1895 two weeks, $399 each week thereafter
Duration: 1+ weeks   **Age:** 16, or younger with an adult
Contact: volunteer@tropicaladventures.com
Learn more: www.tropicaladventures.com
Details: Combine your experience as a volunteer with sightseeing and enjoy the many sights and sounds of nature in Costa Rica. Volunteers in Bambu will be integrated into the local indigenous community while participating in a variety of ongoing sustainable and cultural volunteer projects designed to strengthen the community. Meals and lodging with a host family or in a Cultural Center are included. Take part in local activities with the family that you are living with. You will get the opportunity to improve your Spanish and enjoy this loving culture.

Camaronal Sea Turtle Rescue

Organization: Tropical Adventures
Location: Nicoya Peninsula
Cost: $995 per week, $1,895 two weeks, $399 each week thereafter; Meals and lodging included.
Duration: 1+ week **Age:** 16, or younger if accompanied by adults
Contact: volunteer@tropicaladventures.com

Learn more: www.tropicaladventures.com

Details: As a volunteer at the Camaronal Sea Turtle Project, you will be working on the beach in the National Wildlife Reserve in Guanacaste. You will be involved with the nesting and hatching of sea turtles. When a turtle is found, you will tag and measure it and collect the eggs for transfer to the safety of a hatchery. In addition volunteers have the opportunity to participate in the release of hundreds of hatchlings into the sea. Something else to keep you busy is working in the nearby elementary school with students. They enjoy art classes, English, tutoring, environmental education and sports. This season project is available to volunteers during Oct, Nov and Dec.

Global Health Volunteer in Alajulita

Organization: Foundation for International Medical Relief of Children

Location: Alajuelita

Cost: $925 per week; Housing is provided in homestays with local families.

Duration: 1-3 weeks, longer stays are possible

Contact: missions@fimrc.org   **Learn more:** www.fimrc.org

Special skills: This program is specially focused for undergraduate and medical students.

Details: Immerse yourself in Costa Rican culture while providing much-needed medical assistance to children living in immigrant settlements outside the capital city! Volunteers provide direct assistance in the clinic and are stationed in the examination room, pharmacy area and waiting room. Activities include shadowing the doctor, distributing medications, managing patient intake and taking vital statistics of incoming patients. Volunteers also venture out in the community as part of FIMRC's health education initiative, teaching positive health practices to local children. Numerous opportunities exist for nightlife, sightseeing, hikes and tours during free time.

Wildlife Rescue Center

Organization: Tropical Adventures

Location: La Fortuna, near the Arenal Volcano

Cost: $1,245 per week, $2,490 two weeks, $499 each week thereafter; Meals and lodging with host family included.

Duration: 1+ week

Age: 16, or younger if accompanied by adults

Contact: volunteer@tropicaladventures.com

Learn more: www.tropicaladventures.com

Details: Volunteers at this Wildlife Rescue Center will help with the daily tasks of feeding and caring for animals, care

and evaluation of recently arrived animals, introductions to their new living quarters according to their natural habitats, basic cleaning and maintenance, the daily care and eventual liberation of animals back into the forest, surgeries and medical care. At any given time this "family" is made up of birds, caymans, monkeys, boars, herons, ducks, raccoons, dogs and cats. Volunteers are able to take Spanish classes at an on-site language school allowing you to improve your language skills and learn more about Costa Rican culture. This is an exciting project for volunteers with a passion for working with animals.

Sea Turtle Conservation Project

Organization: Globe Aware
Location: The small Caribbean village of Parismina, Costa Rica
Cost: $1290   **Duration:** 1 week, weekly extensions are available
Age: None - Families welcomed
Contact: info@globeaware.org   **Learn more:** www.globeaware.org
Details: Have fun while helping wildlife! Globe Aware partners with local community leaders to build sea turtle nurseries, maintain the local beaches and watch towers to prevent sea turtle poaching. As a Global Aware sea turtle volunteer you will help with species preservation while learning about the local culture in a beautiful natural setting.

VISIONS Language Immersion Costa Rica

Organization: VISIONS Service Adventures
Location: Costa Rica
Cost: Variable   **Duration:** Customized programs
Age: Teens, customized programs for all ages
Contact: info@VisionsServiceAdventures.com
Learn more: www.VisionsServiceAdventures.com
Details: This is a language immersion program in one of the most verdant Central American countries. Part of this program is on a sea turtle preservation reserve on the Caribbean coast, accessed by boat through winding canals—a quiet, safe sanctuary with 3 kilometers of beach to patrol. Participants assist with turtle patrols and data collection, and in development projects on this remote reserve. The rest of the program takes place in a village further inland, not far from Guayaba National Park in the Cartago Province. In partnership with local associations, participants undertake construction and agricultural work to improve community resources. VISIONS maintains relationships with the host communities, and they are able to create customized programs on a year-round basis.

CCC's Research Programs in Tortuguero

Organization: Caribbean Conservation Corp
Location: Tortuguero at the Phipps Biological Field Station
Cost: $1,599 **Duration:** 3 days to 1 month
Age: 18, or 14 with parent or guardian
Contact: resprog@cccturtle.org
Learn more: www.cccturtle.org
Special skills: None, but volunteer must be good physical condition.
Details: Join one of the Caribbean Conservation Corporation's (CCC) Research Participant Volunteer Programs and discover a very unique travel and research programs and experience an outstanding opportunity to see the depth of CCC's research and to be a part of it! Participant volunteers have helped CCC's research and conservation efforts in Tortuguero since the early 1950s. You can continue that tradition by assisting CCC's biologists study Leatherback sea turtles, Green sea turtles and Tortuguero's bird species. By joining one of CCC's Research Programs you will financially support their research efforts. Participants stay at facilities on-site at the Phipps Biological Field Station, located in a tropical rainforest setting and just steps from the black sand beach. You will work hands-on with research staff on the program of your choice. Please understand that CCC's research programs are scientific research projects, not guided tours or package holidays. Participants will be assisting researchers with scientific field work at a remote field station, and when not working you will have unsupervised free time to relax and enjoy the nature surrounding you.

Costa Rica's Sustainable Coffee

Organization: Earthwatch Institute
Location: Alejuela, Costa Rica
Cost: $2,850+ **Duration:** 15 days **Age:** 18
Contact: info@earthwatch.org **Learn more:** www.earthwatch.org
Details: While conducting field experiments to improve the ecological sustainability of shade-grown coffee, you'll live at a research station nestled below the Monteverde Cloud Forest Reserve. Each day, you'll hike to a variety of coffee plantations, bright with fragrant white flowers in spring and ripe red berries in winter, to conduct bird surveys and estimate fruit and flower availability. February and April teams will also remove fruits and flowers from shade trees in experimental plots, using ladders and pole-saws. April teams will conduct bee surveys and collect coffee flower stigmas for slide preparation.

Sea Turtle Conservation for Teens

Organization: Academic Treks
Location: Tortuguero, Sarapiqui and Drake Bay
Cost: $4,780
Duration: 25+ hours as part of a 20-day Sea Turtle Studies program
Age: Teens finishing grades 9-12
Contact: info@academictreks.com; 919-256-8200 or 888-833-1908
Learn more: www.academictreks.com
Details: Academic Treks college accredited Sea Turtle Studies program takes students to work and study on the beaches of Tortuguero, Costa Rica, the nesting site of more Green turtles than anywhere else in the Western Hemisphere. Assist in the longest continuing sea turtle research program in the world at the John H. Phipps Biological Station, and work tagging turtles alongside researchers during night shifts, tracking inventories and conducting surveys. Students also work on a service project with local children in the community of Tortuguero. They also take time to embark on wilderness adventures and travel to Drake Bay to encounter a wealth of marine mammals in the blue waters of the Pacific Ocean.

Other organizations offering projects in Costa Rica:

Alianza (human rights, trafficking...):
  www.alianzaportusderechos.org
ASVO (conservation): www.asvocr.org
Cross-Cultural Solutions: www.crossculturalsolutions.org
BUNAC: www.bunac.org
GeoVisions: www.geovisions.org
Global Visions International: www.gviusa.com or www.gvi.co.uk
i-to-i: www.i-to-i.com
Institute For Field Research Expeditions: www.ifrevolunteers.org
La Tortuga Feliz (sea turtle protection): www.latortugafeliz.com
Rainforest Biodiversity Group: www.greatgreenmacaw.org
SEE Turtles: www.seeturtles.org
Volunteers for Intercultural and Definitive Adventures (medical,
  dental, veterinary, service & construction):
  www.vidavolunteertravel.org

Cuba

Solidarity Brigades to Cuba

Organization: Cuba Solidarity Campaign (UK)
Location: Varies
Cost: $1,470 *(see details)*
Duration: 2 to 3 weeks, runs twice yearly   **Age:** 18
Contact: finance@cuba-solidarity.org.uk
Learn more: www.cuba-solidarity.org.uk/brigades.asp
Details: Solidarity Brigades are holidays with a difference, as well as undertaking light construction and agricultural voluntary work for part of the time you also get to mix with people of different ages and backgrounds from all over the world, learn about a fascinating country and undertake a full program of cultural and educational visits. Brigades depart in the winter and summer. The price includes return flights with Virgin Airlines from London Gatwick, UK departure tax, visa, transfers to and from Havana International Airport, food, accommodation and most visits.

Other organizations offering projects in Cuba

Cuba Volunteers (ESL teaching): www.cubavolunteer.com
Globe Aware (depending on politics): www.globeaware.org

Dominica

VISIONS Service Dominica

Organization: VISIONS Service Adventures
Location: Carib Territory, Dominica
Cost: $4500+ **Duration:** 4 weeks, and customized programs
Age: Teens, customized programs for all ages
Contact: info@VisionsServiceAdventures.com
Learn more: www.VisionsServiceAdventures.com
Details: The "Nature Island" of the Lesser Antilles, with its lush, unspoiled beauty, stands apart from other Caribbean islands. A rainforest mountain range is the north-south spine of Dominica, alive with rare tropical birds and flowers. Whales and dolphins swim the coastal waters. The volcanic island soil is rich, rainfall is abundant, and hundreds of rivers and streams drain the island. Despite its natural beauty, Dominica's economy is strictly third world. VISIONS

participants live and work on the Carib Reserve, home to the surviving original inhabitants of the Caribbean islands. Service focuses on pressing needs in Carib Territory, such as reforestation, supervising enrichment activities for children, renovating housing and community buildings, and constructing schools, cisterns, roads and shelters.

Community Development in Dominica

Organization: Academic Treks
Location: Dominica and Guadeloupe
Cost: $4,480
Duration: 55+ hours of volunteerism as part of a 21-day service and cultural immersion program   **Age:** Teens finishing grades 9-12
Contact: info@academictreks.com; 919-256-8200 or 888-833-1908
Learn more: www.academictreks.com
Details: On this community service trip, students participate in two ongoing community outreach programs. Students initially work with the Ministry of Education's Youth Development Division in Dominica, working with children on recreational activities, as well as community enrichment projects such as tree planting and mural painting. The second project is in the village of Castle Bruce where students assist Peace Corps volunteers with ongoing community development efforts which range from environmental, historical and youth development projects to ecotourism endeavors. In addition to service work, students engage in adventure activities on Dominica including hiking, sea kayaking, snorkeling, optional scuba diving and a weeklong live-aboard sailing trip to Guadeloupe.

Other organizations offering projects in Dominica:

Ecoteer: www.ecoteer.com
Good News Project (home building): www.goodnewswi.com
i-to-i: www.i-to-i.com
Kiva Fellows Program: www.kiva.org
Project Hope (health): www.projecthope.org
Ready, Willing, Enable (enabling the disabled): www.rwenable.org

Dominican Republic

The DREAM Guzman Ariza Summer School & Camp

Organization: The DREAM Project
Location: Cabarete, Dominican Republic
Cost: $1,800 *(see details)*

Duration: 5 weeks (late June to late July) **Age:** 18
Contact: volunteer@dominicandream.org
Learn more: www.dominicandream.org
Special skills: Teaching experience and/or experience working with children, ability to effectively communicate in Spanish
Details: The camp is held in a poor section of a popular tourist town on the north coast of the Dominican Republic. Volunteers help to provide opportunities for children ages 9-17 to learn about their environment, culture and peers through experiential learning and educational excursions. Camp counselors work with Dominican staff while developing their own specialized educational programs for students. The program includes a week of orientation and four weeks serving in the camp as a teacher, counselor or area instructor. This is a great chance to improve your Spanish, teaching and leadership skills while providing a valuable educational experience for children in need. Cost includes housing, training, airport pick up and drop off, meals during the workweek, field trip fees and transportation.

VISIONS Dominican Republic

Organization: VISIONS Service Adventures
Location: Santo Domingo
Cost: $3,500+ **Duration:** 3 or 4 weeks, and customized programs
Age: Teens, customized programs for all ages
Contact: info@visionsserviceadventures.com
Learn more: www.visionsserviceadventures.com
Special skills: A minimum of two years of high school Spanish
Details: VISIONS Dominican Republic offers service work and language immersion in this Spanish speaking third world country. Past participants have built a medical clinic, homes and schools. Every summer, youth build houses and organize an extensive day camp for Dominican children. During free time, students experience the vibrant culture and beauty in and around Santo Domingo. Swimming, snorkeling, hiking excursions into the interior and evenings of merengue dancing are some of the recreation activities offered. Get to know the people whose lives you impact, and return home a more confident global citizen with genuine appreciation for our multicultural world.

Teaching Children's Literacy

Organization: Orphanage Outreach Teach Corps
Location: Rural areas
Cost: $800 for 1 week, $1,800 for 1 month, $3,500 for three months
Duration: 1 week to 2 years
Age: 18 for individuals, for groups or families - no minimum age
Contact: director@orphanage-outreach.org

Learn more: www.orphanage-outreach.org
Special skills: Spanish
Details: The Dominican Republic was ranked 134th out of 134
countries in the quality of education based on a recent World Economic
Forum study. Orphanage Outreach volunteers are working in
Dominican schools to teach literacy during the school years, and to
provide reading camps during the summer. You'll be living at the
orphanage in summer camp type facilities. The location is far from the
tourist areas and major cities. Full time American and Canadian
Orphanage Outreach leaders will be living and working with you.

Teaching English to Dominican School Children

Organization: Orphanage Outreach Teach Corps
Location: Rural areas
Cost: $800 for 1 week, $1,800 for 1 month, $3,500 for three months
Duration: 1 week to 2 years
Age: 18 for individuals, for groups or families - no minimum age
Contact: director@orphanage-outreach.org
Learn more: www.orphanage-outreach.org
Details: Dominicans are hungry to learn English, as it provides
educational and career opportunities. Unfortunately, there are few
teachers who know English, especially in the rural
areas where Orphanage Outreach works.
Orphanage Outreach volunteers teach basic English
vocabulary lessons in the local grade schools, and
also at their English Institute where 200 5th-8th
graders study English each day. During the
summer, volunteers provide fun and interactive
English immersion camps. You'll be living at the
orphanage in summer camp type facilities. Location
is far from the tourist areas and major cities. Full time American and
Canadian Orphanage Outreach leaders will be living and working with
you.

Summer Learning Camps

Organization: Orphanage Outreach Teach Corps
Location: Rural areas
Cost: $800 for 1 week, $1,800 for 1 month, $3,500 for three months
Duration: 1 week to 2 years
Age: 18+ for individuals, groups or families - no minimum age
Contact: director@orphanage-outreach.org
Learn more: www.orphanage-outreach.org
Details: An Orphanage Outreach summer learning camp is like
Disneyworld for the kids in the Dominican Republic. You will create a

general activities camp, a high energy sports camp, an educational English camp, or some combination. Each camp opens with songs and a theme for the day. Then the kids divide into groups—young girls, older girls, young boys, older boys—and rotate through different learning and activity stations. Volunteers act both as group guides and station leaders. The groups then all come back together for closing songs and lesson. You'll be living at the orphanage in summer camp type facilities. The location is far from the tourist areas and major cities. Full time American and Canadian Orphanage Outreach leaders will be living and working with you.

Other organizations offering projects in Dominican Republic:
Amigos de las Américas: www.amigoslink.org
Global Leadership Adventures (for high school students):
   www.experiencegla.com
Dominican Foundation (medical missions):
   www.dominicanfoundation.com
i-to-i: www.i-to-i.com
Kids Alive International: www.kidsalive.org
Transitions Abroad: www.transitionsabroad.com
Serendib: www.serendib.us
Sister Island Project (cultural & educational):
   www.sisterislandproject.org
Global Leadership Adventures (for high school students):
   www.experiencegla.com
Volunteers for Peace: www.vfp.org

El Salvador

Global Health Volunteer in Las Delicias
Organization: Foundation for International Medical Relief of Children
Location: Las Delicias, El Salvador
Cost: $1,101 per week
Duration: 1 to 3 weeks, longer stays are possible **Age:** 18
Contact: missions@fimrc.org **Learn more:** www.fimrc.org
Special skills: This program is specially focused for undergraduates, medical students and public health students
Details: Las Delicias is an underserved community of approximately 5,000 people located a short drive from San Salvador, the capital city of El Salvador. Volunteers have the opportunity to assist and shadow the clinic doctor while gaining firsthand experience in improving the health

of developing communities. Volunteers will spend part of their time at the clinic site working with the clinic doctor to see patients, and will travel with field staff to perform house calls, conduct community outreach campaigns, collect basic health statistics, and survey families to develop assessments of healthcare needs. Programs run year-round, and free time is included to enjoy nightlife, sightseeing, tours and hikes.

Other organizations offering projects in El Salvador:
ArtCorp: www.artcorp.org
Building New Hope (coffee, fair trade, woman, education...):
   www.buildingnewhope.org
Global Crossroads: www.globalcrossroad.com
Coffee Quality Institute: www.coffeeinstitute.org
Global Volunteer Network: www.volunteer.org.nz
Habitat for Humanity: www.habitat.org
Volunteers for Peace: www.vfp.org

Grenada

Monitoring Nesting Leatherbacks & Hawksbills Turtles
Organization: YWF-Kido Foundation
Location: Carriacou Island, Grenadines of Grenada, West Indies
Cost: $450 for 30 days   **Duration:** +1 month, 5 days per week
Age: 18 - 45 (for under age volunteers parent has to sign a disclaimer)
Contact: marina.fastigi@gmail.com
Learn more: www.kido-projects.com
Special skills: Volunteers should have a keen and genuine interest in conservation and ecology and be animal lovers. Volunteers must be good swimmers, physically fit to walk long distances on soft, sandy beaches and nature trails, while working in all weather conditions.
Details: Volunteers will actively participate in monitoring and data-collection of two critically endangered Sea Turtle Species, Leatherback and Hawksbill, nesting on 5 different beaches on the island; helping to reduce illegal poaching activities of turtles and eggs. (From March to August) Duties include: Night patrolling on foot in a nature park area (8pm to 5am, five nights a week), working with local guides; assisting with tagging post-nesting turtles; carapace measuring and other data collecting; disguising nests against poaching activities; egg counting and mapping nest location, hatchling monitoring and survival rate data collection, nest excavation and early morning beach patrols either on foot or kayak.

Other organizations offering projects in Grenada:
Academic Treks: www.academictreks.com
Ecoteer: www.ecoteer.com
Good News Project (home building): www.goodnewswi.com
Granada SPCA Animal Shelter: www.grenadaspca.org
i-to-i: www.i-to-i.com
Rosalie Forest Eco Lodge: www.3riversdominica.com
World Horizons (service trips for teens & adults):
  www.world-horizons.com
Working Abroad: www.workingabroad.com

Guadeloupe (France)

VISIONS French Language Immersion for Teens

Organization: VISIONS Service Adventures
Location: Les Saintes
Cost: $4,500+ **Duration:** 4 weeks, and customized programs
Age: Teens, customized programs for all ages
Contact: info@VisionsServiceAdventures.com
Learn more: www.VisionsServiceAdventures.com
Special skills: 2 years of high school French.
Details: Guadeloupe is a French language-
immersion experience on a Caribbean island
blending French and Caribbean cultures. VISIONS
works in communities on either mainland Basse
Terre or on Terre de Bas, one of Les Saintes—tiny
islands off the southern tip of the mainland.
VISIONS participants undertake joint renovation
projects on parks and preservation endeavors
designated by local governments and apprentice
with local fishermen and artisans. Besides
swimming and snorkeling, the group explores the
rainforests and mountains of Guadeloupe; the small outlying islands;
colorful, fragrant open-air markets; and the exquisite countryside.
VISIONS challenges every part of participants—the mind, muscles and
heart.

Other organization(s) offering projects in Guadeloupe:

Academic Treks: www.academictreks.com

Guatemala

Children's Health Education

Organization: Primeros Pasos
Special skills: Must have intermediate to advanced level of Spanish
Location: Quetzaltenango
Cost: None   **Duration:** 2+ months   **Age:** 18
Contact: info@primerospasos.org
Learn more: www.primerospasos.org
Details: Primeros Pasos is a non-profit, independent organization that offers quality and affordable health care and health education to the underserved communities of the Palajunoj Valley of Quetzaltenango, Guatemala. With the collaboration of health professionals, health educators, volunteers and community leaders, Primeros Pasos strives to improve access to basic medical services. Generally, health educators work side by side with Guatemalan and foreign volunteers and work directly with Guatemalan students, teachers and community members. Health educators provide in-clinic classes to students (grades K-6) participating in the Primeros Pasos Healthy Schools Program and work with community schools to teach children about nutrition, hygiene, puberty, sexual education, natural disasters, the environment, children's rights, self-esteem, alcohol and drug abuse and other topics.

Nuevos Horizontes Home for Women and Children

Organization: Asociacion Nuevos Horizontes
Location: Quetzaltenango
Cost: None   **Duration:** 4+ weeks   **Age:** 18, families & groups welcome
Contact: nhcoordinadoras@gmail.com   **Learn more:** www.ahnh.org
Details: Work with the children of the Nuevos Horizontes home, Guatemala's first shelter for women & children escaping domestic violence or in the day care center for the children of working mothers. Volunteers devise and organize fun, educational and creative activities for the children. This may include helping with homework, arts and crafts, games, exercise and English classes. Volunteers can also help organize excursions for the children. Assistance is also needed for vital fundraising events in the local area. It's sometimes challenging working with the children, but ultimately it is rewarding. Although they have experienced great difficulties in their lives, the children are excited by the new experiences our volunteers offer them.

Help Guatemala's Only Domestic Animal Shelter

Organization: AWARE (Animal Welfare Association Rescue/Education)
Location: Sumpango
Cost: $5.00 a day for volunteer housing (beds, showers, kitchen, etc.; no food included)
Duration: 2+ weeks if staying on site. No upper limit   **Age:** 18
Contact: xenii-2@usa.net   **Learn more:** www.animalaware.org
Special skills: A love of animals, initiative and willingness to work
Details: Volunteers work at a domestic animal
shelter currently housing 250 dogs and 80 cats. The
basic daily routine consists of attending to any sick
animals (giving meds, cleaning cages and the clinic),
cleaning dog runs, cleaning the cat house, socializing
dogs and cats, cleaning and changing animal
bedding, feeding animals, walking dogs, bathing
dogs, grooming dogs and cats, plus assisting with

veterinary care. On Sundays the shelter is open to the
public, so volunteers can show people around and help potential
adopters find the right animal for them. There are occasional
maintenance or construction jobs around the Shelter where help might
be needed. Volunteers might also be asked to assist with spay/neuter or
rabies vaccination clinics in different villages, or with an educational
intervention in a school.

Manos de Colores

Organization: Asociación Centro de Idiomas El Nahual
Location: Quetzaltenango, in Guatemala's beautiful western
highlands.
Cost: None. However, volunteers may sign up for Spanish classes
and/or homestay option ($160 per week), which provides the
opportunity to live with a local family, eat traditional Guatemalan food
and practice rolling your R's while working with Manos de Colores.
Duration: 1 week to 12+ months, prefer 2 months or more
Age: 18, or accompanied by an adult.
Contact: Volunteer only: manosdecolores@gmail.com, Study and
volunteer: cdl.elnahual@gmail.com, Phone: +502 7765.2098
Learn more: www.elnahual.org
Special skills: We can use any and all skill types, interests, and
former experiences, including teaching, art, music, web design,
photography, building, construction, gardening and more!
Details: Manos de Colores is an intensive educational program offered
to children at their community center in Quetzaltenango as well as
three local public schools. The program was founded in 2004 following
a period of reflection on the dismal state of education in Guatemala,

which is compounded by poverty and the continued marginalization of rural and indigenous peoples. To that end, Manos de Colores seeks to provide children in the community with thoughtful, creative instruction in English, the arts, Spanish and mathematics. Their philosophy is "education for social development". For those individuals who prefer to volunteer without the homestay option, they encourage you to bring donations such as school supplies, bike repair kits, computer parts and/or cash; just a few of the things the center always needs.

El Nahual Community Center Construction

Organization: Asociación Centro de Idiomas El Nahual
Location: Quetzaltenango, in Guatemala's beautiful western highlands.
Cost: None. However, volunteers may sign up for Spanish classes and/or homestay option ($160 per week), which provides the opportunity to live with a local family, eat traditional Guatemalan food and practice rolling your R's while working with Manos de Colores.
Duration: 1 week to 12+ months, prefer 2 months or more
Age: 18, or accompanied by an adult
Contact: Volunteer only: manosdecolores@gmail.com, Study and volunteer: cdl.elnahual@gmail.com, Phone: +502 7765.2098
Learn more: www.elnahual.org
Special skills: Any and all skill types/levels are welcome to help build, paint, decorate and furnish a new community center. Experience with building, electrical wiring and plumbing is a plus but not required.
Details: Asociación de Centro Idiomas El Nahual (El Nahual Community Center) is a nonprofit community center funded by its Spanish language school. They serve as a nexus of support to children and families, offering after-school programs and education (Manos de Colores) for social development on the outskirts of Quetzaltenango. They need passionate, enthusiastic volunteers to help us construct a new community center. In addition to expanding current programs the center will house a free health clinic, a daycare center, a free public sports field and a free or sliding-scale school for children where they can receive a complete education and cultural programming involving workshops to develop practical and technical skills. This expansion will be made possible once the new center is built and El Nahual Community Center is no longer losing money to rent their current location. Due to the costs of labor, they are building the new center brick by brick and need volunteers who can help out any way they can, whether it is through raising cash donations for building supplies or the day to day manual work itself.

Organic Gardening at El Nahual Community Center

Organization: Asociación de Centro Idiomas El Nahual
Location: Quetzaltenango, in Guatemala's beautiful western highlands.
Cost: None. However, volunteers may sign up for Spanish classes and/or homestay option (US$160 per week), which provides the opportunity to live with a local family, eat traditional Guatemalan food and practice rolling your R's while working with Manos de Colores.
Duration: 1 week to 12+ months, prefer 2 months or more
Age: 18, or accompanied by an adult.
Contact: Volunteer only: manosdecolores@gmail.com, Study and volunteer: cdl.elnahual@gmail.com, Phone: +502 7765.2098
Learn more: www.elnahual.org
Details: Any and all skill types, levels, and former experiences are welcome to help tend, grow and harvest organic vegetables from a community garden, which returns 100% of its proceeds back to the projects run at El Nahual Community Center for children and families and Manos de Colores. The program runs five days per week in Quetzaltenango (in addition to three other schools in the area) providing thoughtful, creative instruction to children and adults in subjects they would otherwise not receive: English, mathematics and art, just to name a few. To generate income for these important programs and educate the families about environmentally friendly growing practices, we maintain a 100% organic garden which the community itself is responsible for tending. The produce is also given to families in need of food and nutrition.

Green Building Vocational School

Organization: Long Way Home
Location: 95% Mayan Kachiquel village in Western Guatemalan Highlands
Cost: $50 per week **Duration:** 1+ weeks **Age:** 18-55
Contact: volunteer@longwayhomeinc.org
Learn more: longwayhomeinc.org
Details: Actively engage with a Guatemalan community by assisting in the construction of a vocational school. Built in the Earthship style with dirt-packed tires, this ecofriendly school will provide environmental education and focused skill training to broaden the horizons of the youth in a rural area. The school will equip students with welding, electrical, carpentry, mechanic and masonry experience and then send them into other parts of Guatemala to build environmentally sound, structures. Empowering the youth is an active way to break the cycle of poverty and this vocational school will give them the skills

for job acquisition and the knowledge to be stewards of their habitat. You will work hard and acquire an enriching new perspective.

Community Park Volunteer

Organization: Long Way Home
Location: 95% Mayan Kachiquel village in Western Guatemalan Highlands
Cost: $50 per week + food **Duration:** 1+ week **Age:** 18-55
Contact: volunteer@longwayhomeinc.org
Learn more: longwayhomeinc.org
Details: Volunteer in a recreational space used by the community. Parque Chimiyá provides a venue for sports and outdoor opportunities, giving people of all ages a place to channel their active and creative energies in a positive manner. Onsite there is a community kitchen, botanical garden, plant nursery, basketball court, playground and soccer field playing host to hundreds of Guatemalans a week. Women, men and children of all ages enjoy the facilities and participate in organized and spontaneous activities. Volunteers get to apply their strengths by dedicating energy to our ongoing projects. Long Way Home needs people who appreciate the fruits of a challenge and cooperate easily with others. Interest in the outdoors is a plus and the willingness to try new things is highly encouraged.

Youth Education and Achievement

Organization: Safe Passage/Camino Seguro
Location: Guatemala City, Guatemala
Cost: $50 volunteer fee, $95/week average living expenses
Duration: 5+ weeks **Age:** 18
Contact: volunteer@safepassage.org
Learn more: www.safepassage.org
Special skills: Intermediate Spanish
Details: Come make a difference in the lives of the children of the Guatemala City garbage dump. We need energetic volunteers to support our nursery, primary, and secondary school classrooms. Volunteers are a vital and essential part of our project. They work in collaboration with our Guatemalan staff and other volunteers to provide educational and emotional support for our children. Affordable accommodation are available in the town of Antigua and direct transportation is provided.

English Education Program

Organization: Safe Passage/Camino Seguro
Location: Guatemala City, Guatemala
Cost: $50 volunteer fee, $95/week average living expenses

Duration: 5+ weeks **Age:** 18
Contact: volunteer@safepassage.org,
englishprogram@safepassage.org
Learn more: www.safepassage.org
Special skills: Intermediate Spanish
Details: Come make a difference in the lives of the children of the
Guatemala City garbage dump. We need enthusiastic volunteers to
teach English in our primary and secondary school classrooms. English
teachers conduct several classes a day to the children in our programs,
building their vocabulary and grammar through educational exercises.
Affordable accommodations are available in the town of Antigua and
direct transportation is provided.

Adult Literacy Program

Organization: Safe Passage/Camino Seguro
Location: Guatemala City, Guatemala
Cost: $50 volunteer fee, $95/week average living expenses
Duration: 5+ weeks **Age:** 18
Contact: volunteer@safepassage.org, adultliteracy@safepassage.org
Learn more: www.safepassage.org
Special skills: Intermediate Spanish
Details: Come make a difference in the lives of families living around
the Guatemala City garbage dump. We need dedicated volunteers to
assist with our adult literacy program, teaching parents and
grandparents to read and write in Spanish. Volunteers in the Adult
Literacy program will help our teachers conduct classes and work one-
on-one with the students to build their skills and confidence.
Affordable accommodations are available in the town of Antigua and
direct transportation is provided.

Project Administration

Organization: Safe Passage/Camino Seguro
Location: Guatemala City, Guatemala and Antigua, Guatemala
Cost: $50 volunteer fee, $95/week average living expenses
Duration: 6+ months **Age:** 18
Contact: volunteer@safepassage.org
Learn more: www.safepassage.org
Special skills: Intermediate Spanish
Details: Come make a difference by working with Safe
Passage/Camino Seguro, an organization which supports children and
families living around the Guatemala City garbage dump. We need
experienced and committed volunteers to work in a variety of
administrative positions within our organization, facilitating our
programs and supporting our staff. Check our website for a list of
currently needed positions. Affordable accommodation are available in

the town of Antigua and direct transportation to Guatemala City is provided.

Guatemala Wildlife Rescue Center

Organization: Wildlife Rescue and Conservation Association (ARCAS)
Location: On Lake Peten Itza across from the town of Flores in the Peten region of northern Guatemala
Cost: $125 per week. Optional fee of $250 for airport pick-up and trip to Tikal
Duration: Open **Age:** Under 18 with parent's approval
Contact: arcas@intelnet.net.gt
Learn more: arcas@intelnet.net.gt, www.arcasguatemala.com
Special skills: None required, but wildlife rehab experience is helpful
Details: The ARCAS wild animal rescue and rehabilitation center is one of the premier wildlife rescue centers in the world, handling 300-600 wild animals of 40+ species per year. Volunteers at the Rescue Center help in feeding and caring for the animals at the center

which include parrots, macaws, spider and howler monkeys, margays, ocelots, coatimundis, taras and kinkajous. Nearly all of these animals have been seized from smugglers and are very young, needing constant care and attention. There are also opportunities to take part in veterinary medical treatment, animal releases, environmental education and wildlife surveys, though the scheduling of these activities is irregular and we can't guarantee you will be able to participate.

Alternative Education Project in Mayan Village

Organization: Creative Corners; The Global Arts Project
Location: San Marcos La Laguna
Cost: $1,300 1 month $2,000 2 months, additional months $500
Duration: 1 week to 6+ months **Age:** 20
Contact: enquiries@creative-corners.com
Learn more: www.creative-corners.com
Details: This project based in a Mayan village at Lago Atitlán operates as a permanent creativity workshop and program for the youth of the local community. The project dedicates itself to supporting and facilitating artistic expression, learning, exchange, formation and production with the children and youth of San Marcos and the surrounding rural communities. Run by a permanent team of three and assisted by local and international artists and facilitators the project provides art workshops in schools, public spaces and at their own premises which include a dance/gym studio, classrooms and

workshops spaces. They also provide a unique scholarship program where local students are trained to become arts trainers and facilitators themselves so that this will continue to be a creative and vibrant community.

Hogares Comunitarios in Guatemala

Organization: Experiential Learning International
Cost: $885+ **Duration:** 2+ weeks **Age:** 18
Contact: info@eliabroad.org **Learn more:** www.eliabroad.org
Special skills: Intermediate Spanish Language Skills
Details: The Guatemalan government sponsors this project aimed at helping the children of the very poor by providing daycare and meals. The daycare centers are in the homes of women throughout the country. Each project has an average of 12 children from infants to six years old. The children are either from single parent households or households affected by alcohol or drug abuse. The children are provided with breakfast, lunch, and snacks each day along with educational activities and a safe place to spend the day. Volunteers with this program will lead activities with the children, teach reading skills, and assist with some of the other chores such as cleaning, cooking, and bathing the children. You will need to take initiative and be creative.

Indigenous Women's Assistance in Guatemala

Organization: World Endeavors
Location: Quetzaltenango
Cost: $1,260+ **Duration:** 2 to 12 Weeks **Age:** 18
Contact: inquiry@worldendeavors.com
Learn more: www.worldendeavors.com
Special skills: Minimum intermediate Spanish proficiency is required
Details: Impact indigenous women's lives by contributing to local social initiatives. Volunteers are paired with a local government social worker and assist with workshops for indigenous women. The workshops focus on a variety of subjects, including human rights, women's rights, reproductive health, cooking, handicrafts, and economic development. Those with specialized skills are welcome to share their expertise. Participants have the opportunity to live with

host families, with whom they will share three meals each day. Up to four weeks of Spanish lessons are also included with placements.

Orphanage Assistance in Guatemala

Organization: World Endeavors
Location: Quetzaltnango
Cost: $1,260+   **Duration:** 2 to 12 Weeks   **Age:** 18
Contact: inquiry@worldendeavors.com
Learn more: www.worldendeavors.com
Details: Enrich an orphan's life in Guatemala. Volunteers provide support for orphanage staff. Many volunteers teach English to the children, as well as participate in activities such as health education, games, and art projects. Homestay accommodations (including all meals) give volunteers an opportunity to immerse themselves in Guatemalan culture and to practice their Spanish. Up to four weeks of Spanish lessons are also included with placement.

Mayan Stove Project

Organization: inside/out Humanitourism™ Adventures
Location: Guatemala Highlands
Cost: $2,000-$2,500
Duration: 1 week + 1 week of locally guided active adventures*
Age: No age minimum, determined on an individual basis
Contact: info@theinsideandout.com
Learn more: www.theinsideandout.com
Details: This is your chance to help improve the lives and health of Mayan families living in the Guatemalan Highlands by building and installing stoves which will use less fuel and produce less smoke than traditional Mayan open fire cooking. They reduce the use of wood, providing cleaner burning and reducing respiratory problems. You will spend time with individual families, immersing in traditional Mayan culture and experiencing the colors and textures of this lush and colorful region. There may be additional project work teaching basic computer skills. Inside/Out trips are designed around opportunities to do humanitarian volunteer work on meaningful international projects and are combined with sustainable eco-adventure travel in the local area of the project and people. Their trips are designed to create long-term relationships between communities and travelers.

Other organizations offering projects in Guatemala:

Adventure Minded People Exploring Diversity Abroad:
  www.ampedabroad.com
Ak' Tenamit (indigenous community development):
  www.aktenamit.org

AmeriSpan Study Abroad: www.amerispan.com
As Green as it Gets (environmental sustainable agriculture):
 www.asgreenasitgets.org
The Bio-Cultura Project (reforestation): www.bio-cultura.com
Casa Guatemala (orphanage/school): www.casa-guatemala.org
Common Hope (education to empower): www.commonhope.org
Cross-Cultural Solutions: www.crossculturalsolutions.org
Global Crossroads: www.globalcrossroad.com
Global Visions International: www.gviusa.com or www.gvi.co.uk
Hospitalito Atitlan: www.hospitalitoatitlan.org
Maya Pedal (bicycle technologies): mayapedal.org
Nuevos Horizontes (women's & children's rights): www.ahnh.org
SEE Turtles: www.seeturtles.org
Street School (at risk youth): www.streetschool.net
Trama Textiles (women, fair trade, weaving): tramatextiles.org
Volunteer Peten: www.volunteerpeten.com

Haiti

CENEOH-Haiti

Organization: Kids Worldwide
Location: Port Au Prince, the capital of Haiti.
Cost: $30 booking fee, $350 first one month, $200 subsequent
months **Duration:** A minimum of two weeks, 1 month+ preferred.
Bookings made according to volunteer's need. Dates are flexible.
Age: 18, kids welcome with a parent after prior consultation
Contact: ceneoh@kidsworldwide.org
Learn more: southamerica.kidsworldwide.org/haiticeneoh.htm
Special skills: Child education experience to help train teachers.
French will be an advantage.
Details: CENEOH stands for Centre of Neo Humanist Education. This
project is affiliated with AMURT (Ananda Marga Universal Relief
Team). Their mission is to educate the children based on Neo-
Humanist curriculum that fosters a sense of universalism in the
students and teaches them about the sacredness of all forms of life.
Most of the students come from poor families. Currently, there are
approximately 250 children learning in 9 classrooms, including nursery
and primary levels. The school is staffed by 12 teachers and support
staff members. They need volunteers who have a love for children and
who can help children in the process of their learning.

Other organizations offering projects in Haiti:
Action Against Hunger: www.actionagainsthunger.org
CFH International (humanitarian aid): www.chfhq.org
Christian Veterinary Mission: www.cvmusa.org
Fonkoze (alternative banking for poor): www.fonkoze.org
Healing Hands for Haiti (rehabilitation medicine):
  www.healinghandsforhaiti.org
Kids Worldwide: www.kidsworldwide.org
Practical Compassion: www.practicalcompassion.org
New Frontiers Health Force: www.newfrontiershf.com
Reconstructing Efforts Aiding Children Without Homes:
  www.reach4children.org
Safe Water Plus: www.safewaterplus.org
Twinning Center (HIV/AIDS, medical):
  www.twinningagainstaids.org
Volunteers for Peace: www.vfp.org

Honduras

Jungle School Teachers Assistant

Organization: Helping Honduras Kids
Location: La Ceiba, Honduras
Costs: $100 - A daily lunch only is provided when working
Duration: 2 months to 1 year **Age:** 18
Contact: info@helpinghonduraskids.org
Learn more: www.helpinghonduraskids.org
Special skills: Must speak Spanish and enjoy kids
Details: Helping Honduras Kids is a volunteer organization that is geared toward assisting disadvantaged kids on the Caribbean coast of Honduras. They operate an orphanage with 21 children and a jungle school with over 60 kids. Without help these kids would be either on the street and/or get no formal education. HHK believes that through education they can make a difference in the outcomes of these little lives. This volunteer position requires teaching and/or assisting in teaching approximately 5 days per week and 8 hours per day. This leaves time to explore, enjoy Honduras's amazing jungles, see historic sites and best of all; get to know the people. Expect this to be a life altering experience!

Hogar De Amor Orphanage Volunteer

Organization: Helping Honduras Kids

Location: La Ceiba, Honduras
Costs: $100 - A daily lunch only is provided when working
Duration: 2 months to 1 year   **Age:** 21
Contact: info@helpinghonduraskids.org
Learn more: www.helpinghonduraskids.org
Special skills: Must Speak Spanish and enjoy lots of kids
Details: Helping Honduras Kids is a volunteer organization that works passionately to help disadvantaged kids on the Caribbean Coast of Honduras. They operate an orphanage with 21 children and also provide them with an education. Without help these kids would be on the streets and would have very little hope in their futures. Helping Honduras Kids believes that education can change the outcome of each of their little lives. This position requires lots of love, hugs, nurturing, teaching, cleaning and caring. You will go to Honduras thinking that you will change their little lives, but will in fact you will return changed by them! This position requires you help 10 hours per day, seven days per week. Do you think you can do it?

El Porvenir Kinder and Grandmas Project

Organization: Honduras Children
Location: On the north (Caribbean) coast of Honduras.
Cost: $35 per week to live at the volunteers' beach house.
Duration: 6+ weeks
Contact: volunteer@honduraschildren.org
Learn more: www.honduraschildren.org
Special skills: Experience with children and some Spanish is a plus.
Details: Volunteers work with 'kinder' children in the morning and then offer activities and educational enrichment for older children later in the day. The kinder and Gradmas programs at *Honduras Children* are conducted in the beach community of El Porvenir near the lively La Ceiba area of the north coast. The jungle rivers of the Pico Bonito National Forest and the sun and sand of the Caribbean Sea are just minutes from where our volunteers live and work. Although El Porvenir is rural and poor, the small city of La Ceiba is only 20 minutes away, offering all the modern conveniences. Volunteers purchase and prepare their own food.

Honduras Building Project

Organization: Global Volunteer Network
Location: La Esperanza
Cost: $716 for 2 weeks   **Duration:** 2 to 12 weeks   **Age:** 18
Contact: info@volunteer.org.nz   **Learn more:** www.volunteer.org.nz
Special skills: A basic level of Spanish

Details: On the building program volunteers work with rural communities in the region surrounding La Esperanza to build houses, schools, or extensions to existing buildings. In most cases volunteers work directly with the family or community group they are helping, and use traditional methods of building with materials sourced from the region. Tasks on the building project include renovation, laboring, painting, decorating, making adobe bricks, building walls, digging and building wooden playgrounds. Volunteers will assist with cement mixing, sand sifting, cutting wood, and transporting building materials. There is little equipment. This is mostly manual work.

Honduras Teaching Project

Organization: Global Volunteer Network
Location: La Esperanza
Cost: $716 for 2 weeks **Duration:** 2 to 12 weeks **Age:** 18
Contact: info@volunteer.org.nz **Learn more:** www.volunteer.org.nz
Special skills: A basic level of Spanish
Details: Volunteers can help teach English at one of the eight state schools outside of La Esperanza. Volunteer activities will include assisting the local staff as well as taking on sole responsibility of the classroom. The children are aged from 5 to 12 years old and volunteers may be allocated more than one grade to teach. There is no set curriculum for teaching English in rural areas, and volunteers should expect to come prepared with ideas for classroom activities. The level of English of the students is basic and volunteers will be teaching basic vocabulary, grammar and pronunciation. Volunteers may also be required to help in other areas such as computers, sports, mathematics, art or music.

Honduras Medical Project in Gracias

Organization: Global Volunteer Network
Location: The town of Gracias, 6 hours from Tegucigalpa,
Cost: $716 for 2 weeks **Duration:** 2 to 12 weeks **Age:** 18
Contact: info@volunteer.org.nz **Learn more:** www.volunteer.org.nz
Special skills: Intermediate Spanish, experience and/or qualifications in medicine
Details: This project allows volunteers to help at an underfunded rural hospital. The Gracias Hospital continually struggles to meet demand with its meager budget and is therefore in constant need of assistance. Volunteers will participate in many of the roles associated with

shadowing nurses and doctors, laboratory work, prenatal care, intensive care, physiotherapy and more. The level and scope of your involvement will be determined by your experience and knowledge. All applications need to be accompanied with a copy of your CV (résumé).

Honduras Childcare Project
Organization: Global Volunteer Network
Location: La Esperanza
Cost: $716 for 2 weeks   **Duration:** 2 to 12 weeks   **Age:** 18
Contact: info@volunteer.org.nz   **Learn more:**
www.volunteer.org.nz
Special skills: Basic Spanish
Details: Volunteers will work at a state-run daycare institution whose aim is to take care of orphaned, sick, neglected and poor children in Honduras. The specific institute that GVN is involved with is for children from single parent families that have a net income of around US$100 per month. Volunteer activities include feeding, playing, educating and cleaning the children. The children are from around 5-15 year of age and are in need of love and attention. Volunteers act as older siblings. In addition, they have an ongoing revitalization project at the center. With the continuous help from volunteers they are slowly but surely changing the building by painting and decorating the facilities which are run down due to lack of funds.

Honduras Environment Iguana Project
Organization: Global Volunteer Network
Location: The beautiful tropical island of Utila, nestled in the Caribbean Sea 29 km from the Honduras mainland port of La Ceiba.
Cost: $716 for 2 weeks   **Duration:** 2 weeks to 12 weeks   **Age:** 18
Contact: info@volunteer.org.nz   **Learn more:**
www.volunteer.org.nz
Special skills: Basic Spanish
Details: On this project animal loving volunteers will work at an Iguana Center which is dedicated to the protection and breeding of the

Utila Iguana. Daily activities include feeding the iguanas and educating the local community and school groups about the species and their environment. Volunteers will help with conducting guided tours, working on general maintenance of cages, feeding and cleaning the iguana enclosures, gardening, etc. There may also be the opportunity to get involved in research and data gathering as well as any special projects at the center.

Helping Children through Community Development

Organization: Amigos de las Américas
Location: Intibucá, Honduras near the El Salvador border
Cost: $4,000+ **Duration:** 7 weeks **Age:** 16 by Sept. 1st
Contact: info@amigoslink.org
Learn more: www.amigoslink.org
Details: By partnering with *Save the Children de Honduras,* Amigos spreads a philosophy that to improve the life of one child, you must improve the entire community. The volunteer project aims to improve home and community life for children and is committed to utilizing pre-existing community resources. Intibucá is a beautiful, temperate region and a unique destination for volunteers wishing to experience the authentic natural beauty and culture of Honduras. The entire area is green and mountainous with gorgeous views and many small rivers that cut through the valleys.

Teach Environmental Health to 5-12 Year Olds

Organization: Amigos de las Américas
Location: Various locations within 4 hours of La Paz
Cost: $4,000+ **Duration:** 6 weeks **Age:** 16 by Sept. 1st
Contact: info@amigoslink.org **Learn more:** www.amigoslink.org
Details: Volunteers are needed to facilitate educational activities. This will involve different presentation methods for physical education, art and leadership and team building activities, with an emphasis placed on environmental health. Volunteers will be located in mountain communities south and west of the city.

Youth Fair Collaboration

Organization: Amigos de las Américas
Location: Lempira (Lenca Highlands)
Cost: $4,000+ **Duration:** 6 weeks **Age:** 16 by Sept. 1st
Contact: info@amigoslink.org **Learn more:** www.amigoslink.org
Details: Amigos' project volunteers will collaborate with community youth counterparts from Plan-Honduras to prepare presentations for a

large youth fair. The themes are selected by youth at the beginning of the project (past themes include recycling and local culture). As part of your work, you will implement educational activities 3 times a week with children ages 5-12. This can include environment education, physical education, art, dental hygiene, leadership and team building skills.

Safeguarding the Coral Reefs of Cayos Cochinos

Organization: Biosphere Expeditions
Location: Cayos Cochinos Natural Monument in the Caribbean Sea
Cost: $2,220
Duration: 2 weeks (or join multiple expeditions) **Age:** 18
Contact: info@biosphere-expeditions.org
Learn more: www.biosphere-expeditions.org
Special skills: You need to be a fully qualified diver to take part in this expedition (minimum PADI Open Water or equivalent).

Details: This volunteer expedition will take you to the world's second largest reef system in the middle of the Cayos Cochinos Natural Monument in the Caribbean Sea, off the coast of Honduras. The purpose of the survey program is to provide data on the current biological status of the reefs and of population levels of protected species within the marine protected area. Data collection follows an internationally recognized coral reef monitoring program, called Reef Check, and will be used to make informed management and conservation decisions within the existing marine protected area. The expedition also includes training as a Reef Check Eco-Diver. With this you are also eligible to apply for PADI or NAUI Reef Check Specialty Course certification.

Other organizations offering projects in Honduras:

A Pas de Loup www.apasdeloup.org
Architects without Borders: www.awb.iohome.net
ArtCorps: www.artcorp.org
Bay Island Conservation Association: www.bicautila.org
Bilingual Education for Central America: www.becaschools.org
Brethren Volunteer Service: www.brethrenvolunteerservice.org
Carolina Honduras Health Foundation:
   www.carolinahondurashealth.org
Cofradia Bilingual School: www.cofradiaschool.com
Feed the Children: www.feedthechildren.org
Habitat for Humanity International: www.habitat.org
Iguana Station: www.utila-iguana.de

My Little Red House Bilingual School:
  www.mylittleredhousebilingualschool.com
V.I.P. Central America: vipca.webs.com
Volunteers for Intercultural and Definitive Adventures (medical,
  dental, veterinary, service & construction):
  www.vidavolunteertravel.org
Unite for Sight: www.uniteforsight.org
Utila Community Clinic: www.aboututila.com

Jamaica

Deaf Education in Kingston
Organization: World Endeavors
Location: Kingston, Jamaica
Cost: $1,317+ **Duration:** 2 to 12 weeks **Age:** 18
Contact: inquiry@worldendeavors.com
Learn more: www.worldendeavors.com
Special skills: Individuals with fluent sign language skills are needed
to help tutor fast track students. Participants with little to no signing
abilities are also needed to help facilitate the program.
Details: Impact the deaf community in Jamaica. Volunteers work with
the Jamaica Association for the deaf to develop self-sustaining cycles of
deaf education and leadership skills through advocacy, multicultural
exchange and mentor support. Their goal is to train deaf educators who
can reach deaf children across Jamaica. Participants stay in shared
housing, where groceries are provided and they have access to a
kitchen.

Utilizing Historic Resources for Economic Development
Organization: Adventures in Preservation
Location: Cockpit County, inland Jamaica
Cost: $3,100 **Duration:** 3 weeks **Age:** 18
Contact: workshops@adventuresinpreservation.org
Learn more: www.adventuresinpreservation.org
Special skills: No skills necessary; training provided at the site
Details: Tiny historic houses scattered throughout the unique
limestone landscape of inland Jamaica may provide a financial solution
for this economically depressed region. Biodiversity has been created
by the landscape, and to date over 100 species of plants and animals
found nowhere else in the world have been identified. There is great

potential for developing ecotourism in the area, but facilities for guests are non-existent. AiP volunteers, led by an expert, will learn hands-on building conservation skills and use these skills to repair and restore charming tiny houses for use as B&B's. The workshop fee covers lodging, meals, transportation from the coast, instruction and insurance. Once house restoration is underway, local residents will receive training in hosting and providing services to ecotourists.

Other organizations offering projects in Jamaica:

Amizade: amizade.org
Blue Mountain Project (grassroots with community of Hagley Gap):
 www.bluemountainproject.org
Global Volunteers: www.globalvolunteers.org
International Partnership for Service-Learning and Internship:
 www.ipsl.org
Jamaica Volunteer Vacations: www.jamaicavolunteervacations.com
Projects Abroad: www.projects-abroad.org
World Endeavors: www.worldendeavors.com
World Hope International: www.worldhope.org

Mexico

Love and Time to Stray Dogs of Puerto Escondido

Organization: Perros En Puerto A.C.
Location: Puerto Escondido, Oaxaca, Mexico
Cost: None, volunteer pays own transport and expenses
Duration: 4+ weeks   **Age:** 18
Contact: perrosenpuerto@hotmail.com
Learn more: www.perrosenpuerto.com
Special skills: Knowledge of some Spanish & animal care
Details: This very new shelter and rescue program is seeking people who want to make a difference in the life of a stray dog. Like in many other places the canine friends here are suffering neglect and abuse. The aim is to educate the community, provide population control programs and rescue and care for the many dogs who are still wandering the streets. If you have your heart in the right place and would like to spend quality time with special shelter animals, experience instant gratification when feeding a starving dog on the street, or enjoy teaching adults and children to help end the suffering of the animals, this is your opportunity. Depending on the season and length of stay PEP can provide free accommodation for volunteers.

Shelter for the Shelter: Build Kennels & Structures
Organization: Baja Dogs La Paz
Location: La Paz, Baja
Cost: None **Duration:** Open **Age:** 18
Contact: Dhorea Ryon: BDLP@bajadogslapaz.org
Learn more: www.bajadogslapaz.org
Special skills: Construction background or experience helpful-working with cement, wood, metal, fencing, concrete block walls, etc.
Details: Great dogs need people to build and repair structures at their rescue sanctuary. Baja Dogs needs to protect the dogs from the harsh environmental elements. As in many parts of Mexico, animals are often left to fend for themselves. The numbers are staggering! Since 2005, they have been working to provide food, shelter and medical care for homeless animals, to reduce the number of stray dogs through an aggressive spay/neuter program and teaching children care for and respect for their pets. Run almost completely by dedicated volunteers, 100% of Baja Dog's funding comes from donations by generous, caring people like you. All donations go directly to the care of the dogs; no one but two dedicated Mexican employees receives a single penny of the money raised. Baja Dogs La Paz is a member of WSPA World Society for Protection of Animals. To date over 200 dogs have been placed into loving homes.

Must Love Dogs: Veterinary, Socialization and Care
Organization: Baja Dogs La Paz
Location: La Paz, Baja
Cost: None **Duration:** Open **Age:** 18
Contact: Dhorea Ryon BDLP@bajadogslapaz.org
Learn more: www.bajadogslapaz.org
Special skills: Veterinary students, veterinarians, dog groomers or persons experienced with animal care
Details: Baja Dogs is always looking for veterinary students or others with background/experience to help and train other volunteers with care, exams, and other medical protocol. They also need people who want to come and walk the dogs and help socialize the pups so they will be ready for their new homes! The shelter is run almost completely by dedicated volunteers, and 100% of our funding comes from the donations of generous, caring people like you. All donations go directly to the care of the dogs; no one but two dedicated Mexican employees receives a single penny of the money raised. Baja Dogs La Paz is a member of WSPA World Society for Protection of Animals. To date over 200 dogs have been placed into loving homes.

IT for the Dogs

Organization: Baja Dogs La Paz
Location: La Paz, Baja
Cost: None **Duration:** Open **Age:** 18
Contact: Dhorea Ryon, BDLP@bajadogslapaz.org
Learn more: www.bajadogslapaz.org
Special skills: Office help: emails, internet searches, grant researches
Details: This great organization needs people for general office help: i.e. emails, grant research, internet searches, etc. Baja Dogs La Paz, A.C. is located just outside of La Paz, the beautiful capital city of Baja California Sur. As in many other parts of Mexico, animals are often left to fend for themselves, and the numbers are staggering! It is estimated there are over 10,000 strays in southern Baja alone, and many are neglected, starving, injured or abused. Since 2005, Baja Dogs La Paz has been working hard to provide food, shelter and medical care for homeless animals, and to reduce the number of stray dogs through an aggressive spay/neuter program. They also teach children the importance of caring for and respecting their pets.

La Gloria Sea Turtle Conservation Program

Organization: Tierralegre & University of Guadalajara´s Center for the Sustainable Development of Coastal Zones
Location: An off-the-grid research station on the tropical "Costalegre" (southern coastline of Jalisco state, 1.5 hours south of Puerto Vallarta)
Cost: $500 for two weeks, $850 per month,
Duration: 2 weeks to 6 months; July-December
Contact: davison.collins@gmail.com
Learn more: www.tierralegre.org
Special skills: Conservation biology, bilingual (Spanish and English), ability to walk two miles on a sandy beach, light lifting (up to 25 lbs.). Volunteer training provided.
Details: Help preserve endangered sea turtles, gain knowledge of marine biology, and encounter cross-cultural opportunities—all at "La Gloria," a tropical beachfront research station. Four of the world's seven species of sea turtles (Olive Ridley, Pacific Green, Hawksbill, and Leatherback) are found in this diverse eco-region. All are endangered, mainly due to rampant poaching. The Hawksbill and Leatherback are near extinction! You'll receive detailed training which will enable you to help with research and data collection. Regular beach patrols by foot and ATV quad are conducted to find eggs which are then transplanted to a protected pen. Data has proven that these patrols are critical to raising the survival rates of sea turtles. Three home cooked meals are prepared daily. Accommodations provided are in ecologically designed structures. Showers and bathrooms provided.

Sea Turtle, Crocodile and Iguana Conservation Project

Organization: GAP Experience & Conservation
Location: Central Pacific Coast, in Colima State
Cost: $400+ per week   **Duration:** 1 week to 6 months   **Age:** 18-45
Contact: jc@naturalia.ws   **Learn more:** www.gapec.org
Special skills: Volunteers must enjoy animal conservation, beach and outdoor life and work at patrolling night shifts and day centre duties.
Details: The Wildlife Conservation Center is based on the Colima Coast. GAPEC has recently collaborated with this center dedicated to preserve endangered species all along the mangrove "Estero Palo Verde" situated on the coast of Colima. Activities involve: daily centre duties such as cleaning sea turtles pools, feeding animals, collecting turtle eggs to put them in the nursery, helping baby turtles get into the  water the day they are born, fill out reports with staff help, patrolling the beaches, teaching English to people involved in the project, painting signs, patrolling the lagoon in a raft or kayak for bird watching and identification and classification of environmental problems. You can use weekends for independent travel around the area. There are beautiful beaches, towns and cities all the way along the cost.

Health Clinics and Education in Rural Villages

Organization: Los Medicos Voladores
Location: Northern Sonora and Baja
Cost: $400+   **Duration:** 4+ days   **Age:** 18. Some exceptions made for 14 and over if traveling with parent or guardian
Contact: info@flyingdocs.org or info@.napadentist.com
Learn more: www.flyingdocs.org
Special skills: Nurses, physicians, dentists, audiologists, eye doctors, chiropractors, physical therapists, gynecologists etc. Also, hygienists, medical assistance, pilots, general volunteers, translators...
Details: LMV is a volunteer-based nonprofit organization that helps improve the health and well-being of the people of Mexico and Central America through the provision of no cost, high-quality healthcare and health education clinics in rural villages in northern Mexico (northern Sonora and Baja), El Salvador, Guatemala, and Honduras; and also among migrant labor populations in the Coachella Valley of the southwestern United States (southern California). Since 1975 LMV has offered more than 230 short-term medical, dental, optometry, and other healthcare clinics, treating over 7,000 patients per year. LMV clinics are open to anyone who can reach the clinic during open hours in the areas we serve. They help improve villagers' lives by not only treating their immediate health problems, but also by providing lasting

tools that empower people to help themselves – including health education (especially for women and children) and clinic equipment for ongoing use by local healthcare professionals.

Work in a Children's Shelter

Organization: Kaya Responsible Travel
Location: The southern city of Oaxaca
Cost: $1,270 **Duration:** 2 to 26 weeks **Age:** 18-80
Contact: info@kayavolunteer.com
Learn more: www.KayaVolunteer.com
Special skills: A love for working with Children, patience, and enthusiasm are a must. Volunteers must be comfortable dealing with disabled children and speak basic Spanish (Basic Spanish lessons will be provided)
Details: The shelter is one of the few that houses children 24 hours a day, 7 days a week. They receive and look after children from newborns to 18 years. Most of these youths are abandoned, orphaned, removed from unhealthy homes, have physical disabilities, or are recovering from addiction. The shelter has limited space and resources, but aims to take the best care of every child. With so many children, volunteers are necessary to make up for the shortcomings in staff size. Volunteers can create activities for the kids, do physical therapy, work one-on-one with a particular child, participate and help supervise outings with the kids, help maintain and improve the facilities, tutor, participate in therapy sessions, and provide attention and caring for a happy environment.

Costalegre Conservation and Sustainability Program

Organization: Tierralegre & University of Guadalajara´s Center for the Sustainable Development of Coastal Zones
Location: La Manzanilla / Boca de Iguanas / Tenacatita Bay region on the tropical "Costalegre" (southern coastline of Jalisco state, about 3.5 hours south of Puerto Vallarta)
Cost: $1,000 for two weeks, $1,750 a month
Duration: 2 weeks to 1 year **Age:** 16-80
Contact: davison.collins@gmail.com
Learn more: www.tierralegre.org
Special skills: Conservation biology, natural resource management, permaculture, construction, gardening, landscaping, environmental education, bilingual (Spanish and English), ability to walk two miles on a sandy beach, light lifting (up to 25 lbs.). Volunteer training provided
Details: Help Tierralegre with its mission to protect the natural resources and biodiversity of the Costalegre. Discover the Jaliscan tropical dry forest eco-region which is included in WWF's Global 200 sites. Projects include community recycling, creation of a sustainable

design demonstration center, creation and implementation of environmental education curriculum, plus floral and faunal surveys of mangrove ecosystems to help form a management plan for seven RAMSAR wetland status sites. Projects vary depending upon time of year, interest, funding, etc. Tierralegre works in collaboration with the University of Guadalajara, and has previously hosted Earthwatch Institute´s *Mexican Mangroves and Wildlife Program.* Three meals are provided daily; volunteer crews assist with preparation. Accommodations provided at base house (www.comalabandb.com, click "Cabaña Las Iguanas" in lower left corner), beach camp and/or homestays. Showers and bathrooms provided.

Equine Therapy with Disabled Kids
Organization: Kaya Responsible Travel
Cost: $1,270 **Duration:** 2 to 26 weeks **Age:** 18-80
Contact: info@kayavolunteer.com
Learn more: www.KayaVolunteer.com
Location: The southern city of Oaxaca
Special skills: No special skills are required. Participants must be comfortable around horses and disabled children. Basic Spanish language is useful (Spanish classes will be provided)
Details: This fantastic project combines physical and emotional therapy for kids with horse riding and equine care lessons. Equinotherapy is an alternative therapeutic method that uses horses and their environment for rehabilitating neurological and physical disabilities. These children have a wide range of disabilities, including Down syndrome, schizophrenia, attention deficit disorder, lower body paralysis, and many more. A physical therapist runs the courses. Volunteers can help assist the children while riding the horses in physical therapy, create and organize alternative activities for the children who are waiting to ride, help with general maintenance and care of the horses, and work with the physical therapist.

Oaxaca Environmental Conservation
Organization: Kaya Responsible Travel
Location: The southern city of Oaxaca
Cost: $1,270+ **Duration:** 2 to 26 weeks **Age:** 18-80
Contact: info@kayavolunteer.com
Learn more: www.KayaVolunteer.com

Special skills: No specific skills required. An interest in environmental issues and computer skills are helpful
Details: Oaxaca has the most biodiversity out of all the states in Mexico. Unfortunately, Oaxaca's environment is being abused and exploited. Protect the natural habitat that provides water, climate control and sustenance to those living on and near the San Felipe Mountains in one or more of these three areas: information and exchange, alternative technology, and conservation. Working in conjunction with project staff, volunteers participate in projects designed to address deforestation, soil and water contamination, and urban growth. Program activities include reforestation of native plants, conservation, working with local communities to clean up and preserve nature, helping in the organization of local events and supporting small-scale entities doing unique things to preserve the environment (such as organic egg farms, children's ecological brigades, or home gardens).

Empowering Women

Organization: Kaya Responsible Travel
Location: The southern city of Oaxaca
Cost: $1,270+ **Duration:** 2 to 26 weeks **Age:** 18-80
Contact: info@kayavolunteer.com
Learn more: www.KayaVolunteer.com
Special skills: A basic level of spoken Spanish is required (basic Spanish lessons provided)
Details: As part of traditional machismo society, girls in Oaxaca often do not receive as much education as boys, and females of all ages are burdened by gender inequality. Change the lives of rural women by working in the centre helping women build self-confidence, know their rights and improve their skills and knowledge. The centre offers talks on women's empowerment and independence, provides legal advice

and information on women's health, makes scholarships available, and helps provide access to midwives. Volunteers help bring new perspective to women who have not travelled far outside their homes and are not aware of other ways of life. Offer knowledge, experience, empathy and support and see real results as local women become stronger and more independent, passing those traits along to their daughters.

Casa de los Amigos Center for Peace

Organization: Casa de los Amigos, A.C.
Location: Mexico City
Cost: none **Duration:** 6 months to 1 year **Age:** 18

Contact: amigos@casadelosamigos.org
Learn more: www.casadelosamigos.org
Special skills: Spanish fluency, experience with and dedication to social justice work
Details: The Casa de los Amigos is a Quaker Center for Peace and International Understanding in Mexico City that was founded in 1956. It is a non-profit organization, an active community space with many events and activities open to the public, a social justice-oriented guesthouse, and the seat of the Mexico City monthly meeting (Quakers). The Casa currently has programs in hospitality, migration and economic justice.

Community Nutrition Program
Organization: Amigos de las Américas
Location: Oaxaca
Cost: $4,000+ **Duration:** 8 weeks **Age:** 16 by Sept. 1st
Contact: info@amigoslink.org **Learn more:** www.amigoslink.org
Details: For 28 years, AMIGOS has been building strong ties with communities and public service organizations in the state of Oaxaca, México. In spite of its cultural wealth, Oaxaca remains the second poorest state in Mexico with malnutrition, illiteracy and inadequate medical care effecting large segments of the population. Volunteers will work with women's groups on nutritional education, educate community members about the native grain of amaranth, teach community youth about the native grain of amaranth and continue AMIGOS' work on community-based initiatives.

Preservation of Cultural History via Technology
Organization: Amigos de las Américas
Location: Oaxaca
Cost: $4,000+ **Project Duration:** 8 weeks **Age:** 16 by Sept. 1st
Contact: info@amigoslink.org **Learn more:** www.amigoslink.org
Details: Volunteers with a high level of Spanish proficiency and basic technology skills are required for this special project. Finally techno-nerds have a volunteer project just for them. Help promote and preserve local culture through the use of digital cameras, video cameras, website creation, blogs and more. All equipment you need is provided. Volunteers will train youth on basic computer skills, including Internet use, teach youth basic digital photography skills and host youth technology education classes.

Teen Project: Recreational Work at Oaxacan Orphanage
Organization: Academic Treks

Location: Oaxaca, Mexico
Cost: $4,280
Duration: 30+ hours volunteering in 21-day language & cultural immersion program   **Age:** Teens finishing grades 9-11
Contact: info@academictreks.com; 919-256-8200 or 888-833-1908
Learn more: www.academictreks.com
Special skills: One year high school Spanish
Details: On Academic Treks language immersion adventure in Oaxaca, students spend several days working and playing with children at the Pimpollo Orphanage. Volunteers make a real difference in the lives of the children while having a lot of fun. Prepare for piggyback rides, playing in the rain, soccer, patty-cake, chalk drawing, swimming, dancing and just being a kid again. These niños have few material possessions and little exposure to the outside world. Eager for your friendship, they will embrace your group. They are also quick to help with your Spanish skills! When not working at the orphanage, travelers learn Spanish through cultural exploration and personalized instruction. In addition to classroom learning, participants hike through picturesque mountain villages, enjoy a home stay with an Oaxacan family and attend cultural workshops.

Other organizations offering projects in Mexico:
Access to Empowerment (primary education for impoverished kids): www.accesstoempowerment.org
American Friends Service Committee: www.afsc.org
The Bosque Village (campground, permaculture, farm, ecovillage): www.bosquevillage.com
Case de Los Angeles: casadelosangeles.org
Casa Hagar de los Niño's (Tijuana): www.hogardelosninos.com
Canadian Alliance for Development Initiatives and Projects: www.cadip.org
Global Routes: www.globalroutes.org
Global Volunteers: www.globalvolunteers.org
Grupo Ecológico de la Costa Verde, A.C. (Sea Turtles): www.project-tortuga.org
Habitat for Humanity International: www.habitat.org

Maternal Life International (medical & resource assistance):
 www.mlionline.org
My Pro World: www.myproworld.org
Radiant Futures (orphans): www.radiantfutures.org
SeaAid: www.seaaid.org
SEE Turtles: www.seeturtles.org
Western Ecological Society: www.vallartanature.org
United Planet: www.unitedplanet.org

Netherlands Antilles (Netherlands)

Donkey Care and Rescue
Organization: Donkey Sanctuary Bonaire
Location: Bonaire (Dutch Antilles)
Cost: None   **Duration:** 6+ weeks   **Age:** 18
Email: info@donkeysanctuary.com
Learn more: www.donkeysanctuary.com
Special skills: Must speak Dutch

Details: This desperately under-financed organization has a need for
volunteers who want to help care for more than 400 donkeys in their
sanctuary. You will assist in giving all necessary care to the donkeys,
welcome visitors to the sanctuary and help with daily activities that
need to be done. The sanctuary provides free accommodations for up to
2 people in the middle of their park. Only non-smokers will be
accepted. Work will be 5 days a week from 8 am until 5 pm. Experience
with animal care not needed. Love for the donkeys, the will to exert
yourself and not being afraid of getting dirty or sweaty will do. Travel
expenses and daily needs are not paid by the project.

Caribbean Marine Conservation
Organization: Academic Treks
Location: Saba and Statia, St. Barts
Cost: $4,980
Duration: 25+ hours as part of a 22-day marine conservation
program
Age: Teens finishing grades 9 through 12
Contact: info@academictreks.com; 919-256-8200 or 888-833-1908
Learn more: www.academictreks.com
Special skills: None. Scuba certification a plus.
Details: On Academic Treks Caribbean Marine Conservation program
in the Leeward Islands, students spend 25+ hours working with Statia

and Saba's Marine Parks, assisting with the ongoing management of the reserves. Activities on this college-accredited program include but are not limited to helping to assess coral diseases, bleaching, algae coverage and biodiversity, contributing to the Reef Check Survey Project, participating in Statia's turtle monitoring program, conducting conch research, doing beach clean ups and maintaining permanent moorings for the marine park. Students earn college credit while learning about marine resource management and marine reserves, designed to safeguard marine environments while allowing for their sustainable use. Studies are intertwined with world class diving and island exploration.

Other organizations offering projects in the Netherlands Antilles:

HealthCare Volunteer: www.healthcarevolunteer.com
Saba Conservation Foundation: www.sabapark.org
St. Eustatius Animal Welfare Foundation: www.seawf.com
St. Eustatius National Parks Foundation: www.statiapark.org

Nicaragua

Building and Education in the Quarter of La Prusia

Organization: La Esperanza Housing & Development / Casas de la Esperanza
Location: La Prusia, a quarter of 200 slums near Granada, Nicaragua
Cost: None. Lodging and lunch on workdays provided for free for long stay volunteers.
Duration: 8+ weeks preferred **Age:** 18
Contact: admin@casas-de-la-esperanza.org
Learn more: www.casas-de-la-esperanza.org
Special skills: Some construction or education experience preferred, but not necessary
Details: La Esperanza Housing & Development / Casas de la Esperanza is neither denominational nor political. Its' objective is to assist families in marginal districts of Nicaragua (like La Prusia) to attain sustainable, integral development by helping them improve their homes, receive professional training, and obtain a worthy means of subsistence, thus contributing to eradicate poverty in agreement with the "Objectives of the Millennium." They have helped to build 36 houses, and now have started the infrastructure for 80 more houses. They are also enlarging the school/workshop, and will offer technical education in addition to the development courses that the organization

already offers. La Esperanza Housing & Development / Casas de la Esperanza also has small clinic for the quarter and is starting some micro-enterprises that will create jobs.

Las Mercedes Reforestation Project

Organization: This is a family run project
Location: Las Mercedes, approximately 30 miles south of the border with Honduras - 10 miles south from the beautiful town of Ocotal.
Cost: None **Duration:** 2+ weeks **Age:** 18 to 70
Contact: Rogermendoza74@gmail.com
Learn more: www.lasmercedesnicaragua.blogspot.com
Special skills: None. However, if you are knowledgeable in areas, such as animal care, clean energy production, agriculture, architecture, reforestation, and irrigation systems, this will be very helpful.
Details: The reforestation project has been a dream of the Mendoza family for about 5 years now. This local family has donated approximately 30 acres of land to be reforested in order to help the ecology of Nicaragua and help with its deforestation problem. Because of the lack of vegetation, the local wildlife is suffering as well and much of Nicaragua's wildlife is on the verge of extinction. The Mendoza family has decided to help stop deforestation by transforming their farm land, used for agricultural purposes for many years, back to what it once was, a beautiful forest providing shelter to many animals, producing oxygen, and offsetting our carbon foot print.

Long -Term Alternative Energy Solutions

Organization: blueEnergy
Location: Bluefields, Nicaragua (only accessible by boat or plane)
Cost: $500 registration and $150 per month
Duration: 1 year minimum commitment **Age:** Adults
Contact: volunteer@blueenergygroup.org
Learn more: www.blueenergygroup.org
Special skills: Broad range of skills needed, from engineers to accountants and everything in between
Details: blueEnergy improves lives in marginalized communities using a holistic approach to sustainable energy and related fundamental services. blueEnergy develops wind and solar energy solutions, solar lighting solutions, water filtration systems, communications solutions and provides local capacity building support to communities on the Caribbean coast of Nicaragua. An innovator in the sustainable energy field, blueEnergy manufactures its wind turbines locally, an approach seldom seen but designed to increase the local understanding of, and capacity for, maintaining the renewable energy system. This approach helps build local technical capacity and provides jobs in the local economy. blueEnergy functions in challenging

environments and succeeds thanks to the individual relationship that our volunteers build with the communities while investing their time in building local capacity. Long-term volunteers come with the idea of taking the time to build these relationships and often end up staying for two years or more.

Short-Term Alternative Energy Solutions

Organization: blueEnergy
Location: Bluefields, Nicaragua (only accessible by boat or plane)
Cost: $500 registration and $400 per week
Duration: 2 weeks to 3 months   **Age:** Adults
Contact: volunteer@blueenergygroup.org
Learn more: www.blueenergygroup.org
Special skills: Broad range of skills needed, from engineers to accountants and everything in between
Details: blueEnergy utilizes both wind energy (turbines) and solar energy (solar paneling) to create a hybrid, sustainable solution to rural electrification in unpredictable weather conditions. An innovator in the sustainable energy field, blueEnergy manufactures its wind turbines locally, an approach seldom seen but designed to increase the local understanding of, and capacity for, maintaining the renewable energy system. This approach helps build local technical capacity and provides jobs in the local economy. blueEnergy's engineers have pioneered our cutting edge design, and volunteers will learn what it takes to successfully develop and implement this technology by interacting with the design team and visiting the manufacturing facilities. By volunteering for blueEnergy, you can play an important role in supporting this sustainable, locally focused approach to energy development.

Centro Educativo Ananda Marga

Organization: Kids Worldwide
Location: The heart of Managua, Nicaragua's capital
Cost: $30 booking fee, $350 the 1st month, subsequent months $150
Duration: 2 week minimum, 1+ month preferred, dates are flexible
Age: 18, kids welcome with a parent with prior consultation.
Contact: ceam@kidsworldwide.org
Learn more:
southamerica.kidsworldwide.org
Special skills: Volunteers will need to be able to converse in Spanish.
Details: CEAM is a kindergarten and primary school operated by yogic missionaries of Ananda Marga. They are introducing a new type of education which

includes vegetarianism, yoga and meditation. From 2002 until the present the student enrollment ranges from 100 to 130 children. The school has one room for the kindergarten and six classrooms for primary grades as well as an office for the director. They need volunteers, male or female, who have a love for children and can help children in the process of their learning. Those with child education experience can help train our teachers.

Rural Sustainable Development/Farm Life

Organization: uVolunteer
Location: Area of Mombacho Volcano, Nicaragua
Cost: $755 for the first 2 weeks; $120 each additional week
Duration: 2+ weeks **Age:** 18
Contact: info@uvolunteer.org
Learn more: www.uvolunteer.org
Special skills: Intermediate English
Details: While volunteering for this program you will be involved in a number of different activities. You will help with all of the cooperatives needs, help with the children's homework and become involved in helping out at the farm. On the slopes of Mombacho Volcano there are nine farming cooperatives made up of local farmers (campesinos).
The cooperatives are ground based organizations with well experienced traditional working techniques. Campesinos are struggling to keep both, subsistence agriculture and sustainable development, in this vast natural reservation area. The organization structure at cooperatives is horizontal, with democracy and transparency as their core values.

Orphanage for Girls Run by Nuns

Organization: uVolunteer
Location: Barrio La Sabaneta near Granada, Nicaragua
Cost: $755 for the first 2 weeks; $120 each additional week
Duration: 2+ weeks **Age:** 18
Contact: info@uvolunteer.org **Learn more:** www.uvolunteer.org
Special skills: Intermediate English
Details: Volunteers will be working with nuns in Granada, Nicaragua to help girls who are orphaned and in need of psychological and spiritual healing. Nuns run the Orphanage for Girls, which houses 50 female orphans. Volunteers will work with the nuns, nurses and assistants to support the overall mission of the organization: to provide psychological services, spiritual guidance and various life skills to girls who are orphans, in order to empower them to become happy and healthy young women.

Agriculture and Eco-Tourism Project

Organization: Experiential Learning International
Cost: Starting at $885
Duration: 2+ weeks **Age:** 18
Contact: info@eliabroad.org
Learn more: www.eliabroad.org
Details: Volunteers work at a cooperative with the goals of promoting fair trade in coffee and creating ecotourism centers in order to benefit the local economy without massive environmental damage. Volunteers will assist with chores in the cooperative as well as help develop income generating activities to sustain the cooperative.

Global Health Volunteer in Limon

Organization: Foundation for International Medical Relief of Children
Location: Limon, departamento de Rivas, Nicaragua
Cost: $925 per week
Duration: 1-3 weeks, longer stays are possible **Age:** 18
Contact: missions@fimrc.org **Learn more:** www.fimrc.org
Special skills: This program is specially focused for undergraduates, medical students and public health students
Details: Help provide healthcare to children in Limon, a rural community on Nicaragua's Pacific coast! Volunteers have the opportunity to assist and shadow the clinic doctor while gaining firsthand experience in improving the health of a developing community. Volunteers will spend part of their time at the clinic site working with the doctor to see patients, and will travel with field staff to perform house calls, conduct community outreach campaigns, collect basic health statistics, and survey families to develop assessments of healthcare needs. Programs run year-round, and free time is included to enjoy sightseeing, tours and hikes.

VISIONS Nicaragua for Teens

Organization: VISIONS Service Adventures
Location: Jinotega
Cost: $4,500+ **Duration:** 4 weeks, and customized programs
Age: Teens, customized programs for all ages
Contact: info@VisionsServiceAdventures.com
Learn more: www.VisionsServiceAdventures.com
Special skills: Minimum of 2 years of high school Spanish.
Details: A stunning medley of mountains, craters, lakes, plains, bustling towns, open-hearted people and scenic bus rides, Nicaragua leaves travelers floored by its breathtaking beauty. Nicaragua leads Central America's self-sustaining development evidenced throughout

the country by solar and other 'green' energy initiatives. VISIONS is home-based in the northern mountain town of Jinotega, the strategic coffee production area, a *tranquillo* city encircled by outlying small villages. Participants engage in intensely focused community work— from construction to agriculture to apprenticeships—with Nicaraguan artisans, farmers and others. Participants get to know the people whose lives they impact, and return home a more confident global citizen with genuine appreciation for our multicultural world.

Teen Recreational Work at an Orphanage in Ometepe

Organization: Academic Treks
Location: Ometepe
Cost: $4,580
Duration: 30+ hours of service work as part of 22-day language and cultural immersion program
Age: Teens finishing grades 9-12
Contact: info@academictreks.com; 919-256-8200 or 888-833-1908
Learn more: www.academictreks.com
Special skills: One year high school Spanish
Details: Students on this college-accredited Spanish language and community service program spend several days working with the children of Nuestros Pequeños Hermanos Orphanage on the island of Ometepe. The service work is just part of a 22 day program that spans two beautiful and culturally rich Central American countries from the highlands of Costa Rica to the spectacular volcanic islands of Nicaragua. Learn Spanish through immersion, classroom studies and service as you explore magnificent river valleys, a grand colonial city, tropical rainforests and a verdant island in the middle of Central America's largest freshwater lake. Live for a week with gracious families who welcome you into their community. This Academic Trek highlights the diversity of these two countries and opens your eyes to the colorful cultures of each.

Other organizations offering projects in Nicaragua:

Amigos de las Américas: www.amigoslink.org
Basecamp International Centers: www.basecampcenters.com
Building New Hope (coffee, fair trade, woman, education...):
   www.buildingnewhope.org
Fabretto Children's Foundation: www.fabretto.org
Foundation for Sustainable Development: www.fsdinternational.org
Guardabarranco S.A. Agro-ecological Business (improving local
   agriculture on small farms): eco-nic.com
La Esperanza Granada (children's education):
   www.la-esperanza-granada.org
Raleigh: www.raleighinternational.org

Ranch Ezperanza (energy, organic gardening...):
  www.rancho.esperanza.bvg3.com
Volunteers for Intercultural and Definitive Adventures (medical,
  dental, veterinary, service & construction):
  www.vidavolunteertravel.org

Panama

Leatherback Turtle Conservation

Organization: Rainforest Concern/The Endangered Wildlife Trust
Location: Soropta beach and Playa Larga
Cost: US$150 per week. Prices include meals and accommodation
Duration: 1+ week
Age: 18. Children under 18 must be accompanied by an adult
Contact: Carlos Fernandez: carlos57fer@yahoo.com, +506 224 8568
or info@rainforestconcern.org
Learn more: www.turtleprotection.org
Special skills: A keen interest in conservation required
Details: Volunteers are needed at Playa Larga in Panama to help
protect endangered Leatherback turtles, the largest sea turtles.
Volunteers participate in every aspect of the project. The project offer
an exciting opportunity to be involved in the work and help to protect
turtles which are listed as critically endangered species. Volunteers will
help with beach cleaning, making pathways and building trails, helping
with the wildlife inventories and assisting with projects carried out by
the researchers. During the day the volunteer will search for nest
excavations. To protect the turtles and their nests from poachers, the
beaches are patrolled every night from early March to late September.

M*A*S*H* Save Dogs and Cats - Fifty at a Time!

Organization: Fundacion Spay/Panama
Location: Panamanian beaches
Cost: $400 per week   **Duration:** 1 week   **Age:** 18
Contact: doctor@spaypanama.org
Learn more: www.spaypanama.org
Special skills: Veterinarians and any animal-loving individual

Details: Spay/neuter campaigns at Panama
beaches take place in a M*A*S*H*
environment. You will also have the
opportunity to work side-by-side with local
veterinarians and volunteers trying to put

a stop to the misery and unnecessary death of abandoned animals through an intensive sterilization campaign. This is an excellent learning opportunity for veterinary students. The cost includes airport transportation, all meals, lodging, some sightseeing, dinner at the Miraflores Locks of the Panama Canal or a tour to an Embera Indian community located one hour up the Chagres River.

Panama Children's Project

Organization: Global Volunteer Network
Location: The valley of Boquete, in the western highlands of Panama
Cost: $460 for 1 week   **Duration:** 1 to 12 weeks   **Age:** 18
Contact: info@volunteer.org.nz
Learn more: www.volunteer.org.nz
Special skills: A basic level of Spanish
Details: As a volunteer you will have the opportunity to help children in need and aid in developing and inspiring their minds and hearts. This program works to create growth and development opportunities for children and teenagers in extreme poverty conditions with a focus on children living in orphanages and those who come from low income families. Volunteer opportunities include: working in orphanages assisting with daily activities and childcare duties and performing psychological profiling of new arrivals. Other social service duties include: working with teenage mothers and their newborn children; working as a youth mentor helping with homework and being a friend to confide in and talk too; running Saturday morning soccer; and music classes.

Panama Literacy Project

Organization: Global Volunteer Network
Location: The valley of Boquete, in the western highlands of Panama
Cost: $460 for 1 week   **Duration:** 1 to 12 weeks   **Age:** 18
Contact: info@volunteer.org.nz
Learn more: www.volunteer.org.nz
Special skills: A basic level of Spanish
Details: The ability to read, write and speak English is key for many Panamanians in the workforce or those planning to enter the workforce. It gives them increased levels of self-esteem, enhances personal self-worth and self-confidence to succeed in fulfilling their hopes and desires. Volunteers have the opportunity to teach English and literacy skills. Teaching and reading is done one-on-one or in small groups. This role is suitable for an organized, patient and self-motivated individual. A teaching qualification is not required, but volunteers need to be confident teaching English and preferably have or are studying towards a university degree. Volunteers are not required to speak Spanish however a basic knowledge is beneficial.

Community Outreach Project

Organization: Global Volunteer Network
Location: In the valley of Boquete, in the western highlands of Panama
Cost: $460 for 1 week **Duration:** 1 to 12 weeks **Age:** 18
Contact:info@volunteer.org.nz
Learn more: www.volunteer.org.nz/panama
Special skills: A basic level of Spanish required for certain projects
Details: GVN's partner works with a number of small community based organizations that provide important services to enhance the local community. Volunteers have the opportunity to work with the disabled, animal wildlife programs, nutrition projects, and community recycling. Most projects are not full time, so volunteers can expect to be placed in a combination of projects. Placements will be allocated with volunteers interests in mind, but please note that you will need to be flexible.

Volunteer Vacation on an Organic Farm in Darién

Organization: EcoCircuitos Panama
Location: Darién Province, six hours by car from Panama City
Cost: $850 - $1,285
Duration: 8 days & 7 nights with meals, transportation, lodging & tour **Age:** 21
Contact: annie@ecocircuitos.com
Learn more: www.ecocircuitos.com
Special skills: High energy, knowledge of organic farming, good health, driving skills, computer skills, enjoy outdoors

Details: In the community of Santa Fe del Darien, you will be working on a new organic farm that is trying to promote and market their products in Panama City and other regions. The community center in Santa Fe del Darien owns 6 hectares of farmland and 40 hectares of protected land. This is a great program for couples, families, students and teachers! Volunteers are all ages, from various ethnic backgrounds and of all different professions, such as educators, students, laborers, medical professionals, full-time parents, professionals, artists, bankers and the like. The community is very conservative, traditional and in the small town of Santa Fe respect and reputation are of high importance. EcoCircuitos strives to integrate with the community, maintaining the local culture and avoiding foreign influence; volunteers in this program should take a serious approach to volunteering and blending in with the local community.

Other organizations offering projects in Panama:

Amigos de las Américas: www.amigoslink.org
Bruce Organization (educating street kids, raising financial
   independence of women & eradication poverty):
   volunteerpanama.com
CREA (environmental): www.crea-panama.org
Global Humanitarian Adventures: www.gogha.org
Global Visions International: www.gviusa.com or www.gvi.co.uk
Medo (grassroots, education, health, environmental...):
   medo.awardspace.com
Peregrine Fund: www.peregrinefund.org
The Purple House (hostel work exchanged for room/food):
   www.purplehousehostel.com
Volunteers for Intercultural and Definitive Adventures (medical,
   dental, veterinary, service & construction):
   www.vidavolunteertravel.org

Puerto Rico (United States)

Puerto Rico's Rainforest

Organization: Earthwatch Institute
Location: Rendezvous in San Juan, PR, USA
Cost: $1750+ **Duration:** 1 to 10 days **Age:** 18
Contact: info@earthwatch.org **Learn more:** www.earthwatch.org
Details: Earthwatch volunteers will be trained in a variety of tasks: measuring trees, counting lizards or frogs, helping to tag and identify vine species, and helping to set up new experimental plots for planting different tree and shrub species. You will also have the chance to join a night expedition into the forest to help count coqui frogs. During your recreational time you will be able to enjoy hikes, take dips in nearby rivers, take part in some forest related craft activities, use the project library to learn more about the ecology of the area or just relax. There will also be an opportunity to take a salsa dancing class and to experience the local culture and cuisine.

Other organizations offering projects in Puerto Rico:

Animal Welfare Culebra: animalwelfareculebra.org
Eye on the Rainforest: www.eyeontherainforest.org
Global Works: www.globalworksinc.com
Inland Dogs Inc (fly/escort dogs to a better life):
   www.islanddog.org

Saint Kitts and Nevis

Organizations offering projects in Saint Kitts and Nevis:

Florida Association for Volunteer Action in the Caribbean and the America's: www.favaca.org
Partners of the Americas: www.partners.net
Volunteers for Intercultural and Definitive Adventures (medical, dental, veterinary, service & construction): www.vidavolunteertravel.org

Saint Lucia

Organizations offering projects in Saint Lucia:

Good News Project (home building): www.goodnewswi.com
Health Volunteers Overseas: www.hvousa.org
Partners of the Americas: www.partners.net

St. Vincent and the Grenadines

Organizations offering projects in Saint Vincent and the Grenadines

Good News Project (home building): www.goodnewswi.com
Florida Association for Volunteer Action in the Caribbean and the America's: www.favaca.org
Partners of the Americas: www.partners.net
Volunteers for Intercultural and Definitive Adventures (medical, dental, veterinary, service & construction): www.vidavolunteertravel.org

Trinidad and Tobago

Tobago Coastal Ecosystems Mapping Project

Organization: Coral Cay Conservation
Location: Tobago
Cost: $1,050+, Accommodation, food, dive and science training are all included in the price.
Duration: 2 to 20 weeks **Age:** 16
Contact: info@coralcay.org **Learn more**: www.coralcay.org
Special skills: Enthusiasm and a love for adventure!
Details: Join Coral Cay Conservation's (CCC) Tobago project where you will learn how to dive and survey coral reefs while working closely with the local community, teaching them how to best conserve what is theirs. CCC was invited to set up this project following the 2005 Caribbean-wide bleaching event to survey how the reefs of Tobago were affected, aiming to encourage the revitalization of these beautiful reefs. So, be a part of this unique experience and really make a difference on a 2-20 week project, living on the picturesque shores of Charlotteville and diving some of Tobago's most spectacular reefs, home to a variety of remarkable creatures including manta rays and dolphins!

Other organizations offering projects in Trinidad and Tobago:

Earthwatch Institute: www.earthwatch.org
Habitat for Humanity International: www.habitat.org
i-to-i: www.i-to-i.com
New Frontiers Health Force: www.newfrontiershf.com
SeeTurtles: www.seeturtles.org

United States

Dogtown Doggie Duties

Organization: Best Friends Animal Society
Location: The quaint and beautiful town of Kanab in southern Utah
Cost: None
Duration: Flexible—some volunteers help for a few hours and some stay for days or longer
Age: Under 18 must be with a parent. For safety no helpers under age 5
Contact: volunteers@bestfriends.org or call 435-644-2001
Learn more: www.bestfriends.org

Special skills: Compassion for animals and a desire to help
Details: Are you committed to the care of canines? If so, Best Friends would love to have you spend your vacation volunteering at Dogtown, located at Best Friends Animal Sanctuary in southwestern Utah. This is the same Dogtown that is chronicled in the National Geographic television series. Volunteers can assist by walking and socializing the dogs, brushing, poop scooping and aiding with cleaning and maintenance of runs and buildings. Enjoy a delicious vegetarian lunch in Angel Village each day at noon for $5 and chat with other volunteers and staff who are also dedicated to helping animals.

 ৪ **Editor's note:** As a former Dogtown Caregiver (and volunteer before that), I can recommend Best Friends as a top choice for family-friendly volunteer destinations in the United States. In addition, the town of Kanab is in the heart of the "Golden Circle" of national parks. When you're not on doggie duty, families can visit incredible local sights – Zion, Bryce, The Grand Canyon, Lake Powell and much more.

Feline Friend Functions

Organization: Best Friends Animal Society
Location: The quaint and beautiful town of Kanab in southern Utah
Cost: None
Duration: Flexible—some volunteers help for a few hours and some stay for days or longer
Age: Under 18 must be with a parent. For safety no helpers under age 5
Contact: volunteers@bestfriends.org or call 435-644-2001
Learn more: www.bestfriends.org
Special skills: Compassion for animals and a desire to help
Details: Do you enjoy the company of cats? If you do, you're welcome at Cat World, located at Best Friends Animal Sanctuary in southwestern Utah. Mornings are spent cleaning to make sure that the cats are comfortable. You might be helping empty litter pans, brushing pet furniture, sweeping or mopping, washing dishes and then helping with feeding. You can feast on an inexpensive but delightful vegetarian lunch any day but Sunday, and then return in the afternoon to pet and groom the cats, or to help socialize the shy ones. Best Friends is located 90 minutes or less from The Grand Canyon, Zion, Bryce Canyon, Lake Powell and Grand Staircase Escalante National Monument, so when you finish with your feline friends, you must see the spectacular scenery.

Farm Sanctuary Internship Programs

Organization: Farm Sanctuary
Location: New York and California
Cost: None. $150 refundable deposit **Duration:** 3 months **Age:** 18
Contact: intern@farmsanctuary.org

Learn more: www.farmsanctuary.org
Special skills: Ability to work hard in all weather conditions and to commit to Farm Sanctuary goals
Details: Farm Sanctuary is the nation's leading farm animal protection organization. Since incorporating in 1986, Farm Sanctuary has worked to expose and stop cruel practices of the "food animal" industry through research and investigations, legal and institutional reforms, public awareness projects, youth education, and direct rescue and refuge efforts. Farm Sanctuary shelters in Watkins Glen, NY and Orland, CA provide lifelong care for hundreds of rescued  animals, who have become ambassadors for farm animals everywhere by educating visitors about the realities of factory farming. General shelter projects include, shelter cleaning, shelter laundry, assisting with animal health checks, animal monitoring projects, assisting with farm errands including vet trips, barn cleaning and grounds maintenance. Other internship opportunities also exist.

✍**Editor's note:** Read 'Finding Sanctuary' by K. Angel Horne in *The Voluntary Traveler: Adventures from the Road Best Traveled* and discover one interns Farm Sanctuary experience.

Woolfing – Organic Farming USA Programs

Organization: World Wide Opportunities on Organic Farms, USA
Location: 1,000+ farms throughout the USA, including Hawaii, Alaska, and the US Virgin Islands
Cost: $20 annual membership fee. No money is exchanged between volunteers and farmers.
Duration: Variable. 1 weekend to a season. It's up to the volunteers and farmers to decide.
Age: 18 or accompanied by a parent or guardian
Contact: info@wwwoofusa.org   **Learn more:** www.wwoofusa.org
Details: World Wide Opportunities on Organic Farms, USA (WWOOF-USA) is part of a world wide effort to link volunteers with organic farmers, promote an educational exchange, and build a global community conscious of ecological farming practices. WWOOF-USA publishes a printed and online directory of more than 1,000 farms that host volunteers in exchange for meals and accommodations. This is an opportunity to learn practical farming skills, explore the US, connect with where food comes from, be part of the real food movement and have a fun, inexpensive and meaningful eco-vacation

GVN South Dakota Program

Organization: Global Volunteer Network
Location: The program is located in Eagle Butte, the largest town on the Cheyenne River Sioux Reservation and the center of tribal government
Cost: $797 for 2 months **Duration:** 2 to 6 months **Age:** 18
Email: info@volunteer.org.nz **Learn more:** www.volunteer.org.nz
Details: Global Volunteer Network currently has opportunities to volunteer at a youth center located on the Cheyenne River Sioux Reservation in South Dakota. The nonprofit youth center serves children and families living on the reservation and is a grassroots organization run by members of the Lakota tribe and the surrounding communities. Youth and outreach programs have become vitally important to securing a viable future for the Lakota people. Volunteers will work with children from age 4 to 18. Activities include: library time, arts and crafts, working in the organic garden, outdoor games, serving meals, fundraising drives within the community, etc. In addition, volunteers with particular skills, for example language or sporting skills, will be encouraged to implement their own programs with the children.

Creating Affordable Housing

Organization: Adventures in Preservation
Location: Cairo, Illinois at the southernmost tip of the state
Cost: $1,275 **Duration:** Two weeks **Age:** 18
Contact: workshops@adventuresinpreservation.org
Learn more: www.adventuresinpreservation.org
Special skills: No skills necessary; training provided at the site
Details: Cairo, located at the confluence of the Ohio and Mississippi Rivers, has played a key role in some of America's most significant events, yet like the trucks on the highway that runs through the town, the world is passing it by. The city's rich collection of historic buildings is being dismantled by demolition. Local citizens are fighting back and working to restore vitality to the city. A key strategy is creating affordable housing, and it is working. Volunteers will join AiP, students and faculty of the University of Southern Illinois Carbondale School of Architecture and Department of History, and the Cairo Vision 20/20 Committee to restore a shotgun house, which will then be used for affordable housing and spur the restoration of additional shotgun houses.

VISIONS Alaska

Organization: VISIONS Service Adventures
Location: Alaska Athabascan communities

Cost: $4,000+ **Duration:** 4 weeks, or customized programs
Age: Teens, customized programs for all ages
Contact: info@VisionsServiceAdventures.com
Learn more: www.VisionsServiceAdventures.com
Details: VISIONS challenges every part of you—the mind, muscles, and heart. The coed programs for teens blend community service, cross-cultural immersion, and adventurous exploration in impoverished communities. VISIONS has sites on the northern boundary of south-central Alaska, roughly 4 hours from Fairbanks. Projects in native villages include building playgrounds and recreation facilities, renovating community buildings and elders' homes, and supervising children's activity programs. Participants learn about Athabascan culture and a unique frontier heritage. Recreation includes day hikes, extended backpacking trips in the Wrangell Mountains, an ice-climbing adventure, trips to neighboring towns and wildlife viewing.

Mammoth Graveyard Excavation

Organization: Earthwatch Institute
Location: Rendezvous in Rapid City, South Dakota
Cost: $2,950+ **Duration:** 15 days **Age:** 18
Contact: info@earthwatch.org **Learn more:** www.earthwatch.org
Details: An experienced and enthusiastic team leader, Dr. Larry Agenbroad will give you a complete perspective on prehistoric environments and Pleistocene extinctions. Working with his field staff, you'll learn how to excavate, record and preserve bone fragments from terraces and how to map your finds on a computer. You will also share your knowledge with the many visitors to the site, now a $2.1 million museum and a National Natural Landmark thanks to Dr. Agenbroad's efforts. Expect a warm welcome from Hot Springs locals, who are proud of their mammoths. You will also have a chance to visit natural areas nearby, and perhaps see free-ranging bison, deer, antelope, wild turkeys, and if you are really lucky, bighorn sheep or mountain goats.

✐**Editor's note:** The Mammoth Site of Hot Springs sits on the hill behind my home. Make no mistake about it, this is not a small archeological dig site! If, like me, you have ever sifted for days to unearth a single trade bead or minute pot shard, this place will knock your socks off! You simply must see the Mammoth Site for yourself in order to grasp the excavations impact.

Pueblo Indian Site Archeology

Organization: Crow Canyon Archeological Center
Location: Around Cortez, Colorado
Cost: $1,275 **Duration:** 1 to 3 weeks
Contact: CPatton@crowcanyon.org or travel@crowcanyon.org
Learn more: www.crowcanyon.org
Details: Join professional researchers in the field and lab, contributing to our understanding of the ancestral Pueblo Indians who inhabited the region more than 700 years ago. The mission of the Crow Canyon Archaeological Center is to advance knowledge of the human experience through archaeological research, education programs, and collaboration with American Indians. Their vision is to expand the sphere in which we operate, both geographically and intellectually, and show how the knowledge gained through archaeology can help build a healthier society.

VISIONS Mississippi for Teens

Organization: VISIONS Service Adventures
Location: Gulfport Mississippi
Cost: $4,000+ **Duration:** 4 weeks, and customized programs
Age: Teen, customized programs for all ages
Contact: info@VisionsServiceAdventures.com
Learn more: www.VisionsServiceAdventures.com
Details: VISIONS programs blend ambitious service, cultural immersion and adventure. Know the people whose lives you impact, and return home a more confident global citizen with genuine appreciation for our multicultural world. VISIONS is based in North Gulfport and Turkey Creek, communities rooted in African American history. Purchased by newly emancipated African Americans in 1866, these few acres of swamp land grew into vibrant, self-sufficient neighborhoods with homesteads, businesses, and the first African American school in the Gulfport region. Turkey Creek is a vital watershed that has come under threat from developers, a threat that intensified in the aftermath of Hurricane Katrina. The service work in Mississippi will vary to include construction, renovation, debris clean-up, work with the elderly and children, and with the Mississippi Audubon Society.

VISIONS Northern Passages for 11 to 13 year olds

Organization: VISIONS Service Adventures
Location: Northern Cheyenne Indian Reservation, Montana
Cost: $3,000+ **Duration:** 3 weeks, and customized programs
Age: 11-13, customized programs for all ages
Contact: info@VisionsServiceAdventures.com

Learn more: www.VisionsServiceAdventures.com
Details: Northern Passages is a special program for 11 - 13 years of age who want to get an early start on ambitious community service work. Participants live and work on the Northern Cheyenne Plains Indian Reservation in eastern Montana. Projects include carpentry and construction, social projects, organizing day camp activities for children, and conservation work. Participants learn firsthand about native traditions and history that shape life on and off the reservations. VISIONS challenges every part of participants—the mind, muscles and heart. Their coed programs for teens blend community service, cross-cultural immersion, and adventurous exploration in impoverished communities.

VISIONS Service for Teens in Montana

Organization: VISIONS Service Adventures
Location: Montana Blackfeet Reservation
Cost: $3500+   **Duration:** 3 or 4 weeks, and customized programs
Age: Teens, customized programs for all ages
Contact: info@VisionsServiceAdventures.com
Learn more: www.VisionsServiceAdventures.com
Details: At every VISIONS site, projects encompass construction and other service work such as sustainable development, environmental work in national parks and wilderness areas, volunteering with children; and apprenticeships with local vendors, artisans or health professionals. In Montana, participants live and work on Plains Indian reservations surrounded by abundant natural resources and stunning landscapes. Projects include renovation and construction of tribal buildings and elders' homes, ceremonial structures, and playgrounds for schools and communities; organizing day camp activities for children; and trail work in primitive wilderness. Renowned for its beauty, the "Last Best Place" offers backpacking, rock climbing, horseback riding, rafting, attending powwows, and sharing a sweat lodge with native friends. Participants learn firsthand about native traditions and history that shapes life on and off the reservations.

Mapping Change in California's Mountains

Organization: Earthwatch Institute
Location: Rendezvous at Ontario, California
Cost: $1750+   **Duration:** 8 days   **Age:** 18
Contact: info@earthwatch.org   **Learn more:** www.earthwatch.org
Details: As a volunteer, you'll help collect solid data on what's happening with plants in this area, what plants used to be here and what the effects of current and future management policies could be on the overall health of the ecosystem. Each day you'll be hiking 2-6 miles

through the study area (weather permitting) with scientists and/or experienced field guides, using GIS technology to record precise location data on the plant species you'll encounter. Hikes will follow marked trails and may reach an altitude of 2,000 ft. On non-hiking days, you'll be at the research base helping organize and analyze collected data as well as historical plant data for the region.

Other organizations offering projects in The United States:

American Friends Service Committee: www.afsc.org
Concordia: www.concordia-iye.org.uk
Cultural Institute of America (Hawaii teen opportunities):
*   www.culturalinstituteofamerica.com*
Gibbon Conservation Center (California): www.gibboncenter.org
Global Visions International: www.gviusa.com or www.gvi.co.uk
Good News Project (home building): www.goodnewswi.com
International Primate Protection League (S. Carolina): www.ippl.org
National Tropical Botanical Garden (Hawaii): www.ntbg.org
Save the Chimps: www.savethechimps.org
Service Civil International: www.sci-ivs.org
The Great Basin Institute (conservation):
*   www.thegreatbasininstitute.org*
United Saints Recovery Project (New Orleans): www.unitedsaints.org
Wildlife Survival Sanctuary (big cats in Florida): wildlifesurvival.com

U.S. Virgin Islands (United States)

Organizations offering projects in U.S. Virgin Islands:

Earthwatch Institute: www.earthwatch.org
Eco Abroad: www.ecoabroad.com
Virgin Islands National Parks: www.virgin.islands.national-
park.com
Volunteer Eco Students Abroad: www.vesabroad.com

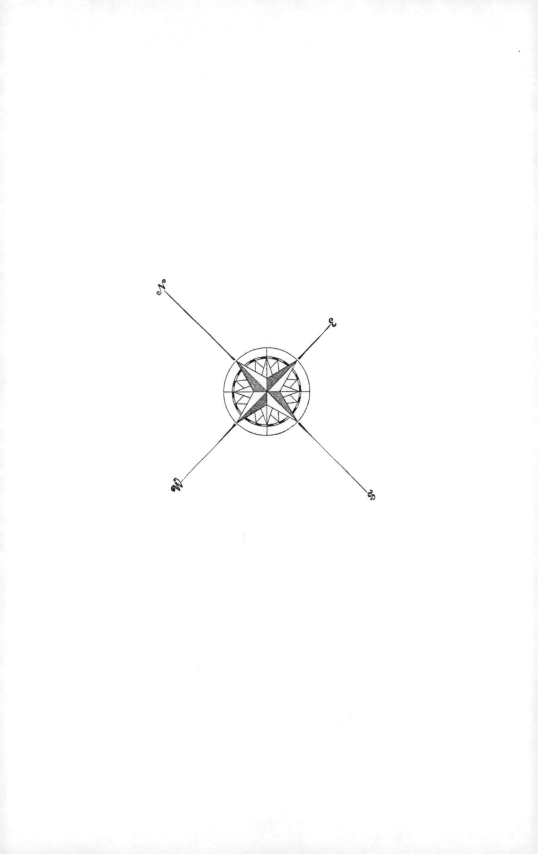

"Walking ten thousand miles of the world is
better than reading ten thousand scrolls."

~ Chinese Proverb

Armenia

Saving Armenia's Architectural Heritage

Organization: Adventures in Preservation
Location: Kumayri Historic District in Gyumri, Armenia
Cost: $2,350 **Duration:** 13 days **Age:** 18
Contact: workshops@adventuresinpreservation.org
Learn more: www.adventuresinpreservation.org
Special skills: No skills necessary; training provided at the site
Details: Armenia is one of the world's oldest civilizations, and over the years has developed a distinctive architectural identity. Much of Gyumri's beautifully crafted traditional architecture was damaged during a 1988 earthquake, and recent recovery has involved more demolition than repair. Concern about the loss of this architectural heritage led to the Kumayri Historic District being named to the World Monument's Watch List of 100 Most Endangered Sites in 2008. AiP volunteers will work under the guidance of an expert to demonstrate that restoration is a viable alternative to demolition, keeping valuable building materials in use. This first in a series of workshops will lead to formation of a field school for Armenian students. Workshop fees cover lodging, meals, transportation from Yerevan, instruction, fieldtrips and insurance.

Global Village Trip to Nshavan

Organization: Habitat for Humanity
Location: Nshavan, Armenia.
Cost: $1,900   **Duration:** 10 days.
Age: 18+ or 14 and be accompanied by a legal guardian or be part of an established group
Contact: gv@habitat.org, 1-800-HABITAT (422-4828), ext. 7530
Learn more: www.habitat.org
Special skills: Global Village teams are open to all with a willingness to work hard, learn new skills and explore a new culture. Trips require strenuous manual labor, so all participants should be in good health.
Details: More than 50 percent of Armenia's families live in deteriorated housing with cramped quarters and limited water and heat. For decades thousands of families have been living in domiks, metal containers that were brought to Armenia as part of the relief effort following the devastating 1988 earthquake. Domiks are unbearably hot in the summer, and only makeshift stoves combat the extreme cold in winter. Habitat for Humanity Armenia has helped hundreds of families through a variety of efforts, including the construction of affordable, efficient houses; the completion of half-built homes; implementation of water and sanitation facilities; advocacy of improved housing policies for low-income families; and engagement of volunteers and other like-minded partners. You will eat Armenian barbecue and fresh pomegranates, dance to the music of a traditional duduk, and explore monasteries in the first Christian nation as you make a difference for Armenian families!

✐**Editor's note:** Habitat for Humanity Global Village teams travel to over 50 countries around the world! If building projects interests you, I encourage you to visit Habitat's website and see the diversity of program locations available.

Other organizations offering projects in Armenia:

Armenian Volunteer Corps: www.armenianvolunteer.org
Earthwatch Institute: www.earthwatch.org
Kiva Fellows Program: www.kiva.org
Service Civil International: www.sci-ivs.org
Transitions Abroad: www.transitionsabroad.com
The Fuller Center for Housing Armenia:
www.fullercenterarmenia.org
Volunteers for Economic Growth Alliance: www.vegaalliance.org

Azerbaijan

Organizations offering projects in Azerbaijan:

Concordia: www.concordia-iye.org.uk
Kiva Fellows Program: www.kiva.org
Service Civil International: www.sci-ivs.org
Volunteers for Peace: www.vfp.org
Volunteers for Prosperity (skilled professionals):
  www.volunteersforprosperity.gov

Bangladesh

Organizations offering projects in Bangladesh:

ChildSite Foundation: www.childsight-foundation.org
Habitat for Humanity: www.habitat.org
Service Civil International: www.sci-ivs.org
Volunteer Association for Bangladesh: vabonline.org
Volunteers for Economic Growth Alliance: www.vegaalliance.org
Volunteers for Peace: www.vfp.org
UNA Exchange: www.unaexchange.org

Cambodia

Rainbow Orphanage
Organization: Working for Children
Location: Rural area of Siem Reap Province in Cambodia
Cost: None. Donations to Rainbow Orphanage are much appreciated
Duration: 4 hours per day for 1 or more days
Age: 18, kids over 12 welcome with their parent or teachers
Contact: orphancambodia@yahoo.com
Learn more: wfc-kh.org
Detail: Working For Children (WFC) is a registered, non-profit charity committed to assisting orphans, poor and vulnerable children in rural communities of Siem Reap province. WFC is a project initiated and staffed by Cambodians, working towards a better future for Cambodian children. WFC is a non-profit humanitarian Khmer group trying to

improve the lives, health and education of the rural poor. It receives no government assistance, but relies entirely on donations from visiting tourists to the Angkor Wat area and interested people from overseas. Teaching English, laboring, agriculture, art and building work are all areas in which we need volunteers.

GVN Cambodia Program

Organization: Global Volunteer Network
Location: Cambodia's capital of Phnom Penh.
Cost: $1,077　**Duration:** 13 weeks　**Age:** 18
Contact: info@volunteer.org.nz　**Learn more:**
www.volunteer.org.nz
Details: Volunteers will be working as language teachers in a school project which provides affordable conversational English language courses for students. The aim of this project is to raise money for a local NGO which works to improve livelihoods in rural communities in Cambodia. Students pay a small fee to attend the classes. In the past, the money raised by the language center has been used to improve water and sanitation, for small livestock and agriculture production and for community environmental awareness in rural Cambodia. Volunteers teach conversational English classes which have around 10 students in each class. All students and teachers have books, from which to learn and teach. There is room for volunteers to include their own exercises/games into each class.

Marine Conservation Cambodia

Organization: Marine Conservation Cambodia
Location: Koh Rung Samleom, Sihanoukville, Cambodia
Duration: 2+ weeks　**Cost:** $200 per week　**Age:** 18
Contact: paul.ferber@marineconservationcambodia.org
Learn more: www.marineconservationcambodia.org
Details: Tropical island life, SCUBA diving and getting to know the locals! With meals and accommodation included, Marine Conservation Cambodia has it all for the adventurous volunteer. While working with other volunteers, specialists and the local fishing community, you will spend time learning about diving then put your skills into practice in the field collecting, collating and analyzing data on the marine environment. Underwater investigative projects include seahorse surveys, biodiversity and abundance surveys. As well as reef and beach clean ups. Terrestrial projects include jungle treks collecting species information and mangrove rehabilitation. All information is submitted to the Cambodian Fisheries Administration Conservation Department. This relationship has already made great steps forward in maintaining and protecting a sustainable marine environment for Cambodia, so join us and make the changes happen.

Volunteer in a Village in Cambodia

Organization: Openmind Projects
Location: 25 km from Siem Reap
Cost: $1,200 per month **Duration:** 1+ months **Age:** 18
Contact: info@openmindprojects.org
Learn more: www.openmindprojects.org or
upload.openmindprojects.org/volunteerpackage
Special skills: An interest in teaching and aid work. Ability to live simply with local village people
Details: Volunteer at a school in a village outside Siem Reap with children who have a basic level of English. Phum Chhuk is a beautiful village with friendly people living in typical Khmer houses. English is taught by volunteers, assisted by local Cambodian boys from Chhuk who speak a little English. The time schedule of the classes varies by season, as children help their families in the rice fields. About 200 children attend classes though the number varies. In addition to, English classes, you should be prepared to give information about hygiene, health and dental care. The Volunteer House is a small Khmer house which belongs to an orphan girl and her younger brother. The volunteers live in the house together with the two orphans.

Volunteer in Children's Art Center

Organization: Greenheart Travel
Location: A beautiful coastal area of Southern Cambodia near Sihoukanville
Cost: $1,250 for 4 weeks; Guest house accommodation is included in the program **Duration:** 4 to 12 weeks **Age:** 18
Contact: info@greenhearttravel.org
Learn more: www.cci-exchange.com
Details: Volunteering with the Children's Art Center in Cambodia is a way to help children experience a safe, supportive environment, while immersing yourself in a culture that will leave you spellbound. This program is ideal for adult participants who have skills and experience with the arts and enjoy working with children. The art center provides neglected, abused and impoverished children ages 5 to 15 with the opportunity to develop their imaginations and skills through painting. Volunteers will assist children with art projects, instruct different painting techniques, lead sports activities and tutor children in math, English and computer skills.

Teach English at Orphanages in Cambodia

Organization: LanguageCorps
Location: Phnom Penh and other locations in Cambodia
Cost: $2,395 for 8 weeks, $150 additional weeks

Duration: 8+ weeks **Age:** 21
Contact: info@languagecorps.com
Learn more: www.languagecorps.com
Special skills: Native English speaker ability
Details: Thinking about an overseas adventure? Want to broaden your horizons, achieve personal goals, and build your resume with a life-changing international experience? The LanguageCorps volunteer program in Cambodia is a chance to impact children's lives and your own as well. The basic program lasts eight weeks and includes an abbreviated TESOL course along with accommodations, excursions, medical insurance, cell phone, Corps Advocate support and placement in an unpaid volunteer position.

Coral Cay Conservation

Organization: Coral Cay
Location: Untouched tropical island of Koh Rong, Cambodia
Cost: $1,050+ **Duration:** 2 to 20 weeks
Contact: info@coralcay.org **Learn more**: www.coralcay.org
Special skills: Enthusiasm and love for adventure!
Details: Since this is their newest project, joining Coral Cay's Cambodia expedition is a chance to be a part of exciting and groundbreaking conservation. Individuals who volunteer with CCC gain hands on conservation experience, learn how to dive and work with local communities teaching them how to best conserve what is theirs so that they go on to use their reefs sustainably. The project is based on the beautiful, remote and undeveloped island of Koh Rong off the coast of Sihanoukville, Cambodia. You can work from 2 to 20 weeks, and you'll be living in truly rustic, and eco-friendly conditions on a beach-fringed bay – accommodation, meals, dive and science training are included in the price.

✐**Editor's note:** Coral Cay is one of three organizations rated as highly recommended under the *'Best Volunteering Organization'* category of the *Virgin Holidays Responsible Tourism Award 2009*

Integrated Orphanage Care, Teaching and Health

Organization: Global Service Corps
Location: Phnom Penh, Cambodia
Cost: 9 weeks $4,820; weekly fee after 9 weeks $365, after 13 weeks $250; Accommodations throughout the program are provided in local hostels.
Duration: 9 weeks to 6 months
Age: 20 or older (18 or 19 with three letters of recommendation)
Contact: cambodia@globalservicecorps.org
Learn more: www.globalservicecorps.org

Details: The program begins with a one week cultural orientation and technical training in Phnom Penh. The orientation includes learning about Khmer customs, including social do's and don'ts, and acquiring basic Khmer conversation skills. During this time participants will tour local historical sites and visit local partner organizations, public hospitals and clinics. Non-professional participants receive training in teaching HIV/AIDS prevention or teaching English in a Cambodian

context. The training is followed by four or more weeks each participating in the Orphanage Care, Teaching English or International Health Program. The program also includes a three day trip to Siem Reap to visit Angkor Wat and other historical sites. Accommodations throughout the program are provided in local hostels.

Orphanage Care Service Learning Program

Organization: Global Service Corps
Location: Phnom Penh
Cost: 5 weeks $3,360; weekly fee after 5 weeks $365, after 13 weeks $250; Accommodations are provided in local hostels.
Duration: 5 weeks to 6 months
Age: 20 or older (18 or 19 with three letters of recommendation)
Contact: cambodia@globalservicecorps.org
Learn more: www.globalservicecorps.org
Details: The Orphanage Care Program begins with a one week cultural orientation and English teaching training in Phnom Penh. The orientation includes learning about Khmer customs, including social do's and don'ts, and acquiring basic Khmer conversation skills. During this time participants will tour local historical sites and visit local partner organizations. Participants are also provided training in teaching English as a Foreign Language (EFL) in a Cambodian context. The training is followed by four or more weeks of mentoring, teaching conversational English, and assisting with arts, crafts and recreational activities with young Cambodian orphans. The program also includes a three day trip to Siem Reap to visit Angkor Wat and other historical sites.

HIV/AIDS Prevention Education Service Learning

Organization: Global Service Corps
Location: Phnom Penh
Cost: 5 weeks $3360; weekly fee after 5 weeks $365, after 13 weeks $250 **Duration:** 5 weeks - 6 months
Age: 20 or older (18 with three letters of recommendation)
Contact: cambodia@globalservicecorps.org

Learn more: www.globalservicecorps.org
Special skills: No special skills required, just a commitment to service
Details: The program begins with a one week cultural orientation and teaching English training in Phnom Penh. The orientation includes learning about Khmer customs, including social do's and don'ts, and acquiring basic Khmer conversation skills. During this time participants will tour local historical sites and visit local partner organizations, public hospitals and clinics. Participants receive training in teaching HIV/AIDS prevention in a Cambodian context. The training is followed by four or more weeks of teaching HIV/AIDS prevention to secondary school students and adults hosted by community based organizations. Opportunities for shadowing health care professionals are at a minimum. The program also includes a three day trip to Siem Reap to visit Angkor Wat and other historical sites. Accommodations throughout the program are provided in local hostels.

Teach English Abroad Service Learning Program

Organization: Global Service Corps
Location: Phnom Penh, Cambodia
Cost: 5 weeks $3360; weekly fee after 5 weeks $365, after 13 weeks $250; Accommodations are provided in local hostels.
Duration: 5 weeks to 6 months
Age: 20 or older (18 or 19 with three letters of recommendation)
Contact: cambodia@globalservicecorps.org
Learn more: www.globalservicecorps.org
Special skills: No special skills required, just a commitment to service
Details: GSC's Teach English Program begins with a one week cultural orientation and teaching English training in Phnom Penh. The orientation includes learning about Khmer customs, including social do's and don'ts, and acquiring basic Khmer conversation skills. During this time participants will tour local historical sites and visit local partner organizations. Participants are also provided training in teaching English as a Foreign Language (EFL) in a Cambodian context. The training is followed by four or more weeks of teaching basic and conversational English to either primary or secondary school students hosted by community based organizations. The program also includes a three day trip to Siem Reap to visit Angkor Wat and other historical sites.

International Health Service Learning Program

Organization: Global Service Corps
Location: Phnom Penh

Cost: 4 week $2,995; weekly fee after 4 weeks $365, after 13 weeks $250; Accommodations throughout the program are provided in local hostels. **Duration:** 4 weeks - 6 months
Age: 20 or older (18 or 19 with three letters of recommendation)
Contact: cambodia@globalservicecorps.org
Learn more: www.globalservicecorps.org
Special skills: Professional licensing, or student of pre-med, medicine or public health
Details: The program begins in Phnom Penh with a one week cultural orientation and introduction to the Cambodia health care system. The orientation includes learning about Khmer customs, including social do's and don'ts, and acquiring basic Khmer conversation skills. Participants also tour historical sites and visit health care facilities and partner organizations. Non-professionals are trained in teaching HIV/AIDS prevention in a Cambodian context. This is followed by four or more weeks providing medical assistance (professionals) or HIV/AIDS prevention and education (non-professionals) in schools, orphanages, health care NGOs, and other community based organization. Shadowing opportunities for non-professionals are at a minimum. The program also includes a three-day trip to Siem Reap to visit Angkor Wat and other historical sites.

Wheelchairs for Land Mine Victims

Organization: Globe Aware
Location: Siem Reap
Cost: $1,200 **Duration:** 1 week, weekly extensions are available
Age: Any - Families welcomed
Email: info@globeaware.org
Learn more: www.globeaware.org

Details: Globe Aware works in Siem Reap, the gateway to the Angkor Wat temples, to build and distribute wheelchairs for community members injured by landmines, victims of polio and other debilitating diseases. Have fun while helping people by building the chairs and distributing them to those in need.

Other organizations offering projects in Cambodia:

Cambodian Children's Painting Project:
   www.letuscreatecambodia.org
Friends without a Border: www.fwab.org
GeoVisions: www.geovisions.org
Globalteer: www.globalteer.org
Habitat for Humanity: www.habitat.org/ivp
i-to-i: www.i-to-i.com

Life and Hope Association: www.watdamnak.org/lha
Medforce: www.medforce.info
Medical Teams International: www.medicalteams.org
Pepy: pepyride.org (Editor's note: Pepy has been consistently ranked
*   as one of the world's top socially responsible tour operators by*
*   multiple organizations)*
Savong's School: www.savong.com
Volunteer in Cambodia: www.volunteerincambodia.org
vMaD: www.madforgood.org
Volunteers for Economic Growth Alliance: www.vegaalliance.org
Where There Be Dragons: www.wheretherebedragons.com
Working for Children: www.wfc-kh.org

China

Hunan Providence Year

Organization: WorldTeach
Location: Changsha and other cities in the Hunan Providence
Cost: $500, subsidized by Hunan Provincial Government
Duration: One Year (Departure in early August) **Age:** 18-65
Contact: info@worldteach.org **Learn more:** www.worldteach.org
Details: WorldTeach volunteers in China teach in secondary schools
(ages 12-18) in Hunan Province. The program is designed to bring
native English speakers to teach students at all socioeconomic levels, as
currently in China the upper classes have more opportunities to learn
from native speakers. Your role will be to build students' confidence in
English through creative, orally-focused English lessons. Volunteers
are also encouraged to contribute to their school community in other
ways. You may want to set up an English club, help in the school library
or computer room, participate in sports or help students prepare for
cultural performances. You may also help local English teachers with
their pronunciation skills. Your host school will provide you with a
furnished foreign teacher's apartment on the school campus. You may
opt to buy lunches from the school dining hall, eat at local restaurants
or cook your own meals.

Panda Keeper Assistants, Interpreters and Clerks

Organization: Panda Club, China Conservation and Research Center
for the Giant Panda,
Location: Bifengxia Giant Panda Base near Ya'an City
Cost: $15 per day per person and $22 to rent uniforms for your work.
Duration: Varies **Age:** 18

Contact: pandaclub@vip.163.com, levy@vip.163.com, bfxpandaclub@163.com **Learn more:** www.pandaclub.net
Special skills: There is a short training for volunteers
Details: One keeper will become your teacher. Volunteers clean the giant panda enclosure and their garden, prepare food: carrot, apples, panda bread and biscuit, collect and carry bamboo. In addition, you may help the scientists to collect behavior data and sometimes you may help the veterinarian to give care to a panda. Volunteer positions also exist as a clerk at Wolong Panda Club and as an interpreter for the Panda Garden. Accommodations & meals are available at a hostel which is within walking distance of the panda preserve. The Panda Club can assist you with transportation from the Chengdu Airport.

China English Program

Organization: Global Volunteer Network
Location: Yantai, a coastal region on the eastern tip of the Shandong Peninsula, located in Northern China, across the Yellow Sea from Japan.
Cost: 1 month $597 **Duration:** 1 to 3 months **Age:** 18
Contact: info@volunteer.org.nz **Learn more:** www.volunteer.org.nz
Details: Based in the stunning coastal region of Yantai, volunteers will be surrounded by picturesque scenery, beautiful beaches and islands, rich culture and traditions and sumptuous food. The need in the Urban Teaching Program is for volunteers to teach English as the Chinese nation has an objective to become bilingual in the next decade. You will find the schools are relatively well resourced with modern facilities. This program is ideal for volunteers who wish to experience the Chinese culture and help Chinese students to learn English in a city with a well developed infrastructure.

Teaching English in Yantai

Organization: uVolunteer
Location: Yantai, northeast part of China in the Shandong Province
Cost: $850 for the first 4 weeks; $95 each additional week
Duration: 4+ weeks **Age:** 18
Contact: info@uvolunteer.org **Learn more:** www.uvolunteer.org
Special skills: Intermediate English
Details: While volunteering in China, you will be assisting an English teacher with the daily lesson plans. Since the schools use integrated education you will have the chance to be involved in science, arts, sports and music. This project provides assistant English teachers to the schools in Yantai, China. Volunteers on this project will be helping the Chinese teacher, with more effective ways to teach the English

language. Chinese students are trained to be disciplined in the school and they show great respect to teachers.

China Summer
Organization: WorldTeach
Location: China- Hunan Province
Cost: $3,990 **Duration:** 2 months (mid June- mid August) **Age:** 18
Contact: info@worldteach.org **Learn more:** www.worldteach.org
Special skills: Fluent in English
Details: WorldTeach volunteers in the China Summer Program teach in secondary school-based summer English camps in Hunan Province. The program is designed to bring native English speakers to teach students from all socioeconomic levels. Your role will be to build students' confidence in English through creative, orally-focused English lessons and to design and participate in cultural activities with your students. Chinese lessons, cultural activities, housing and meals provided by host schools.

Giant Panda Conservation
Organization: Greenforce
Location: Chengdu, in the east of Mt. Qionglai
Cost: $3,000+ **Duration:** 4+ weeks **Age:** 17
Contact: info@greenforce.org
Learn more: www.greenforce.org
Details: This special Panda Reserve, founded with assistance from World Wildlife Fund (WWF), is the earliest, largest and best-known panda reserve in
China. It was placed on the UNESCO Man and Biosphere Reserve Network in 1980. Sixty-seven captive pandas are among 150 pandas in the Giant Panda Reserve managed by the China Conservation and Research Center for the Giant Panda. Following your training, you will work with the panda keepers helping with the day to day running of the sanctuary which involves daily interaction with the Pandas!

People with Disabilities and Orphanage Programs
Organization: Cross-Cultural Solutions
Location: Xi'an
Cost: $2,784 and up **Duration:** 2 to 12 weeks
Age: 18, 8 and older welcome with adult supervision.
Contact: info@crossculturalsolutions.org
Learn more: www.crossculturalsolutions.org
Details: Many residents of underserved rural areas travel to Xi'an in search of better opportunities for their families. As these residents continue to move in to the city, the challenges of overcrowding and

levels of unemployment are only heightened. One of the ways volunteers can make a difference is by caring for children and people with disabilities. When Chinese parents try to adhere to the official "one child" policy, many children are abandoned. Volunteers can work in orphanages that help these children to thrive by providing personal attention and affection. You can also work with children who have mental and physical disabilities to help them overcome the challenges they face. All meals and accommodations are provided.

Other organizations offering projects in China:

Abroad China: www.abroadchina.net
Animals Asia: www.animalsasia.org
Cross-Cultural Solutions: www.crossculturalsolutions.org
Global Crossroads: www.globalcrossroad.com
Global Volunteer Network: www.volunteer.org.nz
Globe Aware: www.globeaware.org
Go Eco: www.goeco.org
HHS International: www.hhscenter.com
i-to-i: www.i-to-i.com
Joy in Action: www.joyinaction.org
Our Chinese Daughters Foundation: www.ocdf.org
Projects Abroad: www.projects-abroad.org
Raleigh: www.raleighinternational.org
Volunteers for China (Christian humanitarian):
  www.volunteersforchina.org

India

Child Labour School, Resource Project, Children's Homes (Internship)

Organization: The Right Now Foundation
Location: Chennai, Tamil Nadu, and Nellore District, Andhra Pradesh
Cost: None **Duration:** Open **Age:** Any
Contact: Stewartbotting@hotmail.com or stewart@rightnow.org.uk
Learn more: Rightnow.org.uk
Special skills: Teaching (English, art and crafts, games)
Details: The Right Now Foundation's projects are all undertaken within four hours of Chennai city. As a volunteer you may opt to work in a wide range of fields and select experiences from teaching in a slum or working with children in child labor, to teaching English in a rural home located in the middle of nowhere. All you need is a willingness to

help children and to offer them (based on your experience) some fun and learning opportunities. This is tough work – heat, culture and language - to say nothing of the plight of the children the program works with, so be bold in this endeavor. It might just change your life!

VSPCA Sanctuary Shelter & Volunteer Office Work

Organization: Visakha Society for Protection and Care of Animals
Location: Visakhapatnam, Andhra Pradesh
Cost: $100 donation **Duration:** 2+ weeks **Age:** 18
Contact: info@vspca.org **Learn more:** www.vspca.org
Special skills: Adaptability, hardiness, a love of animals, vegetarians preferred
Details: Depending on your skills and interest you can volunteer with VSPCA staff at either the office or shelter/sanctuary or a mixture of both. You may be grooming, walking and/or on tender loving care work for the shelter residents and hospital patients: dogs, cats, cows, etc. VSPCA has almost 1,000 animals. Help the shelter staff clean, monitor and perform simple medical tasks. Have office skills? Help improve shelter records for incoming and resident animals. In the office, volunteers can work on a computer and also around town to assist in seminars teaching the public and school children - depending on VSPCA schedules - in humane awareness. Independent ability to take on tasks, ability to feel comfortable in Indian culture and good health a must!

Animal Rescue and Birth Control Program

Organization: Animal Rescue Kerala
Location: Kerala, Southern India
Cost: $145 for any length stay **Duration:** 6+ weeks **Age:** 18
Contact: Odette@ animalrescuekerala.org
Learn more: www.animalrescuekerala.org
Details: ARK has one Vet and one Vet nurse so volunteer veterinarians and vet nurses to help with the workload and animal birth control program would be a great help to them. Other volunteers are needed to walk dogs, detick dogs and puppies and at the same time give them much needed love and affection. Handyman skills would also be very useful to help the rescue with everyday repairs and gardening. Other volunteer opportunities exist for people who are willing to give out leaflets/fliers to tourist on the local beaches.

Mixed Projects for all Nature Lovers

Organization: Himalayan Nature Society
Location: Dharamsala

Cost: None **Duration:** 1+ weeks **Age:** 18
Contact: friendsforanimals@gmail.com
Learn more: www.hnsindia.org
Special skills: Volunteer, visitor, and sponsor must have rabies and tetanus vaccinations plus be able to walk 3 to 4 km. per day.
Details: HNS needs people from all walks of life: veterinarians, vet-nurses, dog catcher or handler, pharmacist, computer expert, shotographer, business developer(MBA), hydrologist, environmentalist, birdwatcher, graphic designer, web designer, rescue expert, animals researcher and writers, etc. Also any people who loves animals and nature. Volunteers clean cages, socialize animals, feed dogs at streets, help with vehicle and building maintained. They have a special need for veterinarians and vet techs to help with our trap, neuter, release (TNR) program. Also we need office help experienced in generating publicity, fundraising, website update, public relation etc.
✒**Editor's note:** Himalayan Nature Society was previously only focused on nature conservation, but local government authorities were organizing mass inhumane killings of stray dogs by poisoning and beating them with bamboo and iron sticks in order to control over population. Then local people came forward in conjunction with HNS to offer an alternative ABC (Animal Birth Control) program.

Arithmetic to Yoga: Educating Street Kids

Organization: SMILE Society
Location: Various
Cost: None **Duration:** 2+ weeks **Age:** 16 or accompanied by a parent
Contact: info@smilengo.org **Learn more:** www.smilengo.org
Details: SMILE has different projects for street, slum and underprivileged kids in India. There are different volunteer opportunities available from 2 weeks to 24 weeks. All volunteers can have a chance to work within the neediest part of the society. As a volunteer you gain a lifetime of experiences and are involved with important welfare activities. At SMILE they treat all volunteers and interns as family members. Students, individuals, groups, seniors and families with children of all ages participate in SMILE projects. Teaching opportunities include math, English, arts and crafts, music, dance and yoga to street and slum kids.

Shelter Veterinarians and Rural Villages

Organization: Darjeeling Goodwill Animal Shelter
Location: Darjeeling
Cost: None expenses **Duration:** 2+ weeks **Age:** 18
Contact: yogesh_24sh@yahoo.co.in or catrina_vear@yahoo.com

Learn more: *via email*
Special skills: Volunteers should be qualified veterinarians, but
veterinary technicians may be considered on a case by case basis.
Details: Darjeeling Goodwill Animal Shelter focuses mainly on a two
tier program: 1) anti-rabies vaccinations and 2) animal birth control of
the street dog population. Dogs are caught from the street, vaccinated,
spayed or neutered, and released back to their original areas with
certain identifying marks such as an ear notch or tattoo number to
identify them as safe to the public. DGAS also performs regular anti-
rabies vaccination camps both locally and in remote villages, open to
owned, street, and community animals that people wish to bring for
vaccination.
DGAS is also available for treatment of owned animals, ranging from
dogs to goats and cows. Puppies on the street are often rescued, made
healthy, and rehomed.

Urban Wildlife Rescue

Organization: People for Animals
Location: Bangalore.
Cost: $5 for membership   **Duration:** 2 weeks   **Age:** Open
Contact: ranjanchacko@rediffmail.com
Learn more: www.pfabangalore.org
Special skills: A passion for animals.
Details: People for Animals, Bangalore is among the few organizations
in India which works at the rescue and rehabilitation of urban wildlife.
Due to the rapid and rampant concretization of our cities and lands, the
delicate balance between man and animal is getting dangerously
tipped. PFA, Bangalore has chosen this niche to work in and to make a
difference to our world and to the Earth. Volunteers help in the upkeep
of our shelter, feeding of the animals, veterinary care, community
awareness programs, fundraising, data upkeep and more.

Animal Welfare and Public Health

Organization: Vets Beyond Borders
Location: Varies and including Project Vet-Train
Cost: None   **Duration:** 2 weeks   **Age:** 18
Contact: *via website*
Learn more: www.vetsbeyondborders.org
Special skills: Volunteers must be veterinarians, veterinary nurses or
veterinary technicians and need to be a member of Vets Beyond
Borders
Details: Vets Beyond Borders is an Australian-based, nonprofit,
incorporated organization established by veterinary volunteers in
2003. Vets Beyond Borders coordinates and runs veterinary based
animal welfare and public health programs in developing communities

of the Asia and Pacific region. VBB projects focus on ABC/AR (animal birth control and rabies) and the clinical training of local veterinary personnel. Experienced volunteers are required to assist these projects and to help with the training and the education of local staff.

Development Education Programme

Organization: Dakshinayan
Location: Roldih Village in Jharkhand, nearest Railhead is Jasidih.
Cost: $300 per month   **Duration:** 1+ months   **Age:** 18
Contact: Dakshinayan@gmail.com
Learn more: www.dakshinayan.org
Special skills: Not required, but a willingness to teach primary level children would be helpful
Details: Dakshinayan is trying to provide basic education to tribal and non-tribal children in a few villages in interior Jharkhand. The education is nonformal. Volunteers should like to spend time with children. Living conditions are basic and meals are simple vegetarian. Volunteers live on the project campus which functions like a commune and are expected to set an example by participating in daily chores.

Aradhana Boys Children's Home

Organization: Kids Worldwide
Location: The children's home is located in the remote village of Tumkur. The project headquarters are in a slum in the city of Bangalore, Southern India.
Cost: $350 1st month, $200 for subsequent months
Duration: 2 week minimum, 1 month+ preferred   **Age:** 18
Contact: aradhana@kidsworldwide.org
Learn more: asia.kidsworldwide.org/indiaaradhana.htm
Special skills: This project needs talented volunteers or couples/families who would like to spend time with rural and tribal, slum women and children
Details: This project is run by the Bethesda Mission, which was started in 1999 in Bangalore. It is registered with the government of India and it is part of a faith-based mission serving the rural, slum and tribal population. There are around 70 boys in their care. You can get

219

involved in the following activities: teaching, training the youngsters in various skills, conducting medical clinics, awareness programmes, screening programmes, vocational training, visiting the houses and slums, immunization programmes and fundraising.

Daya Orphanage
Organization: Kids Worldwide
Location: In the heart of Bhubaneswar city, Orissa state
Cost: $350 1st month, $200 subsequent months
Duration: 2+ weeks, 1+ month preferred.
Age: Older volunteers (30+) preferred, no single women under 30.
Contact: daya@kidsworldwide.org
Learn more: asia.kidsworldwide.org
Special skills: Volunteers should have a love for children, and the character to act as a role model.
Details: The Orphanage of Daya (means compassion) was established in the year 2004. Daya is a Christian based organization which has grown steadily over the last 5 years and now has 2 buildings - one which houses boys, and the other which houses the girls. The children live on site, receiving a Christ centered education, food, clothing and love. The orphanage also runs a school for slum children. There are 20 children at present. Most of the parents of these children are day workers, alcoholic and/or illiterate. Each day the children get snacks and two days a week they receive a free lunch. The majority of these kids are considered lower caste/untouchable according to the Hindu caste system and need your caring open heart to help them to survive and thrive.

Jaipur Orphanage
Organization: Kids Worldwide
Location: Jaipur, also known as the Pink City.
Cost: First month $440, subsequent months $150
Duration: 2+ weeks, 1+ month preferred
Age: 18, or kids welcome with a parent after prior consultation
Contact: malatii@kidsworldwide.org
Learn more: asia.kidsworldwide.org
Special skills: The orphanage prefers female volunteers. You must have a good moral character and respect the local culture.
Details: Currently home to around 13 orphans, this project really has an incredible history. It is the story of one woman (the director who is a yogic nun) who struggled against all odds to do something for the underprivileged. The project started in 2005 and has grown consistently year by year. When you stay with them, you join a family for the time you are there, sharing joys and sorrows, learning about

Indian culture and teaching others about yours. Most of all, you will gain a place in their hearts...when you leave, the children will never forget you and will request you to come back again and again.

Mother Theresa Society for the Handicapped

Organization: Kids Worldwide
Location: Udumalpet, a rural region in Tamilnadu State, India.
Cost: 1st month $350, subsequent months $200.
Duration: 2+ weeks, 1 month+ preferred
Age: 18, kids welcome with a parent after prior consultation
Contact: mothert@kidsworldwide.org
Learn more: asia.kidsworldwide.org
Special skills: They prefer female volunteers who have some experience and knowledge related to disability issues - especially developmental disabilities. They also welcome occupational therapists, neuro-developmental therapists, and physiotherapists to come to help train our staff.
Details: Open since 1988, Mother Theresa Society for the Handicapped-Udumalpet is a small voluntary organization providing care and rehabilitation for rural poor children with disabilities. Currently there are around 65 children in their care. The Mother Theresa Society enables them to lead a meaningful life through the use of systematic methods provided by a dedicated team of caregivers. About 1/3 of the children stay with them for fulltime residential care since the children come from remote villages with irregular transport access. The majority are between 3 and 18 years old and just over half are either mentally disabled or suffer from cerebral palsy.

GVN India Women's & Children's Programs

Organization: Global Volunteer Network
Location: Kolkata
Cost: $747 for 1 month   **Duration:** 1 to 3 months   **Age:** 18-60
Contact: info@volunteer.org.nz
Learn more: www.volunteer.org.nz
Details: The types of projects you could be involved with in India through GVN include their Children's Project, in which you will be working in a local slum school, assisting teachers, developing new lessons, working individually with students in a tutoring setting, etc. Additionally, there is another school which is specifically for disabled children where you would be working with high need youth. The Women's Project: volunteers are needed to work on various projects with women from the red-light district, from teaching English to the women as well as their children, to giving computer training or teaching business skills to small women's groups forming their own

221

businesses. Additionally, volunteers with web design, photography, or jewelry making skills are needed to work with women in the fair trade market.

Animal Shelter and Hospital

Organization: The Tree of Life for Animals
Location: Rajasthan
Cost: $500 to $700 per month   **Duration:** 1+ month   **Age:** 18
Contact: volunteers@tolfa.org.uk   **Learn more:** www.tolfa.org.uk
Special skills: Ideally we are in need of qualified vets and vet nurses, but we are also happy for veterinary students and volunteers who have experience working with animals, as well as people with a bit of time, compassion and any other skills to contribute.
Details: Vets, vet nurses and vet students needed to assist with surgery and animal treatments. Non-vet volunteers will assist with general animal care, feeding, dog walking, cleaning etc. Anyone with other skills that might be of benefit to the shelter should tell them when applying. All help is appreciated!

Teaching English to the Santhal Community

Organization: uVolunteer
Location: Sankiniketan, West Bengal district
Cost: $750 for the first three weeks; $95 each additional week
Duration: 3+ weeks   **Age:** 18
Contact: info@uvolunteer.org   **Learn more:** www.uvolunteer.org
Special skills: Basic English
Details: As a volunteer you will be supporting the development of a Santhal tribal people. Volunteers will be helping the community by teaching basic English to the children of the village. You will be developing daily lesson plans and assisting the teachers. You will also have a chance to help with the craft camps. India is home to 1/3 of world's poor and 25 to 50 percent of its population lives in sheer poverty. Volunteers for this project should be lively and love children.

Bring Education to the Heart of India

Organization: iSPiiCE (Integrated Social Programs in Indian Child Education)
Location: Dharamsala, Himachal Pradesh, North India
Cost: Starting at $490 (2 weeks), $150 per extra week
Duration: 2 to 12 weeks   **Age:** 18
Contact: info@ispiice.com   **Learn more:** www.ispiice.com
Special skills: Proficiency in English and basic Microsoft
Details: Marginalized communities in North India desperately require your help to gain a better standard of education for their children.

iSPiiCE invites international volunteers to teach, raise awareness about the need for regular schooling and provide support to local staff. This is a brilliant opportunity to teach school children in Himachal Pradesh along with children in shelter homes and orphanages. Interacting with them is extremely valuable for children's confidence and also for your learning about the local culture. iSPiiCE offers a unique combination of quality volunteering experience, weekend excursions (to India's most famed landmarks), personal connections with locals and cultural immersion.

Empowering Women in Rural India

Organization: iSPiiCE (Integrated Social Programs in Indian Child Education)
Location: Dharamsala, Himachal Pradesh, North India
Cost: Starting at $490 (2 weeks), $150 per extra week
Duration: 2 to 12+ weeks **Age:** 18
Contact: info@ispiice.com **Learn more:** www.ispiice.com
Special skills: Proficiency in English
Details: iSPiiCE take you to the very heart of India to raise awareness on Women's Empowerment issues. Strong gender inequalities still exist in rural India and women's lack of decision making power is evident in all aspects of their lives. Often girls receive only a few short years of schooling and are sent off to be married at a young age. Education is the most influential tool to raise the status of women. iSPiiCE runs a variety of educational and confidence building activities to benefit women and adolescent girls in the local community. Teaching English and computer classes impart much needed skills to the ladies, increase their self-worth and offer a platform for social interaction, ultimately increasing their social status and employability prospects. Make a real impact on these women's lives and share with them your experiences and skills to help them take control of their futures.

Street Children Work in India

Organization: International Volunteer HQ
Location: Placements available in New Delhi, surrounding rural areas and Palampur
Cost: $250 for 1 week to $2,500 for 6 months; includes food & accommodation **Duration:** 1 week to 6 months **Age:** 18
Contact: volunteer@volunteerhq.org
Learn more: www.volunteerhq.org
Details: School is simply not an option for many children in India as they work the streets with their parents to help stay alive. There are literally millions of street children in India. Every day of the year these

children work the streets with their parents, selling goods, foraging and performing to make a living. The Street Children Program focuses on giving children some enjoyment in their lives. This program is popular with children and their families as it gives them opportunities and perspectives on life they would never have otherwise been provided with. Work consists of giving basic school lessons, playing with the children, providing medical support and introducing them to activities (such as painting) that they would never otherwise have a chance to do.

Indian Animal Welfare

Organization: Help in Suffering, Maharani Farm
Location: Jaipur, Rajasthan
Cost: To be determined   **Duration:** Open   **Age:** Adult
Contact: hisjpr@helpinsuffering.org
Learn more: www.his-india.org.au
Special skills: Previous animal experience is useful and rabies vaccinations are essential
Details: Help in Suffering is a busy animal welfare organization in Jaipur India. Volunteers can expect to help with animal care especially feeding and socializing young dogs, kennel management, bathing of rescues, and possibly assisting with ambulatory clinics tending draught equines and camels. Help may be needed with veterinary treatment of rescued animals, under the guidance of veterinary and technical staff. Volunteers may also be involved in simple shelter maintenance tasks, gardening, repairs etc. Contact Help in Suffering directly to check what specific roles may be required at a given time.

Care for Rural Indian Children in Need

Organization: iSPiiCE (Integrated Social Programs in Indian Child Education)
Location: Dharamsala, Himachal Pradesh, North India
Cost: Starting at $490 (2 weeks), $150 per extra week
Duration: 2 to 12+ weeks   **Age:** 18
Contact: info@ispiice.com   **Learn more:** www.ispiice.com
Details: iSPiiCE gives you the chance to honor your desire to help those less fortunate by providing love, care and affection to neglected children in rural India. Work is available in shelters for street children, orphanages or childcare centers where children often suffer from terrible cases of neglect and poverty. Children need volunteers to provide their love and shelter needs plus some level of education, which is currently nonexistent in their lives. In recognition of the hard work our volunteers put in, they ensure that you receive a quality

volunteering experience. All the main arrangements are included in the program leaving you free to concentrate on volunteer activities. Three weekend excursions are also provided to the Taj Mahal in Agra, the Golden Temple in Amritsar and a Himalayan trek.

Healthcare/Social Work: Women and Children

Organization: iSPiiCE (Integrated Social Programs in Indian Child Education)
Location: Dharamsala, Himachal Pradesh, North India
Cost: Starting at $490 (2 weeks), $150 per extra week
Duration: 2 to 12 weeks or more   **Age:** 18
Contact: info@ispiice.com   **Learn more:** www.ispiice.com
Special skills: Recognized Healthcare/Social Work qualifications
Details: Rural Indian communities lack access to healthcare, putting women and children are at severe risk. This group is among the most disadvantaged in the world in terms of health status. iSPiiCE has volunteers travel into small rural villages to meet with local pregnant women and those with small children, to discuss their situations with regard to general health, difficulties and concerns they may be facing and to determine practical ways of assistance that benefit their specific needs while giving nutritional and healthcare advice. Visits benefit all in terms of increased education/awareness. Volunteers experience, at a grass roots level, the difficulties women of rural India face and offer practical ways of assistance which will ultimately bring benefits to the community as a whole.

Women Empowerment Program in India

Organization: International Volunteer HQ
Location: Placements available in New Delhi
Cost: $300 for 2 weeks to $2,500 for 6 months, includes food & accommodation
Duration: 2 weeks to 6 months   **Age:** 18
Contact: volunteer@volunteerhq.org
Learn more: www.volunteerhq.org
Details: Due to the existing social, cultural, economic and social phenomena of India, a lot of women are deprived of basic human rights including education, health, nutrition, involvement in politics, etc. Violence and rape against women are other critical factors which have been exacerbating the plight of women. A number of homes have been created to shield women from the wrongdoings of society and restore their last sense of pride and self respect. These resource strapped homes badly need volunteers to run their program. Volunteers provide counseling and monitoring and help women by teaching English, beautician work, yoga, stitching, sanitation and health education.

Volunteers make a big difference in the women's lives by sharing their love and warmth with the stressed residents of these homes.

Be a Miracle for Children

Organization: The Miracle Foundation
Location: Varies
Cost: $1,400   **Duration:** 2 to 20 weeks   **Age:** None
Contact: jim@miraclefoundation.org
Learn more: www.miraclefoundation.org
Details: The Miracle Foundation was founded in 2000 by Caroline Boudreaux after she visited India. She found a dire need for the global community to take action and help the millions of children in India with no home, education or proper meals. There are four orphanages and about 500 children being taken care of by the foundation. The main work done by volunteers around the orphanages is small renovations, cleaning, planting, making crafts and games for the children, taking photographs and video footage of the children, having fun and getting to know the kids! Offering three trips per year, the August trip is a Medical Tour centered around doctors and other people in the health professions who would like to use their specific skills to help those who require it in the orphanages, but anyone is welcome!

✍ **Editor's note:** The Miracle Foundation's volunteer trips have been highly recommended by numerous previous participants. For an inside look at the lives of India's street kids and work conducted by Miracle Foundation read *The Weight of Silence: Invisible Children of India* by Shelley Seale. You will be motivated, uplifted and your voluntary spirit will be inspired.

Farm Animals and Beyond

Organization: India Project for Animals and Nature
Location: Nilgiris district
Cost: Up to $700 depending on skills   **Duration:** 1+ weeks   **Age:** 18
Contact: info@uvolunteer.org   **Learn more:** www.uvolunteer.org
Special skills: As a non-veterinary volunteer you need experience in working with animals and handling them. As a working vet you have to be able to spay/neuter dogs and cats and treat domestic livestock. Practical experience in treating horses is beneficial.
Details: General volunteers; socialize animals, groom horses and dogs, assist vets in their treatments, develop animal welfare programs for children and help in generating publicity and fundraising. Vet students interested in animal welfare, mixed animal practice and development of animal health services in the rural areas of developing countries are welcome. Work with vets in the ABC program, Equine Street Clinics, emergency vet service in rural villages and at times teaching the

participants of the vet training program. Every year volunteer veterinarians and vet students join the IPAN team learning about animal health and welfare issues in India. The Hill View Farm Animal Refuge is situated in the Mavanalla village bordering the Mudumalai Wildlife Sanctuary in the Nilgiris district of Tamil Nadu. This is part of the UN designated Nilgiris Biosphere Reserve, world renowned for its birdlife and flora.

Special Needs Children in India

Organization: Experiential Learning International
Location: Chennai, India
Cost: $925   **Duration:** 2+ weeks   **Age:** 18
Contact: info@eliabroad.org   **Learn more:** www.eliabroad.org
Details: In Indian society, children born with mental or physical disabilities are often considered a burden or curse. ELI works with several organizations that provide care and a nurturing environment for children with disabilities. The centers also place an emphasis on educating the families of disabled children to prevent the children from being cast out of their families. Volunteers with this program will assist with the day to day tasks such as feeding the children, dressing the children, helping with clean up, spending time with the kids, and leading activities. Experienced volunteers may also have the opportunity to assist with physiotherapy exercises and occupational therapy activities.

Animal Rescue and Care Tour Program with Yoga

Organization: Greenheart Travel
Location: Jaipur, India
Cost: $2,290 for 4 weeks   **Duration:** 2 or 4 weeks   **Age:** 18
Contact: info@greenhearttravel.org
Learn more: www.cci-exchange.com
Details: Volunteers will tour the city in an animal ambulance which identifies and transports sick and mistreated animals back to the shelter. Volunteers will help manage the animal rescue hotline and aid in vaccinating and sterilizing the animals. They will also assist the adoption center staff in finding homes for the animals and help create community campaigns about the importance of the center and of animal adoption. Accommodations are at the local volunteer house known as the "base-camp." All meals are included and are prepared by project staff. All programs include the following activities: dinner with a local, English-speaking family in Jaipur, guided tour of the Amber, one week yoga session, Indian cooking class, all transportation to/from the excursions are included.

227

Global Health Volunteer
Organization: Foundation for International Medical Relief of Children
Location: Kodaikanal, Tamil Nadu
Cost: $1,299 for 2 weeks
Duration: 2 to 4 weeks, longer stays are possible   **Age:** 18
Contact: missions@fimrc.org   **Learn more:** www.fimrc.org
Special skills: This program is specially focused for undergraduates, medical students, and public health students
Details: Help provide primary medical care to several hundred children living in the southern Indian town of Kodaikanal. Volunteers will gain valuable medical experience at the hospital by shadowing medical professionals, administering medications, taking vital statistics, assisting with patient intake, and accompanying field staff to children's centers to present interactive health lessons. You will help provide additional assistance to these childcare centers by delivering nutritious meals to combat malnourishment and distributing hygiene and personal care supplies to encourage positive lifetime health practices. Opportunities exist for all weeks throughout the year!

Teaching and Empowering
Organization: Greenforce
Location: Himalayas, Rajasthan or Goa
Cost: $2,300   **Duration:** 4+ weeks   **Age:** 17
Contact: info@greenforce.org
Learn more: www.greenforce.org

Details: With education being the foundation of a community's social development, volunteer for Greenforce's teaching project and make a difference to some of the world's least fortunate children. By volunteering on one of these international teaching projects in India, you would be helping those most prone to illiteracy and poverty. Help provide a basic education, and you are playing a key role in empowering those on the fringes of society to help themselves out of the cycle of poverty. Volunteers can choose to work in one of three diverse areas in India: Himalayas, Rajasthan or Goa.

Sunderbans Smiles
Organization: Hands Up Holidays
Location: Bali Islands Sunderbans, North-East India
Cost: $1,800 per person, based on sharing a room
Duration: 4 days volunteering/11 day trip
Age: 16 with an adult
Contact: info@handsupholidays.com
Learn more: www.handsupholidays.com

Special skills: None required, but teaching English as a second language (ESL), building, or horticultural skills are desirable
Details: Delve into rural community life, get to know the people and take part in a wonderful sustainable project. This is the heartwarming story of 'poachers turned conservationists' protecting the wildlife and flora of this unique ecosystem. Assist in maintaining and repairing clay embankments of the dike, planting mangroves to minimize flood damage or you can help construct a 10-bed hospital. To complete a remarkable adventure and to give yourself a taste of India's diversity, guided walks through the peaceful and stunning Bali Island will contrast with the noise, color and energy of the streets of Calcutta. The truly lucky may even be able to add a tiger sighting to your list of experiences.

Women's Empowerment with Greenforce

Organization: Greenforce
Location: India
Cost: $2,300 **Duration:** 4 weeks **Age:** 17
Contact: info@greenforce.org **Learn more:** www.greenforce.org
Details: Volunteer with Greenforce and you will play a firsthand role in combating social obstacles and discrimination which face many women in India. You will empower women by discussing unfair gender norms with families, encourage education and organize special workshops. Help put a halt to gender inequality, and provide more life opportunities for women. Also, explore India's three most visited cities. The routes connecting Delhi, Agra and Jaipur form a triangle aptly labeled 'golden' for the cultural and historical wealth each city has to offer. Experience the hustle and bustle of these three great cities; interact with the locals and experience authentic Indian cuisines.

Himalayan Animal Welfare: Dogs of Dharamsala

Organization: inside/out Humanitourism™ Adventures - Piyara Kutta
Location: Dharamsala, India (Himalayas)
Cost: $2,500+
Duration: 1 week + a week of locally guided active adventures
Age: No age minimum, determined on an individual basis
Contact: info@theinsideandout.com
Learn more: www.theinsideandout.com
Details: You will be an integral part of a singular effort to change the destiny of thousands of homeless animals high in the Himalayas. Volunteers will work with Piyara Kutta, an organization dedicated to improving the lives of dogs in Dharamsala. Piyara Kutta has helped to fund the construction of a shelter and veterinary clinic in Dharamsala

for the sole animal welfare advocate in the region. You will be helping to build an expansion to this facility to provide shelter and veterinary care for additional numbers of animals. Inside/Out trips are designed around opportunities to do humanitarian volunteer work on meaningful international projects and are combined with sustainable eco-adventure travel in the local area of the project and people. Their trips are designed to create longer term relationships between communities and travelers.

Taste of India

Organization: Hands Up Holidays
Location: Delhi
Cost: $2,350 per person, based on sharing a room, excluding flights.
Duration: 4 days volunteering/12 day trip
Age: 16 years unless accompanied by an adult
Contact: info@handsupholidays.com
Learn more: www.handsupholidays.com
Special skills: None required, but teaching English as a second language (ESL) skills are desirable
Details: This volunteer project is a unique opportunity to help the poorest of the poor. Improve the living conditions of people in the slums or devote time to teaching English, math, science, drama or general studies or improve the school. Marvel at the ingenuity of the children as they make toys and play games with the few things they have. Then explore other facets of this fascinating country as you visit the beautiful Taj Mahal, explore the streets of Jaipur the 'Pink City," seek out tigers in the Ranthambore reserve, haggle in bazaars and marvel at the Maharajas Palace. From slums to riches, India has it all.

Ultimate India – In Style

Organization: Hands Up Holidays
Location: Delhi - India
Cost: $5,700 per person, based on sharing a room
Duration: 4 days volunteering/14 day trip
Age: 16 with an adult
Contact: info@handsupholidays.com
Learn more: www.handsupholidays.com
Special skills: None required, but teaching English as a second language (ESL) skills are desirable
Details: This trip offers a fascinating juxtaposition. As you enjoy the luxuries of India and marvel at the myriad of colors, fascinating history and stunning scenery, you have the unique opportunity to help the poorest of the poor. Help improve the education of the impoverished children in the slums or improve the school. Contrast this humbling experience with a visit to the magnificent Taj Mahal. You will be awe-

stuck as you experience the many facet of life in this remarkable country, from the stunning 'Pink City' of Jaipur to a beautiful tiger reserve and some relaxing days spent in the luxurious Chambal lodge

Other organizations offering projects in India:

Calcutta Rescue: (socially & economically) www.calcuttarescue.org
Child Family Health International: www.cfhi.org
Crawl: www.crawlsociety.org
Ekal Vidyalaya Foundation (combats illiteracy): www.ekalindia.org
FairMail (photography to underprivileged teens producing cards to
* earn money): www.fairmail.info*
Global Choices: www.globalchoices.co.uk
Global Contact, ActionAid Denmark: www.globalcontact.dk
Global Visions International: www.gviusa.com or www.gvi.co.uk
i-to-i: www.i-to-i.com
India Study Abroad: www.indiastudyabroad.org
India Volunteer Care: www.indiavolunteercare.com
Kerala Link: www.kerala-link.org
People and Places (Winner 'Best Volunteering Organization' category
* of Virgin Holidays Responsible Tourism Award 2009):*
* travel-peopleandplaces.co.uk*
Projects Abroad: www.projects-abroad.org
Raleigh: www.raleighinternational.org
Volunteering India: www.volunteeringindia.com

Indonesia

Bali Veterinarian and Veterinary Nursing
Organization: Bali Animal Welfare Association (BAWA)
Location: Ubud, Bali, Indonesia
Cost: None **Duration:** 2 weeks to 6 months **Age:** 18
Contact: wendyl@bawabali.com **Learn more:** www.bawabali.com
Special skills: Nurses experience in a vet clinic including emergency procedures, general animal clinic protocol, surgery protocols and standard applications of medicines and drugs. Doctor of

Veterinary Medicine (D.V.M or V.M.D); At least 3 to 5 years work experience.
Details: This is a unique opportunity to volunteer to help animal welfare in a fascinating and rich cultural setting. BAWA aims to relieve suffering, control the population and improve the health of Bali's street dogs

through medical care, spay/neutering street-feeding, puppy adoption and education of school children. They're also involved in rabies eradication in Bali. BAWA staff especially need training in general veterinary staff procedures, emergency procedures, best surgery protocols and administering drugs and medications. They need to become more efficient and improve day to day procedures at the clinic to increase their intake capacity and use clinic space to its maximum benifit. They also need you to train their education staff in the best practices to educate local Indonesians on the care of companion animals, how to prevent rabies and what to do if bitten.

Bali Animal Clinic Helper

Organization: Bali Animal Welfare Association (BAWA)
Location: Ubud, Bali, Indonesia
Cost: None   **Duration:** 1 day or more   **Age:** 16, or under with parents
Contact: wendyl@bawabali.com   **Learn more:** www.bawabali.com
Special skills: Passion for animals a must
Details: This is a unique opportunity to volunteer to help animal welfare in a fascinating and rich cultural setting. BAWA's aim is to relieve suffering, control the population and improve the health of Bali's street dogs through medical care, spay/neutering, street feeding, puppy adoption and education of school children. They are also involved in rabies eradication in Bali. When it comes to animal welfare, there is a lot of work to do in Bali and BAWA is still a relatively new and small organization, so they desperately need all the help they can get. Volunteers assist with the programs running from the clinic. They need you to assist the staff in day to day care of the clinic animals including feeding, cleaning, puppy socialization and dog walking.

Bali Animals Business Management Consultant

Organization: Bali Animal Welfare Association (BAWA)
Location: Ubud, Bali, Indonesia
Cost: None   **Duration:** 3 to 6 months   **Age:** 18
Contact: wendyl@bawabali.com   **Learn more:** www.bawabali.com
Special skills: 5 years experience working in business management for an NGO and a passion for animals
Details: Take part in this unique opportunity to use your business savvy while helping animals in a fascinating and rich cultural setting. BAWA is still a relatively new and small organization. With a business plan and strategic plan BAWA will have a clear map to follow. Help BAWA clarify it's strengths and weaknesses Then, employees will have clear job descriptions and clearly deliniated roles which will make the organization much more efficient and more economically viable. BAWA need to have clear, easy to use standardized computer programs for

greater efficiency and the ability to more easily access information needed for external relations, i.e. press releases, magazine articles, previously written grant applications. With your help the animal clinic will function with greater efficiency and effectiveness benefiting the animals of Bali for years to come.

Animal Rescue Fundraising and Promotion

Organization: Bali Animal Welfare Association (BAWA)
Location: Ubud, Bali, Indonesia
Cost: None   **Duration:** 3 to 6 months   **Age:** 18
Contact: wendyl@bawabali.com
Learn more: www.bawabali.com
Special skills: 5 years of fundraising with NGOs and a passion for animals
Details: BAWA is a relatively new and small organization, desperately needing all the help they can get, especially in capacity building. Through the establishment of sustainable programs for fundraising, BAWA would be able to hire desperately needed staff to run their ambitious and vital programs which will aid the animals of Bali for many years to come and will also have the funding to increase their programs' outreach to all areas of Bali.

✍**Editor's note:** The fledgling BAWA recognizes the need to have volunteers with business skills in order to set up the organization for long-term success, thus benefiting the animals of Indonesia for years to come. If you also have experience in marketing, public relations, product design for merchandising please let them know. You contribution in any aspect of running a successful business can be an invaluable contribution.

Teach and Care for Orphans in Indonesia

Organization: International Humanity Foundation
Location: Bali, Jakarta, Medan and Aceh, Indonesia
Cost: $50 per week, maximum of $600; Room and board included
Duration: 1+ month, no maximum
Age: 18, older with parental permission
Contact: volunteering@ihfonline.org
Learn more: www.ihfonline.org
Details: Learn the realities of international poverty by serving at IHF's orphanage and education center where you will live, learn, teach and play with the children who call it home. At the center tasks and needs vary widely, and you are certain to find a niche according to your skills. Since IHF is entirely volunteer-run, you will be asked to serve on various online task teams, such as advertising and photography, which

233

will grant you unique insight into how an international non-profit operates.

Narayan Seva Childrens Home

Organization: Kids Worldwide
Location: Singaraja, one of the two main cities on Bali.
Cost: $30 booking fee, $510 the 1st month, $370 subsequent months
Duration: 2 week minimum, 1 month+ preferred
Age: 18, families with children also welcome
Contact: narayanseva@kidsworldwide.org
Learn more: asia.kidsworldwide.org/balinarayanseva.htm
Special skills: Kids Worldwide needs talented female volunteers or couples/families who would like to come spend time with our children.
Details: Narayan Seva Children's Home was started in June 2004 with one 4 year old child. They now have 30 children in their care. The home was started with the intention of providing shelter and education for the needy, marginalized and disadvantaged children. Based on the progressive system of Neo-Humanist Education, under the guidance of dedicated teachers, students not only acquire academic skills and knowledge, but also gain strength of character and high ideals. Volunteers should have a love for children and good character through which to act as a role model for the children.

Wildlife Rescue Indonesia

Organization: Tasikoki Wildlife Rescue
Location: North Sulawesi
Cost: $125-$400 per week depending upon length of stay
Duration: 3+ weeks   **Age:** 18
Contact: wildlifevolunteer.indonesia@gmail.com
Learn more: www.tasikoki.org
Special skills: None required, just enthusiasm for animal welfare and reasonable physical fitness to work in a tropical climate. Veterinarians and vet nurses are welcome to support this project
Details: Tasikoki rescue centre was set-up in 2001 to tackle the hub of illegal trade in Indonesian wildlife being smuggled through Sulawesi on its way to the Philippines and then on to the global market. Sadly many of the confiscated animals have nowhere safe to be released and must remain in care at the rescue centre until better protection of Indonesia's forests can be established. Since 2006, Tasikoki Wildlife Rescue has experienced a funding crisis until 2009, when this volunteer project was set-up to help put the project back on its feet. Volunteers assist in the daily care of orangutans as well as many other endangered primates, bears, leopard and a variety of rare bird species. All meals and resort-style accommodation over-looking a fabulous beach are included.

Orangutan Foundation Volunteer Programme

Organization: Orangutan Foundation
Location: Lamandau River Wildlife Reserve, Central Kalimantan
Cost: $1,300 for 6 weeks
Duration: 6 weeks Aug. to Oct.   **Age:** 18
Contact: info@orangutan.org.uk
Learn more: www.orangutan.org.uk
Special skills: No special skills required. Must be a
team player
Details: The Orangutan Foundation Volunteer
Programme offers individuals a unique opportunity
to contribute to the conservation of the orangutan

and its rainforest home. It was established to provide field operations
with an additional committed workforce. Work is of a manual
labor/construction nature and you will not be working with
orangutans. Past teams have built guard posts, accommodation
buildings and an orangutan release site. Accommodation and food are
basic and you will most likely be bathing in rivers. Volunteers are
offered insight into the work of the Orangutan Foundation and get to
go "behind the scenes" of operations. You will work in a team of 12
volunteers plus Volunteer Coordinators and Indonesian staff. Price
includes food and accommodation, plus transport while on the
program.

Bird Rescue North Sulawesi

Organization: Tasikoki Wildlife Rescue
Location: North Sulawesi
Cost: $125-$400 per week depending upon length of stay
Duration: 1+ weeks   **Age:** 18
Contact: wildlifevolunteer.indonesia@gmail.com
Learn more: www.tasikoki.org
Special skills: None required, just enthusiasm for birds and
reasonable physical fitness to work in a tropical climate.
Details: This rescue centre was set-up in 2001 to tackle the hub of
illegal trade in Indonesian wildlife being smuggled through Sulawesi on
its way to the Philippines and then on to the global market. Sadly many
of the confiscated birds, especially those from Papua, have nowhere
safe to be released and must remain in care at the rescue centre until
better protection of Indonesia's forests can be established. Since 2006,
the centre experienced a funding crisis until 2009 when Wildlife
Friends Foundation Thailand (WFFT) set-up this volunteer program to
help put the project back on its feet. Volunteers assist in the daily care
of over 20 rare bird species including parrots, cockatoos and hornbills,

totaling over 150 individuals. All meals and resort-style accommodation over-looking a fabulous beach are included.

Sulawesi Macaque Rehabilitation

Organization: Tasikoki Wildlife Rescue
Location: North Sulawesi
Cost: $125-$400 per week depending upon length of stay
Duration: 1+ weeks **Age:** 18
Contact: wildlifevolunteer.indonesia@gmail.com
Learn more: www.tasikoki.org
Special skills: None required, just enthusiasm for monkeys and reasonable physical fitness to work in a tropical climate.
Details: Tasikoki rescue centre was set-up in 2001 to tackle the hub of illegal trade in Indonesian wildlife being smuggled through Sulawesi on its way to the Philippines and then on to the global market. Volunteers assist in the daily care of several rare species of Sulawesi macaques at the rescue centre, as well as helping in the field with reintroduction projects. All meals and resort-style accommodation over-looking the beach included.

Orangutan Research

Organization: Orangutan Health Project
Location: North Sumatra, Indonesia
Cost: $1,289 **Duration:** 2 weeks **Age:** 18-50
Contact: orangutanhealth@nusa.net.id
Learn more: www.orangutan-health.org
Details: The Orangutan Health Project investigates the special behaviors and ecological conditions necessary for the maintenance of health in wild orangutans. By volunteering with OHP, you will have a special opportunity to see primary rainforest in one of the most beautiful areas in the world while contributing to the research and conservation goals of OHP. Work of this type on orangutans in Indonesia has never been conducted before. The aim is to understand how orangutans combat parasite infections that affect their health, reproduction and, ultimately, their survival. The importance of our research cannot be emphasized enough – it will bring knowledge to basic science, public health and wildlife management and hopefully help to save both flora and fauna. In effect, we will all win.

Bali Bound

Organization: Hands Up Holidays
Location: Bali
Cost: $1,850 per person, based on sharing a room
Duration: 4 days volunteering/12 day trip

Age: 16 with an adult
Contact: info@handsupholidays.com
Learn more: www.handsupholidays.com
Special skills: None required, but teaching English as a second language (ESL), engineering, or building skills are desirable
Details: Join a project devoted to improving the lives of disabled children and young adults. All tasks including administrative work and building repairs have a significant impact on quality of life. If you have specialist skills you may be fortunate enough to directly assist these remarkable youngsters directly. This volunteer project comes toward the end of an adventure-filled trip in Bali. Visit the beautiful village of Ubud, enjoy spectacular scenery as you take a thrilling whitewater rafting trip and revel in a slow-paced mountain bike ride through the villages of Mt. Batur. Finally reminisce about your heart warming volunteer project as you luxuriate at a refreshing health spa.

Other organizations offering projects in Indonesia:

4ᵗʰ World Love: fourthworldlove.org
Canadian Alliance for Development Initiatives and Projects:
   www.cadip.org
Cross-Cultural Solutions: www.crossculturalsolutions.org
Global Visions International: www.gviusa.com
Great Orangutan Project: www.orangutanproject.com
Doorways: www.internationaldoorways.com
i-to-i: www.i-to-i.com
International Humanity Foundation: www.ihfonline.org
Medical Teams International: www.medicalteams.org
Orangutan Tropical Peatland Project: www.orangutantroop.com
PAK Orphanage Project: www.pakorphanage.org/en
People and Places (Winner 'Best Volunteering Organization' category
   of Virgin Holidays Responsible Tourism Award 2009):
   travel-peopleandplaces.co.uk
Volunteer in Asia: www.viaprograms.org
Vets Beyond Borders (veterinary): www.vetsbeyondborders.org

Israel

Free Dental Care for Underprivileged Children
Organization: DVI - Dental Volunteers for Israel
Location: Jerusalem

Cost: None. Accommodations provided, volunteer responsible for transportation and other living costs
Duration: 1 to 4 weeks
Contact: international@dental-dvi.org.il
Learn more: www.dental-dvi.org.il
Special skills: Licensed dentist
Details: DVI, with the help of international dental volunteers provides free state-of-the-art dental care to the indigent children of Jerusalem. If not for DVI, the over 200,000 children in Jerusalem living under the poverty line would not receive any dental care or learn about oral hygiene. DVI provides the perfect opportunity for a volunteering

holiday. Working hours are Sunday – Thursday, 8am – 2pm, leaving enough free time for sightseeing. For the duration of their stay, volunteer dentists are given the use of apartments in prime locations around Jerusalem. By giving of your skill and volunteering at the clinic, you have the opportunity to change a child's life and your own.

Kibbutz Lotan Eco Volunteer Program

Organization: GoEco
Location: Israel, Kibbutz Lotan
Cost: $300 – $400 **Duration:** 2 to 8 weeks **Age:** 18
Contact: goeco@goeco.org **Learn more:** www.goeco.org
Details: The Eco-volunteering program at Kibbutz Lotan is a complete and practical introduction to both ecology and cooperative living. As a participant in the program you will be interwoven into the daily life of the kibbutz and volunteer for the Center for Creative Ecology (CfCE). The CfCE is a unique ecological center that combines hands on, experiential environmental education within the framework of a living community. Utilizing creative recycling and alternative/natural building techniques, the center now includes an ecological theme park, migratory bird reserve, nature trails, recycling center, and constructed wetlands for treating the waste water of the entire kibbutz.

Desert Wildlife Reserve

Organization: GoEco
Location: Israel, Yotvata
Cost: $300 – $400 **Duration:** 4 to 8 weeks **Age:** 18
Contact: goeco@goeco.org **Learn more:** www.goeco.org
Details: The mission of Yotvata Hai-Bar (wildlife preserve) Nature Reserve is to establish reproduction groups for populations of wild animals that are mentioned in the Bible, but have disappeared from the landscape; as well as for other endangered desert animals. The reserve

has three parts: a three acre penned-in open area where herds of herbivorous animals live in conditions similar to those in the wild; the Predators Centre where reptiles, small desert animals and large predators are on display; and the Desert Night Life Exhibition Hall, where night and day are reversed so that visitors can observe nocturnal animals during their active hours. Long-term volunteers are needed to join the Israel Nature & Parks Authority (NPA) staff with its ongoing conservation and animal care work at the Wildlife Preserve.

Ecotourism Development in Nazareth

Organization: GoEco
Location: Nazareth
Cost: $300 – $400 **Duration:** 4 to 8 weeks **Age:** 18
Contact: goeco@goeco.org **Learn more:** www.goeco.org
Details: The Fauzi Azar house is a beautiful 300 year old Ottoman building that was converted into an inn in 2005. The Fauzi Azar Inn promotes ecotourism in Nazareth and works with the community to contribute to its development in various areas. The aim is to introduce in Nazareth, which is the largest Arab city in Israel, a new model of tourism and thus "bridge the gap" between Arabs and Jews. Volunteers will be involved in hosting the guests and reception work. Volunteers will also be encouraged to help with other projects associated with the Inn such as the Jesus Trail. Volunteers can help teach a new language to the staff and members of the coal community.

Other organizations offering projects in Israel:

Leap Now: www.leapnow.org
Israeli Society for Autistic Children: alutfriends.org
LeadEarth: masa.leadearth.org
Safe Haven for Donkeys in the Holy Land:
   www.safehaven4donkeys.org
Service Civil International: www.sci-ivs.org
Silent Arrow Desert Lodge: www.silentarrow.co.il/index_eng.htm
Volunteers for Peace: www.vfp.org
World Horizons International: www.world-horizons.com

Japan

Tennis for Blind Children

Organization: Hands On Tokyo
Location: Ayase, northeast Tokyo
Cost: None **Duration:** 3+ hours **Age:** 15
Contact: info@handsontokyo.org
Learn more: www.handsontokyo.org
Special skills: Some tennis experience; it is not necessary to speak Japanese
Details: As a volunteer on this project, you will help teach visually-impaired children from elementary to high school age to play tennis. Tennis for the blind originated in Tokyo several years ago and new clubs for blind youth are forming each year. With the help of special balls equipped with bells inside, players are able to hear the ball's location and successfully hit to one another. Their determination to excel and their remarkable abilities are inspiring to all volunteers on this project. This is a wonderful way to gain a deeper understanding of Japanese life and culture while helping make a measurable difference in the lives of the young players.

Teach or Interpret Onboard a Chartered Passenger Ship

Organization: Peace Boat
Location: International Boat Trip – Based in Japan
Cost: Personal expenses **Duration:** 3 months **Age:** None
Contact: participate@peaceboat.gr.jp
Learn more: www.peaceboat.org
Special skills: Language teachers who have at least 18 months experience teaching English or Spanish, and interpreters who are highly skilled in Japanese and either English or Spanish.
Details: Peace Boat strives to build a culture of peace around the world through the development of a global grassroots network. Volunteer teachers are needed by our Global English and Español (GET) Program to hold classes onboard for primarily Japanese students who range in age and ability. Volunteer interpreters are needed to facilitate communication for guest speakers from various countries and for our optional programs in ports. The 600-900 participants on each voyage have the opportunity to learn about various issues firsthand while experiencing some of the most beautiful and interesting ports of the world. Music, art, dance, photography, language, and sports are also an integral part of each voyage, as participants have the opportunity to share their skills and interests with

one another and create nearly 100 free events and workshops onboard daily.

Other organizations offering projects in Japan:
Concordia: www.concordia-iye.org.uk
Japan Center for Conflict Prevention: www.jccp.gr.jp
Lattitude Global Volunteering Canada: www.lattitudecanada.org
UNA Exchange: www.unaexchange.org
United Planet: www.unitedplanet.org
Workaway: www.workaway.info
WWOOF Japan (organic farming): www.wwoofjapan.com

Jordan

Organizations offering projects in Jordan:
Canadian Alliance for Development Initiatives and Projects:
  www.cadip.org
International Internship and Volunteer Network:
  www.iivnetwork.com
Jordan Tourist Board North America: www.seejordan.org
True Travellers Society: www.truetravellers.org
United Planet: www.unitedplanet.org

Lao(s)

Organizations offering projects in Lao:
Fair Trek: www.trekking-in-laos.com
Global Visions International: www.gviusa.com
Globe Aware: www.globeaware.org
Lifewater International: www.lifewater.org
Open Mind Projects: www.openmindprojects.org
Travel to Teach: www.travel-to-teach.org
Volunteer in Asia: www.viaprograms.org
Volunteers for Economic Growth Alliance: www.vegaalliance.org

Malaysia

Animal Shelter and Sanctuary Volunteers

Organization: LASSie, Langkawi Animal Sanctuary and Shelter Foundation
Location: Langkawi
Cost: None **Duration:** Varied **Age:** 21 to 41
Contact: info@langkawilassie.org.my
Learn more: www.langkawilassie.org.my
Special skills: A love for animals and their welfare. Qualified veterinarians are very much appreciated.
Details: The Langkawi Animal Shelter and Sanctuary Foundation is set up to receive, rehabilitate and care for neglected, abused and needy animals. The shelter's policy is that for stray cats on the streets, they are trapped and sterilized, then returned to their normal habitat. In this way the Sanctuary hopes to control the stray population. An adoption centre is also operated. Animals put up for adoption are spayed, neutered, dewormed and vaccinated. Any wildlife brought to the shelter are treated and once healthy returned back to nature. Volunteer vets are needed, plus animal lovers to help out in the clinic and dog and cat shelters. Accommodation is provided with a simple breakfast and the main meal of the day at lunch. Volunteers are on their own for dinner.

Juara Turtle Project

Organization: Juara Turtle Project
Location: Kampung Juara, Tioman Island, Malaysia
Cost: $50 per night includes breakfast, lunch, and room/bath
Duration: Open, minimal suggested stay is 2 weeks
Age: 16 (under 18 need guardian permission)
Contact: contact@juaraturtleproject.com
Learn more: www.juaraturtleproject.com
Special skills: None needed, but physically fit and willing are a plus
Details: Juara Turtle Project is a privately run and operated sea turtle conservation project, working with a hatchery, personal food gardens and environmental awareness as their main tools. Located in a quiet area on Tioman Island, volunteers work on relocation of nests into the hatchery compound, immediate delivery of hatchings back to their native nesting beach, research on sea turtles and their nesting habits, and establishment of hatchery protocol. You may also work with visitors to educate them about environmental responsibility, help maintain the facility and the permanent agriculture (permaculture) system for self-sustainability, developing communication with local

people to teach aspects of environmental responsibility, etc. Not run by any organizations, government, or public grants; just a few folks on the beach doing what they can. Good opportunity for gap year students, biology graduates looking for experience, anyone who likes to live by the jungle and ocean or anyone looking to pitch in. Join them and help.

Marine Conservation Expedition, Malaysia

Organization: Blue Ventures
Location: The coral reefs and interior forest of Tioman Island, Malaysia
Cost: $3,600 – $4,000 (with food, accommodation, training and diving)
Duration: 6 weeks (3 to 30 week options available) **Age:** 18
Contact: info@blueventures.org **Learn more:** www.blueventures.org
Special skills: None, full training provided
Details: Blue Ventures is an award-winning marine conservation organization dedicated to conservation, education and sustainable development in tropical coastal communities. Blue Ventures Malaysia's primary aim is to contribute to the conservation of Malaysia's valuable ecological resources. Volunteers carry out year round monitoring of the health of the marine environment of Tioman Island though underwater coral reef surveys as well as hands on reef and beach clean ups. Blue Ventures research volunteers also run a children's environmental education programme and contribute to island-wide events promoting conservation to a variety of stakeholders. With the dramatic backdrop of the forested peaks of the island, volunteers stay in comfortable beach-side chalets overlooking the sparkling waters of the 'coral triangle'.
 ‍ **Editor's note:** Blue Ventures was named as one of three "Highly Recommended" companies in the 'Best Volunteering Organization' category of the Virgin Holidays Responsible Tourism Award 2009.

Other organizations offering projects in Malaysia:

Adventure Heart: www.adventureheart.com
Ecoteer: www.ecoteer.com
Global Visions International: www.gviusa.com
i-to-i: www.i-to-i.com
Lattitude Global Volunteering Canada: www.lattitudecanada.org
Raleigh: www.raleighinternational.org

Maldives

Organization offering projects in the Maldives:

Maldives Whale Shark Research Programme:
  www.scubadivemaldives.com

Mongolia

Media TV Project

Organization: "New Choice" Mongolian Volunteer Organization
Location: Ulaanbaatar
Cost: $495 per month   **Duration:** 2 to 8 weeks   **Age:** 17
Contact: info@volunteer.org.mn, +976 11 314577
Learn more: www.volunteer.org.mn
Special skills: Journalist or media student
Details: "Education TV" is Mongolia's new television channel. The main aim is to produce and present entertainment, sport & youth educational programmes for the Mongolian people. Demand for English language improvement and an exchange of skills is high. New Choice is also interested in a person's skills as a producer, operator, correspondent, illustrator or drawer who can help to create scenes and provide new ideas for these programs. The programmers are eager to add a Western flavor in a variety of ways, from set designs to proper English pronunciations. You might shoot and edit videos and documentaries or work on the floor during newscasts. Some of these shows target at-risk youth, warning them about the dangers of drug and alcohol abuse. This project has been producing sport, live interview and entertainment shows for several years. You'll take a very hands-on role: assisting the director with film production, taking part in editing work, and teaching some English to other staff members. New Choice is a 100% Mongolian NGO and NPO.

Health Project at Children's Hospital

Organization: "New Choice" Mongolian Volunteer Organization
Location: Bayangol district, Ulaanbaatar
Cost: $495 per month   **Duration:** 2 weeks to 3 months   **Age:** 17
Contact: info@volunteer.org.mn, +976 11 314577
Learn more: www.volunteer.org.mn
Special skills: Doctor or Medical student very much in demand

Details: Volunteers will work at The Maternal and Child Medical Research Centre of Mongolia, which was established in 1930 as a Children's Hospital. In 1987, it expanded in all aspects as a Research and Training Centre and was given the name Maternal and Child Medical Research Centre. MCMRC has two main functions: provide specialized medical care for mothers and children and organize post graduate medical training for doctors and nurses to carry out basic research on reproductive, genetics and children's diseases. The MCMRC has three main hospitals with 600 nurses. Volunteers main work is to: 1) Help to take care of children who has mental disabilities or illness, heart deceases and cancer 2) Doctor's assistant 3) Teach informal English language 4) Create a joyful time

Teaching English in Ulaanbaatar

Organization: "New Choice" Mongolian Volunteer Organization
Location: Ulaanbaatar
Cost: $495 per month   **Duration:** 2 weeks to 12 weeks   **Age:** 17
Contact: info@volunteer.org.mn, +976 11 314577
Learn more: www.volunteer.org.mn
Details: Volunteers will work at secondary school in Ulaanbaatar. The school is starting to teach foreign languages with cheerful games and toys. At the same time the pupils of the school will be studying English as a new language. They need the English environment and native speakers. Volunteers will teach English to elementary, pre intermediate, intermediate and upper intermediate students, making an effort to improve the quality of the training by consulting with the teachers and helping to organize the English language levels.

Orphan Children's Summer Camp

Organization: "New Choice" Mongolian Volunteer Organization
Location: Khandgait
Cost: $495 per month   **Duration:** 2 to 10 weeks, every June, July and August   **Age:** 17
Contact: info@volunteer.org.mn, +976 11 314577
Learn more: www.volunteer.org.mn
Details: Children's Orphanage Camp is located in Khandgait a 30 minute drive from Ulaanbaatar, the capital of Mongolia. Orphan children (around 120-150 orphans) come from all over Mongolia for the three month summer camp (June, July and August). The Orphanage Camp provides social, educational, sport and opportunities to the orphaned children during their summer holidays. Volunteers main work is to teach English in the mornings and join in leisure activities in the afternoons and evenings. Also volunteers will join in sports and cultural activities including hiking, singing, etc.

245

Orphanage Volunteer Help

Organization: "New Choice" Mongolian Volunteer Organization
Location: Ulaanbaatar
Cost: $495 per month   **Duration:** 2 to 8 weeks   **Age:** 17
Contact: info@volunteer.org.mn, +976 11 314577
Learn more: www.volunteer.org.mn

Details: This is the only state orphanage for
children ages 6-17 in the whole of Mongolia. The
kids lives at the orphanage all day. The aim is to
provide both a home and education for the
children. When possible the orphanage also tries
to find the natural parents of the children. The
volunteers' main work is to help kids do
homework, wash clothes (daily work), play with
the children, organize activities (song, dance and music) and to teach
English to the children.

Przewalski Wild Horse Repatriation

Organization: Muir's Tours (Nepal Kingdom Foundation)
Location: Hustai Nuruu Steppe Reserve
Cost: $240 registration fee + $86 per day (discount for stays of 21+
days)
Duration: 10 days to 6 months   **Age:** 18
Contact: mo@nkf-mt.org.uk   **Learn more:** www.nkf-mt.org.uk
Special skills: Capable of walking and horseback riding regularly over
long distances, speak fluent English, have the ability to remain quiet
and to sleep in a tent. Most Mongolian meals are non vegetarian.
Details: Volunteers ensure the continued success of the horse
breeding and repatriation to the wild, along with the protection of the
biological diversity of the Mongolian steppe. Several harems of horses
were released into the reserve after being kept under semi wild
conditions. The team rides or hikes over the steppe to monitor the
horses and make sure they are adjusting to their new environment and
to gain a better insight into their behavior. You need to be able to work
without assistance in tracking down the harems by hiking, trekking, or
horse-back riding and compile data on their whereabouts and behavior.
You will also need to help encourage conservation awareness in the
local communities. The majority of the field work is done on foot,
hiking over the steppe. Following the horses on horseback is done for
about 2 hours two or three times a week. You will be asked to work for
about 6 hours a day, the rest of the day is free time. All weekend and
Wednesdays are free time.

Other organizations offering projects in Mongolia:
Earthwatch Institute: www.earthwatch.org
Projects Abroad: www.projects-abroad.org
Service Civil International: www.sci-ivs.org

Myanmar

Organizations offering projects in Myanmar:
Action Against Hunger: www.actionagainsthunger.org
Habitat for Humanity: www.habitat.org
Kids Alive International: www.kidsalive.org
Spain Exchange (student programs in Spain and abroad)
  www.spainexchange.com
Volunteer in Asia (long-term): www.viaprograms.org

Nepal

Bringing Primary Healthcare in the 'Hidden Himalayas'
Organization: The Nepal Trust
Location: Humla District, Nepal
Cost: Depends on time and availability for tailor-made package

Duration: 1+ month **Age:** 18
Contact: admin@nepaltrust.org, Tel: 0131 467 4020
Learn more: www.nepaltrust.org
Special skills: Any person with medical qualifications (e.g. GP, Doctor, Nurse, Medical Student) is welcome and needed!

Details: For the last 15 years The Nepal Trust has been working in Humla District, one of Nepal's most remote and impoverished areas to bring basic healthcare to those in need. The Nepal Trust has been working continuously during this period, despite the disruptions caused by the Maoist conflict. Being one of our volunteers, your main aim is to help our organization and local health workers to reinstate and develop primary healthcare provision, with a main focus on maternal and child health, family planning, control of communicable diseases, poverty reduction and improved nutrition. Your expertise will greatly increase the knowledge of our local health workers (who you

247

will assist in a local Himalayan village), who on their turn can pass their knowledge on within their communities.

Compassion Orphanage

Organization: Kids Worldwide
Location: Phutung, near Kathmandu
Cost: $30 booking, $300 per month and $100 administrative fee upon arrival. A discount will be offered to longer term volunteers.
Duration: 1 month or more **Age:** 18, kids over 10 welcome with parent
Contact: compassion@kidsworldwide.org
Learn more: asia.kidsworldwide.org/nepalcompassion.htm
Details: Contribute you time and skills offering education and shelter to orphans, poor, lower caste and disadvantaged children. Many of the children's backgrounds are full of pain and sorrow. Compassion Nepal helps to educate them and provides them food and accommodations. They will look after the children until they finish their university. Volunteers can teach two hours every morning and two hours in the evening. You can also help by teaching the children different games, songs in English, basic education, drawing and other activities. You can also help with writing newsletters, fundraising and administrative work.

Nandumaya Self-Sustaining Orphan Home

Organization: Kids Worldwide
Location: Phutung, 9 km from the city of Kathmandu.
Cost: $30 booking fee, $250 under 1 month, $350 1 month, $100 for subsequent months
Duration: 1 week to 3 months **Age:** 18
Contact: nandumaya@kidsworldwide.org
Learn more: asia.kidsworldwide.org
Special skills: Those staying in the home should be highly motivated to work with the children. You must present a good, moral character and respect the local culture.
Details: Nandumaya is a self-sustaining model orphanage that was established 5 years ago. It is situated in a village and has a vegetable garden, milking buffalo, 3 goats, honey bees, 200 hundred female chickens that give 160 eggs every day, and mushroom cultivation. There are around 21 children, from 2 years up to 10 years old. It is very important that volunteers rise by 7:30 in the morning. The children view them as teachers and feel strange if the volunteers sleep in while they must get up and go to school. You should plan on helping out at the children's local school until 3:30 pm. In the evening from 6:00 pm until 7:30 pm volunteers also assist

with English, math and/or moral education programs.

Remote Health Post Work in Nepal

Organization: International Volunteer HQ
Location: Rural placements available in Pokhara and Chitwan
Cost: $220 for 1 week to $1,020 for 5 months, includes food and accommodation
Duration: 1 week to 5 months **Age:** 18
Contact: volunteer@volunteerhq.org
Learn more: www.volunteerhq.org
Special skills: Volunteers need to be in healthcare training or qualified in a relevant medical field.
Details: Remote health clinics in Nepal struggle to attract qualified doctors and medically trained personnel let alone sufficient resources such as equipment and medicine. Volunteers working at village health clinics will assist local health staff in performing day to day tasks such as dressing wounds, administering vaccinations, drawing blood, screening and organizing patients, collecting medicines and generally helping in whatever capacity they are required. There is also the need to conduct seminars to motivate and educate local villagers on health initiatives.

Teaching English in Kathmandu, Pokhara and Chitwan

Organization: International Volunteer HQ
Location: Urban and Rural placements in Kathmandu, Pokhara and Chitwan
Cost: $220 for 1 week to $1,020 for 5 months, includes food and accommodations
Duration: 1 week to 5 months **Age:** 18
Contact: volunteer@volunteerhq.org
Learn more: www.volunteerhq.org
Details: More than 80% of children from Nepal's villages and cities are unable to access a good educational system. This is due to a lack of financial and physical resources as well as the remote mountain geography of Nepal. Volunteers participating in the Nepal Premier Teaching English program will teach English at Nepali public or private schools, depending on the need for volunteers at the time. Volunteers can also assist with creating low cost teaching materials for the school and help organize health checkups for students. Teaching English volunteers are more than welcome to participate in other school activities such as sports or sanitation programs while they work at the school. Many volunteers teach English in the mornings before arranging sports, drama and songs in the afternoon.

Nepal English Teaching Project

Organization: Global Volunteer Network
Location: Kathmandu Valley
Cost: $867+ **Duration:** 6 weeks to 5 months **Age:** 18
Contact: info@volunteer.org.nz **Learn more:**
www.volunteer.org.nz
Details: Volunteers who wish to teach in Nepal will be teaching in an adult literacy school. The school is a locally run charity, a partner organization in Nepal that GVN works with. The class is comprised of Nepalese, Tibetan refugees and monks. To teach English at a Nepali school you don't need any formal teaching qualifications. You will however, need a good command of written and spoken English, plenty of initiative, determination, motivation and a lot of patience. A minimum 6 week commitment is required.

Nepal Children's Home Project

Organization: Global Volunteer Network
Location: Kathmandu Valley
Cost: $867 for 2 weeks **Duration:** 2 weeks to 5 months
Age: 18 years old or over
Contact: info@volunteer.org.nz
Learn more: www.volunteer.org.nz

 **Details:** In this program volunteers will be placed in a Children's Home located within a one and a half hour bus ride from the heart of Kathmandu. Volunteers stay with a local Nepali family. Your role at the Children's Home is to be a big brother or sister to the children. Other tasks may include helping with medical visits, cleaning, paper recycling, gardening, teaching the house mothers how to properly clean, doing repairs, mending clothing, after school activities and perhaps preparing meals. Once the children return from school, your role will be to assist and encourage them with their homework as well as play with them.

Nepal Health Education Project

Organization: Global Volunteer Network
Location: Kathmandu Valley
Cost: $867 for 2 weeks **Duration:** 2 weeks to 5 months **Age:** 18
Contact: info@volunteer.org.nz **Learn more:**
www.volunteer.org.nz
Special skills: For this program GVN prefers medical students or advanced degree holders

Details: The main focus of the health education program is prevention of health complications by way of regular basic health checks and teaching children about health, personal hygiene and sanitation. All health volunteers will be based in a children's home and assist the health team in leading health fun days in schools and children's homes, maintaining health records and dealing with health complications as they arise. Depending on experience/qualifications, there are various roles health volunteers can undertake, however this is not a medical program and you should not expect to be performing any medical procedures. Volunteers are required to submit their resume/CV when making an application for this program.

Community Maintenance Projects

Organization: Global Volunteer Network
Location: Kathmandu Valley
Cost: $867 for 2 weeks   **Duration:** 2 weeks to 5 months   **Age:** 18
Contact: info@volunteer.org.nz   **Learn more:** www.volunteer.org.nz
Details: This is an opportunity to help in a wide range of practical village-based projects. Projects are usually partly funded by the communities and partly by GVN's partner organizations and/or volunteer contributions. You will work with other volunteers in small groups, usually with minimal supervision. Often you'll also work alongside villagers, learning about traditional methods of building and working. Examples of projects include school repair and decoration; toilet building; drinking water projects; road drainage projects; recycling projects, etc. You can also take more of an environmental education focus by informing children about appropriate waste disposal, recycling, composting and creating vegetable and flower gardens in the children's homes.

Teaching English in Monasteries

Organization: uVolunteer
Location: Kathmandu, Chitwan or Pokhara
Cost: $1,000 for the first 4 weeks; $50 each additional week
Duration: 4+ weeks **Age:** 18
Contact: info@uvolunter.org **Learn more:** www.uvolunteer.org
Special skills: Intermediate English
Details: While volunteering in Nepal, you will be teaching English to people in monastery schools, so they can explore more scriptures written in English and circulate Buddhist teaching practices to the whole world. Class sizes will typically be from 15 to 40 students. Volunteers will create activities, games, and projects to teach and

promote increased vocabulary to the students and will also be responsible for planning their own lessons.

Provide Health Care and Education

Organization: uVolunteer
Special Skills: Intermediate English and Medical Background
Location: Kathmandu, Chitwan or Pokhara in Nepal
Cost: $1,000 for the first 4 weeks; add $50 for each additional week
Duration: 4+ weeks **Age:** 18
Contact: info@uvolunteer.org **Learn more:** www.uvolunteer.org
Details: The goal of this project is to provide community development assistance to the communities of Kathmandu Valley. Volunteers will assist in educating the local communities on the importance of appropriate health care and sanitation habits because the people of Nepal are unaware of these issues. The main focus preventative measures and guidance in health care and sanitation to apply a proactive method rather than having to react to the result of poor health practices.

Orphanages in Nepal

Organization: Experiential Learning International
Location: Kathmandu
Cost: Starting at $515 **Duration:** 2+ weeks **Age:**18+
Contact: info@eliabroad.org **Learn more:** www.eliabroad.org
Details: Thousands of Nepali children are orphans, and the numbers have been rising in recent years. ELI has been working closely with a few orphanages in the Kathmandu Valley. ELI orphanage volunteers work as activity coordinators: playing with the children, coordinating games, teaching an English, math or art class and giving these children some much needed attention. The children range in age from toddlers to teenagers. This is a great placement for an independent, upbeat volunteer.

Unique Eco Tourism Project in South Nepal

Organization: OpenmindProjects
Location: Chitwan, South Nepal
Cost: $1,200 per month
Duration: 1+ month **Age:** 18
Contact: info@openmindprojects.org
Learn more: www.openmindprojects.org
Special skills: An understanding and interest in ecotourism and environmental/wildlife protection. The abilities to go trekking, on field trips and live with local village people.

Details: Volunteer for an ecotourism project near the famous Chitwan National Park in Nepal working in a community-based sustainable ecotourism and wildlife conservation. The project focuses on preparing the villagers for overseas ecotourists and helping the local school children to learn English. You go trekking with local people and possibly stay overnight in a jungle watch tower with a chance to see wild rhinos and even tigers.

Community Development and Everest Trek

Organization: Greenforce
Location: Nepal
Cost: $3,300+ **Duration:** 5+ weeks **Age:** 17
Contact: info@greenforce.org **Learn more:** www.greenforce.org
Details: Starting in Kathmandu, the Himalayan capital of Nepal, volunteers spend their first week acclimatizing, enjoying cultural visits around the city and attending Nepali classes. You then travel into one of the rural valleys where volunteers work on a rural development project, before heading to the Chitwan National Park, to take an elephant back safari to look for the endangered Bengal Tiger. The final two weeks of the trip is a trek to Everest Base Camp – a once in a lifetime opportunity!

Chairro Gompa (Monastery) Restoration Project

Organization: Cultural Restoration Tourism Project (CRTP)
Location: Nepal
Cost: $1,495 - $2,495 **Duration:** 6 to 12 days **Age:** Any
Contact: info@crtp.net **Learn more:** www.crtp.net
Special Skills: No special skills required, everyone is welcome
Details: This unusual project offers a great opportunity to help Nepali people preserve an important part of their cultural heritage and daily life. The Chairro Gompa (Gompa is the Tibetan word for 'Buddhist monastery') was built in the 1600s and was once the religious center of the Takhali people of the Mustang region. When the Chinese government closed the border to Tibet, the salt traders of the region were forced to relocate their families and the villages along the trade route met with economic hardship. The Chairro Gompa fell into poverty and disrepair. For years the people of the area still came to the monastery to perform their religious practices, but the dwindling population found it difficult to support and maintain it. The last of the resident monks left Chairro in the 1990s and the fate of the gompa was left to the elements and to a handful of local Nepali. Mmake a difference and preserve history.

Other organizations offering projects in Nepal:

Aadharbhut Prasuti Sewa Kendra (Basic Maternity Service Centre):
  www.apskendra.org.np
Base Camp International Centers: www.basecampcenters.com
Friends of Maiti Nepal (combating sex traffic):
  www.friendsofmaitinepal.org
Global Visions International: www.gviusa.com or www.gvi.co.uk
Insight Nepal: www.insightnepal.org.np
Institute for Cultural Ecology (Buddhist Monastery, agriculture and
  orphanage internships): www.cultural-ecology.com
The Mountain Fund: www.mountainfund.org
People and Places (Winner 'Best Volunteering Organization' category
  of Virgin Holidays Responsible Tourism Award 2009):
  travel-peopleandplaces.co.uk
Volunteer Nepal: www.volnepal.np.org
Volunteering Solutions: www.volunteeringsolutions.com
Volunteers Initiative Nepal: www.volunteeringnepal.org
Work and Volunteering Abroad: www.workandvolunteer.com
World Endeavors: www.worldendeavors.com

Palestinian Territories

Permaculture in Palestine

Organization: Bustan Qaraaqa
Location: Wadi Hanna Saad, a green valley in the town of Beit
Sahour, close to the city of Bethlehem in the West Bank of the Occupied
Palestinian Territories.
Cost: $20 per day or $400 per month for longer stays including all
food
Duration: Open –from a few days to a few months or even a year
Age: 18, unless accompanied by an adult
Contact: info@bustanqaraaqa.org
Learn more: www.bustanqaraaqa.org
Details: Bustan Qaraaqa is an initiative to propagate a grassroots
environmental movement in the Palestinian Territories to help address
the pressing humanitarian and environmental crises in the area. Bustan
Qaraaqa is establishing a permaculture centre for demonstration of and
experimentation with cheap and easy techniques for sustainable living
and food production. In addition, they are working with partners in the
local community to help raise environmental consciousness and
implement projects that make a real difference to peoples'
lives. Volunteers will join a lively, international team working both at

the Bustan Qaraaqa farm and in the local community and learning about permaculture and the situation in Palestine

Trek Program
Organization: Paidia International Development
Location: Beit Sahour, West Bank
Cost: $2,850 for 3 months, $4,725 for 6 months, $8,675 for 12 months; includes all living expenses.
Duration: 3 to 12 months   **Age:** 19, or one year of university
Contact: volunteers@paidia.org   **Learn more:** www.pidev.org
Details: Visit Palestine and spend your time making a difference in people's lives! Paidia's Trek Program offers participants the unique opportunity to invest in the lives of a needy community while living in and exploring one of the most fascinating regions of the world. Paidia uses experiential learning and adventure recreation to transform communities by transforming individuals within the community. Participants will live together in dorm style housing in an Arab neighborhood. Paidia's Trek Program offers many opportunities and ways to get involved in the local community, both inside and outside of work hours. Year-round opportunities are available in several different areas, including media projects, development, and program facilitators.

Other organizations offering projects in the Palestinian Territories:
American Near East Refugee Aid: www.anera.org
Karama Organization for Women and Children Development:
  www.karama.org/eng
Palestine Summer Encounters (list of organizations offering projects)
  www.palestinesummer.org/volunteer
Project Hope: www.projecthope.ps
Tent of Nations: www.tentofnations.org
Volunteers for Peace: www.vfp.org

Philippines

Pag-Amoma Childrens Place
Organization: Kids Worldwide
Location: The fruit and orchid city of the south - Davao, Philippines

Cost: 1st month $250, succeeding months $25, includes accommodation, but does not include meals; volunteers stay on site to help with the care of the children.
Duration: 2+ weeks, 1+ month **Age:** 20
Contact: pagamoma@kidsworldwide.org
Learn more: asia.kidsworldwide.org
Special skills: Female only volunteers please. A warm and loving personality, ready to care for toddlers and young children
Details: Pag-Amoma Children's Place provides a nurturing home for "lumad" (indigenous) children who are orphaned, abandoned, neglected or victims of a violent home. They have around 20 children in their care. Children's Place is unique compared to other orphanages in Davao because they are the only ones who are caring for indigenous children. All of the children come from different tribes living in the mountains of Marilog, a 27-30 km hike from the city. The Childrens Place was opened 2 years ago and is one of several projects run by Pag-Amoma to help the indigenous people of the region.

Field of Dreams

Organization: Kids Worldwide
Location: Tugbok, on the outskirts of Davao
Cost: Less than a month $250, 1st month $280, succeeding months $30 Includes accommodations, but not meals
Duration: 2 week minimum, 1+ month preferred
Age: 18+, or kids over 10 welcome with parent
Contact: field@kidsworldwide.org
Learn more: asia.kidsworldwide.org
Special skills: Willingness to participate and learn in all the activities.
Details: Field of Dreams is the newest orphanage in Davao. They currently look after 27 boys ranging in age from 3 - 18 years. They cater exclusively to boys, as there is already a girls home in Tugbok, run by Polish nuns. Along with the children's home, their hope is to provide comprehensive external recreational facilities to enrich the children's lives. Volunteers can assist with some of the following activities: website design, fundraising, tutorials, gardening and farm management. Skills enhancement: dancing, drawing, voice lessons, musical instruments, karate etc. Assist in the kitchen, laundry and help the house mother/father.

City Nutrition Office in the Philippines

Organization: Experiential Learning International
Location: Tacloban City
Cost: Starting at $795 **Duration:** 4+ weeks **Age:** 18
Contact: info@eliabroad.org **Learn more:** www.eliabroad.org
Special skills: Knowledge of nutrition.

Details: This local government office aims to reduce the number of malnourished children in Tacloban City. The office monitors malnourished children throughout the city. Volunteers can work directly with neighborhood nutrition committees directly and organize educational programs for parents, implement community and school vegetable gardens, and conduct weight surveys of children in different areas.

Street Children in Tacloban City

Organization: Experiential Learning International
Location: Tacloban City
Cost: Starting at $695 **Duration:** 2+ weeks **Age:** 18
Contact: info@eliabroad.org **Learn more:** www.eliabroad.org
Details: Neglected, abandoned or run-away children on the streets in Tacloban City, Philippines live a life that is often without love, warmth, safety, protection and parental care. Most of the children who have settled on the streets have families of their own, but turn to the streets for food. Glue-sniffing, known as "rugby", is a common addiction among the street children who turn to this drug to suppress their hunger pains. Volunteers help to change this reality through their involvement in after-school programs that focus on providing the children basic daily care. Volunteers work directly with a social worker from the Department of Social Welfare and may help to administer programs such as English language training, computer training and medical care.

Philippines Childcare Project

Organization: Global Volunteer Network
Location: Various locations in the laid back archipelagic province of Romblon-one of the poorest provinces in Philippines.
Cost: $732 for 2 weeks **Duration:** 2 weeks to 6 months **Age:** 18
Contact: info@volunteer.org.nz **Learn more:** www.volunteer.org.nz
Details: Volunteers will have the chance to work in daycare centers with children ages 3 to 5 for two to four hours a day. You will work alongside the staff at the centers to help with classroom teaching, childcare and the daily running of the daycare. Volunteers will teach the alphabet and basic concepts like colors, shapes, sizes, days of the week. Volunteers are also encouraged to organize subjects of interest such as art and crafts, dance, music, sports or games. This volunteer program is not available during April and May.

Philippines Program Teaching Project

Organization: Global Volunteer Network
Location: Various locations in laid back archipelagic province of Romblon-one of the poorest provinces in Philippines or short-term volunteers will be placed around the capital city of Manila.
Cost: $732 for 2 weeks **Duration:** 2 weeks to 6 months **Age:** 18
Contact: info@volunteer.org.nz **Learn more:** www.volunteer.org.nz
Details: Volunteers on the program teach elementary and high school students in public schools for two to four hours a day. Subjects taught include English, math, science, health and basic computer skills (only in schools where computers are available). Volunteers may teach in a classroom on their own but there will be a local teacher available to assist. This volunteer program is not available during April and May.

Philippines Health Project

Organization: Global Volunteer Network
Location: Various locations in the laid back archipelagic province of Romblon-one of the poorest provinces in Philippines, or short-term volunteers will be placed around the capital city of Manila.
Cost: $732 for 2 weeks **Duration:** 2 weeks to 6 months **Age:** 18
Contact: info@volunteer.org.nz **Learn more:** www.volunteer.org.nz
Details: Health volunteers on this project are asked to live and immerse themselves in the communities where they will conduct

medical missions, especially in the rural placements. This is done to give the volunteers a more holistic appreciation of the people they wish to help, their economic activities, culture, values, issues and struggles. At some point in your programs, you will also be taken to both public and private hospitals to see the problems of the health sector in the Philippines.

School Building and Library Maintenance Project

Organization: Global Volunteer Network
Location: Various locations in the laid back archipelagic province of Romblon-one of the poorest provinces in Philippines or short term volunteers will be placed in and around the capital city of Manila.
Cost: $732 for 2 weeks **Duration:** 2 weeks to 6 months **Age:** 18
Contact: info@volunteer.org.nz **Learn more:** www.volunteer.org.nz
Details: Volunteers on the program will be doing the manual tasks of building. Your time will be spent repairing school buildings, painting roofs, walls, chalkboards, desks, teaching aids and other equipment.

You may help in the installation of water pumps or may also help in the setting up of libraries. Volunteers can start by asking for donations of old books from families, friends, towns, parishes and former schools. You can encourage the use of books to the students through class visitations and regular storytelling sessions. The objective is to introduce to public school students the joys of using a library, which most do not experience until college, if at all.

Philippines Environment Project

Organization: Global Volunteer Network
Location: Various locations in the laid back archipelagic province of Romblon-one of the poorest provinces in Philippines or short-term volunteers will be placed in and around the capital city of Manila.
Cost: $732 for 2 weeks **Duration:** 2 weeks to 6 months **Age:** 18
Contact: info@volunteer.org.nz **Learn more:** www.volunteer.org.nz
Details: The Philippines is one of the world's biodiversity hot-spots. GVN's Marine Sanctuary Project has been set up by their partner in San Agustin (Romblon). The town's main economic activity is fishing but its traditional fishing grounds already show signs of fish stock depletion due to destructive fishing practices, such as the use of fine nets and dynamite fishing. This is now being countered by the establishment of a marine sanctuary between the villages of Carmen and Long Beach. First, volunteers help operate a nursery for the propagation of mangrove seedlings. Second, they help reforest mangrove sites by planting. Third, they help in implementing the marine sanctuary project with regular patrols, beach cleanups and education on the needs and benefits of the project.

Southern Leyte Coral Reef Conservation Project

Organization: Coral Cay Conservation
Location: Southern Leyte
Cost: $1,050+; Accommodation, food, dive and science training are all included in the price **Duration:** 2 to 20 weeks
Contact: info@coralcay.org **Learn more:** www.coralcay.org
Special skills: Enthusiasm and love for adventure!
Details: Join Coral Cay Conservation's team and help survey and contribute towards preserving some of the least disturbed and least researched habitats in the Philippines -  the coral reefs of Southern Leyte. You will be taught how to dive, survey the reefs, and work with the local community to teach them how to best conserve what is theirs and go on to use their reefs sustainably. Since 2002 this highly successful project has

already helped establish several marine reserves within the bay. This is a unique opportunity to spend from 2-20 weeks living in this idyllic setting right on waters that are visited by whale sharks and home to some of the best diving in the Philippines.

✂ **Editor's note:** Coral Cay is one of three organizations rated as highly recommended under the 'Best Volunteering Organization' category of the Virgin Holidays Responsible Tourism Award 2009

Medical Health Projects

Organization: Kaya Responsible Travel
Location: The bustling Leyte capital of Tacloban
Cost: $1,270+   **Duration:** 2 to 26 weeks   **Age:** 18-80
Contact: info@kayavolunteer.com
Learn more: www.KayaVolunteer.com
Special skills: Study or experience in specific medical, healthcare, social work and welfare fields will be required and your skills matched to the placement
Details: Kaya projects work with community health clinics, social and welfare departments and nutritional offices within the city to support the struggling, understaffed health services offered to the poorest of the community. Apply your specific field of knowledge to an environment that can really make use of your skills, in a country where poverty and malnutrition is high and resources are minimal.

Street Children Project

Organization: Kaya Responsible Travel
Location: The bustling Leyte capital of Tacloban
Cost: $1,270+   **Duration:** 2 to 26 weeks   **Age:** 18-80
Contact: info@kayavolunteer.com
Learn more: www.KayaVolunteer.com
Special skills: Study or experience in specific medical, healthcare, social work and welfare fields will be required and your skills matched to the placement
Details: In the Philippines, more than 250,000 children live on the streets. Most of these survive by begging and scavenging in dumpsites for plastic bottles to recycle for money. This project aims to provide safe housing, healthy food, educational support and – with volunteers' help - the love, trust and care these children need to improve their chances in life. The social welfare department has built a facility to house, feed and educate the children, but the ratio of staff to street children does not meet the demand. Many of the children do not get the attention and guidance that they need, and so they return to the streets. Your role will involve working alongside staff to assist them in improving projects, IT skills and English.

Women's Assistance

Organization: World Endeavors
Location: Tacloban City
Cost: $1,237+ **Duration:** 2 to 12 weeks   **Age:** 18
Contact: inquiry@worldendeavors.com
Learn more: www.worldendeavors.com
Details: Make a difference in the lives of disadvantaged women in the Philippines. Volunteers work at a center that provides rehabilitation and support for women and teenage girls who have been victims of exploitation and abuse. A recent project included therapy through artwork; each volunteer is encouraged to contribute his/her unique skills. One of the main goals of the center is to reintegrate the women into the workforce and community by providing skills training. Participants have the opportunity to stay with a local host family who provides two meals a day and help to introduce the volunteer to Filipino culture.

Philippines Health Care in Tacloban City

Organization: World Endeavors
Location: Tacloban City
Cost: $1,237+ **Duration:** 2 to 12 weeks   **Age:** 18
Contact: inquiry@worldendeavors.com
Learn more: www.worldendeavors.com
Special skills: Individuals currently studying or completed a degree in a healthcare-related field
Details: Shadow a medical professional and observe medical practices in the Philippines. Many small town clinics are understaffed, some with only one doctor. Volunteers will assist doctors and interact with patients, while learning about the rural health care system. Participants stay with a local host family who provides two meals a day.

Deaf Education

Organization: World Endeavors
Special skills: Individuals with sign language skills are needed to help tutor students. Participants with little to no signing abilities are also needed to help support the program.
Location: Tacloban City
Cost: $1,237+ **Duration:** 2 to 12 weeks   **Age:** 18
Contact: inquiry@worldendeavors.com
Learn more: www.worldendeavors.com
Details: Deaf students in the Philippines do not have the same opportunities as hearing students. Volunteers help to bridge that gap by providing tutoring at a local school, as well as by teaching computer

261

skills. Participants live with a local host family in the friendly, welcoming country and truly immerse themselves in the local culture.

Orphanage Assistance in the Philippines

Organization: World Endeavors
Location: Tacloban City
Cost: $1,237+ **Duration:** 2 to 12 weeks **Age:** 18
Contact: inquiry@worldendeavors.com
Learn more: www.worldendeavors.com
Details: Empower a child in the Philippines. Through education and compassion, volunteers show children that there is more to life than poverty and exploitation. Volunteers provide basic daily care and educational programs for the orphans. Participants live and eat two meals a day with a local host family, giving them an opportunity to truly connect with their host community.

Street Children Assistance

Organization: World Endeavors
Location: Tacloban City
Cost: $1,237+ **Duration:** 2 to 12 weeks **Age:** 18
Contact: inquiry@worldendeavors.com
Learn more: www.worldendeavors.com
Details: Make a difference in the lives of local Filipino street children. Participants assist with afterschool programs that focus on providing the children with basic daily care, homework assistance, English tutoring, and computer training. Volunteers live with a local host family and spend their free time exploring this beautiful and friendly country.

Other organizations offering projects in the Philippines:

Center for Volunteerism in the Philippines:
  www.volunteerphilippines.com
Global Crossroads: www.globalcrossroad.com
Hands On Manila: www.handsonmanila.org.ph
i-to-i: www.i-to-i.com
International Surgical Missions: ismissions.com
Meaningful Volunteer: www.meaningfulvolunteer.org
Medical Teams International: www.medicalteams.org
Thresher Shark Research and Conservation Project:
  web.mac.com/spoliver/Site/expeditions.html
Volunteer for the Visayans: www.visayans.org
Volunteering Solutions: www.volunteeringsolutions.com

Singapore

Wild Animal Rescue Project

Organization: Animal Concerns Research and Education Society
Cost: $25 per day   **Project Duration:** 1+ weeks   **Age:** 18
Contact: volunteer@acres.org.sg   **Learn more:** www.acres.org.sg
Details: This is your chance to get involved with people passionate about animal rescue. Volunteers are needed to assist with the running of ACRES, i.e. preparing food, cleaning enclosures, feeding and observing rescued wild animals, and general upkeep of the centre (gardening etc.) Volunteers may also assist with giving guided tours and helping to deliver educational programmes to school groups. In addition, ACRES needs help with fundraising, delivering education programmes, manning public road shows, general office duties and organizing and running events.

Other organizations offering projects in Singapore:

International YMCA (Go Global): www.internationalymca.org
Take Me to Volunteer Travel: takemetovolunteertravel.com

South Korea

Angels' Haven Care for Developmentally Disabled

Organization: Inter Cultural Youth Exchange (ICYE)
Location: South Korea
Cost: $6,300 for 6 months or $7,500 for 12 months; dormitory accommodation
Duration: 6 or 12 months   **Age:** 18-30
Contact: international@icye.co.uk   **Learn more:** www.icye.org.uk
Special skills: Must be female and willing to learn the Korean language
Details: The Angels' Haven works through education and training to help people with developmental disabilities to develop and unfold their potential, to become less dependent on others and to participate as much as possible in every aspect of community life. The volunteer on this project works in the kindergarten, organizing play activities for the children and helping with mealtimes. The role also involves providing general care for the disabled.

Other organizations offering projects in South Korea:

Canadian Alliance for Development Initiatives and Projects:
  www.cadip.org
Citizen Development Corps: www.cdc.org
Concordia: www.concordia-iye.org.uk
International YMCA (Go Global): www.internationalymca.org
Service Civil International: www.sci-ivs.org
Volunteers for Peace: www.vfp.org

Sri Lanka

Veterinary Spay/Neuter Field Clinic

Organization: Tsunami Animal-People Alliance
Location: Mobile
Cost: None **Duration:** 2+ weeks
Contact: info@tsunami-animal.org
Learn more: www.tsunami-animal.org
Special skills: Experienced veterinarians, vet nurses and techs only.
Volunteers must be "low maintenance."
Details: TAPA's tented field clinic does about 35 spay/neuters per
day, about 50% street dogs caught with nets, and 50% owner dogs. Vet
and vet nurse volunteers would join our team of ten (which includes
three vets) in conducting the sterilizations and bringing in new
ideas. Their protocols were originally developed by vets from Australia
and New Zealand, and have been refined over time. TOPA's goal is to
vaccinate and sterilize five to six thousand animals per year, educate
regarding responsible pet ownership, and raise awareness of the link
between the welfare of the animals in a community and the welfare of
the people.

Integrated Eco-Cultural Resource Management Project

Organization: The Centre for Eco-Cultural Studies (CES)
Location: Sigiriya (Lion Rock)
Cost: $400 a month plus $100 administrative fee. Includes basic field
accommodation, local meals and field travel within the project site.
Duration: 1 to 3 months. Intake commences on the 1st of each month.
Age: 18-60
Contact: cesvolunteers@hotmail.com or centeco@sltnet.lk
Learn more: www.cessrilanka.org

Special skills: Ability to cope in a traditional rural setting, living and working in a forest environment, adjusting to cultural changes and loneliness among traditional forest communities and wildlife.
Details: Based in the shadows of Sigiriya (Lion Rock), a stunning UNESCO World Heritage Site and wildlife sanctuary bordering the Minneriya National Park, volunteers are invited to engage in diverse eco-cultural applied policy oriented research and development activities ranging from conservation biology, eco-cultural tourism, eco-agriculture, forest-dependent community development, environmental conservation and protected area management. The project has a well-documented track record of contributing policy and community development.

Other organizations offering projects in Sri Lanka:

Global Visions International: www.gviusa.com or www.gvi.co.uk
i-to-i: www.i-to-i.com
Institute for Field Research Expeditions: www.ifrevolunteers.org
Outreach International: www.outreachinternational.co.uk
RCDP: www.rcdpinternationalvolunteer.org
Sarvodaya USA: www.sarvodayausa.org
Vets Beyond Borders: www.vetsbeyondborders.org
Volunteer International: www.volunteerinternational.com
Volunteer Sri Lanka: volunteersrilanka.net

Tajikistan

Organizations offering projects in Tajikistan:

Habitat for Humanity: www.habitat.org/ivp
Medical Teams International: www.medicalteams.org
Volunteers for Economic Growth Alliance: www.vegaalliance.org

Thailand

Fun with Dogs: Shelter Help
Organization: Care For Dogs
Location: Chiang Mai
Cost: None **Duration:** 1+ days **Age:** 18
Contact: contact@carefordogs.org

Learn more: www.carefordogs.org
Special skills: A love of animals and a caring heart
Details: Care For Dogs is a volunteer-based nonprofit organization located outside of Chiang Mai, Thailand which strives to limit the suffering of street dogs through medical assistance, preventative health care, adoptions and spays. By offering your time at the shelter you will have the opportunity to socialize the dogs, improving their social skills, which helps to alleviate boredom, and build up their confidence around people, which makes them more adoptable and sets them up for building successful relationships in their forever homes. You can also help bathe, clean, feed and much more all while learning about the issues faced by animals and animal shelters in SE Asia. Longer term opportunities (1 week or more) for experienced trainers who practice 'positive' training techniques may also be available for the right volunteers.

✍**Editor's Note:** Care for Dogs is one of this author's favorite places to volunteer. The environment is casual. Be it socializing dogs at the shelter or participating in recues among the stunning Wat temples of Northern Thailand, volunteers would be hard pressed to find an easier way to make a difference while escaping the typical trappings of tourism.

Providing Veterinary Care for Street Dogs

Organization: Care For Dogs
Location: Chiang Mai
Cost: None **Duration:** 1+ weeks **Age**: 18
Contact: contact@carefordogs.org
Learn more: www.carefordogs.org
Special skills: Veterinary health experience
Details: Care For Dogs is a volunteer-based nonprofit organization located outside of Chiang Mai, Thailand which strives to limit the suffering of street dogs through medical assistance, preventative health care, adoptions, and spays. In their efforts, CFD relies on dedicated volunteers to assist us with fundraising and staffing of our shelter and clinic. They are seeking experienced veterinarians who are people-oriented (and possibly shelter-experienced!) to volunteer on-site performing physical examinations, diagnosing health issues, deciding on the course of treatment, dispensing medication, and performing spays. CFD also needs veterinary technicians who can assist the veterinarian. This opportunity is a great way to build a resume!

Designers and Fundraisers for Dogs

Organization: Care For Dogs
Location: Chiang Mai
Cost: None **Duration:** 6 months for fundraisers or by the project for design work **Age:** 18
Contact: contact@carefordogs.org
Learn more: www.carefordogs.org
Details: Inspire hope! Care for Dogs relies on volunteers to assist them with creative and productive fundraising. Help the animals of Thailand either onsite or abroad. Spend a few days at CFD and you'll fall in love with the animals, the staff and the work they do. Take that knowledge with you or work onsite in and around Chiang Mai, using your own special talents to help these wonderful animals and to grow the rescue. Give CFD the means to do more for the animals and to teach the community about kindness to animals and responsible pet ownership.

From the Tsunami to the Classroom

Organization: Volunteer Teacher Thailand
Location: Andaman Coast, southern Thailand
Cost: $90 **Duration:** Open **Age:** 18-80
Contact: volunteer.teachers@yahoo.com
Learn more: www.volunteerteacherthailand.org
Special skills: English speaker who can listen
Details: Among the inspirational work of the Tsunami Volunteer Center was an education project, set up to alleviate the loss of 75% of the English speaking Thai people in this area. Renamed as Volunteer Teacher Thailand, the project now educates over 1,000 children in 5 junior schools and a high school, as well as teaching in a children's home and in the community. The project is run by an experienced British teacher. Quality lessons are prepared in advance, and volunteers teach as a team. The group helps you find accommodations and we give full volunteer support. At the end of your stay you will have a certificate and memories that you will always carry with you. Your memories of laughing children and friendly people in this beautiful setting will last a lifetime.

Island Animal Rescue: Clinic Assistant & Veterinary

Organization: Phangan Animal Care (PAC)
Location: Koh Phangan Island in the Gulf of Thailand
Cost: None **Duration:** 2 to 3 months **Age:** 21
Contact: info@pacthailand.org **Learn more:** www.pacthailand.org
Special skills: Hard working, a sense of fun & a love of animals

Details: At PAC the weekly schedule for the clinic assistant depends on the number of assistants available. PAC's clinic workload also depends on whether or not they have a volunteering veterinarian. When a vet volunteers at the facility, the team usually schedules a few days a week as surgery days. Work includes: walking patients (dogs), monitoring health and progress, disinfection of kennels, restraint of patients for treatment, assistance with daily medication, feeding patients, cleaning feed bowls, pick up feces, daily laundry, housecleaning, etc. On surgical days: volunteers help ensure every neutered animal receives a rabies vaccine, an antibiotic injection, a rabies tag, a vaccination card (for owned animals), is restrained for examination and so on. This is a chance for you to help needy animals on the island's only animal care facility. PAC also welcomes volunteer veterinarians willing to share their skill on an island that is paradise for people, but whose dogs need your help.

✍**Editor's note:** PAC is a recommended volunteer experience for dog lovers who want to make a real difference. I have visited PAC and have

experienced Koh Phangan both before and after PAC's establishment. They have made a world of difference for the animals on the island. Read volunteer Tony James Slater's chapter 'Mad Dogs and Irish Women' in *The Voluntary Traveler: Adventures from the Road Best Traveled* and learn why people may travel to the island for the full moon party, but often stay for the animals.

Teach and Care for Orphans in Chiang Rai

Organization: International Humanity Foundation
Location: Chiang Rai
Cost: $50 per week, maximum of $600; room and board at the center are included
Duration: 1+ month   **Age:** 18, or older or parental permission
Contact: volunteering@ihfonline.org
Learn more: www.ihfonline.org
Details: Learn the realities of international poverty by serving at our orphanage and education center where you will live, learn, teach and play with the children who call it home. Center tasks and needs vary widely, and you are certain to find a niche according to your skills. As IHF is entirely volunteer-run, you will be asked to serve on various online task teams, such as advertising and photography, which will grant you a unique insight into how an international nonprofit operates.

Teaching English in Northern Thailand

Organization: International Volunteer HQ
Location: Chiang Rai, Northern Thailand and surrounding hill tribes
Cost: $325 for 2 weeks to $1,275 for 3 months, includes food &
accommodations
Duration: 2 weeks to 3 months **Age:** 18
Contact: volunteer@volunteerhq.org
Learn more: www.volunteerhq.org
Details: In the northern areas of Thailand such as Chiang Rai many of
the local people have not been fortunate enough to have access to any
type of formal education. Therefore there is a real need for volunteers
to assist in the education of not only young children, but also adults
from surrounding hill tribes and local villages. Houe Khom School is
one of the possible placements and is located just outside of Chiang Rai
in a rural village. This school caters to over 300 Thai children ranging
in age from 7 to 12, all from local villages. Volunteers do not need to be
experienced teachers.

WFFT Gibbon Rehabilitation Centre

Organization: Wildlife Friends Foundation Thailand (WFFT)
Location: Petchaburi Province
Cost: $170-$270 a week depending upon length of stay;
accommodation and all meals are included.
Duration: 2+ weeks **Age:** 18
Contact: volunteer@wfft.org
Learn more: www.wildlifevolunteer.org
Special skills: None required, just enthusiasm for animal welfare and
reasonable physical fitness to work in a tropical climate. Graduates of
animal behavior studies are welcome.
Details: Gibbons are small arboreal apes, native to Southeast Asia.
They are becoming more and more endangered due to habitat loss and
poaching for the illegal wildlife trade. Over one hundred gibbons have
been rescued from exploitation in tourism or from neglect in captivity.
Gibons are undergoing rehabilitation on islands at the foundations
centre near Kaeng Krachan National Park. This can be a long process
for intelligent primates and WFFT requires support all year around
from volunteers in order to maintain the care of these cute and furry
little creatures. Scientist-led release programs in other parts of
Thailand, including the northern and western regions, are the final
stage in returning the gibbons back to the wild.

Sanctuary for Southeast Asia's Bears

Organization: Wildlife Friends Foundation Thailand (WFFT)
Location: Petchaburi Province

Cost: $170-$270 a week depending upon length of stay;
accommodation and all meals are included
Duration: 2+ weeks **Age:** 18
Contact: volunteer@wfft.org
Learn more: www.wildlifevolunteer.org
Special skills: None required, just enthusiasm for animal welfare and
reasonable physical fitness to work in a tropical climate
Details: Southeast Asia's bears are becoming more and more
endangered due to habitat loss and poaching for the illegal wildlife
trade. WFFT sanctuary cares for victims of this trade that have been
rescued, but have no safe haven in the wild they can be returned to. The
operation of this project is completely funded through WFFT volunteer
programs. Volunteers assist in the daily care of these fascinating
creatures. Over 25 sun bears and Asiatic black bears have been rescued
over the past 5 years and WTTF plans to rescue twice this amount over
the next 5 years with continued support from volunteers. Volunteers
may also assist developing an education center and giving tours to
visitors at the sanctuary.

Elephant Camp in Chiang Mai

Organization: Experiential Learning International
Location: Chiang Mai, Thailand
Cost: Starting at $1,000 **Duration:** 4+ weeks **Age:** 18
Contact: info@eliabroad.org **Learn more:** www.eliabroad.org
Special skills: Ability to participate in strenuous physical work
Details: The Asian Elephant is only thriving in Thailand due to the
work of a few organizations. This program gives volunteers a chance to
help with this massive effort at a Thai-run elephant camp. Volunteers
live onsite in tree houses that lean out over the
river and they assist the hill tribe staff with bathing
and feeding schedules Monday through
Friday. Volunteers also work to educate visitors
and make sure that they are interacting safely with
the animals. Some volunteers teach an hour or two
of English at the local hill tribe school. Other

volunteers will stay at the park and teach English to the elephant
trainers and other staff. Volunteers may be asked to help out with other
areas of the elephant camp during their volunteer service and should be
open to diversity.

WFFT Wildlife Rescue Thailand

Organization: Wildlife Friends Foundation Thailand (WFFT)
Location: Petchaburi Province
Cost: $170-$240/week depending upon length of stay; shared
accommodations are onsite and all meals are included.

Duration: 3+ weeks **Age:** 18
Contact: volunteer@wfft.org
Learn more: www.wildlifevolunteer.org
Special skills: None required, just enthusiasm for animal welfare and reasonable physical fitness to work in a tropical climate. Veterinarians and vet nurses are encouraged to support this project
Details: Based on the grounds of a Buddhist temple, not far from Thailand's largest national park, this project was set-up in 2001 and has since rescued and treated thousands of animals escaping human conflict as well as victims of the illegal wildlife trade. The wildlife hospital and mobile wildlife clinic work around the clock to care for sick and injured animals, while the rest of the wildlife are taken care of by volunteers at the rescue center until they can successfully be released back to the wild. Species include many primates, birds, reptiles, nocturnal animals, wild cats as well as tigers.

Outdoor Work in Thailand

Organization: International Volunteer HQ
Location: Chiang Rai, Northern Thailand and surrounding hill tribes
Cost: $305 for 1 week to $1,275 for 3 months, includes food & accommodations
Duration: 1 week to 3 months **Age:** 18
Contact: volunteer@volunteerhq.org
Learn more: www.volunteerhq.org
Details: Outdoor work is for those who enjoy getting their hands dirty, physical labor and who appreciate the sense of achievement felt when a job is completed. If outdoor work is not possible due to weather conditions, this is overcome by researching methods of agricultural production to assist the area, project presentations to villagers, promotional work and other work that can be carried out while protected from the elements. Previously completed work by volunteers on this project include: building water tanks, extending water pipe systems, building check dams, building classrooms, painting classrooms, developing a local agricultural project, helping in local vegetable gardens, working on developing plantations, road repairs, repair and maintenance of homes of the elderly and building new houses and toilets for older Thai villagers.

Island Community Eco Education

Organization: Naucrates
Location: Phra Thong Island, South Thailand
Cost: $300 per week **Duration:** 2+ weeks
Age: 18, kids over 10 welcome with parent
Contact: info@naucrates.org **Learn more:** www.naucrates.org

Details: This project aims to introduce environmentally friendly practices to improve the living conditions of the Lion Village Community, strengthening the capacity of the community to implement conservation programs and establishing a positive-sustainable relationship between ecotourism, conservation and community economic development. In parallel with the teaching programme, livelihood activities are organized in the community in order to increase the capacity among local people. In the conservation lessons, the students discuss sea turtles, mangroves, pollution and the importance of recycling and composting. With the supervision of their teacher, Kruu Jiik, the students plant and grow a lush, green garden outside of their school. Using the tools and seeds donated by Naucrates, the children are able to eventually sell their vegetables in town with pride.

Teaching Basic Computer or Advanced IT Skills

Organization: uVolunteer
Location: Phonphisai, Udon Thani
Cost: $600 for the first 2 weeks; $75 each additional week
Duration: 2+ weeks   **Age:** 18
Contact: info@uvolunteer.org   **Learn more:** www.uvolunteer.org
Details: Volunteers will be teaching several different basic and advanced lessons of computer skills to the local students who are excited and eager to learn and develop computer knowledge skills. The new computer center located in Phonphisai needs volunteers with basic or advanced computer skills. Currently there is a teacher teaching basic lessons, and there are about 5 classes and 50 students so far. The center has 16 new computers, 15 for the students and 1 for the teacher. There is also high speed Internet, a projector and overhead for slide shows.

Elephant Refuge and Education Centre

Organization: Wildlife Friends Foundation Thailand (WFFT)
Location: Petchaburi Province
Cost: $330-$420/week depending upon length of stay; accommodation and all meals are included
Duration: 1+ week   **Age:** 18 and over, over 12 welcome if with parent
Contact: volunteer@wfft.org
Learn more: www.wildlifevolunteer.org
Special skills: None required, just enthusiasm for animal welfare and reasonable physical fitness in order to work in a tropical climate
Details: The elephant is Thailand's national symbol, but sadly they are suffering due to habitat loss and exploitation by tourism. WFFT's refuge cares for elephants that have been rescued from a life on the city streets, exploited for begging by their mahouts. The operation of this project is completely funded through the WFFT volunteerprograms,

272

whereby volunteers assist in the daily care of these magnificent creatures in a large and natural forested area next to the wildlife rescue centre. Volunteers may also assist in developing an education center, giving tours to visitors at the refuge and assisting with a forest restoration project.

HIV Orphanage

Organization: Friends for Asia
Location: Chiang Mai
Cost: $695 for two weeks, $100 for each additional week
Duration: 2 to 8 weeks (from mid-March to mid-May only) **Age:** 20
Contact: info@friendsforasia.org
Learn more: www.friendsforasia.org
Details: Your role as a volunteer is to make the children's lives at the orphanage more enjoyable and to educate them through music, sports, computer, English education and art. You will pick one or more of the above areas and with direction from the full time staff, organize lessons or games with the children to enjoy and take part in. Also the orphanage staff asks volunteers to spend individual time with the children, giving hugs, attention and love. Volunteers are asked to be flexible, often times last minute changes or events come up which may disrupt a volunteer initiated or planned activity. Although the children at the orphanage are living with HIV, they show just as much excitement, love and life as children anywhere.

Gibbon Rehabilitation Project

Organization: The Wild Animal Rescue Foundation of Thailand
Location: Phuket, Thailand
Cost: Please contact **Duration:** 3+ weeks **Age:** Above 18
Contact: volunteer@warthai.org
Learn more: www.warthai.org,
www.gibbonproject.org
Special skills: Basic command of spoken
English is essential
Details: The Wild Animal Rescue Foundation of
Thailand (WARF) is a charity founded in 1992
and is dedicated to preventing the maltreatment
of wild animals, relieving their suffering,
providing a caring environment in which rescued
animals can live and ultimately returning healthy animals to the wild. They recruit paying volunteers to help at projects that are devoted to animal care. As a volunteer with WARF you will support the foundation in two ways, with the rehabilitation of animals and with your donation. Their gibbon volunteer work and other animal rescue projects are best

suited to people with a genuine interest in the care and well being of the wildlife.

Thailand Animal Sanctuary Program
Organization: Global Volunteer Network
Location: Kao Look Chang, Petchaburi, near Cha-am & Hua-hin
Cost: $747 for 2 weeks　**Duration:** 2 to 12 weeks　**Age:** 18
Contact: info@volunteer.org.nz　**Learn more:**
www.volunteer.org.nz
Details: The Global Volunteer Network has opportunities available to work with wild animals through their partner organization in Thailand. Most of the animals residing at the sanctuary were maltreated before they arrived here, suffering from abuse, malnutrition, neglect and improper care, rescued from the illegal pet trade, or have previously been exploited for the tourism industry. Many of the animals arrive with permanent disabilities and hence, cannot be returned to the wild. Animals you can expect to work with at the sanctuary include a variety of macaques, two species of gibbon, several species of civets, loris, leopard cats, tigers, bears, crocodiles and exotic birds.

Elephant Helpers, Veterinarians & Vet Students
Organization: Elephant Nature Park
Location: Chiang Mai
Cost: $365 per week; includes accommodations and meals
Duration: 1+ week　**Age:** 18, or accompanied by a parent
Contact: info@elephantnaturepark.org
Learn more: www.elephantnaturepark.org
Special skills: No previous experience with elephants is required.
Details: At Elephant Nature Park the volunteer program is designed for those who wish to work with elephants and gain knowledge about the local conditions and problems facing elephants in Thailand. Tasks include assisting elephant keepers, bathing elephants and general duties around the park and surrounding area. ENP also has volunteer positions for professional veterinarians who have 5 or more years of experience with large animals and for elephant student vets volunteers open to veterinary students as part of their course-work. Office help is also appreciated.
✎**Editor's note:** The Elephant Nature Park volunteer program has been highly recommended by many past volunteers.

Gibbon Rescue Project
Organization: Greenheart Travel
Location: Island of Phuket in Thailand
Cost: $1,830 for 4 weeks　**Duration:** 2 to 8 weeks　**Age:** 18

Contact: info@greenhearttravel.org **Learn**: www.cci-exchange.com
Special skills: Volunteers must be capable of physical labor, walking
long distances and be able to stand high temperatures. Certain
vaccinations are required before joining this project. Your Greenheart
Travel coordinator will give you more details.
Details: Since 1992 this project, founded in cooperation with the Asian
Wildlife Fund, has been rehabilitating rescued gibbons for release back
into the wild. As a volunteer, you will help run and maintain the
facilities. Typical activities include preparing food, cleaning, and
repairing and building new enclosures, and talking to tourists about the
threats gibbons face and the work being done at the center. You may
also assist with the release of animals back to their natural habitat,
which involves observation to ensure the animals are adapting
successfully. Long term volunteers (two months or more) may be able
to assist researchers with behavioral studies. Volunteers live in
bungalows in a tiny village close to the work site. Rooms will be shared
with another volunteer.

Sea Turtle Conservation Project

Organization: Greenheart Travel
Location: The project is located about an hour from the town of
Ranong in a very remote location near Baan Talae Nork, along the
Andaman coastline.
Cost: $1,850 for 4 weeks **Duration:** 3 to 8 weeks **Age:** 18
Contact: info@greenhearttravel.org **Learn**: www.cci-exchange.com
Special skills: Volunteers must be physically fit and able to walk or
hike long distances. Team work is essential to this project, so working
well with others is a must. Volunteers must be at least 18 years old and
have an interest in wildlife conservation. Certain vaccinations are
required before joining this project. Your Greenheart Travel
coordinator will give you more details.
Details: Founded in 2003 with support from the nearby Ranong
Coastal Resources Research Station, this project is based on a
biosphere reserve in Thailand. In addition to restoring the turtle
population in the area, the project plays an important role in
generating local understanding of the value of nature and its
conservation, with the aim of actively involving the community in the
protection of turtles and nesting sites. You will help monitor the beach
for turtle nests, learn how to identify turtle tracks, find nesting turtles,
and record tag numbers. Volunteers live in small huts near the work
site. Rooms will be shared with two to three fellow volunteers. The
work site also has Internet access and satellite television.

Remote Island Sea Turtle Conservation Project

Organization: Naucrates
Location: Phra Thong Island, South Thailand
Cost: $480 per week **Duration:** 2+ weeks
Age: 18, kids over 10 welcome with parent
Contact: info@naucrates.org **Learn more:** www.naucrates.org
Details: This volunteer project provides the opportunity to take an active part in a conservation project in Asia. Naucrates staff and volunteers actively work towards the preservation of nature. You learn about Thai wildlife and conservation, help monitor beaches, teach English and conservation to the local community and enjoy the beauty of a remote tropical island. You will bring skills and knowledge, plus a small economical contribution to cover some expenses of the project. The team helps the local community, encouraging them to understand that ecotourism programs are a precious alternative source of income for their future. This is a homestay program. Volunteers stay in local houses sharing daily life with the community. Thai lessons are given to help you communicate with villagers during your stay.

Environmental and Gibbon Conservation

Organization: uVolunteer
Location: Phuket, Thailand
Cost: $1,470 for the first 3 weeks; $105 each additional week
Duration: 3+ weeks **Age:** 18
Contact: info@uvolunteer.org **Learn more:** www.uvolunteer.org
Special skills: Intermediate English
Details: Help save the Gibbons and their rainforest habitat through rehabilitation and education of the local community. This project's aims to reduce poaching, deforestation, gain support for the continuation of the project and continue the conservation movement of gibbons in Thailand. uVolunteer works with an animal rescue foundation in Thailand that specializes in saving gibbons. The animal rescue foundation works with White-handed Gibbons (Hylobates Lar), the most widespread of the four species of gibbon found in Thailand. This foundation currently houses over seventy gibbons, an effective resource for teaching the local community and foreign tourists and it attracts international students who wish to study gibbons. Planning is from the ground up and involves the employment of local people who act as educators and 'gibbon guardians'.

Elephant Camp Project

Organization: Friends For Asia
Location: Chiang Mai, Thailand
Cost: $995 for two weeks, $250 for each additional week

Duration: 2 to 26 weeks   **Age:** 18
Contact: info@friendsforasia.org
Learn more: www.friendsforasia.org
Special skills: Volunteers do not need any specific qualifications, but should be able-bodied, enjoy working outside and with animals.
Details: As part of this special volunteer experience you will assist and work alongside elephant trainers and camp staff from 7:00–5:00 Monday – Friday. After gaining experience, volunteers may be asked to present different safety precautions to day visitors. Days start early at the Elephant Camp. Six o'clock is elephant bath time, followed by breakfast for the elephants. Once they are fed and before day visitors arrive volunteers and staff sit down to have breakfast and enjoy a cup of northern Thai coffee with a backdrop of the rolling mountains of Northern Thailand. The rest of a typical day at camp consists of cutting grass, making herbal medicines for the elephants, teaching children at a small hill tribe school and English to the staff and elephant trainers.

Teaching Monks

Organization: Friends for Asia
Location: Chiang Mai, Thailand
Cost: $695 for two weeks, $100 for each additional week
Duration: 2 to 26 weeks   **Age:** 18
Contact: info@friendsforasia.org
Learn more: www.friendsforasia.org
Special skills: Volunteers should be proficient in written and spoken English, as well as creative considering there is an incredible lack of teaching materials within the school.
Details: Our volunteers teach novice Buddhist monks, from age 12-18, at five different monastery schools. You will have the choice of either leading your own class or assisting a Thai teacher in his or her daily lessons. Your placement is completely dependent upon your level of comfort within the classroom. Depending upon your educational background, you may also want to teach art or help in other subject areas and activities that may be occurring at the school during you service. It is important to the school administration that volunteers aid in English education at the school, but also that volunteers receive a rich education about Thailand, Thai culture and Buddhism during their service. For this reason, be prepared to learn as much as you teach.

Single Mothers in Crisis & Childcare

Organization: Friends for Asia
Location: Chiang Mai
Cost: $895 for four weeks, $100 for each additional week
Duration: 2 to 26 weeks   **Age:** 20

277

Contact: info@friendsforasia.org
Learn more: www.friendsforasia.org
Special skills: Volunteers must have experience with and a love for young children. Considering that many of the women and children at the home have recently suffered due to mistreatment or abuse by men, the home requests that all volunteers serving in this project be female.
Details: Volunteers assist in supervising the many children at the home, newborn to seven years old. It's important for the women at the home to take part in different classes (ESL, computer, financial management, child care etc.) to learn skills essential to obtaining independent self sufficiency. Volunteers will look after the babies, toddlers and older kids, change diapers, organize simple games and make sure the older children don't get into too much trouble. Volunteers involved in this project will have the chance to experience cradling a newborn ethnic Thai or hill tribe youngster in a bamboo constructed house surrounded by rice paddies and mountains, while the child's mother is learning essential skills to improve her own and her young child's life and future.

Beautification of Chiang Mai

Organization: Friends for Asia
Location: Chiang Mai, Thailand
Cost: $695 for two weeks, $100 each additional week
Duration: 2 to 26 weeks (year round) **Age:** 20

Contact: info@friendsforasia.org
Learn more: www.friendsforasia.org
Special skills: Only men are able to participate in this project. Volunteers do not need any specific qualifications, but should be able-bodied, enjoy working outside and flexible to change. Decisions on events in Chiang Mai City Hall are sometimes made at the last minute which requires a great amount of flexibility and understanding for all involved.
Details: Volunteers in this project work to develop and maintain the nine public parks and green spaces of Chiang Mai and participate in special event planning, preparation, set up and clean up. The old city of Chiang Mai is surrounded by a large square moat, which has been protected because of its beauty and historical significance to the city. Volunteers will assist in the upkeep and beautification of this area and other historical structures within the city. The upkeep and development of these areas will include planting, trimming, watering and fertilizing the flowers and plants (many of which are native to Thailand) in these areas. Many of Chiang Mai's bridges and sidewalks have come under the jurisdiction of the beautification movement. Therefore, volunteers may also assist in the upkeep and planting of flowers and plants in

these areas. This is a great opportunity for people passionate about gardening to learn about landscape in the tropics.

Volunteer and Training Center in North Thailand

Organization: OpenmindProjects
Location: NongKhai
Cost: $900 per month   **Duration:** 1+ month plus   **Age:** 18
Contact: info@openmindprojects.org
Learn more: www.openmindprojects.org or upload.openmindprojects.org/volunteerpackage
Special skills: Adequate computer skills to teach computer basics or more advanced skills to teach special applications, graphic design, programming, etc.
Details: Teach computer skills in NongKhai by the Mekong River, the gateway to Laos. Teach at the project's Volunteer and Training Center, in a Buddhist temple or public schools. You can teach daytime weekdays or evening classes, weekends to adults and young people with an interest in computers. By living at the Training Center you will be a part of the local community and get to know Thai people and culture. In NongKhai Western needs are catered to, but none of its multiethnic Indochinese atmosphere is lost. NongKhai is a popular volunteer location and the Center, with wireless Internet, volunteer office, bedrooms, relaxation area, garden and tennis court makes it the ideal placement for the less experienced volunteer.

Volunteer at a National Park in Thailand

Organization: OpenmindProjects
Location: NongKhai
Cost: $1,200 per month   **Duration:** 1+ month   **Age:** 18
Contact: info@openmindprojects.org
Learn more: www.openmindprojects.org or upload.openmindprojects.org/volunteerpackage
Special Skills: An understanding and interest in eco tourism and environmental/wildlife protection. Ability to go trekking on field trips, IT, Environmental Impact Assessment, Geographic Information System, Watershed Planning
Details: Volunteer at national parks in Thailand, with community based, sustainable ecotourism and wildlife conservation projects. OpenmindProjects works with national parks and specialists such as zoologists, marine biologists, botanists, sustainable ecotourism experts, GIS, EIA, IT/database specialists, are welcome, along with others who have less expertise and a good command of English. Projects focus on preparing the national parks for overseas eco-tourists. Qualified volunteers participate in wildlife surveying marine survey diving,

Environmental Impact Assessment and assisting with Geographic Information System applications.

Marine Research and Rescue Unit

Organization: Wildlife Friends Foundation Thailand (WFFT)
Location: Petchaburi Province
Cost: Trang Province, Thailand
Duration: 2+ weeks **Age:** 18
Contact: volunteer@wfft.org
Learn more: www.wildlifevolunteer.org
Special skills: None required, just enthusiasm for animal welfare and reasonable physical fitness to work in a tropical climate. Marine biologists welcome.
Details: Use of life jackets, accommodation in beach villas and all meals are included. This project has been set up to support marine conservation efforts by studying the coastal populations of whales and dolphins and as a base for rescuing marine wildlife from human conflicts. Volunteers will typically rotate a day at sea followed by a day on land processing and analyzing the data with the resident biologist during the course of this project. Diving opportunities may also be available for those with certification.

English Education Service-Learning Program

Organization: Global Service Corps
Location: Singburi
Cost: 6 weeks $3,140; weekly fee after 9 weeks $415, after 13 weeks $255
Duration: 6 to 6 months
Age: 20 or 18 with three letters of recommendation
Contact: thailand@globalservicecorps.org
Learn more: globalservicecorps.org
Special skills: No special skills required, just a commitment to service
Details: The English Education Program begins with a two day tour of Bangkok and continues with two weeks of orientation and training in Singburi. The first week of the training is dedicated to learning about Thai customs, including social do's and don'ts, and acquiring basic Thai conversation skills. During this time participants will tour local historical sites, get to know the other program participants and be informed in detail about specific program placement and associated projects. In the second week participants are provided training in teaching English as a Foreign Language (EFL). The training is followed by four or more weeks of teaching basic and conversational English to either primary or secondary school students. Semi-private, group and homestay accommodations are available.

Integrated Buddhist, Teaching & Orphanage Project

Organization: Global Service Corps
Location: Various areas in central Thailand
Cost: 6 weeks $3,140   **Duration:** 6 weeks - 6 months
Age: 20 or 18 with three letters of recommendation
Contact: thailand@globalservicecorps.org
Learn more: globalservicecorps.org
Special skills: No special skills required, just a commitment to service
Details: The Integrated Program is for those who want to participate in more than one service learning project by Global Service Corps. The program begins with a two day tour of Bangkok and continues with a two week orientation and training. The first week of the training is dedicated to learning about Thai customs, including social do's and don'ts, and acquiring basic Thai conversation skills. During this time participants will tour local historical sites, get to know the other program participants and be informed in detail about specific program placement and associated projects. In the second week participants are provided training in teaching English as a Foreign Language (EFL). Participants then divide their time between GSC's Buddhist Immersion program, Teach English Abroad program or Orphanage Care projects with a minimum commitment of two weeks each.

Buddhist Immersion-EFL Service-Learning Program

Organization: Global Service Corps
Location: Rajburi Province
Cost: 2 weeks $1480; weekly fee after 9 weeks $415, after 13 weeks $255
Duration: 2 weeks to 6 months
Age: 20 or 18 with three letters of recommendation
Contact: thailand@globalservicecorps.org
Learn more: globalservicecorps.org
Special skills: No special skills required, just a commitment to service
Details: The Buddhist Immersion-EFL Program begins with a two day tour of Bangkok and continues with one or more weeks of living at a wat (monastery) and teaching English to young novice and older monks, as well as visiting monks in training as meditation teachers. Also included is a three day tour to a rural Thai village near the Laos border. Besides teaching English to monks at the wat, participants have opportunity to participate in up to three meditation sessions and one lecture/question & answer session per day. Additionally, participants may participate in morning and evening chanting at the temple with

the approximately 200 novice monks and monks who live on the premise. The wat is located on 90 acres in a beautiful rural setting.

Orphanage Care Service-Learning Program

Organization: Global Service Corps
Location: Singburi
Cost: 6 weeks $3,140 **Duration:** 6 weeks to 6 months
Age: 20 or 18 with three letters of recommendation
Contact: thailand@globalservicecorps.org
Learn more: globalservicecorps.org
Special skills: No special skills required, just a commitment to service
Details: The Orphanage Care Program begins with a two day tour of Bangkok and continues with two weeks of orientation and training in Singburi. The first week of the training is dedicated to learning about Thai customs, including social do's and don'ts, and acquiring basic Thai conversation skills. During this time participants will tour local historical sites, get to know the other program participants and be informed in detail about specific program placement and associated projects. In the second week participants are provided training in teaching English as a Foreign Language (EFL). This is followed by four or more weeks of mentoring, teaching conversational English, and providing recreational, arts, crafts and sports activities for young Thai orphans. Semi-private, group and homestay accommodations are available.

Elephant Sanctuary

Organization: Greenforce
Location: Thailand
Cost: $750+ **Duration:** 1+ week **Age:** 17
Contact: info@greenforce.org **Learn more:** www.greenforce.org
Details: It wasn't long ago that elephants in Thailand were abundant and able to roam freely. Now, there are less than 3000 in the entire country, which are being forced to live in smaller and more confined spaces. Wild elephants have to compete with local villagers and there are now many domesticated elephants must perform tricks for tourists in order to survive. Our team on the ground has adopted several elephants and uses them to raise awareness and to educate the local people. Volunteers are needed to walk, clean and feed the elephants, but more importantly to show them some TLC. With the elephant population dwindling into endangerment, now is your chance to have an elephant shower and to witness why elephants have always been such a sacred animal.

Thailand Hill Tribe Program

Organization: Greenforce
Location: Northern Thailand
Cost: $1,500+ **Duration:** 2+ weeks **Age:** 17
Contact: info@greenforce.org **Learn more:** www.greenforce.org
Details: Participating in the Hill Tribe volunteer program in Northern Thailand gives volunteers the opportunity to visit rural communities while also giving them the chance to truly understand and appreciate the rich culture and traditions of this fascinating region of Thailand. This program is all about discovering Northern Thai traditions. The work is very diverse, from construction to teaching and working with the villagers, depending on the needs of the community and on the volunteer's personal preferences. There is also the opportunity to visit local markets and help local initiatives when they appear.

Elephant Encounter

Organization: Hands Up Holidays
Location: Elephant Nature Park near Chiang Mai
Cost: $1,900 per person, based on sharing a room, excluding flights.
Duration: 4 days volunteering/14 day trip
Age: 16 years unless accompanied by an adult
Contact: info@handsupholidays.com
Learn more: www.handsupholidays.com
Special skills: None required, but veterinary skills are desirable
Details: Elephant Nature Park is a unique project established in the 1990's to provide a sanctuary and rescue centre for elephants. Volunteer jobs are varied, from bathing elephants to basic health care. Help these beautiful creatures and gain an insight into Thai culture as you get to know the people who permanently care for the elephants. Sample the generous hospitality of these remarkable people and immerse yourself in local and tribal lifestyles. This special experience will form an integral part of your trip, and in addition you get to spend the remainder of this journey trekking, bamboo rafting, visiting hill tribes and exploring towns and markets.

Village Vitality

Organization: Hands Up Holidays
Location: Mae Hong Son
Cost: $2,150 per person, based on sharing a room
Duration: 4 days volunteering/in 15 day trip)
Age: 16 years unless accompanied by an adult
Contact: info@handsupholidays.com
Learn more: www.handsupholidays.com

Special skills: None required, but teaching English as a second language (ESL) or civil engineering skills are desirable
Details: Immerse yourself in an ethnic hill tribe community in Mae Hong Son province. Enjoy a fun and authentic journey, learning about the community's relationship with the land and discover how this has influenced their traditional arts and crafts. Your volunteering experience will promote your understanding of these wonderful people, as you work alongside them on varied projects. Enjoy the looks of delight and appreciation on the children's faces as you teach and interact. The intimate moments with the children and the rest of the community will be treasured memories for you. You will also participate in Thai cooking classes, treks, canal trips, city tours and white water rafting.

Tantalizing Thailand
Organization: Hands Up Holidays
Location: Sangkhlaburi, northwest Thailand, near the Burmese border.
Cost: $2,700 per person, based on sharing a room, excluding flights.
Duration: 4 days volunteering/14 day trip
Age: 16 years unless accompanied by an adult
Contact: info@handsupholidays.com
Learn more: www.handsupholidays.com
Special skills: None required, but teaching English as a second language ("ESL") or building skills are desirable
Details: This volunteer project based in Sangkhlaburi near the Burmese (Mynamar) border is a great opportunity to provide children of an orphanage (largely Burmese ethnic minority refugees) with an environment that is conducive to learning and nurtures their inquisitive nature. Let them touch your life as you help rebuild theirs. Your volunteer project is undoubtedly the highlight of this fabulous trip, but there are many more things to explore: you get to visit a sunken temple and an elephant camp, and then make yourself at home on a converted rice barge as it snakes its way down the beautiful Chao Phraya River. You also get to visit local markets and enjoy the hive of activity as villagers trade and socialize.

Thai Travels
Organization: Hands Up Holidays
Location: Khao Lak
Cost: $2,850 per person, based on sharing a room
Duration: 4 days volunteering/15 day trip
Age: 16 years unless accompanied by an adult

Contact: info@handsupholidays.com
Learn more: www.handsupholidays.com
Special skills: None required, but teaching English as a second language (ESL), gardening or medical skills are desirable
Details: On Boxing Day 2004 a huge tsunami devastated vast tracts of coastline in Southeast Asia. Khao Lak was one of the worst affected areas and an orphanage was set up in the aftermath to care for the children who were orphaned by that tsunami. This is a great opportunity to interact with these remarkable children and help make a real difference in their lives. Their courage and resilience is astonishing and their smiles will forever leave fond memories in your heart. Alongside this remarkable volunteer project you will also visit the hill tribes around Chiang Mai, ride elephants, marvel at the lush green hills on a bamboo raft and relax on stunning beaches.

Origins of Angkor

Organization: Earthwatch Institute
Location: Rendezvous in Bangkok, Thailand
Cost: $1,850 - $3,050+   **Duration:** 7 to 14 days   **Age:** 18
Contact: info@earthwatch.org   **Learn more:** www.earthwatch.org
Details: By uncovering Southeast Asia's past, you'll learn how agriculture, technology and changing climates affect civilizations. Volunteers help excavate the rural Thai village of Ban Non Wat, a key site for understanding the origins of the Angkor Empire. Under the shade of a tarp, you will dig for human burials, food remains, pottery, metals and other artifacts. You will also screen and float sediments to isolate microscopic materials and will process your finds in the field lab. You'll work closely with local people and have a chance to truly experience Thai village life. At the end of the work day volunteers are driven back to town to shop at the local market, check your email, take a swim and enjoy a delicious Thai dinner.

Taste of Thailand – In Style

Organization: Hands Up Holidays
Location: Khao Lak
Cost: $3,400 per person, based on sharing a room, excluding flights.
Duration: 3 days (in 9 day trip)
Age: 16 years unless accompanied by an adult
Contact: info@handsupholidays.com
Learn more: www.handsupholidays.com
Special skills: None required, but teaching English as a second language (ESL), gardening or medical skills are desirable
Details: On Boxing Day 2004 a huge tsunami devastated vast tracts of coastline in South East Asia. Khao Lak was one of the worst affected

areas and an orphanage was set up in the aftermath to care for the children who were orphaned by that tsunami. This is a great opportunity to interact with these remarkable children and help make a real difference to their lives. Their courage and resilience is astonishing and their smiles will forever leave fond memories in your heart. This immersion into Thai culture will only serve to heighten your enjoyment of the remainder of the trip. Explore bustling Bangkok, enjoy a tranquil cruise to Ayuthaya, enjoy the magnificent beaches of Phuket or visit the jungle camp at Elephant Hill in nearby Khao Sok.

Other organizations offering projects in Thailand:
Andaman Discoveries: www.andamandiscoveries.com
Canadian Alliance for Development Initiatives and Projects:
*   www.cadip.org*
Cross-Cultural Solutions: www.crossculturalsolutions.org
Cultural Canvas Thailand: www.culturalcanvas.com
Dog Rescue Center Samui: www.samuidog.org
Dragonfly: www.thai-dragonfly.com
Earthwatch Institute: www.earthwatch.org
Global Visions International: www.gviusa.com or www.gvi.co.uk
i-to-i: www.i-to-i.com
Institute for Cultural Ecology (marine biology, disabled persons or
*   journalism internships): www.cultural-ecology.com*
Noistar Thai Animal Rescue Foundation (Koh Tao):
*   www.kohtaoanimalclinic.org*
Rustic Volunteer and Travel: www.rustic-volunteer-travel.com
Volunteer Teaching Thailand: www.volunteerteacherthailand.org
Volunthai: volunthai.com
Wild Animal Rescue Foundation of Thailand: www.warthai.org
Worldwide Veterinary Service: www.wvs.org.uk

Turkey

English at Home
Organization: Tutor and Travel in Turkey
Location: Varies
Cost: $1,800 for 3 months **Duration:** 2 to 6 months **Age:** 18-28
Contact: esra@edurehber.com **Learn more:** tutorandtravel.com
Special skills: Native English speaker
Details: In this homestay exchange you will have room & board and meals are provided in exchange for 20 hours of unofficial English

practice with the family/kids. TTT organizes a Turkey tour at the end of each program. You will have a chance to see at least 10 different cities, visit unforgettable places and have a vacation on some of the most beautiful beaches in the world.

Other organizations offering projects in Turkey:

Concordia: www.concordia-iye.org.uk
Dekeyser and Friends: dekeyserandfriends.com
Educational Volunteers Foundation of Turkey: www.tegv.org/v4/en/
GeoVisions: www.geovisions.org
Volunteers for Peace: www.vfp.org

Vietnam

Wildlife Conservation

Organization: Wildlife at Risk
Location: Chu Chi and Kien Giang Province
Cost: $200 per week form members, $300 for nonmembers
Duration: Open **Age:** 18
Contact: khoi.ngugen@wildlifeatrisk.org or

chris@wildlifeatrisk.org
Learn more: www.wildlifeatrisk.org
Details: Wildlife At Risk (WAR) is dedicated to protecting the biodiversity of Vietnam by combating the illegal wildlife trade, raising environmental awareness and promoting the conservation of endangered species and their habitats. As a volunteer, you will dedicate your time to assisting permanent staff in providing clean, safe, natural environments for the rescued wildlife and be involved in many different activities. Volunteers learn a lot about endangered Vietnamese wildlife and why the animals are at the Rescue Station. The work is not glamorous, but it s certainly rewarding to those with true commitment to the cause.

Youth House School and Disadvantaged Children

Organization: Solidarités Jeunesses Vietnam
Location: Hanoi, Vietnam
Cost: $230+ **Duration:** 2 weeks **Age:** 18
Contact: info@sjvietnam.org **Learn more:** www.sjvietnam.org

Details: Fisher Village, in Long Bien District, is the living place of many poor people from different parts of Vietnam. Most of them are working as a carrier, waste collector, or have a small business in the market, etc. and live in cottages beside the Red River. The children in these families wander the streets begging and collecting rubbish. An entire family barely makes $2 a day. Most of them have little or no education. To help these children have better future than their parents, SJ Vietnam Organization has successfully run this project for 5 years with the help of hundreds volunteers. Youth House School is a special school which was built by SJ Vietnam for 27 children. Teachers are local and international volunteers who share their love, hope and knowledge so these children can have a good future.

Working with Local NGOs

Organization: International Volunteer HQ
Location: Placements available in Hanoi
Cost: $570 for 1 month to $2,220 for 6 months, includes food and accommodation
Duration: 1 month to 6 months   **Age:** 18
Contact: volunteer@volunteerhq.org
Learn more: www.volunteerhq.org
Details: Many small, locally run NGOs (non-governmental organizations) in Vietnam are contributing to the cause of development in both rural and urban areas. These local NGOs, typically new, are shortage of finances, human resources and skills. There is a need for building their capacity in different approaches. Involving a foreigner in the office helps improve their communication skills, working skills and assists in bridging local NGOs with new partners in other countries. There are currently placements in the following sectors; community health, HIV/AIDS, community development and natural conservation. Volunteers' roles vary dependent on the type of organization they work with, but typical work includes: writing proposals/reports, improving the staff's English and communication skills, assisting with fundraising initiatives and networking with international partners.

Friendship Kindergarten for Disadvantaged Children

Organization: SJ Vietnam
Location: Hanoi
Cost: $600   **Duration:** 1 month   **Age:** 18
Contact: out@sjvietnam.org   **Learn more:** www.sjvietnam.org
Special skills: Must speak English, possess teaching skills, love children and have self-discipline
Details: SJ Vietnam volunteers organize English classes and do other activities to help the kindergarten. You may help with cleaning, organizing games for children, etc. Your creativity is highly

appreciated, so you can contribute your ideas about fun games that children can enjoy. It is very important to let these disadvantaged children know and trust you, so you can share an understanding of their hardships in life and make your time there more meaningful. This will also be a good time for all of you to learn about different cultures from other people by working in a group with both Vietnamese and foreign volunteers.

Aspiration Center for Mentally-Disabled Children

Organization: SJ Vietnam
Location: Hanoi
Cost: $300/2 weeks and $450/3 weeks
Duration: 2 to 3 weeks **Age:** 18
Contact: out@sjvietnam.org **Learn more:** www.sjvietnam.org
Special skills: Must speak English, teaching skills, especially skills and experience relating to mentally disabled people
Details: The purpose of the camp is to help mentally disabled children do routine tasks and then integrate these children into the community. At the Center of Mentally Disabled Children some children are heavily handicapped children, unable to speak and some cannot hear. These children have difficulties in moving, holding things and often easily lose their concentration. You will help them improve their muscular strength by taking them for a walk, teaching them to do simple exercises and to play simple games. For not seriously handicapped children, you may organize an English class, teach them to play simple games, sing songs, draw and many other things. You can also teach them to play sports such as badminton in the backyard.

Transporting Instruction and Environmental Camp

Organization: SJ Vietnam
Location: Hanoi
Cost: $375 **Duration:** 2 weeks **Age:** 18
Contact: out@sjvietnam.org **Learn more:** www.sjvietnam.org
Special skills: Must speak English, hard-working to protect environment, and self-discipline
Details: Global warming is leaving people disturbed and calling them to action. When you join the camp in Hanoi, you will support the implementation of PR programs to raise awareness among the local people about the importance of and ways to protect the environment Hanoi tourist spots, for example, Hoan Kiem Lake, Temple of Literature, etc. Also, you will work with a group of Vietnamese volunteers to teach means of transportation on Hanoi's streets during heavy traffic times. It will be a great and fresh experience when you

directly join Vietnamese transportation efforts to instruct local people on means of transportation during busy hours!

Learn Vietnamese Culture at Handicraft Village

Organization: SJ Vietnam
Location: Bell Village specializing in making Vietnamese traditional hat "Nón", Ha Tay Province
Special skills: Must speak English, hardworking to protect environment, love children, and teaching English
Cost: $450/2 weeks, $600/3 weeks, and $750/1 month
Duration: 2 weeks to 1 month **Age:** 18
Contact: out@sjvietnam.org **Learn more:** www.sjvietnam.org
Details: Volunteers have the chance to join in the manufacturing process of Vietnamese traditional hats, Nón. And, to gain deeper understanding into some aspects of the Vietnamese culture and make hats by yourself. Also, you will work as a"green agent" to do PR programs to raise the awareness of the local people to the importance of preserving the surrounding environment via cleaning, gathering rubbish, organizing environmental discussion, or planting trees. Furthermore, you will organize English Classes for the children because many children in Traditional Handicraft Villages are disadvantaged kids who are very eager to learn English. In this camp, volunteers will participate in homestay in a village. You will have a great opportunity to savoring countryside meals, experience the rural lifestyle and enjoy local scenery.

Vietnam Orphanage Program

Organization: Global Volunteer Network
Location: Volunteers have the opportunity of working in orphanages in Da Nang, Tam Ky and Tuy Hoa.
Cost: $997 for 1 month **Duration:** 1 month to 5 months **Age:** 18
Contact: info@volunteer.org.nz **Learn more:** www.volunteer.org.nz
Details: Volunteers share their time between a variety of placements including working with babies, children, and disabled children, as well as teaching English. In the orphanages and support centers there are many children who suffer from mental and physical disabilities. Qualified physiotherapists, occupational therapists, clinical psychologists, behavioral therapists, play therapists, doctors, nurses, orthotists prosthetists, podiatrists and all people with a healthcare qualification are highly sought after in this Vietnam program.

University Teaching Program

Organization: Global Volunteer Network
Location: Volunteers have opportunities to teach in Duy Tan University, Da Nang University, Tuy Hoa Industrial College or Duy Tan College.
Cost: $997 for 1 month   **Duration:** 1 to 5 months   **Age:** 18
Contact: info@volunteer.org.nz   **Learn more:** www.volunteer.org.nz
Details: Volunteers can contribute by teaching in the following disciplines: English for English Major Students (pronunciation, speaking, writing, culture, and literature), English for Non-English Major Students (communication skills, entrepreneurial skills, international marketing and finance, and tourism management), etc. In Tuy Hoa Industrial College, volunteers have the following subjects/workshops that they can be involved in: English teaching, environmental awareness programs, community service and volunteerism programs. There are also opportunities available for French-speaking volunteers to teach French to university students.

Caring for Disabled Children in Vietnam

Organization: International Volunteer HQ
Location: Placements available in Hanoi and Ho Chi Minh City
Cost: $270 for 1 week to $2,220 for 6 months (includes food and accommodation).
Project Duration: 1 week to 6 months   **Age:** 18
Contact: volunteer@volunteerhq.org
Learn more: www.volunteerhq.org
Details: Although Vietnam has now been at peace for many years, effects from war continue to haunt not only the adult population of this beautiful country, but also its children. Volunteers have the opportunity to work in institutions caring for children and young people affected by Agent Orange or in schools and community clinics looking after mentally disabled children. Work is somewhat varied dependent on the institution where the volunteer is placed, however typical examples of jobs and tasks can include; assisting local staff in providing rehabilitation exercises and therapist treatments for children, playing with children and entertaining/educating them with games, music, arts and other exercises, helping to develop fundraising initiatives to ensure

ongoing funding for these institutions and teaching English to local staff.

Center for Disadvantaged Children

Organization: Experiential Learning International
Location: Mekong Delta
Cost: Starting at $885   **Duration:** 2+ weeks   **Age:** 18
Contact: info@eliabroad.org   **Learn more:** www.eliabroad.org
Details: The Mekong Delta is one of the most densely populated regions of Vietnam. Towns in this region float on rivers or stand above the flood plain on tall stilts. Most people living in the Mekong delta are agricultural workers. The labor intensive process of producing rice leaves parents very little time to spend with their young children to provide them with the education needed outside school. Volunteers will work at a center started by a local priest to give the children of Cai Mon a safe place to stay while their parents are working, as well as provide early childhood education. Volunteers will teach English, lead activities and spend time with the children.

Victims of Agent Orange

Organization: Experiential Learning International
Location: Hanoi
Cost: Starting at $930   **Duration:** 2+ weeks   **Age:** 18
Contact: info@eliabroad.org   **Learn more:** www.eliabroad.org
Details: A tragic legacy of the Vietnam War in the 1960s and 1970s is the millions of people affected by Agent Orange. Between 1961 and 1971, the US military dumped millions of gallons of a herbicide nicknamed Agent Orange on Vietnam. Many of the victims are small children whose parents were exposed to dioxin, suffered chromosomal damage and gave birth to children with birth defects. ELI works with organizations committed to helping the victims of Agent Orange. Volunteers in this program will assist in providing day to day care to the children, lead activities for the children and assist the center staff with tasks around the center.

VISIONS Vietnam

Organization: VISIONS Service Adventures
Location: Varies
Cost: $5,600+   **Duration:** 5 weeks, and customized programs
Age: Teens, customized programs for all ages
Contact: info@VisionsServiceAdventures.com
Learn more: www.VisionsServiceAdventures.com
Details: VISIONS Vietnam blends the bustle of historic Hanoi with serene landscapes of rice paddies, rolling hills and mountains, jungles

and the coast. In the older generation's faces are reflected centuries of perseverance and loyalty to tradition while the youthful majority of Vietnamese seek to embrace Western, market-based principles. Service includes improvements to facilities for those disadvantaged and disabled by the cross-generational effects of chemicals such as Agent Orange, and assisting with classes for children. Participants witness the war's remnant legacy while simultaneously experiencing the forward-looking character of the Vietnamese. Exploration includes historical sites; Ha Long Bay, renowned for its beauty and geology; Sapa, an area of multitudes of indigenous groups near the Chinese boarder; the ancient capital of Hue; silk village of Hoi An; the DMZ.

Northern Cycling

Organization: Hands Up Holidays
Location: Hanoi
Cost: $2,200 per person, based on sharing a room
Duration: 4 days volunteering/15 day trip
Age: 16 years unless accompanied by an adult
Contact: info@handsupholidays.com
Learn more: www.handsupholidays.com
Special skills: None required, but teaching English as a second language (ESL), gardening, physical therapy or medical skills are desirable
Details: A cycling trip is the perfect way to get into the natural pace of this stunning country and meet its inhabitants. Your volunteer project is the final highlight. You get to spend four fulfilling days assisting with repairs and renovations, gardening and teaching English at the Vietnam Friendship Village. Some 500,000 Vietnamese children are thought to have been born with birth defects resulting from the use of Agent Orange, a chemical defoliant deployed during the Vietnam War. By volunteering at the Friendship Village, you have the unique opportunity to directly improve the lives of some of those victims by teaching them English, assisting in the organic garden, or, if you have medical or physical therapy skills you can directly help the children's physical conditions.

Hanoi & Hilltribes

Organization: Hands Up Holidays
Location: Sapa
Cost: $1,200 per person, based on sharing a room, excluding flights.
Duration: 3 days volunteering/8 day trip
Age: 16 years unless accompanied by an adult
Contact: info@handsupholidays.com

Learn more: www.handsupholidays.com
Special skills: None required, but teaching English as a second language (ESL) skills are desirable.
Details: The highlight of this adventure is the opportunity to teach English at a local school in a hilltribe village a day's hike from Sapa. Education is invaluable, as ethnic minority youths compete for employment in a rapidly changing world. You interact with these jovial and curious children and feel rewarded as you help build another small step towards their future. You will explore these beautiful northern reaches of Vietnam, noticing the cultural differences between the lowland Vietnamese and the ethnic minority groups of the mountain regions. Enjoy gorgeous scenery and flora as you hike into the remote reaches of the hills surrounding Sapa. Visit small villages and gain an appreciation and understanding for these warm and proud people that continue to hold fast to age-old traditions.

Vietnamese Venture: Friendship Village

Organization: Hands Up Holidays
Location: Hanoi
Cost: $2,400 per person, based on sharing a room, excluding flights.
Duration: 4 days volunteers/in 15 day trip
Age: 16 years unless accompanied by an adult
Contact: info@handsupholidays.com
Learn more: www.handsupholidays.com
Special skills: None required, but teaching English as a second language (ESL), gardening, physical therapy or medical skills are desirable.
Details: Saigon, the beautiful Mekong delta and its friendly inhabitants, charming Hoi An, historic Hue and delightful Hanoi are just some of the wonderful places to experience and enjoy. However, just as the hustle and bustle of Saigon is a symbol of Vietnam's future, some 500,000 Vietnamese children are thought to have been born with birth defects resulting from the use of Agent Orange, a chemical defoliant deployed during the Vietnam War. By volunteering at the Friendship Village, you have the unique opportunity to directly improve the lives of some of those victims by teaching them English, assisting in the organic garden, or if you have medical or physical therapy skills you can directly help local children's physical conditions. Stunning Halong Bay is your final stop.

Other organizations offering projects in Vietnam:

Global Medic Force: www.globalmedicforce.org
Global Routes: www.globalroutes.org
Globe Aware: www.globeaware.org
i-to-i: www.i-to-i.com

Kaya Responsible Travel: www.kayavolunteer.com
Lattitude Global Volunteering Canada: www.lattitudecanada.org
Medical Teams International: www.medicalteams.org
Volunteering Solutions: www.volunteeringsolutions.com

Europe
Volunteer Opportunities

"The real voyage of discovery consists not in seeing new landscapes, but in having new eyes."

~ Marcel Proust

Albania

Saving Albania's Ottoman Architecture

Organization: Adventures in Preservation
Location: Historic section of Gjirokastra, in southern Albania
Cost: $3,100 **Duration:** 2 weeks **Age:** 18
Contact: workshops@adventuresinpreservation.org
Learn more: www.adventuresinpreservation.org
Special skills: No skills necessary; training provided at the site
Details: Albania, tightly closed to the outside world until the 1990's, is now a travel destination not to be missed. For many Albanian cities, the only means of survival is the development of heritage tourism. Gjirokastra is such a town. It depends on its remarkable Ottoman architecture, large stone tower houses built over a period of 500 years, to draw tourists. Once the Ottomans departed, the residents had no resources to maintain these amazing houses, and hundreds have been lost or are on the verge of collapse. AiP volunteers will work with an international team learning hands-on skills and using these skills to restore one of the tower houses. The workshop fee covers lodging, meals, transportation from Tirana, instruction, fieldtrips and insurance.

Other organizations offering projects in the Albania:

Experiment Albania: www.experiment-albania.org
The Italian Scientists and Scholars in North America Foundation
   www.issnaf.org/web
Service Civil International: www.sci-ivs.org
Transitions Abroad: www.transitionsabroad.com
Volunteers for International Partnership:
   www.partnershipvolunteers.org
Volunteers for Peace: www.vfp.org

Bosnia and Herzegovina

Organizations offering projects in Bosnia and Herzegovina:

Concordia: www.concordia-iye.org.uk
Firefly International: www.fireflyinternational.org
Kiva Fellows Program: www.kiva.org
Youth for Life (youth-camp): www.pdvideta.comyr.com

Bulgaria

Animal Rescue for Volunteer Hearts

Organization: Bulgarian Society for Animal Protection and Preservation
Location: Sofia
Cost: None   **Duration:** 1+ week for at least 4 hrs per day   **Age:** 16
Contact: bsappbg@hotmail.com   **Learn more:** www.bsapp.org
Special skills: Must speak English or Bulgarian and love animals.
Details: BSAPP is one of the few animal protection organizations operating in Bulgaria today. Bulgaria has a long history of problems with dog and cat homelessness, neglect and abuse which continues today. The organization's focus is on the rescue of injured, abused, neglected and homeless dogs and cats as well as working to give them a second chance by placing them in loving homes. BSAPP is also a strong supporter of the sterilization of dogs and cats in order to control the population and thus provides low cost, no cost sterilizations at its clinic. They need people who are willing to get themselves dirty, cleaning, feeding, bathing and walking animals. And, if you like to do maintenance, painting and cleaning they would really love our help. A

person who has fundraising or public relations experience and is good at office work is also very useful.

Orphanage Home to 250 Babies and Children

Organization: CAST
Location: In the town of Pleven in northern Bulgaria.
Cost: $375 for 3 weeks
Duration: Runs monthly from the 4th – 29th **Age:** 16
Contact: Amy McCulloch: recruitment@cast-uk.com
Learn more: www.cast-uk.com
Special skills: Volunteers need to have some experience working with children or adults with disabilities before taking part in this project
Details: For this project CAST has partnered with Bulgaria's Abandoned Children's Trust in order to offer volunteers the life-changing opportunity to work with children who are in desperate need of your support. The orphanage is home to 250 babies and children of all ages, many of whom show symptoms of institutionalized autism as well as physical and/or learning disabilities. Volunteers live and work in teams of four and all volunteers are given training in Intensive Interaction and Behavioral & Emotional Management Training prior to the trip.

Occupational Therapy, Applied Sciences, Youth Development and Education

Organization: Isla-International Service Learning Alliance
Location: Kustindil, Bulgaria
Cost: 8 weeks for $3,585; 12 weeks for $4,365
Duration: 2 to 8 weeks for volunteers or 9 to 52 weeks for an internship
Age: 18
Contact: info@isla-serve.org **Learn more:** www.isla-serve.org
Special skills: Applicants with training or experience sufficient to train others in therapeutic methods are encouraged to apply.
Details: Isla has identified the need for care workers to work on an orphanage project with children who are moderately to severely handicapped. The project also seeks therapy trainers to educate care workers in homes for children and adults in methods and practices in occupational therapy, physical therapy, art and music therapy or behavioral management. The opportunity for occupational therapy and

other applied sciences, youth development and education students to serve is an amazing way for aspiring professionals to step outside the box of traditional volunteer work. For example, the need for occupational therapy development compared to the amount of assistance available is so great that Isla volunteers will have the advantage of helping to lay the foundation for successful practices in occupational therapy in rural Bulgaria while developing their own skills in leadership and sustainable development.

Natural Resources and Wildlife

Organization: Isla-International Service Learning Alliance
Location: Varies
Cost: 8 weeks for $3,585; 12 weeks for $4,365
Duration: 2 to 8 weeks for volunteers or 9 to 52 weeks for an internship
Age: 18
Contact: info@isla-serve.org **Learn more:** www.isla-serve.org
Special skills: Strong people-skills and a desire to have fun by serving and learning from new communities and environments via cross-cultural exchange.
Details: Isla offers opportunities for individuals with majors or experience in natural resources, wildlife biology, environmental conservation, environmental education and ecotourism to serve on projects with the following host organizations: Green Balkans, The Bulgarian Society for the Protection of Birds and BlueLink. It is most important to be highly motivated and enthusiastic because the work is

quite demanding. Both BSPB and Green Balkans are looking for people who are very passionate about nature. Candidates should be at undergraduate or graduate levels, though they do have some positions for "gap years", working professionals and retirees. Skills such as IT, GIS, fundraising, business, etc. are also needed.

Bulgaria Teaching Summer

Organization: WorldTeach
Location: Bulgaria
Cost: $3,990
Duration: 2 months (late June- late August) **Age:** 18-24
Contact: info@worldteach.org **Learn more:** www.worldteach.org
Special skills: Fluent English skills
Details: WorldTeach Bulgaria volunteers will spend the summer in urban and rural areas, teaching teenage and younger orphans English,

computer literacy, and practical life skills through interactive approaches stimulating students' creativity and personal development. Volunteers can either teach at local foster homes or participate in the STEP Bulgaria program (Summer Teaching English) which brings together about 40 teenagers from five different orphanages across the country. STEP Bulgaria focuses on developing students' language, technical and practical life skills to facilitate their integration into society once they leave their state institutions. In addition to interacting with their students on a daily basis, WorldTeach volunteers will have the assistance of local Bulgarian university students and high school students also volunteering for the program.

Avgusta Traiana-Beroia-Borui Excavation Project

Organization: Balkan Heritage Field School
Location: Stara Zagora, Bulgaria
Cost: $1,650 for two week period **Duration:** 2 weeks to 1 month
Age: 18, 16 with parental consent
Contact: balkanheritage@gmail.com
Learn more: www.bhfieldschool.org
Details: The Bulgarian city of Stara Zagora, like many towns in Europe and the Mediterranean, was built atop debris from thousands of years of continuous human settlement. Most famously, the modern city hides the remnants of: the major Roman walled town of Avgusta Traiana (originally founded by the emperor Trajan in 107 A.D). Early Byzantine city of Beroia and the medieval Bulgarian town of Borui. Excavations take place at the ancient city's gate, walls, forum and residential areas as well as medieval religious buildings. All participants will be able to take part in: fieldwork and lab work, educational courses (lectures, workshops and trainings in Field and Roman Archaeology), and guided visits to the ancient city of Plovdiv as well as to the Rose Valley and Thracian tombs (UNESCO World Heritage Site).

Restoration & Documentation of Ancient Pottery Workshop

Organization: Balkan Heritage Field School
Location: Emona on the Black Sea
Cost: $1,650 **Duration:** 2 weeks **Age:** 18, 16
with parental consent
Contact: balkanheritage@gmail.com
Learn more: www.bhfieldschool.org
Special skills: Basic drawing skills are a plus
Details: The workshop will guide the participants

through the history of ancient Greek and Roman pottery, its production and consequent stages of archaeological conservation, documentation, study and restoration. Both the theoretical and practical courses will be based on pottery from the museums' inventories, found in various ancient (Ancient Greek, Hellenistic, Roman and Late Roman) sites in present day Bulgaria. The project includes 3 modules: practical work in documentation and restoration of ancient Greek and Roman pottery, educational course (lectures, trainings, study - and behind-the-scenes visits) and excursions to the ancient coastal towns of Nessebar (UNESCO World Heritage Site), Sozopol and Varna. Included are all educational and fieldwork activities, tools and materials, accommodation and meals, excursions, sightseeing tours and entrance fees as well as administrative costs.

Heraclea Lyncestis Excavation Project
Organization: Balkan Heritage Field School
Location: Bitola, Macedonia
Cost: $1,650 for two week period
Duration: 2 weeks to 1 month   **Age:** 18
Contact: balkanheritage@gmail.com
Learn more: www.bhfieldschool.org
Details: Every summer you can help excavate the classical city of Heraclea Lyncestis in southwestern Macedonia. Philip of Macedon, father of Alexander the Great, founded the hilltop site of Heraclea in the fourth century B.C. as a strategic and commercial outpost in the fertile plain of Lyncestis. Under Roman rule, the city expanded greatly and became a key stopping point on the long road between Rome and Asia Minor. All participants will be able to take part in: fieldwork and lab work, educational courses (lectures, workshops and trainings in Field and Classical Archaeology), and guided visits to the Roman city of Stobi as well as the town and lake of Ohrid (UNESCO World Heritage Site). Included are educational and fieldwork activities, accommodations, meals, excursions, sightseeing tours, entrance fees as well as administrative costs.

Fresco-Hunting Photo Expedition to Medieval Churches
Organization: Balkan Heritage Field School
Location: Bankya-Sofia, Bulgaria
Cost: $1,800   **Duration:** 2 weeks   **Age:** 18
Contact: balkanheritage@gmail.com
Learn more: www.bhfieldschool.org
Special skills: Sketching/drawing skills and/or basic knowledge in documental photography
Details: Every May join archaeologists, art historians and conservators as they document the beautiful but rapidly deteriorating frescoes from long abandoned medieval chapels and small churches in western Bulgaria. The project seeks to photograph, document and

study the church frescoes before it is too late. All participants will be able to take part in: fieldwork (database recording, sketching, measuring, and making a photographic record); educational courses (lectures, workshops and training in Southeast European medieval history, Orthodox iconography and fresco restoration), and guided tours of Sofia and Rila monastery (UNESCO World Heritage Site). Volunteer fee includes your educational and fieldwork activities, travel to and from the fieldwork sites, accommodation and meals, excursions, sightseeing tours and entrance fees, transfer from and to Sofia airport, etc.

Other organizations offering projects in the Bulgaria:

Canadian Alliance for Development Initiatives and Projects: www.cadip.org
Community Recycling for Organic Produce: www.cropscheme.org
Concordia: www.concordia-iye.org.uk
Fund for Wild Flora and Fauna (wildlife census, mixed birds, vulture program eco-farm): www.fwff.org
Green Balkans: www.greenbalkans.org
Green Balkans – Wildlife Rehabilitation & Breeding Center: www.greenbalkans-wrbc.org

Croatia

Organizations offering projects in Croatia:

A Pas de Loup: www.apasdeloup.org
Concordia: www.concordia-iye.org.uk
International Student Volunteers: www.isvonline.com
Service Civil International: www.sci-ivs.org
Transitions Abroad: www.transitionsabroad.com
Volunteers for Peace: www.vfp.org

Czech Republic

Organizations offering projects in the Czech Republic:

Concordia: www.concordia-iye.org.uk
Earthwatch Institute: www.earthwatch.org
International Internship & Volunteer Network: www.iivnetwork.com

France

Service-Learning Experience on the French Mediterranean

Organization: Institut Mediterraneen de Langues & Services (IMLS)
Location: Montpellier (France)
Cost: $2,240 - $9,900 including homestay (1/2 board), excursions and insurance **Duration:** 1 to 4 months **Age:** 18
Contact: imls@imls.fr **Learn more:** www.imls.fr
Details: A meaningful project and a growing experience: 1) improve your language skills 2) develop intercultural awareness by living in a homestay family 3) link up theory (course on French institutions) and experience learning by: participating in recreation activities (hospital for children, retirement home), tutoring (hospital for children, schools) and helping out the handicapped persons. This is an unforgettable travel and give-back experience in a region renowned for its rich historical heritage, its prestigious medieval university and cultural festivals on the shores of the Mediterranean.
Other organizations offering projects in France:

AmeriSpan Study Abroad (internship): www.amerispan.com
The Art Farm: www.theartfarm.info
GeoVisions: www.geovisions.org
La Sabranenque: www.sabranenque.com
Transitions Abroad: www.transitionsabroad.com
United Planet: www.unitedplanet.org
Work Away: www.workaway.info

Germany

Teach at the Waldorf School

Organization: Experiential Learning International
Location: Enkenbach-Alsenborn
Cost: Starting at $1,685 **Duration:** 4+ weeks **Age:** 18
Contact: info@eliabroad.org   **Learn more:** www.eliabroad.org
Special skills: Intermediate German skills, fluent English language skills
Details: This is a private elementary and secondary school run according to the anthroposophic principles of Rudolf Steiner. Gain insight into the Waldorf methodology while improving your German language skills. While teaching you will live with a local family. There are endless places to visit and the superb German transportation system makes it easy to see the country.

Other organizations offering projects in Germany:

Amizade (Auschwitz Museum...): www.amizade.org
Canadian Alliance for Development Initiatives and Projects:
  www.cadip.org
Concordia: www.concordia-iye.org.uk
GeoVisions: www.geovisions.org
Transitions Abroad: www.transitionsabroad.com

Greece

Karpathos Island Animal Rescue

Organization: Animal Welfare Karpathos
Location: Karpathos Island
Cost: None **Duration:** Open **Age:** 18
Contact: secretary@animalwelfarekarpathos.org
Learn more: www.animalwelfarekarpathos.org
Details: Animal Welfare Karpathos was started because the island was full of strays. Volunteer vets come twice a year to neuter/spay. After almost a decade, real progress can be seen. AWK welcomes vet techs and veterinarians, but most of their volunteers are not trained. Someone with a farm background would be wonderful, because in addition to dogs and cats, AWK receives sheep, goats, donkeys and cows. There are never enough helpers to give the dogs baths and haircuts or to trim their nails. You can also assist in their clinic or

pick up medications at the pharmacy. During May and September volunteers may trap cats and dogs for neutering/spaying, maintain comprehensive record of where they were found and return them following recovery from surgery.

Transnatura Mountain Bike Stage

Organization: Cultural Triangle of Prespa, the Ecotourism companies of Vitsi and Grammos and the NGO Arcturos.
Location: Regions of Nymphaio-Amytaio, Nestorio-Grammos and the Prespa lakes.
Cost: None. Food and accommodation are provided.
Duration: From three days to one week (5-7 hours per day) at the beginning of September   **Age:** 18
Contact: ctprespa@otenet.gr, +302385051332
Learn more: www.ctp.gr, www.welcometoprespa.com, www.transnatura.gr
Special skills: Activities skills for youth and children (nature, bicycle and orienteering knowledge), logistics skills (knowledge as volunteer in the same type of project).
Details: Transnatura is an annual event that includes a bike race and several animations for the local people and tourists. During the race, the volunteers will be in charge of the organization of several workshops with youth and children: bicycle games, orienteering games, etc and the running and coordinating of the race and extra activities of Transnatura (concerts, festivals and more).

The Ark Rescue of Corfu

Organization: The Ark, Friends of Animals
Location: Corfu Island
Cost: None   **Duration:** 3+ days
Email: info@corfuanimalwelfare.com
Learn more: www.corfuanimalwelfare.com
Details: The Ark was founded in 1997 to help the animals of this beautiful Mediterranean island. They focus on helping dogs and cats and sometimes birds. Due to limited financial means volunteers are most welcome. The rescue can use all kinds of people and expertise: grooming the dogs, giving veterinarian advice, poop scooping in the olive grove, repairing the fences or building dog houses, etc. Volunteers are asked to give at least 4 hours per day and accommodations will be provided if space is available.

Prespa Children, Prespa in Motion

Organization: Cultural Triangle of Prespa (Greece)
Location: Villages in the region of Greek Prespa (there are 12 villages in total)
Cost: None. Food and accommodations are provided.
Duration: 1 week (3 hours per day) to 1 month during Easter and summer holidays   **Age:** 18 and over
Contact: ctprespa@otenet.gr, +302385051332
Learn more: www.ctp.gr, www.welcometoprespa.com
Special skills: Activity skills for children and youth (sports, outdoors, or artistic projects), speaking Greek is not obligatory but would be nice.
Details: Be not a tourist, be deeply integrated into the culture and inhabitants of the Greek Prespa rural area by getting involved in their activities! Prespa has very few leisure opportunities for the locals. The role of the volunteers is to: provide the local children and young people different activities, to socialize with them and increase their interests in art and culture, and organize physical and outdoor activities during their holidays. And, why not make these workshops known to the local community at the end? Arrange presentations, sports competitions, concerts, exhibitions, etc. They are very open to any ideas and collaboration!

Wildlife Hospital

Organization: GoEco
Location: Aegina Island
Cost: $420 **Duration:** 2 to 8 weeks   **Age:** 18
Contact: goeco@goeco.org   **Learn more:** www.GoEco.org
Details: The Wildlife Hospital began its activities in 1984 and today it is the oldest and largest wildlife rehabilitation center in Greece and Southern Europe. The Wildlife Hospital treats 3,000 to 4,500 injured, poisoned or orphaned wild animals from all over Greece. As a volunteer you will gain an unforgettable experience by working with

the animals. You will work with local staff and volunteers from around the world. This is a beautiful, productive opportunity to explore and experience the beauty of Greece on the Island of Aegina.

Ionian Dolphin Project: Delphi's Dolphins

Organization: Tethys Research Institute
Location: Galaxidi, Gulf of Corinth – Ionian Greece
Cost: $410.00 per week **Duration:** 1+ week **Age:** 18
Contact: tethys@tethys.org; istituto.tethys@gmail.com

Learn more: www.tethys.org
Special skills: English speaking; and be in good physical condition, tolerant of hot weather, sun and long periods (up to 4-5 hours) on an inflatable boat.
Details: Since 1991, this project has investigated the ecology, behavior and conservation of two dolphin species in the waters of the eastern Ionian Sea, Greece. You will be trained through lectures and working side by side with researchers and will be involved in field activities that include regular surveys of the study area. You will spot dolphins and other animals during the surveys at sea, and once dolphins are sighted, you will contribute to the data collection. The afternoon is for preliminary analysis of digital photos of the dolphins. The research team investigates dolphin ecology, behavior, feeding habits, interactions with human activities and dolphin response to habitat degradation. Researchers aim to identify the main threats affecting the animals and offer scientific support to management actions that can ensure a favorable conservation status of the dolphins and their ecosystem.

Animal Welfare: Ending the Tragedy for Greek Dogs

Organization: inside/out Humanitourism™ Adventures
Location: Athens, Greece and Ioannina
Cost: $2,500-$3,000
Duration: 5 days + 5 days of locally guided active adventures*
Age: No age minimum, determined on an individual basis
Contact: info@theinsideandout.com
Learn more: www.theinsideandout.com
Details: While you experience the beauty of Greece, you will spend the first part of your trip volunteering at an incredible animal shelter and rehabilitation facility near Athens, working on shelter improvements. Then you'll travel to Ioannina in northern Greece continuing educational work begun in 2009. Efforts in Ioannina will be focused on a leaflet campaign with the local university population, but may also include assistance work, such as spay/neuter, vaccinations, microchipping, care for sick or injured dogs and feeding programs. inside/out trips are designed around opportunities to do humanitarian volunteer work on meaningful international projects and are combined with sustainable eco-adventure travel in the local area of the project and people. Their trips are designed to create longer-term relationships between communities and travelers.

Zakynthos Island Sea Turtle Conservation

Organization: inside/out Humanitourism™ Adventures
Location: Zakynthos Island, Greece
Cost: $3,295

Duration: 1 week + 1 week of locally guided active adventures
Age: No age minimum, determined on an individual basis
Contact: info@theinsideandout.com
Learn more: www.theinsideandout.com
Details: Work on a project to preserve, protect and provide education about the Mediterranean Loggerhead Sea Turtle, an endangered species with nesting grounds on the beaches of the Greek island of Zakynthos. The focus of this tour will be hands on work maintaining and improving nesting areas, including monitoring and reporting turtle activity, a leaflet distributing campaign, a beach cleanup day and helping to build a rescue and rehabilitation facility on the island. You also spend a day at the Sea Turtle Rescue Center in Athens, touring the facility and volunteering with the sea turtles in rehabilitation there. *Inside/Out trips are designed around opportunities to do humanitarian volunteer work on meaningful international projects and are combined with sustainable eco-adventure travel in the local area of the project and people.

Other organizations offering projects in Greece:

A Pas de Loup: www.apasdeloup.org
Earth Sea & Sky (Ionian Nature Conservation): www.earthseasky.org
Earthwatch Institute: www.earthwatch.org
Frontier (broadcasting): www.frontier.ac.uk
Global Visions International: www.gviusa.com
Global Volunteers: www.globalvolunteers.org
Greeka: www.greeka.com
The Silva Project (Corfu Equine Projects): www.thesilvaproject.org

Iceland

Whales and Tourism
Organization: The Húsavík Whale Museum
Location: Húsavík and the Bay of Skjálfandi, Northeast Iceland
Cost: None   **Age:** 20
Contact: info@whalemuseum.is   **Learn more:** www.whalemuseum.is
Special skills: Preferably students or post-graduates in marine biology, biology, museology, graphic design or marketing.
Details: The Húsavík Whale Museum is a non-profit organization established in 1997 to form an educational component to whale watching tours operated from Húsavík. The Museum's mission is to

educate the public about the marine ecosystem and cetacean species inhabiting the world's oceans. The museum has been constantly growing with an emphasis on education and science. The educational component presents informative and attractive exhibits that raise awareness about cetaceans and their environment. The museum operates a research program in cooperation with the University of Iceland Research Centre in Húsavík as well as international institutions. Volunteers play an important part in the museum's research working on data collection, processing and cataloguing. The museum was formally acknowledged as an educational facility by the Icelandic Ministry of Education in 2007. Volunteers travel at their own expense and get lodging on site, but have to provide their own meals.

Reykjavík Photomarathon

Organization: SEEDS Iceland
Location: Reykjavík and around Iceland
Cost: $200 **Duration:** 2 weeks
Age: 18 (under 18 considered with parental consent)
Contact: seeds@seedsiceland.org
Learn more: www.seedsiceland.org
Special skills: None. Volunteers just need a digital camera.
Details: In the past the SEEDS Photomarathon has proved very successful, combining volunteering work around Reykjavík, photography lessons, photography excursions and, finally, a public exhibition of photographs from the camp. The camp is intended to raise awareness of volunteering and environmental issues in Iceland. SEEDS Iceland hopes to expand the Photomarathon project, running more camps over the summer in more locations around the country.

Reykjavík International Film Festival (RIFF)

Organization: SEEDS Iceland
Location: Reykjavík and around Iceland
Cost: $200 **Duration:** 2 weeks
Age: 18 (under 18 considered with parental consent)
Contact: seeds@seedsiceland.org
Learn more: www.seedsiceland.org

Details: Working as a volunteer for the RIFF is
perfect for people interested in film. Volunteers work on many tasks through the festival, from film projection or selling tickets, to driving around supplies or even waiting on film stars at glamorous parties. Volunteers have the chance to visit the film screenings and special events during their free time, and get to enjoy all that Reykjavík and the film festival has to offer.

Conservation and Heritage in The Wild West of Iceland

Organization: SEEDS Iceland
Location: A remote fjord in the west of Iceland
Cost: $200 **Duration:** 2 weeks
Age: 18 (under 18 considered with parental consent)
Contact: seeds@seedsiceland.org
Learn more: www.seedsiceland.org
Details: This project has been running for two years, and has proved very successful. Work revolves around the restoration of a former whaling station in the Westfjords of Iceland, in a remote place only accessible by 4x4 vehicles. The buildings of the whaling station have been abandoned since the early 20th Century and are being preserved as part of the local cultural heritage. Although accommodations are comfortable, the camp has electricity for only part of the day, and campers are encouraged to forage for food in the local area. There are plenty of fish in the fjord and blueberries cover the hills. This camp is perfect for people who want to get in touch with nature and experience the beauty of the Icelandic Fjords.

Conservation and Environment Between the Glaciers

Organization: SEEDS Iceland
Location: Vatnajokull National Park and Thorsmork reserve
Cost: $200 **Duration:** 2 weeks
Age: 18 (under 18 considered with parental consent)
Contact: seeds@seedsiceland.org
Learn more: www.seedsiceland.org
Details: This double project allows volunteers to spend a week each in two of the most beautiful places in Iceland: the Vatnajokull NP at Skaftafell, and Thorsmork reserve, two of Iceland's beautiful glacier parks. Famous for their beauty, SEEDS has been working with local organizations to preserve the natural heritage in the parks, and to open up access to the public. Work involves protecting the natural flora from an invasive introduced species of lupine, intended to prevent erosion, but which is strangling the native flora; as well as work fixing hiking trails in both parks. Volunteers will have plenty of opportunity to explore the beautiful nature and will be shown some of Iceland's most incredible sights.

Nature and Heritage in the East of Iceland

Organization: SEEDS Iceland
Location: A remote nature reserve in the East fjords of Iceland
Cost: $200 **Duration:** 2 weeks
Age: 18 (under 18 considered with parental consent)
Contact: seeds@seedsiceland.org

Learn more: www.seedsiceland.org
Details: In a beautiful and remote nature reserve in the far east of Iceland, volunteers will be working to preserve the local flora and fauna as part of long running project by the owner of the land. They have striven for years to research and preserve the natural environment of the area with help from volunteers and academic researchers from around the world. Work will initially be mainly on reforestation, but it is very likely that on completion of the planting, other activities will be undertaken such as: traditional turf wall construction, stone wall construction, path building and maintenance, lupine control, preparation of an organic vegetable garden and cleaning of the coast line. The beauty of this place cannot be described.

Nature and Heritage in the Reykjavík Area

Organization: SEEDS Iceland
Location: A recreational park in a town close to Reykjavík
Cost: $200 **Duration:** 2 weeks
Age: 18 (under 18 considered with parental consent)
Contact: seeds@seedsiceland.org
Learn more: www.seedsiceland.org
Details: Working using traditional Viking methods, volunteers will be creating recreational spots in a pretty park close to Reykjavík. The park is adjacent to a new town and opening access to the park is a priority for the town's community group. With three successful camps there in 2009, there are great plans for 2010 and beyond. The park surrounds a small trout-fishing lake used regularly by the local residents. And in late summer its woods are full of wild mushrooms. Work may include creating more recreational communal areas in the park, and building hiking trails over the hills and through the woods. Close proximity to Reykjavík also allows volunteers to enjoy all that Iceland's capital has to offer.

Videy Island, a Quiet Haven in Icelandic Capital

Organization: SEEDS Iceland
Location: Videy Island, Reykjavík city
Cost: $200 **Duration:** 2 weeks
Age: 18 (under 18 considered with parental consent)
Contact: seeds@seedsiceland.org
Learn more: www.seedsiceland.org
Details: Videy is the location of a number of our camps throughout the summer in Reykjavík. Work on the island, located 3 minutes by boat from Reykjavík, may include: preparing and tending to a vegetable garden; preparing the facilities on the island for visitor; removing invasive plant species, cleaning the coastline, harvesting and

preparing vegetables grown (at the end of the summer), and preparing Yoko Ono's peace tower sculpture for its opening ceremony. The island enjoys both access to the facilities and fun of Iceland's capital, and the peace and quiet of a getaway island. The views over Reykjavík bay are stunning, and through the summer there are wonderful sunsets. After September, volunteers even have a chance to see the northern lights.

The Path to the Volcanoes, West Iceland

Organization: SEEDS Iceland
Location: West Iceland
Cost: $200 **Duration:** 2 weeks
Age: 18 (under 18 considered with parental consent)
Contact: seeds@seedsiceland.org
Learn more: www.seedsiceland.org
Details: Working with the local university, a number of different jobs will be undertaken. The primary work of 2009 was constructing a hiking trail leading to a small volcano near the campus. Future projects will include the maintenance and extension of this path and the building of new paths in the area, as well as working all around the university to improve the grounds. The area offers many opportunities to explore the natural beauty and geological interest for which Iceland is famous. A lava field flows from the small volcano and there are many opportunities for hiking to waterfalls and the local lake. Volunteers also get full use of the university sports facilities, including the geothermal hotpots.

'Happy Days' in North East Iceland

Organization: SEEDS Iceland
Location: East Iceland
Cost: $200 **Duration:** 2 weeks
Age: 18 (under 18 considered with parental consent)
Contact: seeds@seedsiceland.org
Learn more: www.seedsiceland.org
Details: In the far northeast of Iceland, this camp focuses on environmental works to assist the local environment and community. The project will consist of reforestation work and monitoring reforestation from previous years, as well as cleaning the local beaches. During the camp the volunteers will also assist in the preparations for the local 'Happy Days Festival', a celebration of fun in the town. Past camps here have been great successes thanks to our generous host, always keen to show the volunteers his appreciation; and to the comfortable accommodation, with unrestricted access to the swimming pool and hot tubs. Volunteers also get to see some of Iceland's most famous sights on the journeys there and back.

Nature and Conservation in the Westman Islands

Organization: SEEDS Iceland
Location: Westman Islands, South Iceland
Cost: $200 **Duration:** 2 weeks
Age: 18 (under 18 considered with parental consent)
Contact: seeds@seedsiceland.org
Learn more: www.seedsiceland.org
Details: The Westman Islands archipelago became famous in the 1970s when the eruption of a volcano on Heimaey created a new mountain, covering the island in volcanic ash, and with lava threatening to engulf the town and block the harbor. Thanks to the valiant efforts of locals, and international help, the community was saved and today is still thriving. The work focuses on seeding parts of the volcano and lava field most prone to wind erosion, spreading fertilizer and seeds. The work will be quite demanding but very rewarding, and is an amazing chance to stay in this beautiful place. In the free time, there are plenty of opportunities to hike and to explore the archipelago.

Other organizations offering projects in Iceland:

*Canadian Alliance for Development Initiatives and Projects:
   www.cadip.org
Earthwatch Institute: www.earthwatch.org
Iceland Conservation Volunteers (trail teams, National Parks work):
   english.ust.is
 World Horizons International: www.world-horizons.com
Worldwide Friends Iceland (nature, peace, workcamps): www.wf.is
United Planet: www.unitedplanet.org*

Italy

Sea Turtle Preservation & Education

Organization: A.R.C.H.E
Location: Italian Coast
Cost: From 200 euros per week
Duration: Open **Age** 24
Contact: archeturtle@archeturtle.org
Learn more www.archeturtle.org
Details: The A.R.C.H.E. Association - Research and Educational Activities for Chelonian Conservation was founded in March 2003; it is a non-profit organization. A.R.C.H.E. volunteers get to carry on

educational activities for tourists on the beaches and collect data on sea turtles accidentally captured by local fishermen. You are asked to work a minimum of five hours per day and get one day per week off. Food and accommodations are included.

Cetacean Sanctuary Research

Organization: Tethys Research Institute
Location: Ligurian Sea
Cost: $545 per week **Duration:** 1+ week **Age:** 18
Contact: tethys@tethys.org; istituto.tethys@gmail.com
Learn more: www.tethys.org
Special skills: No experience in the field is required. Volunteers will be trained through specific lectures and work with researchers.
Details: Since 1990, this whale and dolphin volunteer program has been dedicated to investigating the spatial distribution, habitat preferences, ecology and behavior of cetaceans living in the Cetacean Sanctuary - a special marine protected area extending between Italy and France. By volunteering on this program you will contribute towards this vital research and help to protect some spectacular species. Research focuses on beautiful large-fin whales, sperm whales, Risso's dolphins, pilot whales, and striped and bottlenose dolphins. This is conducted by field techniques, which include individual photo identification, remote tracking, distance sampling and behavioral sampling. Intense research activities conducted in this region have also been raising remarkable public awareness. Prices include sleeping on board a 20-m motorsailer and food.

Bottlenose Dolphins of Sardinia Island

Organization: Bottlenose Dolphin Research Institute
Location: Sardinia Island in the Mediterranean Sea
Cost: $100 per day **Duration:** 6 days to 3 months **Age:** 18
Contact: info@thebdri.com **Learn more:** www.thebdri.com
Details: BDRI researchers carry out one of the longest ongoing research projects of a resident dolphin population in the Mediterranean Sea. Volunteers assist researchers with data collection and recording while on the boat, helping to locate and keep track of dolphins, recording behavioural data, environmental information and recording sounds, video or photos. If you are looking for a volunteer opportunity that incorporates boat-based field work, marine mammal research, intensive training and mentoring in marine ecology, and encouragement to work hard, have fun, and learn from the dolphins and each other, then consider volunteering with the BDRI. The fee includes accommodation in an apartment, dolphin research training, certificate of attendance, printed material and all associated field and

laboratory costs during your stay. Food is available at the local supermarkets within walking distance at your own expense

Archeodig Project/Archaeological Field School

Organization: Archeodig and Soprintendenza per I Beni Archeologici della Toscana
Location: Populonia (Piombino-Livorno), Tuscany
Cost: $900 **Duration:** 1+ week **Age:** 16
Contact: info@archeodig.net **Learn more:** www.archeodig.net
Details: Populonia was one of the most important Etruscan cities overlooking the Tyrrhenian Sea. The city was for centuries one of the most flourishing centres of iron smelting and trade all over the Mediterranean. Volunteers enjoy archaeological excavation, increasing the knowledge on Populonia in the Roman Age. Volunteers are needed to help the local community know and save its archaeological heritage. The main objective of the project is to fill as many as possible of the gaps in knowledge of the history of Populonia and its territory, from the early Roman period to the Middle Ages. Volunteers and students will be accommodated in double or multiple rooms, in apartments with all the fundamental comforts. No experience in archaeology or knowledge of Italian is expected.

Other organizations offering projects in Italy:

A Pas de Loup: www.apasdeloup.org
ArcheoSpain (archeology): www.archaeospain.com
Concordia: www.concordia-iye.org.uk
GeoVisions: www.geovisions.org
Global Visions International: www.gviusa.com or www.gvi.co.uk
International Partnership for Service-Learning and Internship:
  www.ipsl.org
Italy Eco Village: www.italyecovillage.com
L.I.P.U. Reggio Calabria (avian anti-poaching, Sardinia):
  www.lipu.it
Mediterranean Center for Art and Sciences: www.saisicily.com
Torre Argentina Roman Cat Sanctuary: www.romancats.com
Transitions Abroad: www.transitionsabroad.com

Poland

Youth Camp in Poland

Organization: Experiential Learning International
Location: Krakow
Cost: $795 **Duration:** 2+ weeks **Age:** 18
Contact: info@eliabroad.org **Learn more:** www.eliabroad.org
Details: You will begin your adventure in Krakow, with 2 days of orientation before heading to a camp located in or very near the Tatra mountains. Once there, you'll join trained Polish counselors who also work and live at the site. Facilities will be simple but adequate. You'll live in summer resort-type housing (not tents) with meals served cafeteria-style. The camp operates July through August, with 4 two-

week sessions in all. There will be approximately 20 children in each session, divided by age into 2 groups. ELI is looking to place two volunteers per session - you can sign up for just one two-week session or the entire two months, it's up to you.

Poland Teaching Summer

Organization: WorldTeach
Location: Varies
Cost: $3,990
Duration: 2 months (late June- late August) **Age:** 18-74
Contact: info@worldteach.org **Learn more:** www.worldteach.org
Special skills: Fluent in English (undergraduates welcome!)
Details: The WorldTeach Poland program offers you the unique opportunity to have an unforgettable summer experience of educational exchange and cultural immersion in communities that uphold hospitality as a core value. As a volunteer, you will mainly teach high school students at your placement site, though some middle school and elementary school students will also participate. Volunteers will be responsible for teaching conversational English, basic grammar and some lessons on American culture. All volunteers will have Internet access, and most will also have computer labs to use for instruction. Classes are open to the entire community, allowing students with a wide range of pre-existing English skills to participate. Housing, meals and language immersion provided with host family.

Other organizations offering projects in Poland:

Global Volunteer Network: www.volunteer.org.nz
Global Volunteer Projects: www.globalvolunteerprojects.org

Habitat for Humanity International: www.habitat.org
IBO Italia: www.iboitalia.org
Lattitude Global Volunteering Canada: www.lattitudecanada.org
Transitions Abroad: www.transitionsabroad.com
Wolves and Humans: www.wolvesandhumans.org

Portugal

One Million Seeds for the Côa Valley

Organization: ATN (Associação Transumância e Natureza)
Location: Faia Brava Reserve, Algodres village, Figueira de Castelo Rodrigo, Guarda district, Northeast Portugal
Cost: $70 registration fee, no extra charge for up to 1 month in duration
Duration: 2+ week **Age:** 18
Contact: voluntarios@atnatureza.org
Learn more: www.ATNatureza.org
Details: Vast areas of Portugal have been devastated by fire. The Faia Brava Reserve, managed by ATN, has been particularly affected by a massive fire in 2003. Today they can still see the effects on the landscape, habitats and biodiversity. ATN has been developing a woodland protection project called Faia Brava Woodland. Now you have the opportunity to actively participate as a volunteer in this project, through the program "1 Million Seeds for the Côa Valley". With your support, they want to work on woodland recovery by planting native trees and sowing seeds directly on the ground. The major goal of this initiative is to collect and sow 1 million seeds of native trees in the next 5 years, in an area of about 500 ha.

Faia Brava Fauna Monitoring Programme

Organization: ATN (Associação Transumância e Natureza)
Location: Faia Brava Reserve, Algodres village, Figueira de Castelo Rodrigo, Guarda district, Northeast Portugal
Cost: $70 registration fee, no extra charge for up to 1 month in duration **Duration:** 2+ weeks **Age:** 18
Contact: voluntarios@atnatureza.org
Learn more: www.ATNatureza.org
Details: ATN has dedicated the last 6 years to the creation of a private nature reserve, which now includes around 600 ha of land. ATN's main

aim is to increase biodiversity levels and to maintain eagle and vulture populations. This area is very important as a breeding site for Bonelli's Eagles and Egyptian vultures. With your support, ATN will do the annual fauna survey at the Faia Brava Reserve (cliff-breeding birds, rabbit, partridge and pigeon populations), cliff-breeders nest surveillance and other secondary tasks (pigeon houses maintenance, horse feeding, etc.). With your help they hope to contribute to the conservation of the traditional agro-forestry mosaic, thus protecting fauna and flora species that depend on it. Support them, by becoming a part of the ATN team!

Faia Brava Woodlands Fire Surveillance & Conservation

Organization: ATN (Associação Transumância e Natureza)
Location: Faia Brava Reserve, Algodres village, Figueira de Castelo Rodrigo, Guarda district, Northeast Portugal
Cost: $70 registration fee, no extra charge for up to 1 month in duration **Duration:** 2+ weeks **Age:** 18
Contact: voluntarios@atnatureza.org
Learn more: www.ATNatureza.org
Details: Vast areas in Portugal have been devastated by fire. The Faia Brava Reserve, managed by ATN, has been particularly affected by a massive fire in 2003. Today, you can still see the effects on the landscape, habitats and biodiversity. ATN has been developing a woodland protection project called Faia Brava Woodland. Protecting the last pieces of natural woodland in the region from fires and overgrazing in a semiarid deforested landscape has been another priority, through the establishment of sustainable practices for domestic and wild grazers. Every summer they invite you to become part of our fire surveillance team, helping ATN in the daily surveillance and secondary tasks (tree watering, pigeon houses maintenance, horse feeding, etc.).

Azores: Studying Whales, Dolphins and Turtles

Organization: Biosphere Expeditions
Location: Azores Archipelago, Atlantic Ocean
Cost: $1,790
Duration: 1 week (can join multiple expeditions) **Age:** 18
Contact: info@biosphere-expeditions.org
Learn more: www.biosphere-expeditions.org
Special skills: Open to all who care enough to become actively involved in conservation
Details: This conservation expedition will take you to the Azores Archipelago in the Atlantic Ocean to study whales, dolphins and

loggerhead turtles. You will photograph whales and dolphins and record
them for local and international monitoring databases as part of a small international team. You will listen to and make recordings of whale and dolphin vocalizations and capture loggerhead turtles in the open ocean for tagging and release. If conditions are right and you would like to help, you may also be asked to collect sperm whale skin samples for DNA analysis without harming the animals by snorkeling to whale dive points or collecting shed skin in nets. The work is to assist with the formulation of effective conservation strategies.

Other organizations offering projects in Portugal:
A Pas de Loup: www.apasdeloup.org
Eco Algarve: www.ecoalgarve.com
GoEco: www.goeco.org
Service Civil International: www.sci-ivs.org
WorldTeach: www.worldteach.org
Volunteers for Peace: www.vfp.org

Romania

Rasarit Kindergarten
Organization: Kids Worldwide
Location: Village of Panatau, and Bucharest, Romania
Cost: $30 booking fee, $36 per week towards the collective food budget **Duration:** 2 weeks minimum, 1 month+ preferred
Age: 18, Kids welcome with a parent after prior consultation.
Contact: rasarit@kidsworldwide.org **Learn more:** kidsworldwide.org
Special skills: Female volunteers only. Volunteers with experience in social work, education and counseling
Details: Rasarit is run by an international aid organization called AMURTEL which began relief work in Romania with the fall of communism in 1989. In1993 two kindergartens were opened, utilizing Neo-Humanist Education, which nurtures creativity, empathy and ecological consciousness. Aside from the kindergartens, they also run a children's home. The children at Familia AMURTEL are between the ages of 10 and 18 years old and are all enrolled and attending school. An after school tutoring center was also recently opened for youth in the village of Panatau where they come for classes in computers and to complete their homework prior to returning home in the evening. The main criteria for volunteers is a love for children and a willingness to work and help the directors in jobs around the centers.

Romania Program with a Christian Mission

Organization: Global Volunteer Network
Location: Galati district about 150 miles from Bucharest
Cost: $1,037 for 6 weeks **Duration:** 6 to 12 weeks **Age:** 21 - 60
Contact: info@volunteer.org.nz **Learn more:**
www.volunteer.org.nz
Details: Volunteers have the opportunity to join a Christian Mission
which cares for disabled orphans, from ten years old to young adults.
The children have suffered so much at a young age, but with your help
they will see a brighter future. Each home is run like a family unit,
where volunteers will act as a mother, father, brother or sister. There
are opportunities to teach, counsel and help with feeding, cooking and
cleaning, depending on your skills and experiences. There is a huge
focus on the children having fun, being happy and enjoying the rest of
their lives. This is in real contrast to the devastating conditions they
have experienced in the state run institutions.

Work with Romania's Abandoned Children

Organization: CAST
Location: Oltania which is an area of Romania situated approximately
three hours west of Bucharest
Cost: $375 **Duration:** 10 days **Age:** 16
Contact: Amy McCulloch: recruitment@cast-uk.com
Learn more: www.cast-uk.com
Special skills: Volunteers need to have some experience of working
with children or adults with disabilities before taking part in this
project
Details: This is CAST's longest standing project and they have been
working with some of the children for nearly six years. Many of the
children previously lived in the state-run orphanages, but after many of
these were closed down the children were moved into smaller homes.
Volunteers split their time between visiting these homes and visiting
the adult institutions which the children are moved to once they reach
eighteen. You live and work in groups of ten to arrange activities for the
children and adults which provide both entertainment and stimulation
in their otherwise monotonous lives. All volunteers are given training
in Intensive Interaction and Behavioral & Emotional Management
Training prior to the trip.

Summer School for Deprived Children in Rural Romania
Organization: CAST
Location: We run four summer schools throughout the summer in four small villages around the town of Bacau in Northeast Romania.
Cost: $275 for eight days
Duration: CAST runs 4 summer schools in July and August **Age:** 16
Contact: Amy McCulloch: recruitment@cast-uk.com
Learn more: www.cast-uk.com
Special skills: Volunteers do not need to have any skills or qualifications. This is a perfect opportunity for people new to volunteering or for young volunteers wanting to volunteer abroad in a supported environment.
Details: Volunteers will work in groups of eight alongside local Romanian volunteers to arrange and carry out fun activities for local children from very deprived families. Most of the children lack the opportunity to relax and have fun in their difficult lives so these summer camps come as a welcome break for both them and their families. You are given the opportunity to organize any activities you want to under the categories of arts & crafts, music, English, sport, dance and drawing and can do the same activities for a week or rotate around the different clubs. This project is a really enjoyable experience and volunteers come back year after year.

Build Homes for the Roma Community
Organization: Globe Aware
Location: The town of Tarlungeni, on the outskirts of Brasov, Romania
Cost: $1,390 **Duration:** One week, weekly extensions available
Age: None - Families welcomed
Contact: info@globeaware.org **Learn more:** www.globeaware.org
Details: Have fun while helping people! Globe Aware partners with local Romanian organizations to help the underprivileged Roma community fight against poverty and injustice. Collaborate with community leaders to build homes for the Roma population in Tarlungeni. Providing safe homes is the first step in helping this community in need access education and economic opportunities.

Other organizations offering projects in Romania:
CFH International (development & humanitarian) www.chfhq.org
Cross-Country Farm: cross-country.ro
Global Water: www.globalwater.org
Medical Teams International: hwww.medicalteams.org
Mondo Challenge: www.mondochallenge.co.uk

Oyster Worldwide: www.oysterworldwide.com
Pro Animals: proanimals.ro/en
Projects Abroad: www.projects-abroad.org
United Planet: www.unitedplanet.org
Valea Plopului (orphanage): www.valeaplopului.com

Russia

Mountain Ghosts: Snow Leopards and other Animals

Organization: Biosphere Expeditions
Location: Altai Mountains of Central Asia
Cost: $2,720 **Duration:** 2 weeks (you may join
for multiple expeditions) **Age:** Adults
Contact: info@biosphere-expeditions.org
Learn more: www.biosphere-
expeditions.org
Special skills: Open to all who care enough
to become actively involved in conservation
Details: Volunteers will journey high into the mountains of
Central Asia to survey Snow Leopards and their prey animals such as
the Argali Mountain Sheep and the Altai Ibex, as well as other animals
including marmots and birds. You will be working as part of a small
international team from a base camp set at 2,300 m at the foot of a
3,500 m remote mountain range and overlooking a vast area of open
steppe. You will be covering ground in Land Rovers and on foot,
looking for tracks, kills, scats and the animals themselves. True
expedition-style base camp conditions, testing but satisfying mountain
surveying, off road driving and variable mountain weather, make this
our most challenging (and very rewarding) expedition.
Editor's note: A first-hand account of this volunteer experience can
be read in *The Voluntary Traveler: Adventures from the Road Best
Traveled.*

Other organizations offering projects in Russia:

Action Against Hunger: www.actionagainsthunger.org
American Jewish World Services: ajws.org
CCUSA (camp counselors): www.ccusa.com
Cross-Cultural Solutions: www.crossculturalsolutions.org
Earth Island Institute: www.earthisland.org
Ecologia Youth Trust: www.ecologia.org.uk
GeoVisions: www.geovisions.org
Great Baikal Trail: www.greatbaikaltrail.org

Habitat for Humanity International: www.habitat.org
Kids Around the World (building playgrounds):
www.kidsaroundtheworld.com
Project Hope (health): www.projecthope.org
Volunteer in Russia: www.volunteer-in-russia.com

Slovakia

Wolf Census Project

Organization: Slovak Wildlife Society
Location: Carpathian Mountains
Cost: $400 for 2 weeks
Duration: 2+ weeks Age: 18-50
Contact: info@slovakwildlife.org
Learn more: www.slovakwildlife.org
Special skills: Need to be physically fit
Details: Learn to track wolves and study their ecology to help local
people better appreciate this misunderstood species. With appropriate
training, much of your time will be spent on long walks in the
mountains searching for wolves and their prey. Collect samples to study
wolf diet as well as to analyze their DNA, which is important to be able
to distinguish different individuals and thus reveal their movements
and interrelationships. If you are lucky, you may even see a wild wolf.
There are also lynx, bears, wild boar, deer, martens, otters, eagles,
chamois and marmots in this beautiful area. The cost covers expert
training, travel within the area and a donation to the project, but
excludes food and accommodation.

The BEARS Project

Organization: Slovak Wildlife Society
Location: Tatra Mountains
Cost: $400 for 2 weeks **Duration:** 2+ weeks **Age:** 18-60
Contact: info@slovakwildlife.org **Learn more:** www.medvede.sk
 Special skills: Volunteers need to be physically fit
Details: This long-term, multi-faceted project seeks to improve the
coexistence of brown bears and local people. Work is based in the Tatra
Mountains, a paradise of unspoiled countryside right at the heart of
Europe. Volunteers have the chance to participate in fieldwork to study
the ecology of bears as well as assisting with education efforts. You
will also see measures that are being implemented to reduce conflicts
with people and find out how this contributes to the bears' long-term

survival. If you are lucky, you may see a bear. There are also wolves, wild boar, deer, martens, otters, eagles, chamois and marmots.
The cost covers expert training, travel within the area and a donation to the project but excludes food and accommodation.

White Wilderness: Winter Wolf and Lynx Tracking

Organization: Biosphere Expeditions
Location: Tatra Mountains of Slovakia
Cost: $1,590 **Duration:** 1 week (can join for multiple weeks) **Age:** 18
Contact: info@biosphere-expeditions.org
Learn more: www.biosphere-expeditions.org
Special skills: Open to all who care enough to become actively involved in conservation
Details: In the Tatra Mountains of Slovakia, you will monitor wolf and lynx populations and their interrelationship with prey species. You will be part of a small international team, working with the local scientist and contributing to an important piece of research. Volunteers track large carnivores through snow in the forest and meadow habitats of the mountains, using snow shoes which are easy to use. You will also learn how to recognize and record other signs of their presence, such as scats and scent markings, collect samples to study their diet and for genetic analysis, and survey prey species, all this is done in an effort to create a sustainable future for these icons of the Carpathian wilderness and to promote greater understanding of their role in European ecosystems.
 ৪ **Editor's notes:** Biosphere Expedition's Winter Wolf and Lynx Tracking expedition appeared in the November 2009 issue of National Geographic Adventure Magazine, featuring the "25 Best New Trips in the World."

Other organizations offering projects in Slovakia:

Concordia: www.concordia-iye.org.uk
Freedom House/AVID: www.freedomhouse.org
People and Water: www.peopleandwater.sk
Service Civil International: www.sci-ivs.org
Volunteers for Economic Growth Alliance: www.vegaalliance.org
Volunteers for Peace: www.vfp.org
Wolves and Humans Foundation (zoologists):
  www.wolvesandhumans.org

Slovenia

Organizations offering projects in Slovenia:

Adventures in Preservation: www.heritageconservation.net
Architects without Borders: www.awb.iohome.net
International Student Volunteers: www.isvonline.com
Volunteers for Economic Growth Alliance: www.vegaalliance.org
Volunteers for Peace: www.vfp.org

Spain

Volunteer in La Casita Verde

Organization: Greenheart Travel
Location: The project is located on the beautiful island of Ibiza
Cost: $1,890 for 6 weeks   **Duration**: 3 to 9 weeks   **Age:** 18
Contact: info@greenhearttravel.org
Learn more: www.cci-exchange.com/travelabroad/index.aspx
Special skills: Volunteers must be in excellent physical condition and willing to engage in heavy manual labor involved with conservation efforts. Volunteers must also have previous outdoor environmental conservation experience.
Details: Volunteers work on a model ecological center called La Casita Verde in one of the most beautiful areas of the island. A working farm created to demonstrate sustainable ecological development; it is powered by wind and sun energy and recycles all the water used by residents and its many visitors. The center supports Greenheart projects in ecological research, as well as volunteer efforts such as beach cleaning and environmental education programs. Sample volunteer projects include: maintaining and improving the farm facilities, installing alternative energy systems, promoting environmental awareness among visitors, cooking for visiting groups and permacultural farming. Modest, rustic housing on site and 3 vegetarian meals daily are provided.

Primate Volunteers Working Weekend

Organization: FUNDACIÓ MONA
Location: Riudellots de la Selva- Girona (Spain)
Cost: $130 per day   **Duration:** 2 to 4 days   **Age:** 18
Contact: info@fundacionmona.org
Learn more: www.fundacionmona.org

Special skills: Just for people who care about primates
Details: During their stay, guests will be made to feel as part of our dedicated team of primate caregivers and they will help out with every type of task involved in the daily care of our rescued primates. They accept a maximum of two guests at a time and our working weekends run all year round.

Other organizations offering projects in Spain:

Adelante Abroad: www.adelanteabroad.com
ArchaeoSpain (archeology): www.archaeospain.com
Canadian Alliance for Development Initiatives and Projects:
  www.cadip.org
Coined-Spain: www.coined-spain.org
Global Crossroads: www.globalcrossroad.com
Global Visions International: www.gviusa.com or www.gvi.co.uk
Pueblo Ingles: www.morethanenglish.com
Sunseed (permaculture technologies to arid/desert regions):
  www.sunseed.org.uk

Ukraine

Orphanage Volunteering/English Teaching
Organization: Ukrainian Humanitarian Initiative
Location: Kiev, Lviv, Simferopol, Odessa, Dnipropetrovsk
Cost: $250 per week   **Duration:** 1 to 6 weeks   **Age:** 17
Contact: golos_ukr@mail.ru   **Learn more:** www.hope.ck.ua
Details: Spend your time with orphan kids and explore a beautiful country. As a volunteer on this project there are going to be loads of different activities you can get involved with. You may help teach English to kids of all ages, play with children so they gain confidence and learn to interact better with people, and arrange extra classes such as dance/music/drama and sports. You can also help with the day to day running of the orphanage, getting involved wherever help is needed. UHI has partnerships with several orphanages where you can volunteer, spend your time in just the one or mix it up. Volunteers have the option of staying with local host families. Local people are well known for their kindness and hospitality and they will help you understand their culture.

Other organizations offering projects in the Ukraine:
Concordia: www.concordia-iye.org.uk

Family Health International: www.fhi.org
Life2Orphans: www.life2orphans.org
Project Hope (health): www.projecthope.org
Reach Ukraine (evangelical): www.reachukraine.org
US Energy Association: www.usea.org
Volunteers for Peace: www.vfp.org

United Kingdom

Scotland Conservation Work Weeks

Organization: Trees for Life
Location: The Caledonian Forest, Scottish Highlands
Cost: From $100 (unemployed/student rate) to $500 full cost
Duration: 1 week **Age:** 18
Contact: info@treesforlife.org.uk, (UK) 01309 691444
Learn more: www.treesforlife.org.uk
Special skills: A reasonable level of fitness is essential and an interest
in conservation would be useful

Details: The Caledonian Forest needs you! Trees
for Life is an award winning conservation charity
based in the north of Scotland carrying out vital
forest restoration work. Volunteers are invited to
join Conservation Work Weeks to help restore the
natural environment. Spend a week in the
Highlands amongst forests, rivers and mountains,
learning about ecological restoration. Work
includes tree planting, felling non-native trees,
fence removal and tree nursery work. Work Weeks run from March –
May & August – November, every year. The cost of the week includes
all food, accommodation and transport from Inverness. No previous
experience required.

Whales and Dolphins of Moray Firth

Organization: Earthwatch Institute
Location: Rendezvous at Banff, Aberdeenshire, Scotland
Cost: $1,950-$2,450+ **Duration:** 11 days **Age:** 18
Contact: info@earthwatch.org **Learn more:** www.earthwatch.org
Details: Working with staff from the Cetacean Research & Rescue Unit
(CRRU), you will take to the Moray Firth in 5.4-meter rigid-hulled
inflatable boats to conduct systematic surveys of the southern Firth.
You will be trained to spot and identify whales and dolphins and to
record data such as the composition and structure of groups, their

behavior and geographic positions. You will also take photographs for individual identification. At the lab, especially during inclement weather, you will help identify individuals from photographs, catalogue images and enter data. Your team may also be called upon to help with live whale or dolphin strandings, as the need arises. In your recreational time, there are rare seabird colonies, coastal wildflowers, castles, and Pictish ruins to investigate.

Other organizations offering projects in the United Kingdom:

AmeriSpan Study Abroad: www.amerispan.com
Global Visions International: www.gviusa.com or www.gvi.co.uk
Lattitude Global Volunteering Canada: www.lattitudecanada.org
Projects Abroad: www.projects-abroad.org

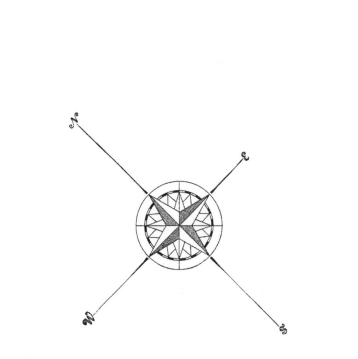

"The best time to plant a tree is twenty years ago.
The second best time is now."

~African Proverb

Algeria

Organizations offering projects in Algeria:
Service Civil International: www.sci-ivs.org
Volunteers for Peace: www.vfp.org

Angola

Organizations offering projects in Angola:
Habitat for Humanity: www.habitat.org
Humana People to People: www.humana.org

Benin

Center for Troubled Youth
Organization: Greenheart Travel

Location: Cotonou
Cost: $1,850 for 8 weeks   **Duration**: 2 to 8 weeks   **Age**: 18
Contact: info@greenhearttravel.org
Learn more: www.cci-exchange.com
Special skills: An intermediate level of French is required. French lessons are available prior to the volunteer project for an additional fee.
Details: Established in 1991, this center currently serves around 60 children from troubled homes, the streets, victims of trafficking or runaways. Help is needed in many different areas including tutoring, organizing recreational activities, leading skills workshops, helping with technical education classes, mentoring and counseling. Volunteers must be patient and open-minded to work with children who come from such difficult situations. The primary focus of the volunteer is to share themselves with the children through encouragement, support and lots of care. Program includes host family accommodations, two meals per day, medical insurance and 24 hour emergency contact.

Regional Hospital in Porto-Novo

Organization: Greenheart Travel
Location: Porto Novo
Cost: $1,850 for 8 weeks   **Duration**: 2 to 12 weeks   **Age**: 18
Contact: info@greenhearttravel.org
Learn: www.cci-exchange.com
Special skills: Volunteers must have some experience or education in the health field. An intermediate level of French is required. French lessons are available prior to the volunteer project for an additional fee.
Details: The large public hospital serves the capital city of Porto-Novo. Equipped with an emergency room, neonatal unit, pediatric center, general medicine department, and many other specialty areas, it is always crowded. Volunteers will be working closely with hospital staff to help with routine checkups, special procedures, administrative duties, and taking care of long-term patients. Volunteer are able to help in any area of the hospital they find most interesting. Volunteers will stay with carefully screened host families for the duration of the program. Two meals during the week and three on weekends with your host family are included in your stay.

Women and Children Center

Organization: Greenheart Travel
Location: Porto-Novo
Cost: $1,850 for 8 weeks   **Duration**: 2 to 8 weeks   **Age**: 18
Contact: info@greenhearttravel.org
Learn more: www.cci-exchange.com
Special skills: An intermediate level of French is required. French lessons are available prior to the volunteer project for an additional fee.

Details: This NGO was created in 1993 to help women and children in the surrounding community. Equipped with a nursery, orphanage, and primary and secondary schools, the center is able to serve many families. Through organizing youth groups, educating young mothers, and a variety of community campaigns and outreach programs (malaria prevention, sexual education, clean water education, HIV/AIDS support), this NGO is working hard to better the situation of so many of its members. Help is needed in tutoring, organizing recreational activities and skills workshops, mentoring, counseling, and assisting with community outreach campaigns. Volunteers will stay with carefully screened host families. Two meals during the week and three on weekends with your host family are included in your stay.

Other organizations offering projects in Benin:

African Rural Development Movement: www.arudmo.org
International Foundation for Education and Self-Help: www.ifesh.org
Service Civil International: www.sci-ivs.org
Students Travel and Exposure South Africa: www.staesa.org
Volunteers for Peace: www.vfp.org

Botswana

Research Assistant with Cheetah Conservation

Organization: Cheetah Conservation Botswana
Location: Mokolodi Nature Reserve, Jwaneng Game Reserve, Ghanzi Farmlands.
Cost: $2,500 per month for room and board
Duration: 1 to 3 months **Age:** 21
Contact: research@cheetahbotswana.com, +267 3500613
Learn more: www.cheetahbotswana.com
Special skills: Wildlife background useful but not essential. Strong passion for conservation and a desire to learn new skills. Ability to work long days, often in heat during summer or cold during winter. Ability to live in the bush with a small group of people.
Details: Cheetah Conservation Botswana (CCB) addresses threats to the long term survival of the national cheetah population and that of other large predators. Using scientific research to inform its community outreach and education programmes, CCB works with communities affected by conflict with predators, to promote the adoption of livestock management practices and non-lethal methods of predator control.

333

Volunteer activities may include assisting with spoor surveys, camera trapping, possible cheetah capture and release, school presentations, community visits, data input, camp maintenance and administration. In addition to the CCB short-term volunteer programme, CCB also has opportunities for researchers interested in carrying out postgraduate research on predator related studies, in collaboration with a university, i.e. MSc's and PhD's.

Cheetah Conservation Administration Assistant

Organization: Cheetah Conservation Botswana
Location: Mokolodi Nature Reserve
Cost: $2,500 per month for room and board
Duration: 1-3 months   **Age:** 21
Contact: info@cheetahbotswana.com, +267 3500613
Learn more: www.cheetahbotswana.com
Special skills: Qualifications and/or proven experience in administrative skills. Experience in charity/NGO office administration, including formal document preparation, funding proposal writing or database maintenance would be a particular advantage.
Details: CCB addresses threats to the long term survival of the national cheetah population and that of other large predators. Using scientific research to inform its community outreach and education programmes, CCB works with communities affected by conflict with predators to promote the adoption of livestock management practices and non-lethal methods of predator control. You will be primarily based at their head office in Mokolodi Nature reserve assisting in basic day-to-day administrative tasks as they arise. If you possess the necessary skills and experience, have an interest in wildlife, can cope with living and working in basic facilities, and wish to experience Africa by volunteering in support of our cheetah conservation efforts in Botswana, then CCB would be delighted to hear from you.

Other organizations offering projects in Botswana:

African Conservation Experience: www.conservationafrica.net
Habitat for Humanity: www.habitat.org
Projects Abroad: www.projects-abroad.org
Service Civil International: www.sci-ivs.org
Students Travel and Exposure South Africa: www.staesa.org
Volunteers for Peace: www.vfp.org
Worldwide Veterinary Service: www.wvs.org.uk
Youth International: www.youthinternational.org
Worldwide Veterinary Service: www.wvs.org.uk

Burkina Faso

Help Build the First Eco-Village in Burkina Faso

Organization: Reciproka
Cost: $750 **Duration:** 1+ month
Contact: infos@reciproka.org
Learn more: www.reciproka.bravehost.com
Details: Reciproka aims at helping West African communities reach economic, social and cultural freedom through reciprocity between people and culture. Along with the local community participants, you will build the first eco-village in Burkina. Participants will also learn about native local plants, the art of Burkinabe's main ethnic groups' traditional building techniques and traditional beer making techniques. One of the poorest countries in the world, landlocked Burkina Faso has few natural resources and a weak industrial base. About 90% of the population is engaged in subsistence agriculture, which is vulnerable to periodic drought.

Other organizations offering projects in Burkina Faso:

African Rural Development Movement: www.arudmo.org
Service Civil International: www.sci-ivs.org
Volunteers for Peace: www.vfp.org

Burundi

Organizations offering projects in Burundi

Doctors without Borders: doctorswithoutborders.org
Habitat for Humanity: www.habitat.org

Cameroon

School and Vocational Instruction

Organization: United Action for Children
Location: Buea, South West Region of Cameroon
Cost: $ 350 for 1 month, $550 for 2 months, $150 each additional month - includes lodging, feeding, transportation to and from the airport
Duration: 1 to 12 months **Age:** 18-55

Contact: unitedactionforc@yahoo.com
Learn more: www.unitedactionforchildren.org
Special skills: Highly motivated volunteers who are ready to experience other cultures
Details: United Action for Children is a child and youth centered organization operating in the South West Region, Cameroon. Its mission is to develop a caring and sustaining society for children and young people through innovative programmes. It is located in the English speaking part of Cameroon. This means English is the working language at UAC. The activities of UAC include the provision of elementary education to orphans and vulnerable children under which they run a nursery/primary school with an enrolment of 620 kids. UAC also runs Vocational Training programmes in woodwork, computer, electricity and painting. These are for rural-based youths with an enrolment of 125 trainees. In addition, their 'School on Wheels' goes into local villages to help children who do not have access to basic education. This is an attempt to minimize failure and school dropout rates among rural kids.

Survey Endangered Gorillas and Chimpanzees

Organization: GVI (Global Visions International)
Location: Lebialem Highlands, Southwest Cameroon
Cost: $1,990+ **Duration:** 1 to 4 weeks **Age:** 18
Contact: info@gviusa.com **Learn more:** www.gviusa.com
Details: Make a difference for two species of Great Apes with one project, Cross River Gorillas and chimpanzees. By joining this African project you will work on the frontline of conservation while working with local staff; using scientific survey methods. Hunting, trapping and the illegal trade of bush meat in particular are endangering these fascinating animals. The aim of this project is to establish community wildlife reserves to protect these great apes from extinction.

 ✍**Editor's note:** Several years ago I booked three of GVI's volunteer projects back to back. When a family member became ill the organization issued me the refund I was due promptly and with absolutely no hassle. Sometimes the best way to judge a company is by how they handle themselves when things go wrong. For this and for their drool-worthy catalog of volunteer programs GVI gets top marks.

Other organizations offering projects in Cameroon:

Afri-Link: www.afri-link.org
Ecoteer: www.ecoteer.com
Global Network for Good Governance: www.gngg.org
Goodness and Mercy Missions: www.gmmafrica.org

Green Cameroon: www.greencameroon.org
RUDEC: www.rudec.org
Students Travel and Exposure South Africa: www.staesa.org
Worldwide Veterinary Service: www.wvs.org.uk

Cape Verde

Sea Turtles Protection Project

Organization: Turtle Foundation
Location: Boavista
Cost: $15 per day for food and basic accommodations
Duration: 2+ weeks (preferably at least 3), nesting season is June through October   **Age:** 18
Contact: *via website*
Learn more: www.turtle-foundation.org
Special skills: Should be able to converse in English or Portuguese (or Spanish) and preferably have basic knowledge of the other language.
Details: Possible duties for project volunteers include: helping with day to day shopping or driving, helping with nocturnal beach patrols (beach walks) together with soldiers from Cape Verde, helping explore beach sectors (during the day by foot or by vehicle) and working out routes for the patrols. Other possible volunteer activities include: data collection to record the numbers of nests and nesting females, cooperation with the local community to help to establish eco-tourism opportunities, and public relations, such as organizing events like beach clean-ups, competitions for kids, etc. Schedules will be arranged by the project management. There is generally a 40-hour work week for volunteers; however, over-time is possible. As some duties have to get accomplished by day, others by night, there are no regular working hours.

Congo

Organizations offering projects in Congo:

Hands at Work Africa: www.handsatwork.org
Volunteers for Peace: www.vfp.org
HELP Congo: www.help-primates.org

Cote d'Ivoire (Ivory Cost)

Refuge for Trafficked Women and Girls

Organization: The Humanity Exchange
Location: Abidjan, The Ivory Coast (La Cote d'Ivoire)
Cost: $1,450 for 1 month, $2,000 for 2 months, $2,550 for 3 months, $3,050 for 4 months.
Duration: 1 to 4 months. Humanity Exchange asks that you keep in mind that the longer you stay, the greater the impact for both you and the host community. **Age:** 18
Contact: director@thehumanityexchange.org
Learn more: www.thehumanityexchange.org
Details: The Ivory Coast is a major destination for young girls and women trafficked within the West African region. Individuals are needed to help run a safehouse located in Abidjan. Here, girls and young women who have been trafficked for the purposes of sexual exploitation can find refuge, a hot meal, and a safe place to rest. You will act as a mentor and help with day to day activities associated with running the safehouse. Comprehensive pre-departure support, fundraising guide, food, lodging, airport pick-up and drop-off, and an Exchange Manager who is available 24/7 are all included in this program. The Humanity Exchange can also set up French classes, help you plan onward travel, and coordinate with your school so you can obtain course credit for the work you do.

Children Are Not For Sale

Organization: The Humanity Exchange
Location: Aboisso, The Ivory Coast (La Cote d'Ivoire)
Cost: $1,450 for 1 month, $2,000 for 2 months, $2,550 for 3 months, $3,050 for 4 months.
Duration: 1 to 4 months. Humanity Exchange asks that you keep in mind that the longer you stay, the greater the impact for both you and the host community **Age:** 18
Contact: director@thehumanityexchange.org
Learn more: www.thehumanityexchange.org
Details: The Ivory Coast is a major destination for children trafficked within West Africa. The people of Aboisso bear witness to child trafficking on a regular basis. In this region, children most often end up selling goods in the market and working as agricultural laborers. You may assist in development of a public awareness campaign, implement public awareness campaigns, conduct farm visits, identify funding opportunities, assist with administrative tasks, etc. These are examples, but needs vary as their work progresses. Comprehensive pre-departure

support, fundraising guide, food, lodging, airport pick-up and drop-off, and an Exchange Manager who is available 24/7 are all included in this program. The Humanity Exchange can also help you plan onward travel, and coordinate with your college or university so can obtain course credit.

Raising Voices with Art and Creative Media

Organization: The Humanity Exchange
Location: Aboisso, The Ivory Coast (La Cote d'Ivoire)
Cost: $1,450 for 1 month, $2,000 for 2 months, $2,550 for 3 months, $3050 for 4 months.
Duration: 1 to 4 months. Humanity Exchange asks that you keep in mind that the longer you stay, the greater the impact for both you and the host community **Age:** 18
Contact: director@thehumanityexchange.org
Learn more: www.thehumanityexchange.org
Special skills: Photography, cinematography, painting, writing or any other skill which can act as a medium to communicate a message in a dynamic and engaging manner.
Details: While the people of Aboisso bear witness to child trafficking on a regular basis, the rest of the world remains largely unaware of this massive trade in children. You are needed to use your talents to tell people what is happening, and that they have the power to do something about it. Your work will have the potential to raise awareness globally, and to raise financial support from donors in North America. Comprehensive pre-departure support, fundraising guide, food, lodging, airport pick-up and drop-off, and an Exchange Manager who is available 24/7 are all included in this program. The Humanity Exchange can also help coordinate with your college or university so can obtain course credit. Local supplies are limited, so you must have the medium for your message such as; painting supplies, camera, laptop to write on.

Speaking Out: Raising Awareness of HIV & AIDS

Organization: The Humanity Exchange
Location: Aboisso, The Ivory Coast (La Cote d'Ivoire)
Cost: $1,450 for 1 month, $2,000 for 2 months, $2,550 for 3 months, $3050 for 4 months.
Duration: 1 to 4 months. Humanity Exchange asks that you keep in mind that the longer you stay, the greater the impact for both you and the host community **Age:** 18
Contact: director@thehumanityexchange.org
Learn more: www.thehumanityexchange.org
Details: Suffering due to HIV/AIDS in the Ivory Coast has been devastating. Despite widespread knowledge of the existence of

339

HIV/AIDS, stigma and misunderstandings are widespread. It's necessary to raise awareness about how HIV is spread and the importance of getting tested. You will be part of a team reaching out, connecting with, and educating people about HIV/AIDS. In your role you will become familiar with the fight against HIV/AIDS as it is taking place in the Ivory Coast, identify target audiences for program delivery, deliver HIV/AIDS awareness as member of an education team, and assist staff in raising awareness in the surrounding community. Comprehensive pre-departure support, fundraising guide, food, lodging, airport pick-up and drop-off, and an Exchange Manager who is available 24/7 are all included in this program. They can also arrange French classes, help you plan onward travel, and coordinate with your college or university so can obtain course credit.

Our Children, Our Future

Organization: The Humanity Exchange
Location: Abidjan, The Ivory Coast (La Cote d'Ivoire)
Cost: $1,450 for 1 month, $2,000 for 2 months, $2,550 for 3 months, $3050 for 4 months.
Duration: 1 to 4 months. Humanity Exchange asks that you keep in mind that the longer you stay, the greater the impact for both you and the host community **Age:** 18
Contact: director@thehumanityexchange.org
Learn more: www.thehumanityexchange.org
Details: Volunteers are needed to work with children orphaned by HIV/AIDS, war, and internal displacement. In your role as a volunteer you will dress and feed children, tutor children in various academic subjects, assist staff in the nursery school and mentor children. Comprehensive pre-departure support, fundraising guide, food, lodging, airport pick-up and drop-off, and an Exchange Manager who is available 24/7 are all included in this program. The Humanity Exchange can also arrange French classes, help you plan onward travel and coordinate with your college or university so can obtain course credit.

Organizations offering projects in Cote d'Ivoire:

Habitat for Humanity: www.habitat.org
International Foundation for Education and Self-Help: www.ifesh.org
Service Civil International: www.sci-ivs.org
Volunteers for Peace: www.vfp.org

Djibouti

Organizations offering projects in Djibouti:
International Foundation for Education and Self-Help: www.ifesh.org

Egypt

Teach English While Experiencing Egyptian Culture
Organization: GeoVisions
Location: Cairo and Alexandria
Cost: $1,380+ **Duration:** 1 to 3 months **Age:** 18
Contact: programs@geovisions.org
Learn more: www.geovisions.org
Details: Volunteers stay with Egyptian families
while teaching them English for 15 hours per
week. This allows you free time to experience this
magnificent culture. The program has a focus on
cultural exchange and host families are not only
excited to learn English, but also love to share the
characteristics of their country, culture and

cuisine. In addition if you would like to study Arabic during your stay
GeoVisions can help to arrange classes at an additional charge. What a
great way to immerse yourself, experiencing the real Egypt beyond the
realm of ordinary tourism.

Medical Mission to Egypt
Organization: Hands Along the Nile Development Service
Location: Varies
Cost: $2,000+ **Duration:** 1 to 2 weeks **Age:** 18
Contact: medmission@handsalongthenile.org
Learn more: www.handsalongthenile.org
Special skills: RN or Doctor with specializations in the following
fields:
women's reproductive health, nurse training (particularly in CPR and
first aid), ophthalmology. Medical students are welcome to apply.
Details: Help people in need while exchanging knowledge and
working alongside your peers. The program consisted in two types of
activities: community health campaigns in which American and
Egyptian medical professionals worked together, and formal teaching

sessions held by US volunteers and attended by Egyptian health care workers and community volunteers involved in health campaigns

Other organizations offering projects in Egypt:

Canadian Alliance for Development Initiatives and Projects:
  www.cadip.org
Habitat for Humanity: www.habitat.org
Learning and Development Center: www.ldc.carpevitam-eg.org
Marhaba: Volunteers in the Middle East: www.gomarhaba.org
Volunteers for Peace: www.vfp.org

Equatorial Guinea

Primate and Sea Turtle Census

Organization: Bioko Biodiversity Protection Program
Location: Gran Caldera de Luba
Cost: $3,000 **Duration:** 3 weeks **Age:** 18
Contact: hearn@bioko.org
Learn more: www.bioko.org
Special skills: Typically, project volunteers are university students with an interest in primates and tropical biodiversity, but other enthusiastic adults with a variety of interests are also welcome.
Details: Every January, Bioko Biodiversity Protection Program organizes a 3-week expedition to Bioko Island's remote, rarely visited, Gran Caldera de Luba. Here staff and volunteers work together to conduct a census of primates and sea turtles. Volunteers participate fully in the primate census, and are expected to maintain their own field notes plus daily logs/journals as an official record of activities. You will be trained in primate and nesting sea turtle census techniques. Volunteers also get experience in operating field equipment including GPS, satellite phones, generators, tape recorders and Zodiac boats.

Ethiopia

GVN Ethiopia Program: Knowledge, Kids & Beyond

Organization: Global Volunteer Network
Location: A suburb of Asko, about 9 km outside of Addis Ababa

Cost: $797 for 1 month   **Duration:** 1 to 3 months   **Age:** 18-59
Contact: info@volunteer.org.nz   **Learn more:**
www.volunteer.org.nz
Details: Volunteers will be involved in tutoring children after school
with a focus on conversational English, grammar, science, and
mathematics. Additionally, volunteers with musical and computer skills
are needed to instruct the children in these areas. Volunteers need to be
able to develop new and creative projects, as well as techniques for
instructing children with special needs. In addition, volunteers will
work in staff development, finance and accounting, computer training,
and/or grant writing. Once a week volunteers have the opportunity to
serve at a local feeding center where meals are provided to the street
community, a large percentage of who are children

Other organizations offering projects in Ethiopia:

Art in Ethiopia (teaching): www.artinethiopia.org
International Foundation for Education and Self-Help: www.ifesh.org
Habitat for Humanity: www.habitat.org

The Gambia

Organizations offering projects in Gambia:

Mondo Challenge (community-based projects):
   www.mondochallenge.co.uk
People and Places (Winner ' Best Volunteering Organization' category
   of Virgin Holidays Responsible Tourism Award 2009):
   travel-peopleandplaces.co.uk
Safari Guide: www.safari-guide.co.uk
Student Travel and Exposure South Africa: www.staesa.org
Tostna (unusually long-term social transformation work):
   www.tostan.org
Worldwide Veterinary Service: www.wvs.org.uk

Ghana

Teach, Empower and Impact
Organization: The Bridge Foundation
Location: Accra

Cost: $8 per day   **Duration:** 3+ months   **Age** 16
Contact: planet35@hotmail.com, tbfghana@yahoo.com
Learn more: www.thebridgefoundationghana.org
Details: The Bridge Foundation (TBF) is a registered humanitarian non-profit organization in Ghana. Their primary objective is promoting human resource development, focusing on assisting disadvantaged and less privileged children/youth in deprived communities through educational, vocational skills training support and sports development, empowering them to assert abilities and capabilities required to improve their livelihood and to grow into responsible adulthood. Volunteers are needed to assist in the sharing of knowledge in math, English and physical education to children in Roman Ridge (Maamobi Junior High School) – Accra Ghana. Volunteers are needed with knowledge in sports/physical training, computers and with knowledge of environmental management. Volunteers are also needed to assist in the promotion of the organization as well as sharing ideas and helping to acquire funds, equipment and partnerships with other organizations around the globe.

Economic and Political Empowerment

Organization: African Rural Development Movement
Location: Accra and rural Ghana
Cost: $600 - $1,000 per month
Duration: 3 months to 1 year   **Age** 18
Contact: volunteers@arudmo.org   **Learn more:** www.arudmo.org
Details: ARUDMO works on implementing initiatives and sustainable development projects in economic empowerment, political empowerment and personal empowerment. The programs work with other local NGOs and focus on education, training and development to ensure the sustainability and economic viability. ARUDMO believes international volunteers enrich the project with their expertise, their independent views and life experiences. The projects of ARUDMO are directed by local communities themselves and were developed in response to the needs and demands of the NGOs and local officials.

Daddy's Modern Academy

Organization: Kids Worldwide
Location: The school is located in the Amasaman District - on the outskirts of Accra – the capital city of Ghana.
Cost: Under 1 month $300, 1 month $350, subsequent months $150.
Duration: 2+ weeks, 1+ month preferred   **Age** 18
Contact: daddys@kidsworldwide.org
Learn more: www.kidsworldwide.org

Special Skills: Patient and caring volunteers - both male & female, experience working in early childhood education is desired but not required.
Details: In October 2006, Daddy's Modern Academy Community Primary School opened its doors and began operating. They currently have 5 class levels from Kindergarten to Standard 2, which are divided into three rooms. The children range in age from 2 to 9 years. Volunteers are encouraged to start their own initiatives and be involved in sustaining the project once they have finished volunteering. Your participation and ideas are very much welcomed at the academy!

Namaskar Primary School

Organization: Kids Worldwide
Special Skills: Qualified teachers are especially encouraged!
Location: Ejura, 2 hours north of Kumasi, the capital of the Ashanti Region
Cost: Under 1 month $300, 1 month $400, 2 months $500, 3 months $600
Duration: Term 1: Mid September to mid December Term 2: Early January to early April Term 3: Early May to early August **Age:** 18
Contact: namaskar@kidsworldwide.org
Learn more: www.kidsworldwide.org
Details: There are currently 400+ kids from kindergarten to junior secondary school level attending Namaskar Primary School. Children range from 3 to 19 years old (some started school late) so it's common to have children of various ages in the same class. Volunteers will mainly assist with remedial teaching. They will take children for tutoring in small groups. In mid 2009 a new computer lab with 20 computers was installed at Namaskar House (3 minutes from the school). Volunteers are responsible for teaching information communication technologies (ICT) to the children and teachers of the school and maintaining the computers. There is also a small boys' home located at Namaskar House, where 7 boys from ages 11-22 live. The school would like to have volunteers come for at least one term, from start to finish. Volunteers wanting to travel around should plan time to do so either before or after the semester.

AMURT Clinic Project - Akwakwaa

Organization: Kids Worldwide
Location: Amidst coconut plantations in Akwakwaa, 2 hours north of Accra
Cost: Under 1 month $200, 1-3 months $350, 3-6 months $450
Duration: 2+ weeks, 1+ month preferred **Age:** 18
Contact: clinics@kidsworldwide.org
Learn more: www.kidsworldwide.org

Special skills: Nurses, midwives, doctors, nursing and medical students
Details: Over the past 20 years, AMURT and AMURTEL-GHANA have been serving rural areas in Ghana through provision of health care (primary health clinics and outposts) and preventative health care such as focusing on the provision of clean drinking water. Community ownership and management is an important factor in our work, as well as being financially self-sustainable. Volunteers will receive patients, diagnose and treat them, train local staff and organize community outreach programmes to teach hygiene, sanitation, nutrition, family planning, AIDS awareness, etc. Volunteers at Akwakwaa can also visit and assist in the local orphanage down the road if they wish. Volunteers more interested in community outreach work should apply for Mafi-Seva. Meals are not included.

AMURT Clinic Project – Mafi-Seva

Organization: Kids Worldwide
Special Skills: Nurses, midwives and doctors, nursing and medical students
Location: Mafi-Seva, 4 hours east of Accra in the Volta region
Cost: 1+ month $250, 1+ month $350, subsequent months $100, includes food and accommodation
Duration: 2+ weeks, 1+ month preferred **Age:** 18
Contact: clinics@kidsworldwide.org
Learn more: www.kidsworldwide.org
Details: Over the past 20 years, AMURT and AMURTEL-GHANA have been serving rural areas in Ghana through provision of health care (primary health clinics and outposts) and preventative health care such as focusing on the provision of clean drinking water. Community ownership and management is an important factor in our work, as well as being financially self-sustainable. Volunteers will receive patients, diagnose and treat them, train local staff and organize community outreach programmes to teach hygiene, sanitation, nutrition, family planning, AIDS awareness, etc.

Triumph Care & Development Centre

Organization: Kids Worldwide
Location: The village of Mowire, 18 km out of Kumasi in the Ashanti Region
Cost: Under 1 month $300, 1+ month $400, 2 months $500, 3 months $600, 4 months $650, 5 months $700, 6 months $750, additional months free
Duration: 2+ weeks, 1+ month preferred.

Age: 18, or kids over 10 welcome with parent
Contact: triumph@kidsworldwide.org
Learn more: www.kidsworldwide.org
Special skills: Experience working in early childhood education is desired but not required
Details: Triumph Care and Development Centre is a school and orphanage. The school has a nursery, kindergarten, primary and junior secondary school 1- 3. There are approximately 380 students. Of the students 45 board or live at the school; of which 30 are orphans. 14 teachers work for the school. There is a new school library and computer lab where volunteers can assist. The main role of the volunteers will be to teach supplementary lessons for the children at the school and orphanage. The ability to speak English gives children in Ghana a head start in life, especially in rural communities, increasing their chances of continuing education and eventually finding work.

Kwahu Tafo: UVO

Organization: Kids Worldwide
Location: Kwahu Tafo, a small village about 4 hours drive north of Accra
Cost: Under 1 month $230, 1 month $555, 2 months $785, subsequent months $230
Duration: 2+ weeks, 1+ month preferred. Bookings made according to volunteer's needs. Dates are flexible.
Age: 18, or kids over 10 welcome with parent
Contact: ghanakwahutafo@kidsworldwide.org
Learn more: www.kidsworldwide.org
Special skills: A love of children and desire to participate in all activities.
Details: Volunteers choose from four projects: 1) The UVO Primary School teaches underprivileged children for free, and provides them all with a lunchtime meal. This is a very new and small school with only 3 classrooms at present. 2) The Culture Centre caters to approximately 60 children, also sponsored to attend school during the day, who meet each afternoon to learn traditional Ghanaian dancing and drumming. 3) The Football Academy has a U12, U14, and a U17 squad. The children are housed and fed in our hostel here in Tafo 4) The Health Program provides all the children with health insurance, and the volunteers can also educate them on a variety of health issues.

Human Rights Advocate

Organization: Volunteer Partnerships for West Africa
Location: Accra
Cost: $587 per month **Duration:** 1+ month   **Age:** 18
Contact: info@vpwa.org   **Learn more:** www.vpwa.org

Special skills: Prior study in law, human rights and related activity
Details: Volunteers are needed to help with human rights work at the grassroot level in Ghana. Volunteers will assist in investigating complaints of violations of fundamental rights and freedoms in the public and private sectors, injustice, abuse of power and unfair treatment of any person by a public officer in the exercise of his/her official duties by using mediation, negotiation, compromise and other alternative dispute resolution mechanisms. Participants also investigate instances of alleged or suspected corruption and misappropriation of public monies by officials and to take the appropriate steps resulting from such investigations and educate the public as to their fundamental human rights and freedoms.

Teach In Ghana (TIG)

Organization: Volunteer Partnerships for West Africa (VPWA)
Location: Accra
Cost: $587 per month   **Duration:** 1+ month **Age:** 18
Contact: info@teachinghana.org
Learn more: www.teachinghana.org
Special skills: English Language skills
Details: VPWA efforts to help local Ghanaian schools that lack teachers led to the launch of an acclaimed project (Teach In Ghana), dedicated to finding international volunteers with an inclination to teach and help the increasing number of enrolled student. Currently there are few or even no teachers available in some schools. This program is designed to help offer you an opportunity to contribute your knowledge to the disadvantaged children in these schools. Volunteers are requested to teach English, mathematics, science and creative arts among many other subjects.

Health Care Delivery

Organization: Volunteer Partnerships for West Africa (VPWA)
Location: Accra
Cost: $587 per month   **Duration:** 1+ month   **Age:** 18
Contact: info@vpwa.org   **Learn more:** www.vpwa.org
Special skills: Nursing and medical students, doctors, nurses
Details: VPWA is offering volunteers an opportunity to work with a local medical facility in Ghana providing their services to help in health care delivery in the country while sharing best practices with local colleagues. Persons applying for this opportunity must be professionals in this field or students studying courses related to medicine/nursing in a university or college. If you have a strong base of medical knowledge and want field experience, but have not started formal classes yet, you may also apply. However you'll need to demonstrate a strong commitment and competence. Services provided by the hospitals and

clinics are mostly in the areas of: general health consulting, child welfare, surgical care, family planning, cervix care, nutritional care, community psychiatric work, dental clinic, antenatal and postnatal care.

Orphanage and Child Care

Organization: Volunteer Partnerships for West Africa (VPWA)
Location: Accra
Cost: $146 week **Duration:** 1+ weeks **Age:** 18

Contact: info@vpwa.org **Learn more:** www.vpwa.org
Details: Volunteers wishing to spend some time in an orphanage or lend a hand at a child care facility in a local school are welcome to provide love and teach kids different songs and games that stimulate their thinking and mental growth. This is very important at this early stage of their lives. VPWA locations for this work are diverse. By visiting their website you can learn about a mixed lot of opportunities and select a program that most interests you.

HQ International Teaching in Ghana

Organization: International Volunteer HQ
Location: In the coastal city of Accra and rural villages in the countryside.
Cost: $220 for 1 week to $2,220 for 6 months, includes food & accommodation
Duration: 1 week to 6 months **Age:** 18
Contact: volunteer@volunteerhq.org
Learn more: www.volunteerhq.org
Details: Although Ghana is an English speaking country, many children cannot communicate effectively in the English language. This is a common phenomenon in both rural and urban areas, hence the need to recruit and place volunteers in communities where there are simply not enough teachers to cater to the number of children. This project seeks to stimulate interest in children to study and speak proper English while also offering foreign volunteers a unique opportunity to learn and experience the Ghanaian culture. Music, math, arts and sports education are also incorporated into the program and volunteers are encouraged to bring resources that can assist with teaching. You are effectively placed in rural and urban communities where you will teach solo and also assist the few available teachers.

GVN Ghana Teaching Program

Organization: Global Volunteer Network
Location: Participating schools can be found in several towns & villages of the following regions in Ghana: Greater Accra, Central, Eastern, Volta & Ashanti.
Cost: $897 for 1 month **Duration:** 1 to 6 months **Age:** 18-65
Contact: info@volunteer.org.nz **Learn more:** www.volunteer.org.nz
Details: The Global Volunteer Network currently offers volunteer teaching opportunities in local schools throughout Ghana, teaching a variety of subjects through their partner organization. Volunteers have the opportunity to participate in the development of Ghana's young people and can teach in preschools, primary, secondary and technical  schools all over Ghana. The teaching projects range from preschool (4 and 5 year olds), primary (6-11 years), to junior secondary (12-14 years)

Ghana Community Development Program

Organization: Global Volunteer Network
Location: In the town of Ho, the capital of the Volta Region
Cost: $947 for 1 month **Duration:** 1 to 6 months **Age:** 18-60
Contact: info@volunteer.org.nz **Learn more:** www.volunteer.org.nz
Details: This GVN program for those interested in development projects who wish to play a leadership role and get highly immersed in a local project. Volunteers will bring the most value in their organizational skills, reliability, project and people management and basic enthusiasm. You will work with one of the various local groups GVN's partner is connected with. These groups each have their own individual goals which include educating orphans, providing vocational training, protecting the local environment through eco-tourism initiatives or starting a youth center.

Teach in Small Town Ghana

Organization: Experiential Learning International
Location: Ghana
Cost: Starting at $1,125 **Duration:** 4+ weeks **Age:** 18
Email contact: info@eliabroad.org **Learn more:** www.eliabroad.org
Details: Ghanaian schools face the same challenges that most schools in Africa face: overcrowding, lack of materials and lack of teacher training. In many classrooms, the student-teacher ratio can be as high as 60-70 students for every teacher. Ghanaian schools also face

shortages of books, paper, pencils, and other school supplies. Teachers rarely have the opportunity to pursue further training. Most teaching placements are in smaller towns and villages where the need is greatest. ELI offers both volunteer teaching placements and a year-long teaching internship.

Health Care and Medical Clinics

Organization: uVolunteer
Location: Koforidua, capital of Ghana's Eastern Region
Cost: $1,300 for the first 4 weeks; $95 each additional week
Duration: 4+ weeks **Age:** 18
Contact: info@uvolunteer.org **Learn more:** www.uvolunteer.org
Special skills: Basic English and a medical background
Details: While working with health care in Ghana, you will work alongside medical professionals in hospitals and clinics throughout the country. You will have the opportunity to help in a variety of sectors within the hospitals and clinics including: the consulting room, outpatient care, maternal and childcare, physiotherapy, and routine examinations and medical practices. The patient to doctor ratio is rather high so the hospitals are in need of worthy volunteers to donate their time and care.

Children's Home/Orphanage

Organization: uVolunteer
Location: Several locations in and around Accra
Cost: $1,300 for the first 4 weeks; $95 each additional week
Duration: 4+ weeks **Age:** 18
Contact: info@uvolunteer.org **Learn more:** www.uvolunteer.org
Special skills: Basic English
Details: Volunteers will be working in an orphanage, helping with the educational and emotional development of the orphans in Ghana. You will be a role model, teach English and assist staff members. Volunteers on this project provide support and guidance by helping the children with their homework, leading recreational activities, aiding in meal preparation, and assisting the staff members. This is a chance for you to create meaningful bonds and emotional ties with these children and help to change their lives for the better. The homes vary in size from 15-20 children up to 150 children depending on the location.

Youth Soccer Coaching

Organization: World Endeavors
Location: Kumasi
Cost: $1,308+ **Duration:** 2 to 12 weeks **Age:** 18
Contact: inquiry@worldendeavors.com

Learn more: www.worldendeavors.com
Details: Connect with children and teens in Ghana through the universal language of soccer. This sport offers these children a respite from their hard daily lives, and volunteers provide coaching and training support for the team. Volunteers live and eat with a local host family, giving them a unique insight into Ghanaian culture. English is the national language of Ghana, though many languages are spoken throughout.

Health Care and Health Education in Ghana

Organization: World Endeavors
Location: Kumasi
Cost: $1,308+ **Duration:** 2 to 12 weeks **Age:** 18
Contact: inquiry@worldendeavors.com
Learn more: www.worldendeavors.com
Details: Support efforts to educate residents of Ghanaian villages about AIDS and malaria prevention, or assist in a local clinic or hospital. Volunteers with no medical experience can assist local non-governmental organizations in education and training on important health issues, traveling to villages throughout the central region of Ghana. Volunteers live with host families, who provide three meals each day. English is the national language, though many local and regional languages are also spoken.

Teaching Children in Ghana

Organization: World Endeavors
Location: Kumasi
Cost: $1,308+ **Duration:** 2 to 12 Weeks **Age:** 18
Contact: inquiry@worldendeavors.com
Learn more: www.worldendeavors.com
Details: Teach English and many other subjects to elementary school children. Volunteers shadow a local teacher during their first week and then teach independently when they are ready. They also provide one-on-one tutoring support for students wishing to improve their English. Housing and meals are provided with local host families, giving volunteers a meaningful experience of Ghanaian culture and hospitality.

Business Development: Design and Merchandising

Organization: Isla-International Service Learning Alliance
Location: Okurase in the West Akyem Municipal of the Eastern Region
Cost: 8 weeks $3,585; 12 weeks $4,365

Duration: 2 to 8 weeks for short-term volunteer, 9 to 52 weeks for an internship **Age:** 18
Contact: info@isla-serve.org **Learn more:** www.isla-serve.org
Special skills: Candidates should be undergraduate or graduate college students, though "gap-year" students, working professionals and retirees will be considered. It is most important to be highly motivated and enthusiastic because the work can be quite demanding.

 **Details:** Isla offers a unique opportunity to live, learn and serve in Ghana with a local host organization, Project Okurase. Immerse yourself in a short-term volunteer project (2-8 weeks) or an internship (9-52 weeks) in a rich cultural, service learning experience that combines cross-cultural and community–based sustainable development training with a hands-on service project. Project Okurase offers short-term volunteer work and internships in Ghana using a service learning model. Individuals with an interest and background in business, social enterprise and/or apparel design and merchandising will help create a small social and sustainable enterprise based on a new line of clothing designed for Project Okurase's fundraising efforts.

Small Business Development

Organization: Kaya Responsible Travel
Location: The vibrant beachside town of Cape Coast
Cost: $1,270+ **Duration:** 2 to 26 weeks **Age:** 18–80
Contact: info@kayavolunteer.com
Learn more: www.KayaVolunteer.com
Special skills: Experience or study in business and enterprise is essential, as well as a motivational, confident approach.
Details: Many people in the communities of the Cape Coast have fantastic skills from dressmaking and carpentry to cooking, but lack the know-how to develop their skills into a business. This project is designed to help these men and women in starting up and growing small sustainable businesses. Help to promote stimulus and sustainability for economic growth in the communities. Volunteers will assist in workshops advising on where to derive funds, how to search and apply for grants, how to promote and market their business, and how to work with basic accounting and budgets. You can help improve local economies by providing your skills to guide them through this process and generate ideas to improve and expand their start-up enterprises.

Education and Youth Development

Organization: Kaya Responsible Travel
Location: The vibrant beachside town of Cape Coast
Cost: $1,270 **Duration:** 2 to 26 weeks **Age:** 18-80

353

Contact: info@kayavolunteer.com
Learn more: www.KayaVolunteer.com
Special skills: Experience or study in business and enterprise is essential, as well as a motivational, confident approach.
Details: Help vulnerable youth to receive a higher quality education than their circumstances normally provide. Schools serving low-income students receive fewer resources, face greater difficulties attracting qualified teachers, have many more challenges in addressing students' needs, and receive less support from parents. You will be able to help the futures of these children by assisting to provide quality teaching, and the funds from your placement fee will help pay for new resources that the school desperately needs. This Kaya project places volunteers in orphanages and rural primary schools to implement fun social activities for the children, to help teach English, science, mathematics, arts and sports.

Conversational English and Assisting Teachers

Organization: Cross-Cultural Solutions
Location: Volta Region
Cost: $3,142+   **Duration:** 3 to 12 weeks
Age: 18, over 8 welcome with a parent or guardian
Contact: info@crossculturalsolutions.org
Learn more: www.crossculturalsolutions.org
Details: Cross-Cultural Solutions is a non-profit organization that enables volunteers to make a meaningful contribution to the community by working side-by-side with local people, while gaining a new perspective and insight into the culture and themselves. In Ghana, volunteers provide extra support by teaching children, teaching conversational English, or assisting teachers of special education. As with many public services in the area, the schools are often overcrowded, leaving many children without the personal attention and assistance they need. Learning English from a native English speaker is so appealing that the sheer presence of international volunteers can increase attendance at local schools. All meals and accommodations are provided.

Other organizations offering projects in Ghana:
Elghana: www.elghana.com
Global Routes: www.globalroutes.org
Global Visions International: www.gviusa.com
Habitat for Humanity: www.habitat.org
International Foundation for Education and Self-Help: www.ifesh.org
Children Better Way: www.childrenbetterway.org
Envision Change Network: www.ecnvolunteer.org
Worldwide Veterinary Service: www.wvs.org.uk

Guinea

Organizations offering projects in Guinea:

Batafon Arts (music & dance): www.batafonarts.co.uk
Chimpanzee Conservation Centre:
   chimpanzeeconservation.wildlifedirect.org
International Foundation for Education and Self-Help: www.ifesh.org
Tostna (unusually long-term social transformation work):
   www.tostan.org

Kenya

Teach and Care for Orphans

Organization: International Humanity Foundation
Location: Nakuru
Cost: $50 per week, maximum of $600
Duration: 1+ month, no maximum
Age: 18, or parental permission
Contact: volunteering@ihfonline.org
Learn more: www.ihfonline.org
Details: Learn the realities of international poverty by serving at an orphanage and education center where you will live, learn, teach and play with the over 100 children who call it home. The center's tasks and needs vary widely, and you are certain to find a niche according to your skills. The center is also heavily involved in fighting malnourishment. Every month you will travel into arid East Pokot to deliver staple foods to, and purchase animals for, the neediest tribal people. As IHF is entirely volunteer-run, you will be asked to serve on various online task teams, such as advertising and photography, which will grant you a unique insight into how an international non-profit operates. Room and board at the center are included in the fee.

Internally Displaced Persons (IDP) Camp Project

Organization: Global Volunteer Network
Location: The suburbs surrounding Nairobi.
Cost: $847 for 4 weeks   **Duration:** 4 weeks to 6 months   **Age:** 25
Contact: info@volunteer.org.nz   **Learn more:**
www.volunteer.org.nz
Details: Volunteers are needed to help rebuild the lives of those who were forced to flee their homes during the post election violence in

Kenya in 2007. Still unable to return to their homes, 1000s of internally displaced persons found refuge in IDP Camps across the Great Rift Valley. Volunteers will work in the IDP camp offering help to children, youth and adults. There are two key areas where volunteers are needed: 1) *Community Program*: Volunteers are needed to provide counseling, youth mentoring and education while being supervised by local camp staff. 2) *Medical Program*: Volunteers will be working together with the nurse doing basic medical procedures such as writing prescriptions, giving out medicine and attending to the patients.

Kenya's Maasailand Teaching &/or Medical Program
Organization: Global Volunteer Network
Location: Varies
Cost: $847 for 4 weeks   **Duration:** 4 weeks to 6 months   **Age:** 18
Contact: info@volunteer.org.nz   **Learn more:**
www.volunteer.org.nz
Details: The Maasai have largely managed to remain outside of mainstream African culture and preserve their traditional ways, although this becomes more challenging each year. For this reason Maasai are increasingly seeking the opportunities African society has to offer. With little government support, Maasai struggle to find teachers and medical professionals to work in their schools and medical clinics. *Teaching Program*: Volunteers have the opportunity to educate children at primary school level. Subjects taught include English, math, science and social studies. Volunteers are also encouraged to initiate extra-curricular activities. *Medical Program*: Medically qualified volunteers are needed to work in community clinics to increase access to basic healthcare and promote health education in the local community.

Colobus Monkey Care and Eco-Volunteer
Organization: The Colobus Trust
Location: Diani Beach
Cost: Varies by program   **Duration:** 3 weeks to 1 month
Age: 18 for eco-volunteers, 22 for Colobologists
Contact: volunteers@colobustrust.org
Learn more: www.colobustrust.org
Special skills: Anyone with a passion for wildlife conservation
Details: The Colobus Trust's goal is to promote, in close co-operation with other organizations and local communities, the conservation, preservation and protection of primates, in particular the Angolan Colobus monkey (*Colobus angolensis palliates*). Volunteers clean

cages, assist with rehabilitation of nonhuman primates, prepare feed rations, change linen, help with environmental enrichment, etc. You may also work in the capture and care of injured monkeys for the rehabilitation centre, (under the supervision of a veterinarian or trained assistant), help in planting indigenous tree seedlings in local forest patches, work closely with traditional kaya (holy forests) elders, monitor troops in the Diani forest, remove of snares, assist with anti-poaching campaigns, etc.

Teaching at Kaloleni Junior Academy

Organization: Touch Africa International
Location: Kaloleni (coastal province)
Cost: $900 per month   **Duration**: Varies   **Age**: 18
Contact: touchafrica1@gmail.com
Learn more: www.helptouchafrica.com
Special skills: Teaching, physical education training &/or peer counseling
Details: Take pride in being part of this socially responsible program by becoming a volunteer teacher at a local primary school in Kenya. By offering your time as a teacher you will learn more of the countries education system, as well as take part in extracurricular activities at the school. Share and experience classroom set up and learn more of the Swahili language. Part of the cost covers your food and accommodation with a family near the school for the whole duration of your volunteer experience. While with the project volunteers will visit historic sites, white sand beaches, Fort Jesus Museum and are able to take a safari at the end of the their stay. Have a real Africa experience by being a part of this Touch Africa vision and mission.

Orphans and Vulnerable Kids Scholarship Project

Organization: Touch Africa International
Location: Kaloleni (coastal province)
Cost: $900 for 4 weeks   **Duration**: 1 month   **Age**: 16
Contact: touchafrica1@gmail.com
Learn more: www.helptouchafrica.com
Special skills: Social workers, teachers or anyone interested in working within a community setting
Details: Make the best of your resources and time as you participate in this well thought out, beneficial project aimed at bringing up kids from less fortunate families, helping them to get a better education and to change their lives through giving them support both morally and via education. Feel a sense of belonging in this world. A part of the work is doing social mapping, data collection and getting reports from schools and families where the children come from. As you volunteer you'll learn more about other cultures, traditions and a systematic approach

geared towards conflict resolution, leadership and working for a purpose. Volunteer for this one common cause; betterment of lives via knowledge.

One Million Trees: Planting and Beach Cleaning

Organization: Touch Africa International
Special skills: Open to everyone, schools, individual volunteers and organized groups
Location: Tsunza Island, Kwale
Cost: $900 per month   **Duration**: 1 month   **Age:** 18
Contact: touchafrica1@gmail.com
Learn more: www.helptouchafrica.com
Details: Tsunza is one of the forgotten islands in Kenya, with beautiful estuaries stretching out to the Indian Ocean. Unfortunately it has been marginalized and residents have encroached on this important ecosystem, cutting down the mangroves which they use for construction of houses and cooking. In response, Touch Africa along with the coastal development authority has come up with a module to plant trees of an indigenous nature which are adapted to the salinity of the soil and water table. Now they are now calling for volunteers to visit the island and help plant those trees, helping them to reach their target goal of one million trees, as well to advocate for a clean environment around the region and especially along the Indian Ocean. Don't miss out on this 'feel good' chance to help out on a tropical island with like-minded volunteers.

Integrated Rehabilitation Center

Organization: Greenheart Travel
Location: Southwest of Nairobi at the southern tip of the Rift Valley.
Cost: $1,890 for 8 weeks **Duration:** 2 to 8 weeks   **Age:** 18
Contact: info@greenhearttravel.org
Learn more: www.cci-exchange.com
Details: The Tania Center is a home for rehabilitating many disabled children, street children, orphans and young Maasai girls rescued from early marriages. The main goal of the center is to provide education, shelter, food and care to the children and equip them with skills to give them a more independent and successful future. Volunteers are needed to help teach students, and also be involved with guidance and counseling activities, music and games, and promotion of HIV/AIDS awareness campaigns. This project includes guest house accommodations with meals included. Medical insurance and 24 hour emergency contact is also provided.

Nursery School Building for Orphaned/Vulnerable Kids

Organization: Touch Africa International
Location: Walea Kaloleni
Cost: $980 for 4 weeks **Duration:** 4 weeks **Age:** 16
Contact: touchafrica1@gmail.com
Learn more: www.helptouchafrica.com
Special skills: Open to all: individuals, groups, organizations
Details: Involve yourself with an initiative born by a local community, to upgrade a deserted school for minors with the hands of volunteer workers. The aim is towards building and reinforcing classrooms with better materials so that there is more strength and sustainability to the building. You will stay with a local host family, where you are expected to be a part of the daily routine of the family and play roles as in a normal family set up. You will also experience learning in Africa, social work and be exposed to many variants of life in the community in general. Be part of this noble cause - uplifting education in Kenya.

Health Care and Medical Clinics

Organization: uVolunteer
Location: Nairobi, Nakuru or Nyeri
Cost: $850 for the first 2 weeks; add $100 for each additional week
Duration: 2+ weeks **Age:** 18
Contact: info@uvolunteer.org **Learn more:** www.uvolunteer.org
Special skills: Intermediate English and a medical background
Details: This is a great opportunity for volunteers to donate their skills and time to helping others in need, while gaining hands-on medical experience and learning about medical care in Kenya – common diseases, treatments, and issues affecting healthcare in this beautiful country. This program places medical volunteers in clinics that treat a wide range of patients. You will help provide services such as maternal and child health, family health, curative health care, primary health care, voluntary counseling, testing and training in health and HIV/AIDS awareness and family planning. Skilled help will be greatly appreciated.

Teaching in Kenya

Organization: International Volunteer HQ
Location: Urban and rural placements available all over Kenya
Cost: $250 for 1 week to $2,220 for 6 months, includes food & accommodations
Duration: 1 week to 6 months **Age:** 18
Contact: volunteer@volunteerhq.org
Learn more: www.volunteerhq.org

Details: The introduction of free primary school education in Kenya left the Kenyan Government faced with a dilemma -a large number of students entitled to education and a comparative lack of teachers. Volunteers are placed in community schools, public schools or orphanage schools. Many of these schools worked are constantly understaffed and always in need of volunteers. You can work alone or alongside other teachers and volunteers. Typical subjects include English, math, science, social studies, art and physical education. Teaching at a rural school is an experience like no other. Giraffes often wander freely around school grounds and it is no big deal to have wild animals burrow holes through the school fields overnight. Volunteers are not required to be qualified or experienced teachers.

Medical Work in Kenya

Organization: International Volunteer HQ
Location: Urban and rural placements available all over Kenya
Cost: $250 for 1 week to $2,220 for 6 months, includes food & accommodations
Duration: 1 week to 6 months   **Age:** 18
Contact: volunteer@volunteerhq.org
Learn more: www.volunteerhq.org
Special skills: Volunteers need to be in training or qualified in a relevant medical field.
Details: Healthcare is neither easily accessible nor affordable for many Kenyans living in rural villages and slums such as Kibera. Poverty creates a large barrier to the acquisition of healthcare in general, but in rural areas in particular. The Kenyan Government has authorized a partner program to place medical students and professionals in their clinics and hospitals. These facilities and hospitals have very basic equipment and facilities. Volunteers are placed according to their medical training and experience. Saikeri Medical Clinic is a possible placement in a remote Maasai village (two hours from Nairobi); this is the only medical establishment for miles servicing thousands of people. The work includes basic first aid, outpatient services, maternity services and HIV/AIDS testing and counseling.

HIV/AIDS work in Kenya

Organization: International Volunteer HQ
Location: Nairobi
Cost: $250 for 1 week to $2,220 for 6 months, includes food & accommodations
Duration: 1 week to 6 months   **Age:** 18
Contact: volunteer@volunteerhq.org

Learn more: www.volunteerhq.org
Details: HIV/AIDS is responsible for thousands of deaths each year in Kenya. In an effort to combat this deadly disease, many hospitals and local NGOs run HIV/AIDS testing, counseling and awareness campaigns. Our HIV/AIDS program aims to give care and support to those infected and also create awareness to vulnerable groups about the dangers of HIV/AIDS through outreach programs. These outreach programs are done through schools and community groups and work consists of; visiting patients in homes, helping with medical care and food, conducting lessons to educate people on the dangers of HIV and how to prevent themselves from getting infected. This program is organized in collaboration with government institutions, NGOs, and community-based organizations who work very closely with the communities and HIV/AIDS patients.

Sports Education Program

Location: Urban and rural placements available all over Kenya
Cost: $250 for 1 week to $2,220 for 6 months, includes food & accommodations
Duration: 1 week to 6 months   **Age:** 18
Contact: volunteer@volunteerhq.org
Learn more: www.volunteerhq.org
Details: The Sports Education Program is designed for people who wish to work with children and in schools, but not necessarily spend all of their time teaching in a classroom. The program consists of volunteers working in local schools to broaden the children's knowledge of sports, teach "foreign" sports and games to the children, and to educate children about general fitness, health and wellbeing in addition to teaching general lessons at the school. It is up to the volunteer to plan lessons and design the teaching of their sports program. While football is extremely popular in Africa, many volunteers have found it rewarding to teach children in the schools different sports (or popular sports from the volunteer's home country). These children are extremely enthusiastic and willing to learn!

GVN Kenya Medical/Health Program

Organization: Global Volunteer Network
Location: The suburbs surrounding Nairobi.
Cost: $647 for 2 weeks   **Duration:** 2 weeks to 6 months   **Age:** 18
Contact: info@volunteer.org.nz   **Learn more:** www.volunteer.org.nz
Special skills: A medical qualification is required for the Medical/Health Program. For Internally Displaced Persons (IDP) programs volunteers must be over 25 years of age

361

Details: Volunteers have the opportunity to be closely involved in a variety of projects in the GVN Kenya program, including: children's, HIV/AIDS, teaching, medical/health and IDP camp projects. For those who have a particular interest in the Massai tribe and its culture, Global Volunteer Network also provides teaching and medical placements in Massailand, in which volunteers have the opportunity of immersing themselves in this unique society. This program offers diverse opportunities for those who are passionate about making a difference in the lives of Kenyan people.

Kenya Program: Children's Project

Organization: Global Volunteer Network
Location: The suburbs surrounding Nairobi.
Cost: $647 2 weeks   **Duration:** 2 weeks to 6 months   **Age:** 18
Contact: info@volunteer.org.nz   **Learn more:**
www.volunteer.org.nz
Details: You have the opportunity to help children in need. These are children who have lost their parents to HIV/AIDS, children who have been abused by their parents and children whose parents are not able to provide for them. As a volunteer you will mentor by becoming a big brother or sister to kids in a children's home. You will work alongside local staff to help with classroom teaching and homework help, childcare and the daily operation of the running of the home. Volunteers are also encouraged to initiate their own work by organizing art and crafts, music, dance, games, sports activities and day trips for the children.

Kenya Program: Teaching Project

Organization: Global Volunteer Network
Location: The suburbs surrounding Nairobi
Cost: $647 for 2 weeks   **Duration:** 2 weeks to 6 months   **Age:** 18
Contact: info@volunteer.org.nz   **Learn more:**
www.volunteer.org.nz
Details: Quality education for both boys and girls is crucial in reducing poverty and promoting gender equality. As a volunteer you will help to empower girls and boys by giving them the skills they need to overcome poverty and to make their voice heard. GVN has opportunities for volunteers to assist with teaching at preschool, primary and secondary levels. At primary and secondary levels volunteer teachers can teach core subjects, such as English, mathematics, science, social sciences, and can initiate extra-curricular activities. Volunteer preschool teachers will teach basic English skills and carry out basic childcare duties. A teaching qualification is not required (except for secondary teaching) but volunteers need to be

confident in the above subjects and preferably have or are studying towards a university degree.

Kenya Program: HIV/AIDS Project

Organization: Global Volunteer Network
Location: The suburbs surrounding Nairobi
Cost: $647 for 2 weeks   **Duration:** 2 weeks to 6 months   **Age:** 18
Contact: info@volunteer.org.nz   **Learn more:**
www.volunteer.org.nz
Special skills: A background in HIV/AIDS and basic health care is required.
Details: The goals of the HIV/AIDS program are to decrease the spread of HIV through raising awareness and education and to increase access to homecare and providing emotional support to those affected by HIV/AIDS within the community. Volunteers have the opportunity to work in a community HIV/AIDS organization to assist with homecare visits to HIV positive people, and to educate and counsel community and school groups as well as individuals. This role is suitable for a caring, motivated and self-directed person. Medical training is not necessary for all aspects of the program, but a background in HIV/AIDS and basic healthcare is required.

Nairobi Area Medical Health Project

Organization: Global Volunteer Network
Location: The suburbs surrounding Nairobi.
Cost: $647 for 2 weeks   **Duration:** 2 weeks to 6 months   **Age:** 18
Contact: info@volunteer.org.nz   **Learn more:**
www.volunteer.org.nz
Special skills: Must be medically qualified
Details: Malaria, typhoid, pneumonia and tetanus are treatable diseases yet many still die in Kenya as a result of not receiving proper medical care. Government-run hospitals and medical clinics are ill equipped to handle the volume of people in need of care. As a medically qualified volunteer you can help by sharing your medical skills and working alongside local staff to provide those in need with basic medical care. Volunteers have the opportunity to work in the areas of general medical practice, maternal health, minor surgery and laboratory work.

Work Camps in Kenya

Organization: Experiential Learning International
Location: Kenya
Cost: $695   **Duration:** 2 or 3 weeks   **Age:** 18
Contact: info@eliabroad.org   **Learn more:** www.eliabroad.org

Details: The International Work Camp Program is a low-cost alternative that gives volunteers the opportunity to work on a three week long project with other volunteers from all over the world. The projects are organized by the Kenya Voluntary Development Association and serve all areas of Kenya. Volunteers meet in Nairobi for a 1-day orientation before heading off to the work camp site as a group. ELI, along with many other organizations worldwide, provides volunteers for these projects.

Children's Home/Orphanages in Nairobi

Organization: uVolunteer
Location: Nairobi, Nakuru or Nyeri
Cost: $850 for the first 2 weeks; $100 each additional week
Duration: 2+ weeks **Age:** 18
Contact: info@uvolunteer.org **Learn more:** www.uvolunteer.org
Special skills: Intermediate English
Details: During your volunteer project you will be working with underprivileged children in one of Kenya's many orphanages. The program cares for children who have lost their parents to HIV/AIDS and/or who have been abused by their parents. Volunteers assist with the daily running of these homes; cleaning, bathing, cooking, etc. The

evenings are spent playing with the children and helping them with their homework. Volunteers also take on a role as a sibling to the children - a relationship that is often taken for granted. The orphanages have their own schools and volunteers will teach the children English and basic math classes. Volunteers also help in refurbishing facilities and help in the general welfare of the children's home in Kenya.

Health Care and Medical Clinics

Organization: uVolunteer
Location: Nairobi, Nakuru or Nyeri
Cost: $850 for the first 2 weeks; add $100 for each additional week
Duration: 2+ weeks **Age:** 18
Contact: info@uvolunteer.org **Learn more:** www.uvolunteer.org
Special skills: Intermediate English and a medical background
Details: This is a great opportunity for volunteers to donate their skills and time to helping others in need, while gaining hands-on medical experience and learning about medical care in Kenya – common diseases, treatments and issues affecting healthcare in the country. This program places medical volunteers in clinics that treat a wide range of patients. They provide services such as maternal and child health, family health, curative health care, primary health care, voluntary

counseling and testing, training in health and HIV/AIDS awareness and family planning. Help will be greatly appreciated.

Orphanages in Nakuru

Organization: Experiential Learning International
Location: Nakuru
Cost: $885+ **Duration**: 2+ weeks **Age:** 18
Contact: info@eliabroad.org
Learn more: www.eliabroad.org
Details: UNICEF estimates that approximately 2.3 million children in Kenya are orphans. These children turn to the street or an orphanage for refuge. ELI works with orphanages in Nakuru, Nairobi, and the base of Mt. Kenya as well as with day centers for street children in Nakuru. These organizations all place a large emphasis on the education and empowerment of the children. Volunteers at these organizations will assist with the daily tasks such as feeding the children, making sure everyone is clean and properly clothed, leading activities, helping with homework, and other tasks. You may also organize classes and educational activities. Volunteers have the chance to serve as a role model and mentor as well as to motivate the children to study.

Kenya Medical and Community Assistance

Organization: African Impact
Location: Limuru, Kenya
Cost: $2,260 for 4 weeks **Duration:** 2 to 4 weeks or more **Age:** 18
Contact: info@africanimpact.com
Learn more: www.africanimpact.com
Special skills: None required, although medical experience is helpful
Details: Kenya's population is hugely affected by the struggles of HIV/AIDS, poverty and unemployment. There are countless possibilities to impact the lives of those that are affected by these problems, such as in Nairobi's slums, surrounding orphanages, schools and in hospitals. As a volunteer, you will spend two days of the week in the Nairobi slums involved in a community support programme. The rest of your time as a volunteer will be split up between Kikuyu Hospital, government hospitals, clinics and orphanages and pre-schools in Limuru. This will give you the chance to make a positive impact on health services in Nairobi, to gain unique medical experience and to make a profound difference in the lives of the surrounding community.

Habitat Global Village Trip

Organization: Habitat for Humanity
Location: Kenya offers six different project locations.

Cost: $1,600 to $1,900, not including airfare.
Duration: 12 days.
Age: 18, or at least 14-years-old and be accompanied by a legal guardian or be part of an established group.
Contact: gv@habitat.org, 1-800-HABITAT (422-4828), ext. 7530
Learn more: www.habitat.org/gv
Special skills: Global Village teams are open to all with a willingness to work hard, learn new skills and explore a new culture. Many of the trips require strenuous manual labor, so all participants should be in good health.
Details: Kenya experienced destructive post election ethnic violence in early 2008 forcing many people from their land and homes. Kenya faces many challenges including high disease prevalence, high unemployment; rising urbanization and a widening gap between the rich and poor. Moreover, millions of Kenyans face periodic hardships due to drought and flooding as a result of climate change. Nearly 60 percent of Kenya's 37 million residents are rural subsistence farmers and live on less than $2 a day. Although parts of the country are lush, green fields of healthy crops, many people in the rural areas suffer extreme poverty. Habitat for Humanity Kenya (HFHK) began building houses in Kenya in 1982. Since that time, HFHK has built over 2,900 homes in partnership with families in need through over 70 local community groups in seven regions: Bomet, Bungoma, Kisii, Machakos, Maua, Naivasha and Runyenjes.

Safari Explorer

Organization: Hands Up Holidays
Location: Voi
Cost: $4,000 per person, based on sharing a room
Duration: 4 days volunteering/14 day trip
Age: 16 years unless accompanied by an adult
Contact: info@handsupholidays.com
Learn more: www.handsupholidays.com
Special skills: None required, but teaching English as a second language (ESL), or building skills are desirable
Details: This is an opportunity to immerse yourself in a local community and help them deal with current issues. The warmth of these impoverished people will forever change you. Assist with painting or building a classroom, teach or partake in many other tasks. Get to know the people as you work alongside them and feel satisfaction and their gratitude. This amazing community experience is complemented by a visit to three of the world's finest game reserves: the elephant-abundant Tsavo National East Park, the gorgeous Amboseli National Park on the doorstep of Mt. Kilimanjaro and the world renowned Maasai Mara National Reserve.

Captivating Kenya

Organization: Hands Up Holidays
Location: Watamu
Cost: $4,750 per person, based on sharing a room, excluding flights.
Duration: 4 days volunteering/16 day trip
Age: 16 years unless accompanied by an adult
Contact: info@handsupholidays.com
Learn more: www.handsupholidays.com
Special skills: None required, but environmental conservation or building skills are desirable
Details: Watamu, which means "sweet people" is a reference to the practice of using candy to lure locals in to become slaves. It is now the site of an inspiring environmental conservation project. Hands Up Holidays lures volunteers to assist with bird monitoring and tagging, tree planting and maintaining a footbridge to a bird lookout point. Along with this rewarding project you also get to explore the gorgeous east coast beaches of Kenya, and three of the best game reserves in the world: the elephant-abundant Tsavo East National Park, the gorgeous Amboseli National Park on the doorstep of Mt. Kilimanjaro and the world renowned Maasai Mara National Reserve.

Elephants of Tsavo

Organization: Earthwatch Institute
Location: Varied, rendezvous at Nairobi, Kenya
Cost: $4,050 - $4,450+ **Duration:** 11 days **Age:** 18
Contact: info@earthwatch.org **Learn more:** www.earthwatch.org
Details: Help researchers monitor the behavior and range of elephants in the breathtaking Kenyan savannah. Your team will spend four days in Tsavo East National Park, two days in Rukinga Wildlife Sanctuary and one day along the boundaries, conducting elephant surveys from a

vehicle. When elephants are spotted, you'll work with your team to record GPS coordinates, group size, composition, behavior and the state of the vegetation. You'll also identify other nearby wildlife and the GPS coordinates and status of waterholes throughout the study sites. Through informal lectures, you'll learn about wildlife conservation issues in the region. A recreational day in the middle of the expedition is yours for relaxing back at the lodge, helping input data or exploring the colorful markets of Voi town.

Other organizations offering projects in Kenya:

American Friends Service Committee: www.afsc.org
Global Crossroad: www.globalcrossroad.com
Global Visions International: www.gviusa.com
International Foundation for Education and Self-Help: www.ifesh.org
i-to-i: www.i-to-i.com
Institute of Field Research Expeditions: www.ifrevolunteers.org
Pamoja International (workcamps throughout Kenya):
  www.pamoja-international.org
Touch Africa International: www.helptouchafrica.com
United Planet: www.unitedplanet.org

Lesthotho

Organizations offering projects in Lesotho:

Habitat for Humanity: www.habitat.org
Service Civil International: www.sci-ivs.org
Volunteers for Peace: www.vfp.org
UAN Exchange: www.unaexchange.org

Liberia

F-SHAM of Faith Girls Academy

Organization: Kids Worldwide
Location: Soul Clinic Community, Paynesville City, Monrovia
Cost: Under 1 month $300, 1 month $400, subsequent months $100.
Duration: 2+ weeks, 1 month+ preferred **Age:** 18
Contact: george@kidsworldwide.org
Learn more: www.kidsworldwide.org
Special skills: Qualified teachers and general volunteers are all welcome
Details: F-SHAM of Faith Girls Academy is an all girl's school located in Monrovia, the capital of Liberia. The school was founded in the year 2000 and was the idea of five women educators. About five hundred female students between the ages of 1 and 18 attend the school. F-SHAM runs from nursery school to elementary, junior high and senior high level. It runs both academic and vocational training programs. The

vocational training program allows other women (i.e. non regular students) to enroll for special skill training. You will teach small classes in either the nursery or upper classes. The civil war in Liberia has been over for several years. This is a terrific chance to explore a portion of the world not often traveled in the past and bring your voluntary spirit to a whole new land.

Other organizations offering projects in Liberia:

Children Better Way: www.childrenbetterway.org
Envision Change Network: www.ecnvolunteer.org
International Foundation for Education and Self-Help: www.ifesh.org
Rural Shelter Assistance Program: rsapliberia.wordpress.com

Madagascar

Health Care Volunteering in Northern Madagascar

Organization: Maventy Health International
Location: Northern Madagascar: Anivorano Nord- Diana Region, Diego Suarez- Diana Region, Nosy Be Island – Diana Region
Cost: None   **Duration:** 2 weeks to 12 months   **Age:** 16- 75
  Contact: info@maventy.org, drm@maventy.org

Learn more: www.maventy.org
Special skills: Interested applicants can be students, trainees and professionals in various fields which may include but are not limited to social, environmental sciences, technology, engineering, medicine, dentistry, public health, international business and development.
Details: MHI has projects focused on improving health care delivery and infrastructure in Northern Madagascar. The organization combines modern technology (mobile and web applications) with on the ground action. Volunteers come from all over the world and experience life changing, hands on work in projects related to prevention, diagnosis and treatment of malnutrition, malaria, family planning, sexually transmitted diseases and tuberculosis as well as in development of healthcare infrastructure. Eligible volunteers initially receive online training.

Volunteer in a Rural Village

Organization: Mada Clinics
Location: Northern Madagascar
Cost: $250 per week   **Duration:** 2 to 12 weeks   **Age:** 18-70
Contact: info@madaclinics.org   **Learn more:** www.madaclinics.org

Special skills: Healthcare worker, environmental specialist, teacher, any able -bodied person

Details: Mada Clinics International was set up to offer free health care and education to the people of Northern Madagascar. They welcome people who wish to spend time in a small village, living a simple lifestyle, eating simple food, sleeping in simple huts and sharing a common goal with the people who work at Mada Clinics to help the local people in whatever way they can. Opportunities are available in: 1) Assisting at our Medical Clinic in a rural village 2) Teaching at the village infant school 3) Assessing the biodiversity of the local forest 4) Assisting in a local town's very basic hospital. A typical volunteer is someone with a thirst for adventure combined with an aim to help people worse off than themselves.

Coral Reef Monitoring Project

Organization: ReefDoctor.org
Location: Southwest Madagascar
Cost: $1,600 for 4 weeks   **Duration:** 3 to 12 weeks   **Age:** 18
Contact: volunteer@reefdoctor.org or info@reefdoctor.org
Learn more: www.reefdoctor.org
Special skills: A general enthusiasm for hands on conservation and ability to live/work in tropical environment in simple but comfortable conditions. The ability to speak French is preferable, but not essential. No previous experience required. Necessary skills are taught on the project.
Details: Volunteer work includes scuba-based monitoring of coral reefs and associated ecosystems to land based activities as part of marine management, community education and community development project. You will be working with local fishermen in a fishermen's association to empower them to manage their resources, with women on alternative income generation projects and with children on marine and environmental education and alternative opportunities from the public schools to a kid's club and sports association.

Community Development and Conservation

Organization: AZAFADY
Location: Varies throughout Madagascar
Cost: $840+ **Duration:** 2 to 10 weeks   **Age:** 18
Contact: info@azafady.org **Learn more:** www.voluntours.co.za
Special skills: No previous experience required. All necessary skills are taught on the project.
Details: Building schools, wells and fuel efficient stoves; health and environmental education; sustainable livelihoods initiatives such as

community vegetable gardens; English teaching; tree planting; lemur research and conservation. By volunteering with us it could help you to choose a new direction in life or to develop a career path you may already be on. It could be both a personal highlight and a practical stepping stone in a gap year or for anyone at any time, a great way to go abroad for more than just a holiday.

Marine Conservation Expedition

Organization: Blue Ventures
Location: Small fishing village of Andavadoaka, Southwest Madagascar
Cost: $3100 – 3600 (includes food, accommodation, training and diving)
Duration: 6 weeks (3-50 week options available)
Age: 18 (under 18 with guardian)
Contact: info@blueventures.org **Learn more:** www.blueventures.org
Special skills: None, full training provided
Details: Blue Ventures is an award-winning marine conservation organization dedicated to conservation, education and sustainable development in tropical coastal communities. For the past 6 years Blue Ventures has been supporting the indigenous fishing communities of Southwest Madagascar in their aim to manage and conserve local marine resources for the future. Research volunteers monitor the local coral reefs, mangroves and seagrass habitats as well as getting involved in local community groups such as the environment clubs for young people, lessons at school and women's associations. Volunteers stay in beach cabins close to the village of Andavadoaka where they can join in village life, learn to fish, sail African canoes and take a trip through the spiny forest to see iconic boabab trees.

Lemur Volunteer Venture

Organization: VOLUNTOURS
Location: Beautiful lakeside camp of Lanirano in Fort Dauphin Madagascar
Cost: From $2,600 for 4 weeks **Duration:** 4 or 8 weeks **Age:** 18
Contact: info@voluntours.co.za **Learn more:** www.voluntours.co.za
Details: Unique research and conservation program designed to discover more about the threatened lemur species and endangered forest habitats of southeast Madagascar, where you gain on-the-ground experience with an organization that has a proven track record in conservation. The program offers the opportunity to live and work amongst some of the most beautiful and remote parts of Madagascar on a number of exciting research and conservation initiatives. Volunteers

work on an extensive range of projects from the collection of data on endangered lemur species to environmental education with local communities and tree planting for reforestation purposes. During which you will get close to the three main species of diurnal lemur you are likely to encounter in the bush - Verreaux's sifaka, Ring-tailed lemurs and Brown lemurs.

Other organizations offering projects in Madagascar:

A Pas de Loup: www.apasdeloup.org
EarthWatch: www.earthwatch.org
Global Visions International:
www.gviusa.com
Habitat for Humanity: www.habitat.org
People and Places (Winner 'Best
Volunteering Organization' category of
Virgin Holidays Responsible Tourism Award 2009): travel-
peopleandplaces.co.uk

Malawi

Provide Health Care and Education

Organization: uVolunteer
Location: Migowi
Cost: $650 for the first 2 weeks; add $75 for each additional week
Duration: 2+ weeks   **Age:** 18
Contact: info@uvolunteer.org   **Learn more:** www.uvolunteer.org
Special skills: Intermediate English
Details: While volunteering at the Children's Home in Malawi you will help nurture and enhance the lives of children of all ages, emotionally and academically. While volunteering you will be working with the Children's home to provide assistance to not only children who have been orphaned, but whose parents are not capable of caring for them and the community as a whole. You will give advice to mothers in need of help with raising their newborns or children. You will also be organizing other educational and recreational activities for the children and the community.

Other organizations offering projects in Malawi:

African Conservation Trust: www.projectafrica.com
Global Seekers Volunteer Vacations: www.globalseekersvv.com
International Foundation for Education and Self-Help: www.ifesh.org

Students Travel and Exposure South Africa: www.staesa.org
Volunteers for Peace: www.vfp.org
Volunteering Solutions: www.volunteeringsolutions.com
Wildlife Action Group: www.wag-malawi.org

Mali

Health Programs Coordinator

Organization: The Mali Health Organizing Project
Location: Sikoro, a slum on the outskirts of Bamako
Cost: None to volunteer. Most volunteers spend about $10 a day (total) on food, transport and housing. **Duration:** 1 year   **Age:** 20
Contact: information@malihealth.org
Learn more: www.malihealth.org
Special skills: High level of French, college degree
Details: The Mali Health Organizing Project partners with slum communities to support residents in designing, implementing and evaluating their own health programs. Year long volunteer coordinators live with host families and are responsible for projects ranging from health radio programs and waste management to community health outreach.

Mali Volunteer Vacation

Organization: The Tandana Foundation
Location: Kansongho
Cost: $2,500   **Duration:** 2 weeks   **Age:** 12+ are welcome with a parent
Contact: tandanafoundation@gmail.com
Learn more: www.tandanafoundation.org
Details: Join a small group of dedicated, open-minded people and spend time working with the village of Kansongho, Mali on projects that help them protect their environment and improve food security. With villagers, volunteers plant many kinds of native and fruit trees to support their efforts to achieve reforestation and mitigate the advance of the desert. Help construct anti-erosion dikes in the fields to preserve topsoil. Get dirty, live in local villages and be amazed at the generosity and hospitality of your new friends. Before and after work, enjoy a tour of Mali's spectacular and diverse countryside, meet all kinds of people and learnabout local arts. Visit a remote, magnificent region and give back by supporting local efforts.

Customized Group Service Project in Mali

Organization: The Tandana Foundation
Location: Mali's Dogon Country
Cost: Variable, depending on the project
Duration: Variable, depending on the group's needs
Age: 15+ welcome with adult chaperones
Contact: tandanafoundation@gmail.com
Learn more: www.tandanafoundation.org
Details: Let your group make a difference in the lives of rural Malians while becoming part of the community you serve. Experience village life, eat local foods with your hosts, and help villagers' plant fruit trees or build anti-erosion dikes in their fields. Learn to dance Dogon style, try spinning and weaving, and teach new games to children. Be amazed at the joy that is shared. Whether you have a class, school group, church group, or set of friends--any group that wants a new experience and a chance to make friends by helping out-- Tandana Foundation can coordinate a service project and a unique learning experience for you.

Other organizations offering projects in Mali:

African Rural Development Movement: www.arudmo.org
Halley Movement (child welfare): www.halleymovement.org
Students Travel and Exposure South Africa: www.staesa.org

Mauritius

Mauritian Dolphin Volunteer Experience

Organization: VOLUNTOURS
Location: Black River, near Tamarin Bay on the tropical isle of Mauritius
Cost: from $2,500　**Duration:** 2 to 12 weeks　**Age:** 18
Contact: info@voluntours.co.za　**Learn more:** www.voluntours.co.za
Details: Ever wanted to volunteer with dolphins, but wanted to do more than just swim with them? Field research with this nongovernmental organization is combined with office-based analysis of fin profiles, notch characteristics and the efficient placing of animals within catalogues. This provides valuable information on the animals' migration patterns and social groups and habits. Support scientific research, conservation and awareness programmes and generate funds for ongoing research ensuring continuity. Ongoing educational work coupled with scientific study of the dolphin populations and coral reef

work is the backbone of this volunteer project. Their work extended from the need to sensitize the local dolphin watching operators to the two species of dolphin, which are the focus of their industry, and the importance of codes of behavior when encountering them.

Other organizations offering projects in Mauritius:

African Conservation Experience: www.conservationafrica.net
Service Civil International: www.sci-ivs.org

Morocco

Good Community Good Work

Organization: Elbassma Association
Location: Errachidia, Morocco
Cost: $230   **Duration:** 2 to 3 weeks   **Age:** 18-40
Email: info@elbassma.org   **Learn more:** www.elbassma.org
Details: The Elbassma Association for social and voluntary work helps children who live in the poorest areas. These are the youth who can't travel or enjoy the kids' camps in the region because of poverty. These kids need activities in summer to help them gain useful skills and knowledge and to spend holidays as a normal child, creating memories and having some fun. If you are outgoing, open, friendly and interested in learning about the Moroccan culture and people, the Elbassma Association needs your help to complete this work. With an open mind and heart volunteers will find whatever they are looking for while opening new worlds to the lives of impoverished children. A reasonable knowledge of English is needed.

Taste of Morocco

Organization: Hands Up Holidays
Location: Talamenzou
Cost: $1,950 per person, based on sharing a room
Duration: 3 days volunteering/9 day trip
Age: 16 years unless accompanied by an adult
Contact: info@handsupholidays.com
Learn more: www.handsupholidays.com
Special skills: None required, but teaching English as a second language (ESL) or building skills are desirable
Details: You can help the Berber people in the non-tourist village of Talamenzou. Take the opportunity to interact with the children, who will be thrilled to have you helping them develop their school building, where three rooms are under construction: a library, a computer room

375

and a reading room.

The itinerary for the rest of this trip is seasonal. In the spring, summer, autumn, hike the stunning Atlas Mountains and enjoy magnificent views. In the winter, explore old Berber towns and Kasbahs then travel along the life giving Dades River. All year round you have time at the end of your adventure to relax on the beautiful Essaouira beaches and reflect on a magnificent trip.

Fostering a Love of Learning

Organization: Cross-Cultural Solutions
Location: Rabat, Morocco
Cost: 1 week: $1,853; 2 week programs start from $2,784
Duration: 1-12 weeks   **Age:** 18. Over 8 welcome with adult supervision.
Contact: info@crossculturalsolutions.org
Learn more: www.crossculturalsolutions.org
Details: Cross-Cultural Solutions volunteers in Morocco work side-by-side with local people, contributing directly to community-based projects. In Morocco, the national literacy rate remains below 70 percent, and high dropout and repetition rates persist. Volunteers help to encourage a love of learning amongst all age groups. Volunteers can aid teachers in an organization designed specifically for educating street children so that they can be reintegrated into local schools, and have positive role models. You also assist teachers of special education students in an organization that strives to combat the social stigmas that surround disabilities in Morocco. The opportunity to exchange cultures and perspectives is one of the most important parts of the volunteers' work. All meals and accommodations are provided.

Other organizations offering projects in Morocco:

Projects Abroad: www.projects-abroad.org
Concordia: www.concordia-iye.org.uk
Service Civil International: www.sci-ivs.org
Volunteers for Peace: www.vfp.org

Mozambique

Rensida-Rede Nacional de Organizacoes de Pessoas vivendo com HIV

Organization: Inter-Cultural Youth Exchange
Location: Varies
Cost: Cost: $6,300 for 6 months or $7,500 for 12 months
Duration: 6 or 12 months   **Age:** 18-30
Contact: international@icye.co.uk   **Learn more:** www.icye.org.uk
Special skills: Prior knowledge of HIV/ AIDS/ STDs required.
Portuguese language skill is an advantage.
Details: Resida is a national network of organizations of people living
with HIV/AIDS. Resida is dedicated to the prevention of HIV/AIDS
and the provision of home care counseling. It also assists with civic
education and awareness campaigns for HIV/AIDS. The activities that
the volunteer will participate in will vary according to the needs of the
particular local organization they work with. These activities can vary
from campaigning and education projects to tackling prejudice
experienced by those living with HIV/AIDS to teaching English and
computer skills to local staff members. The volunteer will stay with a
host family.

Pre-School and English Teaching

Organization: African Impact
Location: Vilanculos
Cost: $1,980 for 4 weeks   **Duration:** 2 to 4 weeks or more   **Age:** 18
Contact: info@africanimpact.com
Learn more: www.africanimpact.com
Special skills: None. Past teaching experience is helpful
Details: This project has a very rural feel and involves various aspects
of community work and development in and around the coastal town of
Vilanculos. Volunteer involvement includes: teaching at the primary
school (developmental playtime; craft activities, singing and dancing),
conducting English and life skills lessons with some of the older
children in the community; working with the children in a local
orphanage; building homes for needy families; and working together
with an outreach programme that aims to develop trade skills among
HIV positive women. Focus is on educating children at the pre-school
level as well as teaching adult literacy. There are also opportunities to
coach sports for the kids and play games with them.

Preschool Teaching and HIV/AIDS Awareness

Organization: Kaya Responsible Travel
Location: The rural coastal town of Vilanculos, Mozambique
Cost: $1,326+ **Duration:** 2 to 26 weeks **Age:** 17-80
Contact: info@kayavolunteer.com
Learn more: www.KayaVolunteer.com
Special skills: None required other than the enthusiasm and flexibility to get involved in multiple projects
Details: Work with a rural Mozambique fishing community in a number of key local projects. Visit preschool classes in the morning to help local teachers educate young children in creative ways. Then work with secondary schools and community groups to conduct HIV/AIDS education and awareness workshops. These workshops are crucial in fighting the spread of the disease. You will also participate in monthly community testing days with a medical group. Volunteers working on these projects may also be required to help with occasional needs at the local orphanages and building projects. In a small community the need for volunteers provides a diverse and involved community experience.

Whale Shark Conservation

Organization: Kaya Responsible Travel
Location: The seaside village of Tofo
Cost: $2,958+ **Duration:** 4 to 26 weeks **Age:** 17-80
Contact: info@kayavolunteer.com
Learn more: www.KayaVolunteer.com
Special skills: Volunteers must be competent swimmers and prepared to take a PADI diving course
Details: Be involved with marine conservation to learn more about the world's largest fish, the whale shark. Working alongside research staff you will be required to obtain a PADI open water diving certificate and use the skills you learn for monitoring and data capture projects for turtles, manta rays and coral reefs as well as the whale shark.

Volunteers will also be involved with education in the local community to encourage the awareness of the conservation issues surrounding marine life and the Mozambique coast.

Other organizations offering projects in Mozambique:

GeoVisions: www.geovisions.org
Global Visions International: www.gviusa.com or www.gvi.co.uk
DolphinCare-Africa: www.dolphincare.org
EarthWatch: www.earthwatch.org
Ecoteer: www.ecoteer.com

People and Places (Winner 'Best Volunteering Organization' category
of Virgin Holidays Responsible Tourism Award 2009):
travel-peopleandplaces.co.uk
United Planet: www.unitedplanet.org
Work and Volunteer: www.workandvolunteer.com

Namibia

Desert Elephant / Human Cohabitation Project

Organization: Elephant – Human Relationship Aid
Location: Brandberg in the ephemeral Ugab River Park
Cost: $800 per 2 weeks   **Duration:** 2 weeks to 3 months   **Age:** 18
Contact: elephant@iway.na **Learn more:** www.desertelephant.org
Details: This project is part of a long-term initiative to find solutions
to the ever growing problem of facilitating the peaceful cohabitation
between subsistence farmers and desert adapted elephants. Working
from mobile base camps in the vicinity of the Brandberg in the
ephemeral Ugab River, the volunteer teams immerse themselves in
pioneer conservation work. This project is not for those interested in
bottle feeding cuddly baby elephants. This is about real, spearhead
conservation work in a harsh desert environment where small bands of
secretive, desert-adapted elephants roam vast wilderness areas. This is
a place where subsistence farmers eke out an existence and need all the
help they can get in their confrontations with the elephants competing
for precious water resources.

Namibia Teaching Year

Organization: WorldTeach
Location: Mostly rural communities
Cost: $5,990   **Duration:** One Year (Departure in late December)
Age: Any with a bachelor's degree
Contact: info@worldteach.org **Learn more:** www.worldteach.org
Special skills: Native English speaker, bachelor's degree
Details: WorldTeach volunteers work as English, mathematics,
science, and computer studies teachers in a wide range of schools,
including primary schools, secondary schools and adult training
facilities. Most volunteers will be responsible for 20-25 hours of
classroom teaching, including lesson preparation and grading. You may
also be asked to work in the school library or computer room. In
addition to their subject teaching, interested volunteers are also
encouraged to serve as HIV/AIDS resource teachers. Volunteers are
typically placed at government, community-based and church-affiliated

schools. Volunteers are placed in a variety of living situations. At government schools, volunteers may share a house with other teachers on school property. A few live in the community, either alone, with housemates or with a host family. Some volunteers live and eat at mission stations, which, in remote areas, often provide the only room and board options.

Namibia Teaching Semester

Organization: WorldTeach
Location: Placements in mostly rural communities
Cost: $4,990 **Duration:** One semester (late June through mid-December) **Age:** 18-74
Contact: info@worldteach.org **Learn more:** www.worldteach.org
Special skills: Native English speaker, bachelor's degree
Details: WorldTeach volunteers work as English, mathematics, science, and Computer Studies subject teachers in a wide range of schools, including primary schools, secondary schools, and adult training facilities. Most volunteers will be responsible for 20-25 hours of classroom teaching, including lesson preparation and grading. You may also be asked to work in the school library or computer room. In addition to their subject teaching, interested volunteers are also encouraged to serve as HIV/AIDS resource teachers. Volunteers are typically placed at government, community-based and church-affiliated schools. Volunteers are placed in a variety of living situations. At government schools, volunteers may share a house with other teachers on school property. A few live in the community, either alone, with housemates, or with a host family. Some volunteers live and eat at mission stations, which, in remote areas, often provide the only room and board options.

Namibia Teaching Summer

Organization: WorldTeach
Location: Varies
Cost: $4,490
Duration: 2 months (early June- early August) **Age:** 18-74
Contact: info@worldteach.org **Learn more:** www.worldteach.org
Special skills: Fluent English (undergraduates welcome!)
Details: The Namibia Summer Program is an incredible opportunity to acquire experience in the field in a developing country and be integral to the implementation of a national initiative. The program is run in close coordination with the Ministry of Education's nationwide plan to deploy Information and Communication Technology (ICT) in all educational institutions. Volunteers will lead computer literacy training for teachers at primary and secondary schools to develop their basic computers skills as required by the Ministry. You will be among

the first to train teachers using the newly developed computer literacy curriculum developed by the Ministry. Volunteers can also choose to teach HIV/AIDS awareness classes, subject classes (as based on the needs of the school), athletics, and work remedially with learners that need extra assistance in certain areas, like reading. Housing and meals provided at school or with host family.

Other organizations offering projects in Namibia:
Biosphere: www.biosphere-expeditions.org
Eco Tracks: www.ekotracks.com
GeoVisions: www.geovisions.org
Global Visions International: www.gviusa.com
Namibian Nature Foundation: www.nnf.org.na
Yomps: www.yomps.co.uk
Youth International: www.youthinternational.org
Volunteers for Peace: www.vfp.org

Nigeria

Mental Health Matters
Organization: Amaudo UK
Location: Southeastern Nigeria
Cost: Varies by length of stay   **Duration:** Varies, often long-term
Contact: amaudouk@btconnect.com
Learn more: www.amaudouk.org
Details: Amaudo has a strong need for mental health nurses, occupational therapists, physiotherapists and financial administrators.

Volunteer support staff may also be needed. Please check with Amaudo UK for their needs at any given time.

Nigerian Red Cross Society

Organization: Inter Cultural Youth Exchange (ICYE)
Location: Lagos
Cost: $6,300 for 6 months or $7,500 for 12 months
Duration: 6 or 12 months   **Age:** 18-30
Contact: international@icye.co.uk   **Learn more:** www.icye.org.uk
Details: The Nigerian Red Cross is involved in humanitarian activities from disaster relief and emergency medicine to providing care for orphaned children. The volunteer will assist with essential fundraising projects and work with local young people with health education matters, particularly related to HIV/AIDS. You will also have the opportunity to be involved with the local 'Mother's Club', which cares for motherless babies in the area. Volunteers stay with nearby families.

Vaccinations and Education on Farms in Abeokuta

Organization: Volunteer Club of Nigeria
Location: Ilisan Remo, Ogun State, Abeokuta
Cost: $350+   **Duration:** 2 to 16 weeks   **Age:** 16
Contact: volunteer4naija@yahoo.com, evans@vcnprojects.org
Learn more: vcnprojects.org
Special skills: From high school graduates to experts in the field of veterinary medicine

Details: This project for underfunded farms in Abeokuta is open to volunteers from every part of the world. This particular project runs throughout the year. Volunteers come to assist locals on the good practice of veterinary medicine. You will help in checking and vaccinating animals at poultry farms, fisheries, pig farms and educating the locals on animal health practices. They also engage volunteers in educating locals on the use of modern farm techniques that will improve crop yield and help in alleviating poverty in rural Africa. This is an opportunity to affect societies that need your service by improving farm yields and educating others regarding animal vaccinations, operations, laboratory work, post-mortems, meat inspections and the routine treatment of domestic farm animals and pets. Whether you are a high school student considering a career in veterinary medicine, an undergraduate, on a career break or an expert in the field, working as a veterinary volunteer or with farmers will allow you to teach and gain invaluable experience.

Other organizations offering projects in Nigeria:
Brethren Volunteer Service: www.brethrenvolunteerservice.org
International Foundation for Education and Self-Help: www.ifesh.org
Habitat for Humanity: www.habitat.org
Service Civil International: www.sci-ivs.org
Teachers Without Borders: www.teacherswithoutborders.org
United Planet: www.unitedplanet.org

Rwanda

Rwanda Teaching Year
Organization: WorldTeach
Location: Varies
Cost: $5,990
Duration: 1 year (Departure in late December) **Age:** 18-74
Contact: info@worldteach.org **Learn more:** www.worldteach.org
Special skills: Native English speaker, bachelor's degree
Details: Volunteers will be primarily teaching math and science subjects in high schools, though there will be opportunities to teach English and ICT as well. A few primary school placements may be possible as well. Volunteers are also expected to join and lead extracurricular activities such as HIV/AIDS clubs, sports teams, library committees, etc. Housing accommodations may vary depending on the placement site. The most common arrangement is school-provided housing or a furnished apartment. Volunteers will have their own room, although they might share common rooms with other teachers or staff. Buildings typically have cement walls and electricity, but not necessarily running water; volunteers may need to use the community water well. Most schools have been built since the genocide and are in quite good condition. Many even have an Internet connection. Cell phones work and have good reception throughout the country.

Rwanda Literacy Program
Organization: Global Volunteer Network
Special skills: Basic French is required for the literacy program
Location: The program is located in the Kigali province, primarily in the capital of Kigali (Nyarugenge), Kicukiro and Gasabo districts.
Cost: $697 for 2 weeks **Duration:** 2 weeks to 3 months **Age:** 18-65
Contact: info@volunteer.org.nz **Learn more:**
www.volunteer.org.nz
Details: The grade for schools in Rwanda is unsatisfactory. Many of them lack books, scholastic and teaching materials and school

equipment. In fact, war and genocide caused heavy losses at the level of human and material resources as well as the decrease of the social capital. Volunteers will work alongside local primary teachers to improve the level of English, math, health, hygiene and science skills amongst students. Volunteers will also be involved in improving teacher's level of English. You are not required to have a teaching qualification, but experience in subject areas like English, math, health, hygiene and science and French would be advantageous.

Rwanda HIV/AIDS Program

Organization: Global Volunteer Network
Location: The program is located in the Kigali province, primarily in the capital of Kigali (Nyarugenge), Kicukiro and Gasabo districts.
Cost: $697 for 2 weeks   **Duration:** 2 weeks to 3 months   **Age:** 18-65
Contact: info@volunteer.org.nz   **Learn more:** www.volunteer.org.nz
Details: Volunteers have the opportunity to work with community mobilizers to assist with counseling and taking care of patients both at home and in hospitals. This will involve taking patients to the hospitals and doing a follow up of their nutritional needs. No medical training is required for volunteers in this program, but volunteers should have a compassionate spirit, HIV/AIDS knowledge and basic counseling skills. There is also opportunity to work with local women's associations in income generation activities such as local soap making, basket weaving for commercial purposes and subsistence farming. Volunteers will work closely with these associations to bring in new business ideas, providing training on small scale business practices. Volunteers should have a basic knowledge in management of small scale income generating activities.

Gender-Based Violence Program

Organization: Global Volunteer Network
Location: The program is located in the Kigali province, primarily in the capital of Kigali (Nyarugenge), Kicukiro and Gasabo districts.
Cost: $697 for 2 weeks   **Duration:** 2 weeks to 3 months   **Age:** 18-65
Contact: info@volunteer.org.nz   **Learn more:** www.volunteer.org.nz
Details: Gender-based violence (GBV) has been a widespread problem for women both during and after the genocide. Volunteers will be involved in promoting education to GBV victims through counseling, visitation, follow-up and school programs. Volunteers will also tutor English and mentor a group of youth, many of whom are from child headed families. Volunteers should have knowledge of GBV, plus good listening and communication skills.

Other organizations offering projects in Rwanda:

American Friends Service Committee: www.afsc.org
Global Visions International: www.gviusa.com
Habitat for Humanity: www.habitat.org
Kiva Fellowship Programs: www.kiva.org/about/fellows-program

Senegal

Volunteer and Cultural Homestay Programs

Organization: Association Sénégalaise des Volontaires Unis
Location: Dakar, Thies, Louga, Fatick, Ziguinchor
Cost: $725 for 4 week volunteering/$925 for 4 week cultural homestay
Duration: 4+ weeks   **Age:** 18
Contact: senevolu@hotmail.com   **Learn more:** www.senevolu.org
Details: The association SENEVOLU is dedicated to promoting community tourism by welcoming volunteers and travelers to discover the cultural differences a West African country like Senegal has to offer, while being part of the community. Therefore, the organization offers both a cultural and volunteer homestay program. Thanks to its programs, local trips and African Workshops SENEVOLU allows travelers to be immersed in the Senegalese culture with host families and colleagues. In the meantime the program gives an opportunity for Senegalese to benefit from community tourism.

Other organizations offering projects in Senegal:

International Foundation for Education and Self-Help: www.ifesh.org
Mondo Challenge: www.mondochallenge.co.uk
Projects Abroad: www.projects-abroad.org
Senecorps: www.senecorps.org
Volunteering Solutions: www.volunteeringsolutions.com

Seychelles

Marine Conservation Volunteer Program

Organization: Global Visions International
Location: Cap Ternay Marine National Park
Cost: $3,990 for 5 weeks   **Duration:** 5 to 10 weeks
Age: 18
Contact: info@gviusa.com

Learn more: www.gviusa.com
Details: Location! Location! Location! This GVI volunteer journey's base is located within the inner granitic islands of the Seychelles. Learn how to identify fish and coral in the Indian Ocean; visiting and diving amongst deserted tropical islands. Join critical conservation efforts on this marine expedition and be an active member of GVI's marine research team in the Indian Ocean.

Other organizations offering projects in the Seychelles:
Nature Seychelles: www.natureseychelles.org
Responsible Travel: www.responsibletravel.com

Sierra Leone

Children in Christ Services School &/or Clinic Work
Organization: Kids Worldwide
Location: Tankatopa Makama Safronko Chiefdom in the Port-Loko Distract
Cost: Under 1 month $400, 1+ month $450, subsequent months $150
Duration: 2+ weeks, 1+ month preferred   **Age:** 18
Contact: cics@kidsworldwide.org
Learn more: www.kidsworldwide.org
Special skills: Qualified teachers and general volunteers are all welcome - teachers who would like to organize inservice training for local staff, volunteers with a medical background to work in the community clinic, nursery specialists, etc. Being able to learn a foreign language is an added advantage.
Details: Children In Christ's Services organization is geared towards caring for needy children (orphans, street kids, disadvantaged and war affected children). The organization has a school in Kambia village in the Port Loko District about 80 miles from Freetown. Forty-five children currently attend this school. The name of the school is CICS Primary School For Needy Kids. There are about 60-80 houses in Kambia Village with a population of around 1000 villagers. There is no electricity supply and water is fetched from a well. Ninety percent of the people in Kambia are Muslims but they are highly tolerant of other religions and very receptive to strangers, especially those who come to help them and their kids. In addition, volunteers with a medical background are needed to work in the community clinic. Being able to learn a foreign language is an added advantage

Fundraising/Office for Children in Christ Services

Organization: Kids Worldwide
Special Skills: Experience in fundraising activities.
Location: East end of Freetown
Cost: Under 1 month $400, 1 month $450, subsequent months $150
Duration: 2+ weeks, 1+ month preferred   **Age:** 18
Contact: cics@kidsworldwide.org
Learn more: www.kidsworldwide.org
Details: Children In Christ's Services organization is geared towards caring for needy children (orphans, street kids, disadvantaged and war affected children). The organization has a school in Kambia village (TMS Chiefdom) in the Port Loko District (about 80 miles from Freetown). For the head office they need volunteers who have in-depth knowledge and experience in fundraising activities.

Other organizations offering projects in the Sierra Leone:

Extra Mile: www.extra-mile.org
Kiva Fellowship Programs: www.kiva.org/about/fellows-program
Tacugama Chimpanzee Sanctuary: www.tacugama.com
Youth Action International: www.youthactioninternational.org

South Africa

Children's Programs in South Africa

Organization: Experiential Learning International
Location: Cape Town
Cost: $695   **Duration:** 16+ weeks   **Age:** 18
Contact: info@eliabroad.org   **Learn more:** www.eliabroad.org
Details: Orphanage volunteers and teachers aides coordinate group activities, assist students with homework, teach English classes, mentor and provide some much needed emotional support. The organizations ELI has partnered with specifically support abandoned, abused, terminaly ill and refugee children from Rwanda, Angola and the Democratic Republic of Congo. These positions are available to long-term volunteers (minimum commitment is four months) and are primarily located in townships outside of the city. It is strongly recommended that volunteers in this program do not rely on public transit.

Primate Sanctuary Build, Garden, Cook & Video

Organization: International Primate Rescue - South Africa
Location: Pretoria
Cost: $286 per week includes accommodations and 3 meals a day
Duration: Ongoing **Age:** 18
Contact: s.a@iprescue.org, Tel: 00 27 78 1424 711
Learn more: www.iprescue.org
 Details: IPR sanctuary recently relocated from Polokwane to Pretoria and is rebuilding and improving all enclosures, volunteer quarters, etc at the new site. Enjoy the fruits of your work watching the primates released into their new, large enclosures. If you enjoy gardening, this is for you. Help us build a massive green house and create a jungle for our little marmosets. Also be part of creating a massive habitat for the large

baboons. Chef or cook, we need you to feed the hard working laborers and the sanctuary primates. We hope to make a documentary of the progress. This would be a great opportunity for a cameraperson and documentary producer. Whatever your skills we need you. Don't miss out on this exciting project.

HIV/AIDS and TB Medical Project

Organization: Edge of Africa
Location: The coastal town of Knysna in the Beautiful Garden Route
Cost: $890 **Duration:** 2 to 4 weeks **Age:** 18
Contact: info@edgeofafrica.com **Learn more:**
www.edgeofafrica.com
Special skills: Edge of Africa is looking for dedicated, hard working, mature and motivated volunteers that care! Volunteers should be of good health and physical fitness. Specific experience is not necessary, however medical students or professionals will benefit from the project. Professional medical and nursing staff will need to be registered with the South African government regulatory bodies in order to perform invasive procedures and tasks.
Details: Learn about the effects of HIV/AIDS in Africa, create awareness in rural communities, assist in static and mobile clinics and make a real difference to the HIV/AIDS and TB epidemic in the area. Volunteer duties include educating patients, developing income generated projects and the business plans thereof, administrative tasks, simple health tasks such as measuring patients' weight, checking adherence to therapy, and supporting pregnant mothers and their children. Tasks will vary, but be assured that you will experience something life changing as you work alongside this team of hard

working and very dedicated team of medical professionals. Food, accommodation and project related transport is included.

Dolphin Studies Program

Organization: Centre For Dolphin Studies
Location: Plettenberg Bay, South Africa
Cost: $320 per week   **Duration:** 4+ weeks   **Age:** 18
Contact: Charlie Kimber, cdsthecoordinator@yahoo.com
Learn more: www.dolphinstudies.co.za
Details: Learn about marine mammals in the lovely setting of Plettenberg Bay. Research is conducted on Bottlenose and Humpback Dolphins, Southern Right Whales, Humpback Whales and Brydes Whales. There is also ongoing research with a seal colony containing 4000+ seals. There is a lecture course where Dr.Cockcroft will teach you all about Marine Mammal Diversity and Research Techniques used. The center also conducts dissections of animals that have been stranded on the beach and were not helped back to the wild. Your accommodation while at the Centre For Dolphin Studies is set at Elephant View Farm, where you will be neighbors to the Knysna Elephant Park. The elephants can be viewed from the farm and you'll awake to their trumpeting serenade each morning.

Township Project in Capetown

Organization: Greenheart Travel
Location: The project is located in a township in Capetown.
Cost: $1,250 for 4 weeks   **Duration:** 2 to 8 weeks   **Age:** 18
Contact: info@greenhearttravel.org
Learn More: www.cci-exchange.com
Specific skills: Experienced travelers who are willing and able to adapt to rustic conditions and an environment where poverty and substance abuse are common. A resume is required.
Details: This program is perfect for more seasoned travelers. The holistic community development project runs a tutoring and activity center for school age children, a facility for young children, sustainable building projects, an organic permaculture community garden, a soup kitchen, and cultural programs that aim to revive and preserve the indigenous arts and traditions of the community. The township itself is underdeveloped and conditions are rustic, and there is no running water. All new building and development is designed to be environmentally sound and sustainable. Solar ovens and composting toilets have been introduced to the community, and new building projects utilize sustainable materials. The shacks typically found in townships are slowly being replaced with well-insulated, solar and wind powered "eco cottages."

Marine Rescue of Penguins and other Seabirds

Organization: Greenforce
Location: South Africa
Cost: $2,600   **Duration:** 6 weeks   **Age:** 17
Contact: info@greenforce.org
Learn more: www.greenforce.org

Details: Set across the expansive bay from Cape Town, in Table View, this penguin rescue centre has cared for over 83,000 seabirds during its 38 years in operation. Primarily set up to rehabilitate African Penguins during major oil spills, the centre now has a mandate from the South African government to oversee the rehabilitation of a number of seabirds, including pelicans and even the odd albatross! Volunteers learn how to catch, handle, feed, tube and administer medication to a variety of seabirds, as well as assisting in the intensive care unit. Past volunteers have sailed to Robben Island (where Nelson Mandela was imprisoned) to release penguins into one of the world's largest penguin colonies.

South Africa Teaching Summer

Organization: WorldTeach
Location: Cape Town Peninsula (Western Cape)
Cost: $4,490   **Duration:** 2 months (late June - August)   **Age:** 18-74
Contact: info@worldteach.org   **Learn more:** www.worldteach.org
Special skills: Fluent in English
Details: The central objective of the summer project is to provide and support educational initiatives in poor communities in the Southern Peninsula of Cape Town. In the first phase of the program, WorldTeach runs various courses during the winter school holidays in the very poor Masiphumelele township. These have included an English literacy program for grades 1–3, computer training for all ages and math for grades 8–12. We also run special projects. Most of the work takes place at the library, which is a modern facility in the heart of the township. In Phase 2, for the remaining five weeks, volunteers are placed at a number of different primary and secondary schools in the southern Peninsula, including the 'coloured' Ocean View area and Simonstown school, where the volunteers also live on campus in a school hostel. During orientation, volunteers will move to their host families for the duration of the program. Families routinely cook breakfast and dinner, and volunteers can make their own packed lunch.

Sports Development in Underprivileged Communities

Organization: Edge of Africa
Location: The coastal town of Knysna on the beautiful Garden Route
Cost: $1,050   **Duration:** 2 to 4 weeks   **Age:** 18

Contact: info@edgeofafrica.com **Learn more:**
www.edgeofafrica.com
Special skills: Interest or experience in sports and a basic fitness is
essential. You should love working with children and should have an
interest in new cultures & the environment as well as working in a third
world country.
Details: Give underprivileged kids the opportunity to develop their
love of sports and learn about aspects of sports development in
Africa. Experience not only the sports culture but the heritage and
traditions of Africa while working in one of the most beautiful areas
of South Africa. Join soccer clinics, assist with cricket coaching or
teach the kids a game from your homeland! You will be amazed at
what you can achieve with these kids in only 4 weeks! There is
always an opportunity to initiate new sports in the area. Whatever
skills or background you have please let us know! Food,
accommodation and project related transport is included.

Wildlife Conservation, Community & Sports Combo

Organization: Edge of Africa
Location: The coastal town of Knysna on the beautiful Garden Route
Cost: $2,825 **Duration:** 8 weeks **Age:** 18
Contact: info@edgeofafrica.com **Learn more:**
www.edgeofafrica.com
Details: Can't decide how you want to help? Perhaps you and your
spouse have different interests, but you want to experience a volunteer
adventure together. This may be the trip for you! This project strives for
maximum positive impact while exploring all aspects of South Africa's
heritage. Your days will be split between assisting teachers with local
kids in various preschools, working on a Big 5 Wildlife & Conservation
Project, inspiring kids in a youth development project for the homeless
and disadvantaged, working at an elephant orphanage, playing games,
teaching English and helping with the school syllabus. Other projects
include community conservation programs and conservation education
workshops. Most afternoons are spent developing sports skills in the
schools including soccer and cricket. It all makes for an unforgettable
African experience! Food, accommodation and project related
transport is included.

Everything Elephant-Work with Elephants

Organization: Edge of Africa
Location: The coastal town of Knysna along the beautiful Garden
Route
Cost: $1,065 **Duration:** 2 to 4 weeks **Age:** 18
Contact: info@edgeofafrica.com **Learn more:**
www.edgeofafrica.com

Details: Volunteers contribute to all aspects of elephant conservation. From the creation of sustainable community projects directly linked to elephant tourism to the hands on maintenance of the parks. As an Everything Elephant Volunteer, you will be learning everything from how an elephant uses its trunk to the complex history that has influenced elephant numbers in Africa, more specifically Addo Elephant National Park. You will assist with the day to day running of an elephant park which provides a home for rescued elephants as well as studying elephants in an untouched wild environment. Food, accommodation and project related transport is included.

South Africa Youth Program

Organization: Global Volunteer Network
Location: The main town of Thohoyandou and its surrounding villages: Manamani, Dzwerani, Shayandima and Itsane. The Soweto project is located in the Southwest area of Johannesburg in a suburb called Orlando West.
Cost: $1,077 for 2 weeks   **Duration:** 2 weeks to 6 months   **Age:** 18
Contact: info@volunteer.org.nz   **Learn more:** www.volunteer.org.nz
Details: Youth during the apartheid era in South Africa played a significant role in bringing about democracy. Today, South Africa's national legislation and policies in its post-apartheid period directs its focus specifically at youth development realizing that previously very little attention focused on matters relating to youth. Volunteers will contribute their valuable time as teaching assistants and tutors in primary and secondary schools, and childcare workers in daycare centers in Venda and in primary schools in Soweto, South Africa. You will have the opportunity to be directly involved in the motivation and development of young people's lives and ultimately helping to bridge gaps and influence change in the 'New South Africa'.

South Africa Youth Primary Teaching Program

Organization: Global Volunteer Network
Location: The main town of Thohoyandou and its surrounding villages: Manamani, Dzwerani, Shayandima and Itsane. The Soweto project is located in the Southwest area of Johannesburg in a suburb called Orlando West.
Cost: $1,077 for 2 weeks   **Duration:** 2 weeks to 6 months   **Age:** 18
Contact: info@volunteer.org.nz   **Learn more:** www.volunteer.org.nz
Details: Volunteers with varying skills will be able to help in areas of academic and skill development through mentoring and tutoring activities. There are opportunities for volunteers to assist with teaching at preschool, primary and secondary levels. At primary and secondary

levels, volunteer teaching assistants can help teach core subjects, such as English, mathematics, life skills, health and hygiene and science. The subjects will be relative to each school's needs; however the greatest need is typically in math and science, particularly at the secondary school level. Volunteer preschool teachers will teach basic English skills and carry out basic childcare duties. At this time, a teaching qualification is not required but volunteers need to be confident in the above subjects and preferably have, or are studying towards a university degree.

South Africa Youth Childcare Program

Organization: Global Volunteer Network
Location: The main town of Thohoyandou and its surrounding villages: Manamani, Dzwerani, Shayandima, and Itsane. The Soweto project is located in the Southwest area of Johannesburg in a suburb called Orlando West.
Cost: $1,077 for 2 weeks   **Duration:** 2 weeks to 6 months   **Age:** 18
Contact: info@volunteer.org.nz   **Learn more:** www.volunteer.org.nz
Details: Volunteers may work in settings such as day care centers or "places of safety" in the community. The town's Children's Home and certain foster home situations are referred to locally as "places of safety". As a volunteer, you can help by working with children ages 2-6, helping with general caretaking like handing out porridge and brushing teeth, teaching English, reading, writing and pronunciation. Simple math and counting, body hygiene, crafts and educational games for younger children may be available as well. Volunteers will be able to use this time to display their mentoring experience, and motivate the students toward a positive future.

Housing Initiative

Organization: Willing Workers in South Africa (WWISA)
Location: The Crags/Kurland Village – Garden Route of South Africa
Cost: $1,050 for two weeks – group discounts available
Duration: 2+ weeks **Age:** 18
Contact: volunteers@wwisa.co.za **Learn more:** www.wwisa.co.za
Special skills: Motivation and enthusiasm
Details: There are over 400 families waiting to be allocated government housing within Kurland and this number continues to grow with the growth in population. There are currently plans to provide just 250 houses. While there is an obvious need to build more houses, there is also the need to renovate existing houses that were some of the first to be built in the village, and as such, do not qualify the residents for the new larger, better equipped houses. Houses need to be waterproofed, repaired and made safe. Most residents are not

able to afford these necessary upgrades. The only way these projects can work is with more volunteers! You will not be required to carry out any major building works yourself, but with your participation a job is created and you assist the local tradesman with all renovations. This is a hands-on project that allows the volunteer to work side-by-side with people in the village.

Zero to Hero Sports Adventure & Volunteering

Organization: Edge of Africa
Location: The coastal town of Knysna on the beautiful Garden Route
Cost: $1,450 **Duration:** 2 to 4 weeks **Age:** 18
Contact: info@edgeofafrica.com **Learn more:**
www.edgeofafrica.com
Details: Experience a fantastic mix of sports volunteering, sports lessons & excursions. You will have the opportunity to teach the sports you enjoy in the local community and learn or practice sports you are interested in. They say you should try something different every day – here is your chance! You will have the opportunity to take lessons in kite surfing, power boating and surfing. Other sports you can enjoy on the project include canoeing, mountain biking and golf. In between the adrenalin of these sports, you will be assisting with soccer, cricket and fitness clinics in the local community! Reach your dreams and help the kids of the Knysna community do the same! Food, accommodation and project related transport is included.

Big 5 Wildlife and Conservation

Organization: Edge or Africa
Location: Near the coastal town of Mosselbay along the Garden Route
Cost: $1,490 **Duration:** 2 to 4 weeks **Age:** 18
Contact: info@edgeofafrica.com **Learn more:**
www.edgeofafrica.com
Details: This project offers you the opportunity to get up close and personal with Africa's most charismatic mammals. The

reserve gives you an incomparable experience in practical knowledge and diverse hands on volunteering. You assist with the conservation of Africa's endangered cheetah, work with orphaned elephants, learn about wildlife nutrition and are needed in the everyday running and maintenance of this malaria-free reserve. Veterinary volunteering is also an option and a short wildlife immobilization course is included in the program. You will be based on the reserve in a very comfortable farm style volunteer house. There is an honesty bar and lapa (courtyard) where plenty of socializing takes place. The house features satellite TV and Internet. All food, accommodation and project related transport is included.

Marine Conservation in Plettenberg Bay

Organization: ORCA Foundation
Location: Garden Route jewel seaside village of Plettenberg Bay
Cost: $500 per week includes all project costs, full board & accommodations **Duration:** 2 to 12 weeks **Age:** 18
Contact: bookings@orcafoundation.com
Learn more: www.orcafoundation.com
Special skills: Passion for marine wildlife; willingness to help less fortunate children; an open mind
Details: Volunteers will participate in creating a partnership with the local community; developing a conservation model in Plettenberg Bay to sustain marine and costal resources through improved management and will work in research and education programs. This includes fish tagging and counts on the reef, whale and dolphin identification, turtle rehabilitation, gathering water samples in the estuary, alien tree removal, tree planting and children's education in outdoor classroom on the ocean, beach and tidal rocks. Volunteers leave with an understanding of what it takes to preserve fragile coastlines and will have the knowledge needed to improve the lives of children and help the environment where they live.

Cape Town Teaching and Community Development

Organization: African Impact
Location: Southern Peninsula of Cape Town, South Africa
Cost: $2260 for 4 weeks **Duration:** 2 to 8 weeks or more **Age:** 18
Contact: info@africanimpact.com
Learn more: www.africanimpact.com
Special skills: A love for children and a passion for community upliftment
Details: Your volunteering mission with The Cape Town Teaching and Community Development Project will help to uplift the community through education, health care, building projects and contribute to child development of the community through assistant teaching at local schools within the underprivileged communities on the outskirts of Cape Town. Make a meaningful difference and give a disadvantaged child the individual attention they deserve, but hardly ever get. This is your invitation to the opportunity to educate them, to entertain them and love them!

Abused Animal and Veterinary Assist Project

Organization: African Impact
Location: Southern Peninsula of Cape Town, South Africa
Cost: $2,260 for 4 weeks **Duration:** 2 to 8 weeks or more **Age:** 17
Contact: info@africanimpact.com
Learn more: www.africanimpact.com
Special skills: No special skills required, just a love for animals!
Details: Be part of a rescue organization whose main focus is to assist distressed pets from the surrounding townships and provide care for them. Get involved with hands on tasks such as feeding, exercising and caring for animals in need, work alongside vets who will train you in veterinary practice and educate people from the disadvantaged communities on animal care whilst experiencing the local culture. Volunteers will have the opportunity to make a tangible difference in the lives of Cape Town's neglected animals by being part of this rescue shelter whose core aim is to rescue, rehabilitate and re-home abandoned, abused and neglected dogs and cats. On an average day the shelter cares for around 170 dogs and puppies and 130 cats and kittens!

Wildlife, Conservation & Community Volunteering

Organization: Edge of Africa
Location: The coastal town of Knysna along the Garden Route
Cost: $3,600 **Duration:** 6 weeks **Age:** 18
Contact: info@edgeofafrica.com **Learn more:** www.edgeofafrica.com
Details: Join Africa's BIG 5 Wildlife and Conservation project and work with Africa's most famous species. Then apply yourself to a specialized elephant park housing orphaned elephants and assist with a number of hands on duties. Next, become part of the rehabilitation team as you work closely with the community to develop and rehabilitate an environmental area in the centre of Kayalethu Township. And lastly, apply the idea that conservation relies on community appreciation and understanding. Through a 'Workshops with Local Kids' project, you can help sow the seed of respect and passion for South Africa's natural heritage. The project allows you to experience and contribute towards every aspect of conservation in South Africa! Food, accommodation and project related transport is included.

St. Lucia Wildlife Photography and Conservation

Organization: African Impact
Location: St. Lucia, South Africa
Cost: $2,690 for 4 weeks **Duration:** 4 weeks **Age:** 18
Contact: info@africanimpact.com

Learn more: www.africanimpact.com
Special skills: Enthusiasm for photography and conservation
Details: Photography buffs, just say, "Wow!" St. Lucia is situated within the iSimangaliso Wetland Park, a beautiful area declared as South Africa's first Natural World Heritage Site by UNESCO. Within this impressive setting volunteers are offered the opportunity to photograph the phenomenal wildlife in the area and to help raise awareness in the local community about the importance of conservation. After being given an intensive photography course by a professional wildlife photographer, volunteers will begin to take photographs of local flora and fauna, which will be added to a picture database; the Green Vision Foundation and African Impact aim to create a complete ecological database for the area. Volunteers will also visit local schools giving classes and workshops about the reason for, and methods of conservation and assist at conservation centers.

Soweto Grassroots Volunteering

Organization: VOLUNTOURS
Location: Soweto, our most populous urban township outside of Johannesburg, near Nelson Mandela's home
Cost: $2,340+ for 4 weeks **Duration:** 1 to 12 weeks **Age:** 18
Contact: info@voluntours.co.za **Learn more:** www.voluntours.co.za
Special skills: Screening and matching of skills required
Details: Volunteers will learn that Soweto in many ways sets trends in fashion, music, dance and language and is also known for its political history. Soweto has grown hugely as a tourist destination with many experiencing the vibrancy of Soweto where people mingle and interact on the streets. Volunteer in a community-based NGO that provides grassroots holistic support to children and families affected by the with HIV/AIDS pandemic in three main project areas - home based care, orphans and vulnerable children support and a public works project. Volunteers are needed that will add value to the programme, staff and the community. Volunteers will gain exposure to the issues facing communities by working with local service providers and sharing skills in a mutually benefiting way.

Soweto Pre-School Volunteering

Organization: VOLUNTOURS
Location: Soweto, our most populous urban township outside of Johannesburg, near Nelson Mandela's home
Cost: $2,340+ for 4 weeks
Duration: 1 to 12 weeks **Age:** 18

Contact: info@voluntours.co.za
Learn more: www.voluntours.co.za
Special skills: Screening and matching of skills required
Details: Founded in 2001 the preschool is run by Ubaba "Daddy" Meyers and his wife Mildred. They provide a much needed service to over 90 children from their community. The preschool is run from their home and provides a safe environment for the children utilising 2 small inside rooms, an outside shelter and minimal play structures. The ages of the children range from 6 months to 5/ 6 years. All kinds of volunteer support is needed from qualified education professionals to those with an interest in childcare. Our volunteers will contribute to the mentoring and upskilling of the staff; improving the infrastructure, stimulating the children, and working with the teachers and parents to provide first rate support and advice regarding their health and school readiness.

Great White Shark Conservation

Organization: Greenforce
Location: South Africa
Cost: $1,900+ **Duration:** 2 to 4 weeks **Age:** 17
Contact: info@greenforce.org **Learn more:** www.greenforce.org
Details: If you have an interest in research and conservation and are not afraid of working closely with Great White Sharks then this is the program for you! The Great White Shark is undoubtedly the greatest predatory force of the seas, cloaked in myth, misunderstanding and fear; this awesome animal remains a mystery to man. This project is a unique opportunity to view the Great White Shark in its natural environment, either from a boat or an underwater cage. You'll learn a lot about the Great White, their behavior and biology, and then you'll put that knowledge to use by assisting in conservation and research into this remarkable animal.

Rural Community Pre-School Volunteering

Organization: VOLUNTOURS
Location: Ndlalane, Klipgat, 40 km northwest of Pretoria, North West Province, South Africa
Cost: $2, 150+ for 4 weeks **Duration:** 1 to 12 weeks
Age: 18, 16 with parental consent, individuals, families and groups welcome
Contact: info@voluntours.co.za **Learn more:** www.voluntours.co.za
Special skills: Screening and matching of skills required
Details: Multiple award winning projects in a semi-rural community. Stay in a local home or in traditional Ndebele tribal community that

was forcibly moved under the Apartheid government in 1952. It may take a while to come to terms with much of the hardships and realities of rural life in South Africa, however, the riches you gather are well worth it. Provide education support and training at this preschool owned and run by a local community member. Our volunteers will contribute to the mentoring and upskilling of the staff; improving the infrastructure, stimulating the children, and working with the teachers and parents to provide first rate support and advice regarding their health and school readiness.

Life Skills Volunteering

Organization: VOLUNTOURS
Location: Ndlalane, Klipgat, 40 km north-west of Pretoria
Cost: $2, 150+ for 4 weeks **Duration:** 1 to 12 weeks
Age: 18, 16 with parental consent, individuals, families and groups welcome
Contact: info@voluntours.co.za **Learn more:** www.voluntours.co.za
Special skills: Screening and matching of skills required
Details: Multiple award winning projects in a semi-rural community. Stay in a local home or in traditional Ndebele tribal community that was forcibly moved under the Apartheid government in 1952. It may take a while to come to terms with much of the hardships and realities of rural life in South Africa, however, the riches you gather are well worth it. Your skills, hobbies and interests are likely to be benefits the community. A few typical areas that you may get involved in are: teaching and tutoring primary and secondary children after school in a range of subjects, adult basic education and training, computer literacy, sports, art, music, drama, business skills, DIY and so much more. Health professionals are also needed in the greater community.

Bicycle Volunteer Project

Organization: VOLUNTOURS
Location: Ndlalane, Klipgat, 40 km north-west of Pretoria, North West Province, South Africa
Cost: $2,150+ for 4 weeks **Duration:** 1 to 12 weeks
Age: 18, 16 with parental consent, individuals, families and groups welcome
Contact: info@voluntours.co.za **Learn more:** www.voluntours.co.za
Special skills: Screening and matching of skills required
Details: Multiple award winning projects in a semi-rural community. Stay in a local home or in traditional Ndebele tribal community that was

forcibly removed under the Apartheid government in 1952. It may take a while to come to terms with much of the hardships and realities of rural life in South Africa, however, the riches you gather are well worth it. Share your love of bicycles, related sporting activities and small business skills at this community run project. The bicycle shop provides important infra-structural, retail, small business and recreational support to the local rural community. Help teach youth how to maintain and repair bicycles as well as design and make load carrying bicycle trailers with the help of community members. Metalwork and DIY skills are also needed.

Solar Cooker Volunteer Project

Organization: VOLUNTOURS
Location: Ndlalane, Klipgat, 40 km north-west of Pretoria
Cost: $2,150+ for 4 weeks **Duration:** 1 to 12 weeks
Age: 18, 16 with parental consent, individuals, families and groups welcome
Contact: info@voluntours.co.za **Learn more:** www.voluntours.co.za
Special skills: Screening and matching of skills required
Details: Stay in a local home or in traditional Ndebele tribal community that was forcibly moved under the Apartheid government in 1952. It may take a while to come to terms with much of the hardships and realities of rural life in South Africa, however, the riches you gather are well worth it. The rising cost and instability of electricity supply means that many local households cannot afford to cook their daily meal. Help save the environment and stop the use of local firewood being used as fuel by building a simple but effective solar cooker and educating households on the value of solar cooking. Help roll out this environmental project to the greater community.

Wildlife Volunteer Experience

Organization: VOLUNTOURS
Location: Private Game Reserve – 60 km from Port Elizabeth, Eastern Cape Province, South Africa
Cost: $2,450+ for 4 weeks **Duration:** 1 to 12 weeks
Age: 18-62 or 16 with parent. Families and groups welcome
Contact: info@voluntours.co.za **Learn more:** www.voluntours.co.za
Details: Gain first-hand experience of how a game reserve is managed from a unique behind the scenes viewpoint. You are the student and the classroom is the reserve! Get involved in game and conservation management, learn new life skills and interact with the children from the local orphanage. One main focus area is monitoring the integration of the lions into the reserve by tracking and recording their behaviour.

You can experience wildlife - up close and personal - as very few people will. Our partner is proudly Fair Trade Tourism South Africa (FTTSA) accredited. This fifth generation, family run game reserve will ensure you a hospitable experience while creating a wildlife adventure, which will capture your imagination, refresh your soul and conserve our natural heritage!

Dolphin Volunteer Experience
Organization: VOLUNTOURS
Location: Plettenberg Bay, nestled along the picturesque Garden Route, Western Cape Province, South Africa
Cost: $1,810+ for 4 weeks   **Duration:** 4 to 12 weeks
Age: 18–62, 16 with parental accompanying, families and groups welcome
Contact: info@voluntours.co.za   **Learn more:** www.voluntours.co.za
Details: A unique opportunity to volunteer on this dolphin, whale, seal and marine life project. The "extra-hands" from their volunteer programme has helped fund research by this nonprofit research organization since 2002. You get hands-on experience in the everyday running of a research organization. Volunteers gain exposure to a range of activities from the routine, to the "CSI-like" fin-matching computer programme, to the spectacular! Volunteers get involved in ongoing research projects that involve monitoring the occurrence, movements, numbers and habitat of Bottlenose and Humpback Dolphins and other marine life in the bay. The course includes a 12 module theoretical component. The course content includes lectures, practical workshops, collection and analysis of data.

Shark Volunteer Experience
Organization: VOLUNTOURS
Location: Gaansbaai Bay, situated at the southernmost tip of Africa, Western Cape Province, South Africa
Cost: $2,450+ for 4 weeks   **Duration:** 1 to 12 weeks   **Age:** 18
Contact: info@voluntours.co.za   **Learn more:** www.voluntours.co.za
Details: Our volunteers get really close up to the Great White Shark and learn to protect and conserve the great white sharks' environment and promote its status as an endangered and declining species. Shark populations worldwide are increasingly threatened, and in scientific circles there is still research needed to fully understand and interpret shark behavior. You will play a pivotal role in observing, collating data and promoting these graceful and majestic creatures. The programme will enable you to see sharks in their natural environment, either from a boat or from a cage. Our volunteers participate in a wide variety of

tasks and activities. Learning about coastal eco-systems in the region, and about what work is going on to help preserve them and the declining African Penguin population.

Orphanage Volunteer Tutoring

Organization: VOLUNTOURS
Location: Midrand, between Pretoria and Johannesburg, Gauteng Province
Cost: $2,750 for 4 weeks   **Duration:** 1 to 12 weeks   **Age:** 18
Contact: info@voluntours.co.za   **Learn more:** www.voluntours.co.za
Special skills: Screening and matching of skills required
Details: Volunteer at a small and intimate orphanage that has a homey, non-institutional feel. Their goal is to improve education levels. We need volunteers who have a desire to assist children with their learning, homework, computer work and clear stumbling blocks in various subjects. You don't need to be a teacher to volunteer and give these children the gift of education-thereby ensuring a better future and breaking the cycle of poverty and abuse of the past. Primary and secondary school tutoring and teaching assistance needed. People able to impart various life, craft, technical and DIY skills are also wanted. It may be the relationship that you have formed with a particular child that could result in the "breakthrough" rather than previous teaching experience.

Helping South African Women

Organization: Cross-Cultural Solutions
Location: Cape Town
Cost: 3 week programs start from $3,142   **Duration:** 3 to 12 weeks
Age: 18 or over 8 welcome with adult supervision.
Contact: info@crossculturalsolutions.org
Learn more: www.crossculturalsolutions.org
Special skills: No special skills required. Proficient knowledge of the English language preferred.
Details: Cape Town is the legislative capital of South Africa, and the influences from the many different cultures of the nation can be seen throughout the city. However, the effects of apartheid persist as many communities remain divided. Volunteers share their professional skills and experience and can work with women's groups in Cape Town. Many women are affected by domestic violence, and others are looking for income-generating opportunities to help provide for their families. Volunteers work in local shelters and organizations that provide a safe and supportive place for the women. Volunteers offer companionship, help with household duties, and provide child care so that the women

can focus on gaining new life skills and training. All meals and accommodations are provided.

Meerkats of the Kalahari

Organization: Earthwatch Institute
Location: Upington, South Africa
Cost: $3,750 - $3,950+ **Duration:** 14 days **Age:** 18
Contact: info@earthwatch.org **Learn more:** www.earthwatch.org
Details: You'll help observe six habituated colonies of meerkats in South Africa's Kuruman River Reserve. You'll learn how to radio-track, conduct focal sampling, use a Global Positioning System, and weigh meerkats. The data you collect will help researchers evaluate how cooperative breeding affects the survival of both pups and helpers. Supplementing the meerkat studies, you'll help conduct biodiversity, invertebrate, and plant surveys, and spend time recording the size and activity of social bird colonies like pied babblers and weavers, in response to rainfall levels. You'll help with outreach efforts to assist the local primary school. These adventures will be set against a backdrop of gemsbok, hartebeest, springbok, duiker, steenbok, bat-eared foxes, three kinds of mongooses, birds and other fantastic creatures of the Kalahari night.

African Wildlife Conservation for Teens

Organization: Academic Treks
Location: Enkosini Wildlife Sanctuary and beyond
Cost: $5,380
Duration: 40+ hours of volunteerism as part of a 22-day wildlife conservation program **Age:** Teens finishing grades 10-12
Contact: info@academictreks.com; 919-256-8200 or 888-833-1908
Learn more: www.academictreks.com
Details: Students on this Academic Trek project study and assist with
 efforts to conserve, protect and increase African wildlife populations that are threatened by habitat destruction, development, poaching and hunting. Living at the Enkosini Wildlife Sanctuary, you work and learn alongside conservationists, researchers and veterinarians as they strive to rescue, rehabilitate and provide sanctuary for Africa's endangered creatures including giraffes, zebras, rhinos and elephants. Explore Kruger National Park, one of Africa's oldest, largest and most renowned national parks in search of impalas, lions, buffaloes and hippos. Teach local schoolchildren about the importance of wildlife conservation. Students also take an excursion to navigate inflatable kayaks through the dramatic Blyde River Canyon, the site where the

prehistoric Gondwanaland super-continent tore apart, creating Africa, Asia and one of Africa's natural wonders.

Southern Hospitality: In Style

Organization: Hands Up Holidays
Location: Cape Town
Cost: $5,000 per person, based on sharing a room
Duration: 3 days volunteering/9 day trip
Age: 16 years unless accompanied by an adult
Contact: info@handsupholidays.com
Learn more: www.handsupholidays.com
Special skills: None required, but teaching, medical or gardening skills are desirable
Details: You can choose from three inspiring volunteer projects and gain a better understanding for the less fortunate inhabitants in and around Cape Town: 1) Help with repair and renovation work, and also help relieve the daily burden at an AIDS orphanage; 2) Help prepare and serve meals in a community kitchen or assist with health and nutrition in a township; 3) Help on an environmental conservation project. Regardless of the project you choose, you will be touched by the people you meet. In addition to your meaningful volunteer project, you also explore the highlights of Cape Town staying in luxury boutique accommodations, taste the full bodied wines of Stellenbosch and seek out the 'Big 5' animals in a luxury game reserve.

Other organizations offering projects in South Africa:

GeoVisions: www.geovisions.org
Global Visions International: www.gviusa.com
Global White Lion Protection Trust: whitelions.org
i-to-i: www.i-to-i.com
International Foundation for Education and Self-Help: www.ifesh.org
Lajuma Research Centre (biological/archeological research)
    www.lajuma.com
Nkombi Volunteers on Mankwe Wildlife Reserve:
    www.mankwewildlifereserve.net
People and Places (Winner 'Best Volunteering Organization' category
    of Virgin Holidays Responsible Tourism Award 2009):
    travel-peopleandplaces.co.uk
Sanccob (penguin rescue): www.sanccob.co.za
Worldwide Veterinary Service: www.wvs.org.uk

Sudan

Volunteer Teachers of English Language

Organization: Sudan Volunteer Programme
Location: Universities in Khartoum and smaller northern towns
Cost: $100 towards insurance **Duration:** 7+ months, start dates
from September or early January **Age:** 22
Contact: david@svp-uk.com **Learn more:** svp-uk.com
Special skills: Graduates who are native English speakers, nationality
is not a problem. TEFL certificate and knowledge of Arabic are not
required.
Details: SVP works with undergraduates and graduates who are native
English speakers and who wish to teach English in Sudan. Teaching
tends to be informal in style, with only 4-5 hours of contact a day.
Volunteers can plan their own teaching lessons, such as arranging
games, dramas, competitions and tests for assessing skills learned by
the students. It is preferred that volunteers have already had
experience travelling in developing countries. Volunteers are required
to write a report of their experiences and to advise new volunteers.
Host institutions cover living expenses and accommodation. SVP
covers insurance beyond the initial three months.

Other organizations offering projects in Sudan:

British Education Institutes (English Instruction):
  britisheducationsudan.com
Sudan-Reach Woman's Foundation:
  sudanreach.org/volunteering.htm
Transitions Abroad: www.transitionsabroad.com
Volunteering Solutions: www.volunteeringsolutions.com

Tanzania

Kahama Donkey Welfare Project

Organization: Tanzania Animals Protection Organization -TAPO
Location: Kahama District, Shinyanga Region Western Tanzania
Cost: $100 **Duration:** 1 week to 6 months **Age:** 18
Contact: yohanakashililah@yahoo.com
Learn more: www.tanzania-animals-protection-org.blogspot.com
Details: TAPO helps ease the suffering of donkeys at Kahama by
educating the owners and students in throughout the whole district.

TAPO is also a rescue and treats abandoned and street animals. TAPO cannot provide volunteers with meal or accommodations, but there are places to stay nearby and the work is highly rewarding and enjoyable.

La No Che Projects

Organization: La No Che Orphans and Youth Camp Trust
Location: Kibaha on the coastal region of Tanzania, approximately 50km from Dar es Salaam
Cost: $250 for 2 weeks   **Duration:** 2 weeks to 3 months   **Age:** Open
Contact: lanochecamp@yahoo.com, camplanoche@hotmail.com
Special skills: No experience is required, but you must be willing to work hard and love children and have fun with them. The ability to work in construction and in building maintenance is also very useful.
Details: La No Che's needs include help with social work, and educating the children: teaching games, counseling, cooking, sharing their activities and showing love to them. Helping with the orphanage vegetable garden and orchard adds to the diversity. If you prefer construction email them about current projects. They frequently work with local villagers on various hand-on opportunities such as wells and building construction, even a chicken coop.

Watoto wa Africa

Organization: Kids Worldwide
Location: Mwanza, the 2nd largest town in Tanzania on Lake Victoria
Cost: $300 per month   **Duration:** 2+ weeks, 1 month+ preferred
Age: 18, or kids over 10 welcome with parent
Contact: watoto@kidsworldwide.org
Learn more: www.kidsworldwide.org
Special skills: A love of children and a desire to change people's lives. They ask volunteers to come ready for a challenge and to be willing to put in some hard work.
Details: Watoto Wa Africa Organization (meaning "Children of Africa") was founded in the year 2000. The primary focus of Watoto wa Africa is caring for orphaned and other vulnerable children. The orphanage is currently home to 45 orphans and street children. Volunteers can teach important skills, such as fine and gross motor skills, sports, computers, music and singing. The children are very eager to learn. The main role of the volunteers will be to teach supplementary English and math lessons to the children at the Buswelu orphanage. They also ask volunteers to try to organize a fund raiser before you come, to support both the orphanage and your expenses.

Music/Video Production and Promotion

Organization: Aang Serian Studio
Location: Arusha, Tanzania
Cost: $860 for 1st month **Duration:** 1 month or more
Age: 18, 16 with parental consent

Contact: enolengila@yahoo.co.uk
Details: Aang Serian Studio was founded in 2002 with the aim of preserving and promoting indigenous knowledge and traditional skills through audio and video recording. They need people to assist with sound recording, mixing and producing music, training young people to use media equipment, recording video footage and editing movies. They also need volunteers to assist with fundraising. Breakfast and dinner are included. Accommodations are not included, but are available nearby.

All Aspects of Running a School: Teach, Build, Fundraise

Organization: Noonkodin Secondary School
Location: Eluwai, a very rural Maasai community
Cost: $995 for 1st month **Duration:** 1+ month
Age: 18, 16+ with parental permission and emotional maturity
Contact: enolengila@yahoo.co.uk
Learn more: www.serianuk.org.uk
Special skills: Previous teaching experience (especially in English as a Second Language) is welcome, although not essential. They particularly need qualified teachers. Volunteers should be emotionally mature, flexible, and able to handle challenging situations with good humor.
Details: Noonkodin Secondary School was founded in 2004 in the Maasai village of Eluwai. It currently has around 150 students between 14 and 25, most of them from Maasai pastoralist families. The school teaches the full Tanzanian national curriculum, but the students also take part in supplementary activities such as research on local culture and herbal medicine, visual arts, drama and music. It is located in a remote rural area and there are few 'comforts'. The staff house currently has solar power to provide lighting and cell phone charging facilities, but there is no other electricity supply or running water. They need volunteers to teach English as a Second Language, mathematics, chemistry, biology and physics (all in English) to 14-18+ years. They also welcome volunteers able to help out with manual labor, e.g. building classrooms, painting, carpentry, digging pits for water tanks, gardening, farming, etc. There is also a need for people to assist with fundraising and with administration of summer camp programs.

Teaching in Tanzania

Organization: International Volunteer HQ
Location: Urban and rural placements in and around Arusha
Cost: $250 for 1 week to $2,420 for 6 months, includes food and accommodations
Duration: 1 week to 6 months **Age:** 18
Contact: volunteer@volunteerhq.org
Learn more: www.volunteerhq.org
Details: Volunteers are placed in exciting community schools, public schools or orphanage schools. Many of the schools we work with are constantly understaffed and are always in need of new volunteers. In this program, volunteers can work by themselves or alongside other teachers and volunteers. Typical subjects taught include English, math, science, social studies, art and physical education. School in Tanzania runs for three terms a year (Term One runs January to April, Term Two runs May to August, Term Three runs September to November).There are short breaks between terms during which time volunteers can take a break, travel, engage in tourist activities such as a safari, take tutorials for senior students or participate in another placement. Volunteers do not need to be a qualified or experienced teacher.

Orphanage Work in Tanzania

Organization: International Volunteer HQ
Location: Urban and rural placements in and around Arusha.
Cost: $250 for 1 week to $2,420 for 6 months, includes food & accommodations
Duration: 1 week to 6 months **Age:** 18
Contact: volunteer@volunteerhq.org
Learn more: www.volunteerhq.org
Details: Sub-Saharan African countries are suffering from huge numbers of orphans left behind after their parents die from illnesses such as HIV/AIDS. This results in a larger number of orphanages in countries such as Tanzania. Contributing to this disproportionate number of orphanages is the fact that in some cases the parents are simply unable to provide for the children or they have been abandoned, increasing the number of orphans in Tanzania. Volunteers who work in an orphanage help with general work and daily chores. Your participation in an orphanage project is not only appreciated by the children but also by the orphanage administration. This work ranges from cooking and cleaning to farm work, assisting with feeding programs, caring for children and babies, as well as teaching.

Reforestation with the Maasai in Tanzania

Organization: Experiential Learning International
Location: Maasailand
Cost: Starting at $795 **Duration:** 2+ weeks **Age:** 18
Contact: info@eliabroad.org **Learn more:** www.eliabroad.org
Details: The greater part of Maasailand is now so dry from ongoing droughts that many areas are fast becoming semi-desert. The trees of the savannah are also being cut to make charcoal at an alarming rate, leaving the land vulnerable to further erosion and loss of moisture. Many families have homesteads with no trees. Volunteers with this project will assist in planting trees both on homesteads and on the plains of Maasailand in order to help improve life for future generations. Volunteers will also assist with ongoing education programs focusing on the importance of tree conservation. Please note that this project is only available from February to July, during the rainy season.

Dar es Salaam Community HIV Education

Organization: Experiential Learning International
Location: Dar es Salaam
Cost: Starting at $885 **Duration:** 2+ weeks **Age:** 18
Contact: info@eliabroad.org **Learn more:** www.eliabroad.org
Details: In its most recent report, UNAIDS estimates over 1.4 million people in Tanzania are HIV positive. Urban centers have been hit much harder that rural areas with some neighborhoods reporting adult infection rates as high as 40%. ELI works with a community center in the Tandale neighborhood of Dar es Salaam where volunteers can assist with HIV prevention activities as well as support activities for HIV positive community members. The center uses dance, street theater and home visits as a means to educate the community on issues such as HIV prevention, life skills, and safe sex practices. The organization is also linked to a clinic which provides STD testing and some basic medical care to members of the surrounding community.

HIV/AIDS and Sustainable Agriculture

Organization: Global Service Corps
Location: Arusha
Cost: 9 weeks core integrated program $5,230; weekly fee after 9 weeks $315; weekly fee after 13 weeks $245 **Duration:** 9 weeks to 6 months
Age: 20 (18 or 19 with three letters of recommendation)
Contact: tanzania@globalservicecorps.org
Learn more: globalservicecorps.org

Special skills: No special skills are required, just a commitment to service

Details: This program combines the HIV/AIDS Prevention and Nutrition Education and the Sustainable Agriculture and Food Security Programs offered by GSC. It includes a total of two weeks of participant cultural orientation and technical training in HIV/AIDS and sustainable agriculture followed by two or more weeks of training local community groups in each subject. These community trainings often take place in rural areas rarely accessed by tourists or volunteers. Program participants spend part of the first week of their program living in a comfortable local hostel and the remaining time living with a local Tanzanian host family or camping during the rural trainings. Your host family will generously introduce you to the culture, traditions and cuisine of Tanzania. A day safari to a local game reserve is also included.

Sustainable Agriculture and Food Security Service

Organization: Global Service Corps
Location: Arusha
Cost: 4 week program $3,455; additional weekly fee $315; 9 week long-term or Internship Program $5,030; weekly fee after 13 weeks $245
Duration: 4+ weeks
Age: 20, 18 with three letters of recommendation
Contact: tanzania@globalservicecorps.org
Learn more: globalservicecorps.org
Special skills: No special skills are required, just a commitment to service
Details: This program includes one week of  participant cultural orientation and technical training followed by three or more weeks of training local community and farming groups in organic agriculture practices. These community trainings often take place in rural areas rarely accessed by tourists or volunteers. Program participants spend part of the first week of their program living in a comfortable local hostel and the remaining time living with a local Tanzanian host family or camping during the rural trainings. Your host family will generously introduce you to the culture, traditions and cuisine of Tanzania. A day safari to a local game reserve is also included. Long-term and internship programs are available from nine weeks up to six months.

Community Development, HIV/AIDS or Sustainable Ag

Organization: Global Service Corps
Location: Arusha
Cost: 13 week $6290; weekly fee after 13 weeks $245

Duration: 3 to 6 months
Age: 20+, 18 with three letters of recommendation
Contact: tanzania@globalservicecorps.org
Learn more: www.globalservicecorps.org
Special skills: No special skills are required, just a commitment to service
Details: The Community Development Program is designed for individuals who are specifically interested in international development and gaining first-hand experience working with specific community development projects. The program begins with one week of cultural orientation and technical training followed by time in the field providing community training in either HIV/AIDS or sustainable agriculture. Participants devote their remaining program to exploring the intricacies of international development by assisting in the development of one of GSC's sustainable community development or partnership projects. The program could include assisting GSC in-country staff with program development, supporting GSC's Peer Education Health Clubs with HIV/AIDS prevention training and materials, working with the local organization NGOs, and working with local orphanages. Homestays and a one-day safari are included.

Wildlife Tracking in Tanzania – Live with a Maasai Tribe

Organization: Greenforce
Location: Tanzania
Cost: $2,500+ **Duration:** 3 to 10 weeks **Age:** 17
Contact: info@greenforce.org **Learn more:** www.greenforce.org
Details: The project begins with lessons from a Maasai warrior about their language and culture. Volunteers then head into to the Maasai village where they will live. Here volunteers undertake vital conservation work on behalf of the African Wildlife Foundation in an area often referred to as the Mini Serengeti due to its high abundance of wildlife. Volunteers survey wildlife and their movement patterns between two national parks, enabling the AWF to understand the migration routes of the animals and therefore ensure their protection. Volunteers also assist in a cultural awareness programme with the Maasai, teaching in their schools and learning from their warriors. The end of the expedition is a real treat: volunteers venture to Zanzibar to relax and enjoy some snorkeling before departing.

HIV/AIDS Prevention & Nutrition Education Service

Organization: Global Service Corps
Location: Arusha

Cost: 4 weeks $3,455; additional weekly fee $315; 9 week long-term or Internship Program $5030; weekly fee after 13 weeks $245
Duration: Four weeks to six months
Age: 20+, 18 or 19 with three letters of recommendation
Contact: tanzania@globalservicecorps.org
Learn more: globalservicecorps.org
Special Skills: No special skills are required, just a commitment to service
Details: This program includes one week of participant cultural orientation and technical training followed by three or more weeks of training students, teachers and local community groups in HIV/AIDS prevention and nutrition. These community trainings often take place in rural areas rarely accessed by tourists or volunteers. Program participants spend part of the first week of their program living in a comfortable local hostel and the remaining time living with a local Tanzanian host family or camping during the rural trainings. Your host family will generously introduce you to the culture, traditions and cuisine of Tanzania. A day safari to a local game reserve is also included. Long-term and internship programs are available from nine weeks up to six months.

International Health Program

Organization: Global Service Corps
Location: Arusha
Cost: 9 weeks $5,230; weekly fee after 9 weeks $315; weekly fee after 13 weeks $245
Duration: 9 weeks to 6 months
Age: 20, 18 or 19 with three letters of recommendation
Contact: tanzania@globalservicecorps.org
Learn more: www.globalservicecorps.org
Special skills: Interested in pursuing a career in health and a commitment to service
Details: This program is designed for health professionals and students interested in pursuing a career in health, especially international health. The first week includes cultural orientation and technical training followed by three weeks of community training on HIV/AIDS prevention and nutrition. Participants are then placed in a healthcare facility or hospital where there may be opportunities for shadowing medical staff while teaching staff basic computer skills and usage of telemedicine software. Participants spend part of the first week of their program in a comfortable local hostel and the remaining time living with a local Tanzanian host family. Your host family will generously introduce you to the culture, traditions and cuisine of Tanzania. A day safari to a local game reserve is also included.

Maasai Experience & Mt. Kilimanjaro

Organization: inside/out Humanitourism™ Adventures
Location: Maasailand, Africa
Cost: $4,250+ **Duration:** 1 week + guided climb of Mt. Kilimanjaro
Age: No age minimum, determined on an individual basis
Contact: info@theinsideandout.com
Learn more: www.theinsideandout.com
Details: You will work side-by-side with the Maasai people planting trees that will be used for biofuel on a parcel of land that flanks Mt.

Kilimanjaro. The purpose of this endeavor is to assist a community of Maasai people in developing an economic opportunity that will benefit the local village, while providing stewardship for the land and environmental sensitivity. You will have the opportunity to be immersed in the local culture while having the security of English-speaking guides and organizers. A climb of Mt. Kilimanjaro and a safari completes the adventure. inside/out trips are designed around opportunities to do humanitarian volunteer work on meaningful international projects and are combined with sustainable eco-adventure travel in the local area of the project and people. Their trips are designed to create longer-term relationships between communities and travelers.

Other organizations offering projects in Tanzania:

Art in Tanzania: www.artintanzania.org
Foot 2 Africa: www.foot2afrika.com
Global Routes: www.globalroutes.org
Habitat for Humanity: www.habitat.org
i-to-i: www.i-to-i.com
Institute of Field Research Expeditions: www.ifrevolunteers.org
Rustic Volunteer and Travel: www.rustic-volunteer-travel.com
Volunteering Solutions: www.volunteeringsolutions.com

Togo

Community Building, Education and Helath

Organization: Association Togolaise des Volontaires au Travail,
Location: Varies
Cost: None **Duration:** 1 to 6 months **Age:** 18
Contact: astovoct@yahoo.com **Learn more:** www.astovot.org
Special skills: Some French and English

Details: Volunteers will work in a variety of programs. Among these are: community mobilisation against STDs/AIDS, reforestation, school sessions, assisting mentally handicapped and deaf/mute children, construction, renovation of schools buildings, education and teaching.

Other organizations offering projects in Togo:

A Pas de Loup: www.apasdeloup.org
Association Togolaise des Volontaires au Travail: www.astovot.org
African Rural Development Movement: www.arudmo.org
Canadian Alliance for Development Initiatives and Projects:
   www.cadip.org
Global Crossroads: www.globalcrossroad.com
Projects Abroad: www.projects-abroad.org

Tunisia

Organizations offering projects in Togo:
Service Civil International: www.sci-ivs.org
Volunteers for Peace: www.vfp.org

Uganda

Training Veterinary Nurses in Kamapala
Organization: Uganda Society for the Protection and Care of Animals
Location: Kampala
Cost: None. You provide your own food & accommodations
Duration: 6 months   **Age:** 18
Contact: Katiasteve@yahoo.co.uk uspca2003@yahoo.com
Learn more: *See editor's note*
Special skills: Need to be an experienced veterinary nurse
Details: This came from the group when they were contacted about the book project. "There are no veterinary nurses in Kampala and we really need the knowledge!" Obviously the need is great and goes beyond nursing. Before 1996, no established animal welfare groups existed in Uganda. There were several scattered shelters, a legacy of the East African Society for the Prevention of Cruelty to Animals, but many dissolved during the upheaval in the late 1960s and into the late 1980s. The Humane Society International website does offer information on

Uganda Society for the Protection and Care of Animals for those who would like to learn more.

🖎 **Editor's note:** Imagine the courage and tenacity it takes to establish the first organization of this type in an entire country. Yes, their information is sparse. Together we can fix that. No website? If you have the skills, why not offer to build them one? It is a great volunteer opportunity that you can create for yourself and you don't even need to be a veterinary nurse. Not a web designer? No worries. Ask yourself this: What can I do?

Physical Therapy Internship Program

Organization: Busoga Integrated Development and Care Foundation
Location: Iganga District, Uganda
Cost: None   **Duration:** 2 to 8 weeks/30-40 hrs per week   **Age:** 18
Contact: bidcaf@hotmail.com   **Learn more:** www.bidcaf.org
Special skills: University or graduate student with medical electives
Details: As a Physical Therapy volunteer you'll work alongside medical personnel who will provide advice, healthcare and education to families living with HIV. The scheme is a highly progressive project that aims to increase people's knowledge and understanding of the disease, and provide practical physical care to terminally ill children and adults. You'll visit families in their homes, treating common illnesses faced by patients such as malaria, cough, and skin infections among others. Keep in mind that though skills are important, a sincere willingness to learn and work is often required to make a valuable contribution.

Orphan Care & Child-Headed Household Outreach

Organization: Uganda Rural Fund (URF)
Location: Kyetume Village, Masaka, Uganda
Cost: $300 a month with host family, accommodation + meals
Duration: 1+ months   **Age:** 18, under 18 with a parent
Contact: jmlugemwa@ugandaruralfund.org
Learn more: www.ugandaruralfund.org
Special skills: Passion for education of orphans
Details: Do you love playing with kids? Are you passionate about the plight of kids, about their education? This is the place you've been looking for. Combine a host family and orphanage live-in experience with a rural setting. You will assist kids with laundry, cleaning, tutoring, games, meals, etc at the orphanage. Your work also involves visiting child-headed family households (orphans living by themselves without an adult) and assessing their needs and finding sponsors. Volunteers help these families with gardening, house construction or repair and tutoring. You may also assist at other projects such as: youth and women empowerment, teaching high school, village banking,

415

crafts, agriculture, AIDS awareness, nonprofit administration, etc to get a feel for community development at the grassroots level.

Women Empowerment & Village Banking

Organization: Uganda Rural Fund (URF)
Location: Kyetume Village, Masaka, Uganda
Cost: $300 a month with host family, accommodation and meals
Duration: 1+ months   **Age:** 18, under 18 with a parent
Contact: jmlugemwa@ugandaruralfund.org
Learn more: www.ugandaruralfund.org
Special skills: Passion for rural development
Details: Get more out of your volunteer experience for less. Living with a host family you will be immersed in the local culture and experience community development at its grassroots level. You will work with wonderful and resilient African women who have chosen to stand up against poverty for the good of their children. Volunteers coordinate with local leaders to facilitate workshops, home visits, program evaluations, dialogue with the women to get a better understanding of their situation – joys, dreams and needs – and with URF, figure out strategies to address these challenges. Workshop topics may include: AIDS awareness, parenting skills, human rights, general health, malaria, entrepreneurship, farming, adult literacy, etc. You can also assist with other projects like village banking, crafts, teaching, orphanage and child sponsorship.

Youth Empowerment & Community Service

Organization: Uganda Rural Fund (URF)
Location: Kyetume Village, Masaka, Uganda
Cost: $300 a month with host family, accommodation and meals
Duration: 1+ months   **Age:** 18, under 18 with a parent
Contact: jmlugemwa@ugandaruralfund.org
Learn more: www.ugandaruralfund.org
Special skills: Passion for rural development
Details: Are you passionate about youth activism, leadership and personal development? You will work with resilient African youth who have chosen to stand up against poverty through education, leadership, community service, and entrepreneurship. Volunteers collaborate with local teams to facilitate youth camps, workshops, home visits, program evaluations, dialogue with the youth to get a better understanding of their situation – joys, dreams and needs – and with URF, figure out strategies to address these challenges. Workshop topics may include: AIDS awareness, leadership, career guidance, human rights, health, malaria, entrepreneurship, etc. You can also assist with other community projects. Here is a chance to empower Africa's generation

of responsible leaders. Living with a host family will immerse you in the local culture and experience community development at its grassroots.

Orphans' Education & Skills Development

Organization: Uganda Rural Fund (URF)
Location: Kyetume Village, Masaka, Uganda
Cost: $300 a month with host family, accommodation and meals
Duration: 1+ months **Age:** 18, under 18 with a parent
Contact: jmlugemwa@ugandaruralfund.org
Learn more: www.ugandaruralfund.org
Special skills: Passion for rural development
Details: Do you believe that education is the best way to empower Africa's AIDS orphans to break the cycle of poverty? URF does and invites you to experience how education is transforming rural Uganda at the grassroots. You will work on both formal and informal education projects: teaching in an afterschool program or high school, vocational skills, crafts, adult literacy, entrepreneurship and small business management, leadership skills, career guidance, etc. They run a high school for kids who had dropped out of school. It has a community library and computer center. You will help prepare student sponsorship profiles, assist teachers by typing exams, teach computer classes, construction, music, crafts, sports programs and any needed work. You may also work on other projects like women's empowerment, orphanage assistance, village banking, and more.

Sustainable Agriculture for Rural Farmers

Organization: Uganda Rural Fund (URF)
Location: Kyetume Village, Masaka, Uganda
Cost: $300 a month with host family, accommodation and meals
Duration: 1+ months **Age:** 18, under 18 with a parent
Contact: jmlugemwa@ugandaruralfund.org
Learn more: www.ugandaruralfund.org
Special skills: Passion for rural development
Details: Over 80% of Ugandans depend on subsistence farming. It's a no brainer that any real development efforts must focus on sustainable agriculture at the grassroots level. You will work with URF on strategies to help smallholder rural farmers learn improved farming practices, crop and animal care, and proper planning as away to improve yields which ultimately improve living conditions for farmers and the ability to educate their children. Current programs include: piggery, poultry, seed loans, goat keeping, and growing of crops like corn, beans, potatoes, bananas, vegetables, etc. The program is looking at implementing drip irrigation during drought seasons. You will research useful information for farmers such as better breeds, markets, small

loans, diseases, etc. You may also work on other projects like women's empowerment, orphanage assistance, village banking, and more.

Funding for Sustainable Development Projects
Organization: Uganda Rural Fund (URF)
Location: Kyetume Village, Masaka, Uganda
Cost: $300 a month with host family, accommodation and meals
Duration: 1+ months   **Age:** 18, under 18 with a parent
Contact: jmlugemwa@ugandaruralfund.org
Learn more: www.ugandaruralfund.org
Special skills: Fundraising, grants research & writing along with a passion for rural development.
Details: It's exciting to see all wonderful things accomplished at a project and the impact it's making on hundreds of lives. However, the lifeblood of any successful project is a steady stream of funding to make the programs sustainable. URF is looking for individuals or groups who desire to change lives through fundraising and grant writing. They need funding for income-generating projects to ensure sustainability of the organization while creating job opportunities and empowering local residents with substantial skills. The goal is to help people help themselves. To achieve this, we need to empower them to launch projects that generate income locally instead of relying on donations. You will have the opportunity to work on outreach projects putting you in touch with the people you advocate for.

Promo Video & Kids' Music/Dance Video Production
Organization: Uganda Rural Fund (URF)
Location: Kyetume Village, Masaka, Uganda
Cost: $300 a month with host family, accommodation and meals
Duration: 1+ months   **Age:** 18, under 18 with a parent
Contact: jmlugemwa@ugandaruralfund.org
Learn more: www.ugandaruralfund.org
Special skills: Video production
Details: URF has achieved a lot in its short lifespan of four years, basically building the organization from scratch with little funding. They have implemented programs that are changing lives for hundreds of children and adults including a school, water system, women empowerment, etc. When this story is told it will raise awareness, help

them gain visibility and be a valuable tool for reaching out to supporters. They are looking for an individual or group to help produce a promotional video. The organization would like to produce videos of kids' music, dance and theater productions. Kids are talented and need exposure, getting their stories to a broader audience. You may also teach kids video recording, editing and production so that in the future they can produce short videos themselves.

Construction of Childrens' Lavatories at School

Organization: Foundation for Young Orphans
Location: Mukono District, Kiggugo village
Cost: $2,000 **Duration:** Varied, depends on resources **Age:** 18
Contact: volunteers@thefyo.org **Learn more:** www.thefyo.org
Details: Volunteers are needed in many aspects of working with local builders on the construction of new school toilets which are in "critical condition." The current bathroom is constructed with wood and all the wood is spoiled putting users at risk. Volunteer's fee pay depending on duration of stay. The program fee that is paid includes a donation to the project, airport pick up, on-going support and supervision and emergency medical insurance. You will stay with a host family or special arrangements can be made at an extra cost.

Microfinance in Busia

Organization: East Africa Metamorphosis Project
Location: Busia
Cost: $15-$30 a day depending on duration of trip
Duration: 1 week to 6 months **Age:** 18 (or accompanied by an adult)
Contact: rick@eastafricametaproject.org
Learn more: www.eastafricametaproject.org
Details: Make a difference and leave a changed person! Microcredit is quickly gaining momentum as an effective way to empower those trapped in extreme poverty. EAMP has recently launched a microcredit program in Uganda and they would love volunteers to come join them. You may help facilitate weekly meetings with the current participants, work with staff to interview new participants to the program, conduct interviews with the new applicants to gather data on their current economic situation or even interview participants in the program to assess hindrances to their business. Your work aides EAMP in assessing new ways to solve some of the issues facing those in extreme poverty.

Extreme Poverty Research Program

Organization: East Africa Metamorphosis Project (EAMP)
Location: Busia

Cost: $15-$30 a day depending on duration of trip
Duration: 1 week to 6 months **Age:** 18 (or accompanied by an adult)
Contact: rick@eastafricametaproject.org
Learn more: www.eastafricametaproject.org
Details: Conduct field research in Busia, Uganda
on issues related to EAMP's mission of serving
orphans and vulnerable children caught in
extreme poverty. Working in groups or
individually, volunteers will interview members
of the local community to answer such questions

as A) "Approximately how many orphaned and vulnerable children live
in Busia?" B) "What are the living conditions of orphans and vulnerable
children in Busia" C) "What are the primary causes of poverty in
Busia?" D) "What has been the impact of HIV/AIDS?" E) "How do
single mothers provide for their children?" F) "How many children are
receiving a quality education?"

Child Education Program

Organization: East Africa Metamorphosis Project (EAMP)
Location: Busia
Cost: $15-$30 a day depending on duration of trip
Duration: 1 week to 6 months **Age:** 18+ (or accompanied by an
adult)
Contact: rick@eastafricametaproject.org
Learn more: www.eastafricametaproject.org
Details: EAMP's Child Education Program is carried out in
partnership with New Hope Orphanage. New Hope houses a primary
school teaching children ages 6-13. In our education program,
volunteers work side-by-side with current New Hope teachers to train
the children in English, math, science and creative writing. The goal
for volunteers is not only to teach the children, but to help the teachers
improve their teaching skills and mastery of the subjects. Volunteers
will work primarily with Ugandan textbooks and follow the Ugandan
national curriculum; however, volunteers are also highly encouraged to
bring educational resources (text books, dictionaries, calculators, etc.)
with them to New Hope.

St Paul KAASO

Organization: Kids Worldwide
Location: Rakai District, 5 hours south of Kampala, near Tanzanian
border
Cost: Under 3 weeks $250, 1st month $350, 2nd month $150, 3rd
month $100, subsequent months $80.
Duration: 2+ weeks, 1+ month preferred
Age: 18, children accompanied by a parent are also welcome

Contact: kaaso@kidsworldwide.org
Learn more: www.kidsworldwide.org
Special skills: Community development, teaching (in English), development techniques, social work and counseling, administrative work, nutrition, public health education, grant writing and research, IT and library skills to help manage the computer centre and community library.
Details: St. Paul KAASO (Kabira Adult Attention & School of Orphans) Project was first intended for orphans and adults who never had the opportunity to attend school or those who partially attended. Their current community projects include: The women's empowerment group, adult literacy groups (for adults between the age of 18-60 years), and the maize mill project which currently sees that 154 farmers are supplied with seeds, fertilizers, herbicides and pesticides to grow their own crops of maize and cassava. The piggery project is a breeding program for pigs to be supplied and sold to members of the above groups to promote community income and teach general business skills. Micro loans, the community library and computer lab, provide guidance and counseling to restore hope.

Bula Children's Home

Organization: Kids Worldwide
Location: Kampala
Cost: Under 3 weeks $250, 1st month $350, 2nd month $150, 3rd month $100, subsequent months $80
Duration: 2+ weeks, 1+ month preferred
Age: 18+, or kids over 10 welcome with parent
Contact: bula@kidsworldwide.org
Learn more: www.kidsworldwide.org
Special skills: Tutoring/homework help, extracurricular activity organization (sports, arts/crafts, music, etc.), counseling, program development (health education, skill training), health and medical care.
Details: BULA cares for 27 orphaned and vulnerable children, ranging in ages from 8 to 18 years old. The Home, located in Kampala, was newly established in early 2009 to alleviate the conditions and hardships endured at the children's prior setting. BULA Children's promotes religious freedom, gender equality, cultural sensitivity and free will. The home welcomes all volunteers committed to its vision that all orphans and vulnerable children deserve to live to their potential and enjoy their rights and aspirations to the fullest.

Community Support, Awareness and Development

Organization: Kyosiga Community Christian Association for Development (KACCAD)
Location: in Wakiso and Mpigi Districts

Cost: $650 for the first month, $450 each additional month
Duration: 1+ month **Age:** 18
Contact: kyosigacommunity@gmail.com
Learn more: www.volunteerkaccad.org
Special skills: Volunteers must speak English
Details: KACCAD's goal has been to create awareness and development projects to raise the standard of living of underprivileged people in Wakiso and Mpigi Districts of Uganda. They offer many opportunities for you to support their work and share your skills. Volunteer opportunities are open to all regardless of ability. To join our volunteer team you will email KACCAD your resume, a list of your skills/interests and tell us why you want to live and volunteer in Uganda. They are especially looking for people to help support these types of projects: farm house construction and repairs, home repairs, health/HIV/AIDS education, reproductive health information, voluntary counseling and testing, immunization programs, youth and child education, animal rearing, water and sanitation (including well construction), construction of a volunteer center, vocational skills development, business planning and budget management skills, project planning and management, fundraisers or other skills that can help transform a community. KACCAD is an all volunteer run and supported organization. Volunteerism is central to sustaining them as an organization. The fee covers your airport pickup, transport to the volunteer house, food and accommodation while volunteering, supervision, and a donation to KACCAD.

Care and Support to People Living with HIV/AIDS

Organization: Kiyita Family Alliance for Development (KIFAD)

Location: Nansana, Wakiso District, Uganda, East Africa.
Costs: $222 **Duration:** 2+ weeks **Age:** 18
Contact: kifad_project@yahoo.com **Learn more:** www.kifad.org
Special skills: Motivation and attitude
Details: KIFAD is an HIV/AIDS project. Their main goal is to contribute to increased access to comprehensive HIV/AIDS treatment, home based care and to provide support to people with HIV/AIDS. They are looking for people who can assist KIFAD towards increasing the provision of care and support to people infected and affected by HIV/AIDS in order to mitigate the effects of the epidemic. People with skills in project proposal writing and resource mobilization, monitoring and evaluation, project planning and management, HIV/AIDS, community development, counseling, health workers, IT, data base management and rural development are all welcome and needed! Benefits:

certificate; recommendation letter, practical and hands on HIV/AIDS experience, cultural orientation and induction. Costs cover, local meals (breakfast, lunch and supper), airport pick and drop, accommodation in a host family.

Village Primary School Teacher

Organization: The Real Uganda
Location: Programs based in Mukono, Wakiso District, Jinja District Masaka District and in Kyazanga.
Cost: $650 first month, $600 second and third months
Duration: 1 to 3 months, school terms vary but are approximately as follows: Feb 1 to April 15, May 15 to August 15, Sept 15 to November 30.
Age: 18-80
Contact: therealuganda@hotmail.com
Learn more: www.therealuganda.com
Special skills: Experience working with children: mentoring, afterschool groups, camp counseling, formal classroom work
Details: We work with community based organizations that provide education for orphaned and underprivileged children. Volunteers teach arts and crafts, structured play, music/singing, sports, health, and academics. Volunteers plan lessons using government curriculum and textbooks, but should bring any supplies, teaching materials, or instruments they wish to use. The main focus is to provide children with a loving, creative and interactive environment in which to flourish. Accommodation and daily meals are provided at school. No more than 2 volunteers will be placed together in any village placement.

Village Outreach Worker

Organization: The Real Uganda
Location: Programs based in Mukono, Wakiso District, Jinja District Masaka District and in Kyazanga.
Cost: $650 first month, $600 second and third months
Duration: 1 to 3 months   **Age:** 18-80
Contact: therealuganda@hotmail.com
Learn more: www.therealuganda.com
Special skills: Volunteers must be self starters, motivators, independent workers, and confident in their own ideas
Details: Work with community based organizations that provide counseling, care and education for rural people. Placements include youth mentoring, team building, HIV prevention and AIDS care, sanitation and hygiene and general public health. Volunteer activities include home visiting, designing education materials, conducting seminars, and maintaining wells and other village infrastructure. A village placement is particularly appropriate for volunteers with great ideas and enthusiasm for grassroots development. This is a real

opportunity for deep cultural exchange. Accommodation and daily meals are provided within the village of placement, and will range from private apartments to rooms in private homes. No more than 2 volunteers will be placed together in any village placement.

Orphanages in Uganda

Organization: Experiential Learning International
Location: Iganga
Cost: $885 **Duration:** 2+ weeks **Age:** 18
Contact: info@eliabroad.org **Learn more:** www.eliabroad.org
Details: According to the World Bank over 1 million orphans are growing up in Uganda. Orphans living with their extended families often face a bleak future of hard work and little opportunity for education. ELI works with several organizations aimed at assisting and empowering these children through education programs, skills training and other activities. Volunteers are welcome to assist with teaching, and are encouraged to lead other activities such as sports and arts in order to enrich the lives of the children. The orphanages provide food, shelter and education to hundreds of children from infants up to teenagers. They operate on very modest budgets, and at times struggle to provide enough food for the children.

Income Generation and Small Business Development

Organization: Experiential Learning International
Location: Iganga
Cost: $885+ **Duration:** 2+ weeks **Age:** 18
Contact: info@eliabroad.org **Learn more:** www.eliabroad.org
Details: Participants in this project will work directly with small village organizations to help facilitate the development of small businesses in rural areas. Interns can pursue a wide variety of projects in collaboration with the local organization including business skills development, microloans, developing business plans and project monitoring and evaluation. This internship is an incredible opportunity to learn firsthand about small scale economic development projects while also playing a role in poverty reduction in rural Uganda.

Global Health Volunteer

Organization: Foundation for International Medical Relief of Children
Location: Bumwalukani
Cost: $1,266 for 2 weeks
Duration: 2 to 4 weeks, longer stays are possible **Age:** 18
Contact: missions@fimrc.org **Learn more:** www.fimrc.org

Special skills: This program is specially focused for undergraduates, medical students, and public health students.

Details: Help provide direct healthcare to a community of approximately 25,000 individuals in rural Uganda, all of whom live on $200 a year or less. The clinic and adjoining primary school are situated on a mountainside about 30 miles from the city of Mbale. Volunteers play a crucial role in streamlining the clinic's operations by managing patient intake and providing basic assistance to the clinic's medical staff. Preventative health education initiatives are a major part of every mission; volunteers will become engaged in the effort to teach basic health maintenance to children and adults in the community.

Organizations offering projects in Uganda:

American Friends Service Committee: www.afsc.org
Come Kuona International: www.comekuona.org
Foundation for Sustainable Development: www.fsdinternational.org
Global Crossroads: www.globalcrossroad.com
Global Visions International: www.gviusa.com
i-to-i: www.i-to-i.com
Meaningful Volunteer: www.meaningfulvolunteer.org

Zambia

Malalo (Bridge) Sports Project

Organization: Youth Press and Development Organization
Location: Lubengele, Chililabombwe
Cost: Budget $40 per day accommodation, $8 for food and $3 for transport
Duration: 4 weeks from mid January to mid February   **Age**: 25
Contact: kebby.shampongo@gmail.com, administrator@fypdo.org
Learn more: fypdo.org
Special skills: Sports education (soccer)
Details: The Youth Press and Development Organization is a non-profit, nongovernmental organization formed in 2003. The YPDO runs Information Technology projects, education projects and a soccer project. The soccer project caters to about 120 children from 12 years to 18 years who want to have a career in soccer. The under 18 team participates in the copperbelt soccer league of 24 teams while the under 15 team participates in the district league of 12 teams. YDPO wants participating youth to develop a technical knowledge of soccer as they

aspire towards their soccer career goals. The volunteer shall also experience cultural practices and visit the monkey orphanage at Chimfunshi.

Hope for Dogs

Organization: Ndola S.P.C.A.
Location: Ndola
Cost: None
Duration: 10 days to 1 month   **Age:** 20
Contact: ndolaspca@yahoo.com
Learn more: Join Ndola SPCA on Facebook
Special skills: Anyone who enjoys working with animals. Dog handling skills would be a great asset however.
Details: Ndola SPCA exists on a shoestring. Their income is generated from providing boarding for security dogs and the pets of Ndola residents going out of town. They have also received some donations from the community. The Ndola SPCA's facilities are very old and basic, but they provide important help for suffering animals in a place where human life is also cheap. There is scope for all sorts of projects in their community, but they are limited mainly due to a lack of volunteers. For this reason Ndola S.P.C.A. must limit activities to promoting proper pet care, vaccinations and neutering. Volunteers help socialize animals, feed, assist the veterinarian and help with maintenance. There are too many possibilities to mention. The group assures volunteers that everyday will be an adventure and your help could not be more appreciated or needed!

Livingstone Sports Development

Organization: African Impact
Location: Livingstone
Cost: $2,260 for 4 weeks
Duration: 2 to 4 weeks or more   **Age:** 18-40
Contact: info@africanimpact.com
Learn more: www.africanimpact.com
Special skills: Enthusiasm for sports
Details: Sports volunteers spend their time doing physical education and sports training at local schools (which is sorely neglected due to the lack of trained teachers), as well as working with sports teams in the Livingstone community. Sports are an essential and effective tool to teach about various subjects such as HIV, nutrition and a healthy lifestyle. The sports project consists of three main areas of work: physical education within schools, training the team and HIV education in sport. As a sports volunteer you will also be involved with community projects in Livingstone which include the following: family support, building, painting, refurbishing, home

based care, farming, adult literacy, as well as HIV Education - all to support, unite and build up the local community as a whole.

African Lion Rehabilitation and Release Program

Organization: Kaya Responsible Travel
Location: Mosi-oa-Tunya National Park, Livingstone
Cost: $1,832+ **Duration:** 2 to 26 weeks **Age:** 17-80
Contact: info@kayavolunteer.com
Learn more: www.KayaVolunteer.com
Special skills: No specific skills required other than a passion for wildlife and conservation
Details: This program works with key lion research organizations to address the issue of rapidly declining lion populations in the African wilds. The project trains and prepares the offspring of animals that

have been brought up in captivity to allow them to be released as self-sufficient wild animals back into the national park. Volunteers will assist in all aspects of care for the animals, including cleaning, feeding and training as well as taking part in research and monitoring projects within the national park, and conservation activities and education within the local community.

Sports Development and Rural Community Work

Organization: Kaya Responsible Travel
Location: The community of Livingstone
Cost: $1,432+ **Duration:** 2 to 26 weeks **Age:** 17-80
Contact: info@kayavolunteer.com
Learn more: www.KayaVolunteer.com
Special skills: No specific skills required other than a passion for wildlife and conservation
Details: Teach children about health, hygiene, nutrition as well as important lessons about HIV and AIDS through sports coaching. This approach is used in schools and community groups within the Livingstone area and the project trains local people to become coaches and local teams to compete against rival towns to promote the spread of interest in sport that can enhance these opportunities for health education, personal development and it reaches out to the most vulnerable children. Volunteers will be hands on and immersed in the local community in an unforgettable and very valuable project.

Organizations offering projects in Zambia:

A Broader View: www.abroaderview.org

Ecoteer: www.ecoteer.com
Global Visions International: www.gviusa.com
UNA Exchange: www.unaexchange.org
Volunteers for Peace: www.vfp.org

Zimbabwe

Donkey Care, Health and Community Education

Organization: Donkey Protection Trust
Location: Travels to various rural areas
Cost: None   **Duration:** 1+ month   **Age:** 18
Contact: donkey@zol.co.zw
Learn more: spana.org/countries/zimbabwe.html
Details: The Donkey Protection Trust is the only organization in
Zimbabwe serving the needs of over a half a million donkeys. In order
to fulfill that need they are mostly a mobile service spending usually a
week or more at a time in our rural areas concentrating on education
and primary health care. Their objectives are to prevent the suffering
and abuse of these hardworking animals. The work is simple, but at
times arduous. Volunteers will be travelling as part of the
team wherever required and organizing and assisting in clinics and
primary health care activities.

Painted Dog/African Wild Dog Conservation

Organization: Painted Dog Conservation
Location: Dete (arrive at Victoria Falls)
Cost: $1,500 (budget $450 extra for park fees & transport to/from the
project site)
Duration: 3 weeks   **Age:** 18
Contact: info@ painteddog.org   **Learn more:** www.painteddog.org
Details: Painted Dog Conservation's mission is to protect and increase
the range and numbers of painted dogs through hands on conservation,
education, community involvement and international support. Project
volunteers will learn about and assist with radio telemetry, daily
tracking of packs in and around Hwange National Park, maintenance
work and feeding and enrichment programmes. Flexibility and
initiative are vital. Entering data/photographs acquired. Assist at the
rehabilitation facility as work can and does arise on a daily basis.

Black Rhino Station

Organization: African Impact

Location: Marondera, Zimbabwe (about 1.5 hours drive east of Harare)
Cost: $2,375 for 4 weeks   **Duration:** 2 to 6 weeks or more   **Age:** 18
Contact: info@africanimpact.com
Learn more: www.africanimpact.com
Details: This black rhino breeding station offers volunteers the amazing opportunity of hands on work with black rhinos, an endangered species, as well as the ranch's few adopted elephants. Volunteers will also have a chance to engage with the local school through conservation education. As a volunteer you will live in close contact with black rhino, elephants, buffalo and all the other species of wild animal on the 10,000 acre conservancy. You will witness incredible animal relationships, hear their sounds, record vital information, and learn the appreciation of simplicity from the surrounding rural communities. All in all the ranch has handled a total of 32 black rhino since the project began in 1987 and has returned 10 rhino back to the Matusadona National Park in Zimbabwe.

Victoria Falls Lion Rehabilitation and Conservation

Organization: African Impact
Location: Victoria Falls, Zimbabwe
Cost: $3,200 for 4 weeks   **Duration:** 2 to 8 weeks   **Age:** 18
Contact: info@africanimpact.com
Learn more: www.africanimpact.com and www.lionalert.org
Special skills: A passion for wildlife and conservation is important
Details: At the Victoria Falls Lion Rehabilitation & Conservation Project volunteers will have the unique opportunity to walk and work with lions, exposing the cubs to the African bush as they hone their natural skills. You will also be involved in research of lion behavior and work with the staff on what is said to be the world's only programme for their release into the wild. You assist with conservation tasks such as clearing of alien invader plant species in the Victoria Falls National Park, and conservation education at a local primary school is also needed. There are opportunities aplenty to enjoy the wide range of adventure activities available around the Falls, which is one of Africa's adrenaline capitals.

Lion Breeding and Rehabilitation

Organization: Kaya Responsible Travel
Location: Antelope Park, Gweru
Cost: $1,824+   **Duration:** 2 to 8 weeks   **Age:** 17-80
Contact: info@kayavolunteer.com

Learn more: www.KayaVolunteer.com

Special skills: No specific skills required, other than a passion for wildlife and conservation

Details: This program works with key lion research organizations to address the issue of rapidly declining lion populations in the African wilds. The project trains and prepares the offspring of animals that have been brought up in captivity to allow them to be released as self-sufficient wild animals back into the national park. Volunteers will assist in all aspects of care for the animals, including cleaning, feeding and training as well as taking part in research and monitoring projects within the national park, and conservation activities and education within the local community.

Organizations offering projects in Zimbabwe:

Action Africa: www.action-africa.org
Animal Welfare Trust: www.awaretrust.org
Chimfunshi Wildlife Orphanage: www.chimfunshi.org.za
HIV/Aids Zimbabwe: www.hivaidszimbabwe.com
Pathfinders: www.pathfindersafrica.com/zimbabwe
Service Civil International: www.sci-ivs.org

Oceania
Volunteer Opportunities

"We are all visitors to this time, this place. We are just passing through. Our purpose here is to observe, to learn, to grow, to love... and then we return home."

~ Australian Aborigines Proverb

American Samoa (United States)

American Samoa Teaching Year

Organization: WorldTeach
Location: Varies by placement – see details
Cost: None, fully funded by the American Samoa Department of Education
Duration: 1 year (departure in mid-July) **Age:** 18-74
Contact: info@worldteach.org **Learn more:** www.worldteach.org
Special skills: Native English speaker, bachelor's degree
Details: In this program, you will have the opportunity to teach English, math and science in public high schools and elementary schools through the Department of Education. Because American Samoa is a territory of the United States, it has access to many federal programs. In particular, there are sufficient texts, teacher manuals and school equipment and supplies. Additionally, all schools, even those on the outer islands, have unlimited Internet access. Cell phones can be used throughout the islands. Volunteers live in furnished houses on local families' properties. Each volunteer has his or her own bedroom and in most cases two or three volunteers (depending on the number of bedrooms) share an apartment. In a few placements a volunteer has his

431

or her own apartment or house. Fifteen of the volunteers are assigned to schools on the main island of Tutuila and the other five to schools on the outer islands.

Australia

Wild Tasmania Devil Management

Organization: Save the Tasmanian Devil
Location: Tasmania
Cost: None   **Duration:** 2 weeks   **Age:** 18
Contact: DevilDisease.Enquiries@dpipwe.tas.gov.au
Learn more: www.tassiedevil.com.au
Special skills: None, however first aid and 4WD experience area always welcome.
Details: Devilish volunteers are involved in field monitoring and wild management of Tasmanian devils, helping with trapping at various sites across Tasmania. A typical survey lasts 11 - 12 days. While team leaders trap and release Tasmanian devils, volunteers assist with scrubbing and cleaning traps and scribing. Not so glamorous? Well, the days can be long, the weather unpredictable and mobile phone coverage will be limited or non-existent. You will, however, four-wheel-drive into breathtakingly beautiful places that very few people get to see and help an amazing endangered animal that is full of personality. Everyone who works with them grows to love them! Food, accommodations and transport from Hobart to the worksite and back are included. You will need to finance travel to Tasmania.

Wombat Protection

Organization: Wombat Protection Society
Location: Quaama, NSW
Cost: None
Duration: Open   **Age:** None specified
Contact: research@wombatprotection.org.au
Learn more: www.wombatprotection.org.au
Special skills: Depends on the work being undertaken. Any handling of wombats requires training and a good level of fitness. We have sedentary volunteer positions available.
Details: Wombats are the most amazing creatures. They live in beautifully engineered temperature controlled burrows from where they fossick for grass, roots and fungi after dark returning before daybreak. Growing up to 40 kilos in weight from a jelly bean less than a gram when born, the joey makes a perilous journey from mum's cloacca

to her pouch where it attaches to a teat and remains safely in her backwards facing pouch until about nine months old. A wide range of volunteer skills can be used here to help protect these amazing, yet comical, creatures, from administrative- including publicity and fundraising to field research and monitoring to working on release sites -which may involve building wombatoriums, fencing as well as research assistance in burrow monitoring, wombat sighting and some direct care.

Wwoofers and Volunteers

Organization: Eagles Nest Wildlife Sanctuary
Location: Queensland
Cost: None   **Duration:** Open
Contact: eagle_save@hotmail.com
Learn more: www.wildlife-sanctuary.info
Details: Eagles Nest Wildlife Sanctuary was founded in 2001 as a place for injured, sick, orphaned and unreleasable wildlife. The animals get medical treatment, are fed with love and are finally released into the wild again, with special preparation for the young ones. Researchers, scientists and volunteers are always welcome. You can help with the daily work, building, gardening, landscaping or with general farm maintenance in exchange you get free accommodation and meals.

Go Batty at a World Class Bat Hospital

Organization: Tolga Bat Hospital
Location: Atherton, Southwest of Cairns
Cost: $40 per day   **Duration:** Varies by project   **Age:** 22
Contact: jenny@tolgabathospital.org
Learn more: www.tolgabathospital.org
Special skills: Appreciation for unique animals.
Details: Volunteers are needed every year during tick paralysis season, and to a lesser extent throughout the year. From October to January they usually need the equivalent of 4 full time people. In February they need 2-3 volunteers. Throughout the rest of the year the hospital takes occasional volunteers. During tick paralysis season, volunteers typically work 7 days per week for an average of about 10 -12 hours per day. Every effort is made to give long-stay volunteers a break for a few days during the season. Outside of tick season the atmosphere is far more flexible, but the work may be less varied. Days off for excursions or a break can be easily accommodated. All volunteers are expected to help with preparing and cleaning up evening meals.
✍**Editor's note:** Volunteers at the bat hospital need to be vaccinated for rabies at least one month prior to arrival. This involves a series of 3 intramuscular injections. Rabies is rare in Spectacled Flying Foxes.

Only two bats have ever tested positive. However rabies vaccines are a condition of their permit and are good standard practice for volunteers at all international animal rescue projects.

Dolphins of Western Australia

Organization: Travellers Worldwide
Location: Koombana Bay
Cost: $1,900-$4,865 **Duration:** 6 to 12 weeks **Age:** 18
Contact: info@travellersworldwide.com
Learn more: www.travellersworldwide.com
Special skills: You must be adaptable, enthusiastic, fit and healthy, and have lots of initiative. You need to be fluent in English and enjoy talking to people
Details: This project is based at a nonprofit Centre in Bunbury committed to dolphin research, education, conservation and tourism. As a volunteer you get to meet people from all around the world, not to mention the dolphins! However, your time as a volunteer will involve a lot more than being in the water with the dolphins. Talking and answering questions is a very important part of your role. Eighty percent of your day will involve talking to people who come down to the beach to see the dolphins, thus educating them about their characteristics and making them aware of how crucial it is to conserve these wonderful animals. You'll learn a great deal through the training course which covers a wide range of issues and skills and includes presentations from a selection of guest speakers relevant to the operation of the Centre. Regular volunteer meetings are held to ensure you are kept up-to-date with the latest issues regarding marine mammal management and the operations of the Centre.

Quintessential Queensland: In Style

Organization: Hands Up Holidays
Location: Mapoon - Australia
Cost: $6,500 per person, based on sharing a room, excluding flights.
Duration: 4 days volunteering/14 day trip
Age: 16 unless with an adult
Contact: info@handsupholidays.com
Learn more: www.handsupholidays.com

Details: Enjoy a fantastic opportunity to get involved in an Australian aboriginal community, learn about their customs, hear stories about the 'dream time' and help them with their turtle conservation project. In addition, explore some of the amazing sights northern Australia has to offer. Dive or snorkel on the world-renowned Great Barrier Reef and marvel at a magnificent World Heritage rainforest. Enjoy an Aboriginal-run boat trip in the stunning Arukun Wetlands and deepen your knowledge of the fascinating indigenous people. Finally spend a few days discovering or relaxing on Haggerstone Island a natural gem in the gorgeous Great Barrier Reef.

Other organizations offering projects in Australia:

Australia Zoo: www.australiazoo.com.au
Conservation Volunteers Australia:
* www.conservationvolunteers.com.au*
Cultural Embrace: www.culturalembrace.com
Go Eco: www.goeco.org
Greenheart Travel: www.cci-exchange.com
Green Volunteers (lists multiple volunteer opportunity providers):
* www.greenvolunteers.org*
Greening Australia: www.greeningaustralia.org.au
i-to-i: www.i-to-i.com
International Partnership for Service-Learning: www.ipsl.org
International Student Volunteers: www.isvonline.com
Ozforce: www.ozforce.org
Palms Australia: www.palms.org.au
Roo Gully: members.iinet.net.au/~roogully
Volunteer Abroad: www.volunteerabroad.com
Willing Workers on Organic Farms Australia: www.wwoof.com.au

Cook Islands (New Zealand)

Vet Treks & Animal Care in the South Pacific
Organization: Esther Honey Foundation
Location: Rarotonga to remote outer islands and beyond!
Cost: None **Duration:** 2 weeks to 1 year
Contact: info@estherhoney.org
Learn more: www.estherhoney.org
Details: The world-renound Esther Honey Foundation needs: veterinarians, administrative volunteers and Clinic
Assistants (technicians, veterinary students, animal care), an outreach coordinator, student interns. Detailed position descriptions are included in the application on their website. The wonderful work of EFH has been the focus of countless magazine articles, newspaper reports, noted in veterinary journals and even covered in documentaries. Their tireless efforts on behalf of island animals will make any volunteer proud to say they were a small part of the work carried out in the middle of the South Pacific.

Other organizations offering projects in the Cook Islands:

Global Volunteers: www.globalvolunteers.org
Health Care Volunteer: www.healthcarevolunteer.com
Vets Beyond Borders: www.vetsbeyondborders.org
Work Away: www.workaway.info

Fiji

Marine Conservation Expedition

Organization: Blue Ventures
Location: The castaway island of Leleuvia in the heart of Fiji
Cost: $3,600 – $4,000; includes food, accommodation, training and diving
Duration: 6 weeks (3 – 30 week options available)   **Age:** 18
Contact: info@blueventures.org   **Learn more:**
www.blueventures.org
Special skills: none, full training provided
Details: Blue Ventures is an award-winning marine conservation organization dedicated to conservation, education and sustainable development in tropical coastal communities. Volunteers to Leleuvia will work closely with local and international scientists from Blue Ventures and the University of the South Pacific in collecting vital data on the rich, but threatened marine life found on the coral reef systems in the 'Heart of Fiji'. As well as conducting underwater surveys, volunteers will also conduct environmental education sessions on neighboring islands and help establish alternative livelihoods and management systems with the local fishing communities. The teams stay in traditional beach huts (bures) on a small tropical island and take part in Fijian kava kava ceremonies, local challenge rugby matches and the relaxed and friendly island life.

Marine Conservation & Learn to Dive in Fiji

Organization: Greenforce
Location: Fiji
Cost: $3,800+   **Duration:** 6, 8 or 10 weeks   **Age:** 17
Contact: info@greenforce.org

Learn more: www.greenforce.org
Details: Working in partnership with the Wildlife Conservation
Society, Greenforce Fiji is surveying the reefs surrounding this remote
South Pacific Island to create a UNESCO Seascape multi-use reserve.
Living in traditional 'bures' on the beach, volunteers will be welcomed
to the village with the traditional 'sevu sevu' ceremony with the local
'ratu' or chief. After completing their PADI Open Water, Advance and
Emergency First Response dive qualifications, volunteers will begin to
carry out survey dives completing up to 2 dives a day Mon-Fri.
Saturday offers a chance for fun dives and on Sunday you visit the local
village to attend church, have lunch with local families or even brace
the odd rugby match!

Fiji Explorer

Organization: Hands Up Holidays
Location: Suva
Cost: $2,500 per person, based on sharing a room
Duration: 5 days volunteering/15 day trip
Age: 16 unless with an adult
Contact: info@handsupholidays.com
Learn more: www.handsupholidays.com
Special skills: None, but teaching or building skills are desirable
Details: You will choose between two incredible projects in and
around Suva. Either assist at an organization dedicated to the welfare
of solo mothers and their children or help out at an orphanage.
Activities range from building and repair work to teaching and
environmental projects, so there is something for everyone. Spend your
time working, learning and enjoying the company of Fiji's beautiful
people. Complete this marvelous experience with a spot of adventure,
exploration and relaxation. Raft the magnificent Navua River, snorkel
at the stunning Coral Coast, hike the gorgeous Ngoda Highlands and
then relax as you cruise the unique Yasawa Islands.

Taste of Fiji: In Style

Organization: Hands Up Holidays
Special Skills: None required, but teaching or building skills are
desirable
Location: Suva
Cost: $2,100 per person, based on sharing a room
Duration: 3 days volunteering/9 day trip
Age: 16 unless with an adult

Contact: info@handsupholidays.com
Learn more: www.handsupholidays.com
Details: Dedicate your time to one of two rewarding projects around the city of Suva. Either assist at an orphanage and help manage all aspects of the children's lives from cleaning and feeding right through to teaching. Or, help in a home for single mothers and their children, where you improve their lives by carrying out building work, environmental projects and baking. The beautiful islands are also a perfect place to luxuriate, relax, cruise, golf or shop.

Other organizations offering projects in Fiji:
Academic Treks: www.academictreks.com
Earthwatch Institute: www.earthwatch.org
Fiji Diving & Volunteering: www.diving-fiji.com
Madventurer (sports, teaching & community projects):
  www.madventurer.compage
Projects Abroad: www.projects-abroad.org
Volunteer Eco Students Abroad: www.vesabroad.com
World Horizons International: www.world-horizons.com

Marshall Islands

Marshall Islands Teaching Year
Organization: WorldTeach
Location: Placements in outer islands and in urban centers
Cost: None. Fully funded by Marshall Islands Department of Education
Duration: 1 year (Departure in mid- July) **Age:** 18-74
Contact: info@worldteach.org **Learn more:** www.worldteach.org
Special skills: Native English skills, bachelor's degree
Details: Volunteers teach in public elementary schools, high schools, and occasionally vocational schools in Majuro and on the outer islands. Volunteers should be prepared for the challenges of teaching in the Marshalls. Schools on the outer islands lack basic supplies that are taken for granted in the United States, and volunteers often purchase pens, paper, and markers before leaving for the country. Furthermore,  volunteers may have to teach students with a wide range of English skills. While these circumstances may be frustrating at first, successful volunteers will be adept at finding solutions that enable them to teach effectively despite the limited resources of the islands. Most volunteers live with host families, while some will live in

teacher housing provided by their school. Houses are basic, but wherever possible volunteers will have their own room or sleeping area.

Micronesia

Federated States of Micronesia Teaching Year

Organization: WorldTeach
Location: Kosrae & Phonpei
Cost: None, Fully funded by Kosare & Pohnpai Departments of Education
Duration: 1 year (Departure in mid-July) **Age:** 18-74
Contact: info@worldteach.org **Learn more:** www.worldteach.org
Special skills: Native English Speaker, Bachelor's degree
Details: Volunteers should be prepared to teach math, science or English and be flexible to the needs of the school. Applicants with college classes in math and science will be given preference, although a math or science degree is not a requirement. Pohnpeian and Kosraen are the native languages, but English is commonly spoken throughout the FSM, especially on Pohnpei. High school students will know English to varying degrees from fluent to beginner. Classes will be taught in English. You will live in Kolonia, the main town on Pohnpei or in Madolenihmw or Kitti, the sites of the two rural high schools on the island. Volunteers will live together in apartments or houses and not with host families. There are also positions available to teach English/math at the College of Micronesia (Master's degree required).

Other organizations offering projects in Micronesia:
Earthwatch Institute: www.earthwatch.org
Habitat for Humanity International: www.habitat.org
Leap Now: www.leapnow.org

New Zealand

Rainforest Recovery and Sustainable Living Project

Organization: Earthwise Living Foundation New Zealand
Location: Earthwise Valley, Coromandel Peninsula, New Zealand
Cost: Variable, a sliding scale donation is requested

Duration: 6 weeks to 6 months   **Age:** 18
Contact: volunteer@earthwisevalley.org
Learn more: www.earthwisevalley.org

Special skills: Just enthusiasm and willingness to give of oneself

Details: At Earthwise Valley they're taking direct action to create an ecologically sound Centre for Sustainable Living. This includes revitalizing degraded farmland by replanting rainforest species, growing and planting fruit trees, controlling animal pests and weeds, using organic and permacultural techniques. The Valley relies on your support and needs your donations, advice and physical volunteer labor to make a difference. The Residential Volunteer Programme suits people interested in learning about sustainable living, enjoying the outdoors, and living a saner, richer and simpler life. Earthwise Valley runs ecoAdventure trips – one per week and a big one every 6 weeks – sea-kayaking, rock-climbing, hiking, camping, and more. Take part as a residential volunteer and you'll experience New Zealand in a very special way while making a real contribution to nature.

New Zealand Nature Program

Organization: Global Volunteer Network
Location: New Zealand's capital city of Wellington, which is perched on the shores of a deep natural harbor surrounded by wooded hills.
Cost: $697 for 2 weeks   **Duration:** 2 weeks to 3 months   **Age:** 18
Contact: info@volunteer.org.nz   **Learn more:** www.volunteer.org.nz
Details: This program is located in one of the most picturesque cities in the world. You will join a small team of volunteers working to preserve, monitor, and reestablish the natural environment in the Wellington region and beyond. Prepare yourself to encounter the challenges of 'hands on' conservation and environmental restoration work in native forests, nature reserves and rugged coastlines. Two of these projects, however, provide the opportunities to work in other regions of New Zealand. The work that you will be involved with is typically a combination of direct habitat restoration (e.g. predator control, tree planting, invasive weed removal) and monitoring re-vegetation growth rates etc.

Heal the Earth Program

Organization: Global Volunteer Network
Location: New Zealand's capital city of Wellington, which is perched on the shores of a deep natural harbor surrounded by wooded hills.

Cost: $697 for 2 weeks   **Duration:** 2 weeks to 3 months   **Age:** 18
Contact: info@volunteer.org.nz   **Learn more:**
www.volunteer.org.nz
Details: Volunteers will work in the GVN Wellington office alongside
their environmental team. You will educate, debate and take action by
expressing your views. Work is tailored to the individual and may
involve article writing, public lectures, discussions, presentations,
research and involvement in local environmental groups. This is an
opportunity to develop your own ideas and to educate and raise
awareness of environmental issues as well as seeing efforts within the
local community. As well as your work in the office, you will spend
several days a week working alongside volunteers within the New
Zealand Nature Program. On these days you will have the opportunity
to aid local organizations in their work, getting first hand, on-the-
ground experience in New Zealand's own conservation and
environmental restoration efforts.

Southern Encounter

Organization: Hands Up Holidays
Location: Catlins, on New Zealand's, South Island
Cost: $3,000 per person, based on sharing a room.
Duration: 4 days volunteering/15 day trip
Age: 16 years unless accompanied by an adult
Contact: info@handsupholidays.com
Learn more: www.handsupholidays.com
Details: New Zealand is famed for its remarkable scenery of lakes,
mountains and volcanoes, and friendly, welcoming people. Enjoy the
rewards and fun of working on an environmental conservation project
in a "hidden gem" part of New Zealand; help to ensure the ongoing
existence of native species, including Yellow-Eyed Penguins, restore
natural habitats and reduce the threat of pests. One of the highlights
following your conservation volunteer project is a visit to the world-
renowned Doubtful Sound. An overnight cruise is the best way to
discover the fur seals and bottlenose dolphins frolicking in the coves.
For the thrill seekers, the adrenalin capital of Queenstown is the next
stop.

Other organizations offering projects in New Zealand:

Conservation Volunteers of New Zealand:
  www.conservationvolunteers.co.nz
i-to-i: www.i-to-i.com
International Student Volunteers: www.isvonline.com
Transitions Abroad: www.transitionsabroad.com
Travelers Worldwide: www.travellersworldwide.com
United Planet: www.unitedplanet.org

Volunteers for International Partnership:
www.partnershipvolunteers.org

Papua New Guinea

Habitat Global Village Trip

Organization: Habitat for Humanity
Location: Teams are able to work at seven different project locations.
Cost: $1,700 to $1,800 **Duration:** 12 days
Age: 18, international trip participants must be at least 14-years-old, and be accompanied by a legal guardian or be part of an established group.
Contact: gv@habitat.org, 1-800-HABITAT (422-4828), ext. 7530,
Learn more: www.habitat.org
Special skills: Global Village teams are open to all with a willingness to work hard, learn new skills and explore a new culture. Many of the trips require strenuous manual labor, so all participants should be in good health.
Details: Eighty-five percent of Papua New Guinea's population live in rural areas and make their livelihood from subsistence agriculture and cultivation of export crops. Habitat for Humanity Papua New Guinea was formed in 1983 in Port Moresby. HPNG uses the Community Build housing microfinance model to involve an entire village or neighborhood in a house building or renovation program. In Papua New Guinea, where land and raw materials are owned by an entire village and two or three families share one house, Community Build helps to leverage resources and reduce housing costs. Habitat also uses the Save and Build model, in which 10 to 12 families form a savings group to save for the cost of building houses and construction materials. Home partners are also expected to put in their own labor to build their own houses.

Other organizations offering projects in Papua New Guinea

Australian Volunteers International: www.australianvolunteers.com
Catholic Medial Mission Board: www.cmmb.org
CUSO-VSO: www.cuso.org
Kids Alive International: www.kidsalive.org
New Frontiers Health Force: www.newfrontiershf.com
OceansWatch: oceanswatch.org
Samaritan's Purse: www.samaritanspurse.org
Volunteers for Economic Growth Alliance: www.vegaalliance.org

Samoa

Organizations offering projects in Samoa
South Pacific Business Development: www.spbd.ws
Transitions Abroad: www.transitionsabroad.com

Vanuatu

Family Volunteers: Turtles & Community Development
Organization: Global Visions International
Location: Moso Island
Cost: $2,320 for 4 weeks   **Duration:** 2 to 4 weeks
Age: Due to the varying group dynamics of different families (for example the number of children and ages of children), each application is dealt with on a case-by-case basis. Please call GVI directly to discuss your family's volunteer travel requirements.
Contact: info@gviusa.com   **Learn more:** www.gviusa.com
Special skills: Global Village teams are open to all with a willingness to work hard, learn new skills and explore a new culture. Many of the trips require strenuous manual labor, so all participants should be in good health.
Details: Volunteering with turtles as a part of vital sea turtle conservation will take you to the turquoise waters and golden sands of Vanuatu, voted the 'happiest place on earth' in 2006 by the New Economics Foundation. This grassroots effort to protect sea turtles is run by the inhabitants of Tasiriki village on Moso Island, from the long-term nesting survey that was started in 2006 in conjunction with Wan Smolbag and GVI. Joining this volunteer program will also give you the chance to try your hand at many other activities that occur in the village, such as reef surveying, teaching at the village school and cooking local food. In your spare time you can snorkel on tropical reefs, learn to dive or just sit with your new friends in the village.

Other organizations offering projects in Vanuatu:
Service Civil International: www.sci-ivs.org
Habitat for Humanity International: www.habitat.org
OceansWatch: oceanswatch.org
Project Marc (medical): www.project-marc.org

Archeology and Historical Preservation

South America
Easter Island (Rapa Nui) Culture – Chile
North America
Preservation of Cultural History via Technology – Mexico
Creating Affordable Housing – United States (IL)
Mammoth Graveyard Excavation – United States (SD)
Pueblo Indian Site Archeology – United States (CO)
Asia
Saving Armenia's Architectural Heritage – Armenia
Chairro Gompa (Monastery) Restoration Project – Nepal
Origins of Angkor – Thailand
Europe
Saving Albania's Ottoman Architecture – Albania
Avgusta Traiana-Beroia-Borui Excavation Project – Bulgaria
Restoration & Documentation of Ancient Pottery Workshop – Bulgaria
Heraclea Lyncestis Excavation Project – Bulgaria
Fresco-Hunting Photo Expedition to Medieval Churches – Bulgaria
Conservation and Heritage in The Wild West of Iceland – Iceland
Nature and Heritage in the East of Iceland – Iceland
Archeodig Project/Archaeological Field School – Iceland

Social Awareness, Human Rights, Peace

South America
Support Communities Affected by Mining – Argentina
Women's Rights Center – Argentina
Reproductive Health Campaign – Peru
Human Rights Campaign Against Racism in Peru – Peru
Promoción de Derechos Humanos – Uruguay
Youth Care, Community and Conservation – Venezuela
North America
Prevention of Child Abuse Program – Belize
Indigenous Women's Assistance – Guatemala

Empowering Women – Mexico

Asia

Empowering Women in Rural India – India
Women Empowerment Program in India – India
Women's Empowerment with Greenforce – India

Africa

Refuge for Trafficked Women and Girls – Cote d'Ivoire (Ivory Caost)
Children Are Not For Sale – Cote d'Ivoire (Ivory Cost)
Raising Voices with Art and Creative Media – Cote d'Ivoire (Ivory Cost)
Human Rights Advocate – Ghana
Gender-Based Violence Program – Rwanda
Helping South African Women – South Africa
Women Empowerment & Village Banking – Uganda

Media: Writing, Music, Photography, Video & Communications

South America

Community Radio Operator – Argentina
Street Kids' Music Project – Bolivia
Media and Art Projects – Bolivia
Teaching 9th Graders Computer & Communication Skills – Columbia
Surf and Volunteer in Peru – Peru

North America

Family planning and HIV Education – Belize
Handbook and Film Creation – Canada
Manos de Colores – Guatemala
Preservation of Cultural History via Technology – Mexico

Asia

Mixed Projects for all Nature Lovers – India
Be a Miracle for Children – India
Media TV Project in Mongolia – Mongolia
Trek Program – Palestinian Territories

Europe

Reykjavík Photomarathon – Iceland

Africa

Raising Voices with Art and Creative Media – Cote d'Ivoire (Ivory Coast)
Health Programs Coordinator – Mali (French language health radio program)
Primate Sanctuary Build, Garden, Cook & Video – South Africa
St. Lucia Wildlife Photography and Conservation – South Africa
Music/Video Production and Promotion – Tanzania
Promo Video & Kids' Music/Dance Video Production – Uganda

Computers & IT Skills

South America
Collaboration on Solidarity Website Development – Argentina
Brazilian Rainforest Conservation Center – Brazil
Teaching 9th Graders Computer & Communication Skills – Columbia
North America
IT for the Dogs – Mexico
Asia
Mixed Projects for all Nature Lovers – India
Empowering Women in Rural India – India (teach)
Street Children Project – Philippines
Teaching Basic Computer or Advanced IT Skills – Thailand
Volunteer and Training Center in North Thailand – Thailand
Africa
Training Veterinary Nurses in Kamapala – Uganda
Care and Support to People Living with HIV/AIDS – Uganda

Teaching: Long-Term/Traditional Education in Schools

South America
Patagonia Sur Year – Chile
Chile DuocUC Year – Chile
Chile Ministry of Education Year – Chile
Chile Ministry of Education Semester – Chile
Columbia Teaching Year – Columbia
Ecuador Teacher Year – Ecuador
Guyana Teaching Year – Guyana

North America
Costa Rica Teaching Year – Costa Rica
Cloud Forest School – Costa Rica
Teacher's Assistant Intern at an Environmental School – Costa Rica
Costa Rica Teaching Summer – Costa Rica
Jungle School Teachers Assistant – Honduras
Asia
Hunan Providence Year – China
China Summer – China
Europe
Bulgaria Teaching Summer – Bulgaria
Poland Teaching Summer – Poland
Africa
Teach, Empower and Impact – Ghana
Namaskar Primary School – Ghana
Triumph Care & Development Centre – Ghana
Kwahu Tafo: UVO – Ghana
Teach In Ghana (TIG) – Ghana

GVN Ghana Teaching Program – Ghana
Teach in Small Town Ghana – Ghana
Education and Youth Development – Ghana
Kenya's Maasailand Teaching &/or Medical Program – Kenya
Teaching in Kenya – Kenya
Kenya Program: Teaching Project – Kenya
F-SHAM of Faith Girls Academy – Liberia
Namibia Teaching Year – Namibia
Namibia Teaching Semester – Namibia
Namibia Teaching Summer – Namibia
Rwanda Teaching Year – Rwanda
South Africa Teaching Summer – South Africa
Village Primary School Teacher – Uganda
Oceania
American Samoa Teaching Year – American Samoa
Marshall Islands Teaching Year – Marshall Islands
Federated States of Micronesia Teaching Year – Micronesia

Teaching in/out of Schools, Shorter-Term, Assistants...

South America
Arutam Rainforest Reserve – Ecuador
Work in a Hostel and a School – Ecuador
Small Indigenous Community Volunteering – Ecuador
Teaching Rural Schools for the Andean Bear Project – Ecuador
Teachers´ Assistants for the Andean Bear Project – Ecuador
School Support Program – Ecuador
Summer Volunteer Program (English & Math) – Ecuador
Teaching Children in Guayaquil – Ecuador
Work with Nursery Children – Peru
Teaching Primary Grade School – Peru
The Mountain School – Peru
CEP Shanty Town School – Peru
Peruvian Elementary School Volunteer Program – Peru
Home for Teenage Mothers – Peru
Youth Care, Community and Conservation – Venezuela
North America
Campus Volunteer at an Environmental School – Costa Rica
Teaching English in Low Income Schools – Costa Rica
At-Risk Children's Programs – Costa Rica
DREAM Guzman Ariza Summer School & Camp – Dominican Republic
Children's Health Education– Guatemala
Manos de Colores – Guatemala
Youth Education and Achievement – Guatemala
CENEOH – Haiti

Teaching Children in Ghana – Ghana
Education and Youth Development – Ghana
Conversational English and Assisting Teachers – Ghana
Teach and Care for Orphans – Kenya
Internally Displaced Persons (IDP) Camp Project – Kenya
Kenya's Maasailand Teaching &/or Medical Program – Kenya
Teaching at Kaloleni Junior Academy – Kenya
Integrated Rehabilitation Center – Kenya
Teaching in Kenya -- Kenya
Kenya Program: Teaching Project – Kenya
F-SHAM of Faith Girls Academy – Liberia
Volunteer in a Rural Village – Madagascar
Pre-School and English Teaching – Mozambique
Preschool Teaching and HIV/AIDS Awareness – Mozambique
Namibia Teaching Summer – Namibia
Rwanda Literacy Program – Rwanda
Children in Christ Services School &/or Clinic Work – Sierra Leone
Children's Programs in South Africa – South Africa
South Africa Teaching Summer – South Africa
Wildlife Conservation, Community & Sports Combo – South Africa
South Africa Youth Program – South Africa
South Africa Youth Primary Teaching Program – South Africa
Cape Town Teaching and Community Development – South Africa
Soweto Pre-School Volunteering – South Africa
Rural Community Pre-school Volunteering – South Africa
Life Skills Volunteering – South Africa
Orphanage Volunteer Tutoring – South Africa
All Aspects of Running a School: Teach, Build, Fundraise – Tanzania
Teaching in Tanzania – Tanzania
Orphans' Education & Skills Development – Uganda
Village Primary School Teacher – Uganda

Special Education & Handicapped Assistance

South America
Bring Happiness to Disable Kids – Bolivia
Children with Physical and Learning Disabilities – Bolivia
Special Education Program – Ecuador
Children with Down's Syndrome (& other disabilities) – Peru
St. Toribio School for Special Needs Children – Peru
Peru Childcare Project – Peru
Youth Care, Community and Conservation – Venezuela (Therapeutic Horseback Riding)
Assisting People with Disabilities – Argentina
Helping Children with Speech and Hearing Impairments – Bolivia
Deaf Education Program in Guayaquil – Ecuador

North America
Deaf Education in Kingston – Jamaica
Equine Therapy with Disabled Kids – Mexico
Community Outreach Project – Panama
Asia
Wheelchairs for Land Mine Victims – Cambodia
People with Disabilities and Orphanage Programs – China
Daya Orphanage – India (runs school for slum children)
Mother Theresa Society for the Handicapped – India
Special Needs Children in India – India
Tennis for Blind Children – Japan
Health Project at Children's Hospital – Mongolia
Deaf Education – Philippines
Angels' Haven Care for Developmentally Disabled – South Korea
Aspiration Center for Mentally-Disabled Children – Vietnam
Caring for Disabled Children in Vietnam – Vietnam
Victims of Agent Orange – Vietnam
Europe
Orphanage Home to 250 Babies and Children – Bulgaria
*Occupational Therapy, Applied Sciences, Youth Development and
    Education – Bulgaria*
Romania Program with a Christian Mission – Romania
Work with Romania's Abandoned Children – Romania
Africa
Fostering a Love of Learning – Morocco
Community Building, Education and Health – Togo
Physical Therapy Internship Program – Uganda

Teaching: Skills, Workshops & Specialty Classes

(Music, sports, arts, dance, computers, literacy, handicrafts, photography, parenting, conservation, communications, life-skills, vocational, etc.)

South America
Tutoring Children and Teenagers – Argentina
Helping Hands – Argentina
Child Minding Center – Bolivia
Helping Children with Speech and Hearing Impairments – Bolivia
Creative Education – Bolivia
Work with Youth in a Detention Center – Bolivia
Working in a Favela (Squatter Community) in Rio – Brazil
Casa do Caminho – Brazil

Arts, Sports and Dance Projects in Favellas – Brazil
Fostering Leadership in Street Youth – Columbia
Caring for Children and Adults with Special Needs – Ecuador
Street Children Work – Ecuador
Paraguarí, Paraguay: Health – Paraguay

Honduras Teaching Project – Honduras
Panama Literacy Project – Panama
Asia
Rainbow Orphanage – Cambodia
GVN Cambodia Program – Cambodia
Volunteer in a Village in Cambodia – Cambodia
Teach English at Orphanages – Cambodia
Orphanage Care Service Learning Program – Cambodia
Teach English Abroad Service Learning Program – Cambodia
Teaching English in Yantai – China
Child Labour School, Resource Project, Children's Homes –- India
Teaching English to the Santhal Community – India
Empowering Women in Rural India – India
Bali Bound – Indonesia (tour with volunteering)
*Teach or Interpret Onboard a Chartered Passenger Ship –
   Japan/Global*
Teaching English in Ulaanbaatar – Mongolia
Orphan Children's Summer Camp – Mongolia
Teaching English in Kathmandu, Pokhara and Chitwan – Nepal
Nepal English Teaching Project – Nepal
Teaching English in Monasteries – Nepal
Unique Eco Tourism Project in South Nepal – Nepal
From the Tsunami to the Classroom – Thailand
Teaching English in Northern Thailand – Thailand
Elephant Camp in Chiang Mai – Thailand

Elephant Camp Project – Thailand
Teaching Monks – Thailand
Single Mothers in Crisis & Childcare – Thailand
English Education Service-Learning Program – Thailand
Integrated Buddhist, Teaching English, & Orphanage Op – Thailand
Buddhist Immersion-EFL Service-Learning Program – Thailand
English at Home – Turkey
Working with Local NGOs – Vietnam
Friendship Kindergarten for Disadvantaged Children – Vietnam
University Teaching Program – Vietnam
Center for Disadvantaged Children – Vietnam
Europe
Teach at the Waldorf School – Germany
Orphanage Volunteering/English Teaching – Ukraine
Africa
Teach English While Experiencing Egyptian Culture – Egypt
GVN Ethiopia Program: Knowledge, Kids & Beyond – Ethiopia
HQ International Teaching in Ghana – Ghana
Conversational English and Assisting Teachers – Ghana
Good Community Good Work – Morocco

Pre-School and English Teaching – Mozambique
Volunteer teachers of English Language – Sudan
Watoto wa Africa – Tanzania

Teaching & Tutoring Languages (non English)

South America
Teach French to Eager Kids – Peru
Adult Literacy Program (Spanish) – Guatemala
Asia
Teach or Interpret Onboard a Chartered Passenger Ship –
 Japan/Global (Spanish)
University Teaching Program (French) – Vietnam
Africa
Refuge for Trafficked Women and Girls – Cote d'Ivoire (French)
Good Community Good Work – Morocco (French)

Sports Programs, Teaching & Events

South America
Coaching Sports and Physical Education - Bolivia
Arts, Sports and Dance Projects in Favellas- Brazil
Teaching Sports and Physical Education – Peru
North America
Summer Camp for Disadvantaged Kids – Belize
Community Park Volunteer – Guatemala
Asia
Tennis for Blind Children – Japan
Europe
Transnatura Mountain Bike Stage – Greece
Prespa Children, Prespa in Motion – Greece
Summer School for Deprived Children in Rural Romania – Romania
Africa
Kwahu Tafo: UVO – Ghana
Youth Soccer Coaching – Ghana
Teaching at Kaloleni Junior Academy – Kenya
Sports Education Program – Kenya
Sports Development in Underprivileged Communities – South Africa
Wildlife Conservation, Community & Sports Combo – South Africa
Zero to Hero Sports Adventure & Volunteering – South Africa
Bicycle Volunteer Project – South Africa
Malalo (Bridge) Sports Project – Zambia
Livingstone Sports Development – Zambia

Zoological & Environmental Education

South America

Outdoor Activities and Education – Argentina
Brazilian Rainforest Conservation Center – Brazil
Teaching Rural Schools for the Andean Bear Project – Ecuador
Teachers´ Assistants for the Andean Bear Project – Ecuador
La Hesperia Reserve Project – Ecuador
Congal Biological Reserve – Ecuador
Island Conservation – Ecuador
Amazon Rainforest Wildlife Rehab & Relocation – Peru
Saving the Environment in the Sacred Valley of the Incas – Peru
Surf and Volunteer in Peru – Peru

North America

Furry Felines for Fuzzy Feelings – Belize
Environmental and Cultural Preservation– Belize
Domestic Animal Rescue and Education – Costa Rica
Environmental Educator – Costa Rica
Campus Volunteer at an Environmental School – Costa Rica
Cloud Forest School – Costa Rica
Teacher's Assistant Intern at an Environmental School – Costa Rica
Teach Environmental Health to 5-12 Year Olds – Honduras
Costalegre Conservation and Sustainability Program – Mexico
Tobago Coastal Ecosystems Mapping Project – Trinidad and Tobago

Asia

Coral Cay Conservation – Cambodia
Juara Turtle Project – Malaysia
Marine Conservation Expedition – Malaysia
Community Maintenance Projects – Nepal
Wild Animal Rescue Project – Singapore
Island Community Eco Education – Thailand
Elephant Refuge and Education Centre – Thailand
Transporting Instruction and Environmental Camp – Vietnam
University Teaching Program – Vietnam

Europe

Natural Resources and Wildlife – Bulgaria
Reykjavík Photomarathon – Iceland
Sea Turtle Preservation & Education – Italy
The BEARS Project – Slovakia

Africa

Coral Reef Monitoring Project – Madagascar
Community Development and Conservation – Madagascar
Marine Conservation Expedition – Madagascar
Lemur Volunteer Venture – Madagascar
Wildlife Conservation, Community & Sports Combo – South Africa
Marine Conservation in Plettenberg Bay – South Africa

Oceania
Wwoofers and Volunteers – Australia
Rainforest Recovery and Sustainable Living Project – New Zealand

Ecological Reserve Development, Flora/Fauna Census

South America
Amazon Reserve Project – Ecuador
Galapagos: San Cristobal Reserve – Ecuador
La Hesperia Reserve Project – Ecuador
Bilsa Biological Reserve – Ecuador
Congal Biological Reserve – Ecuador
Lalo Loor Biological Reserve – Ecuador
Saving the Environment in the Sacred Valley of the Incas – Peru
Animal and Environmental Conservation – Peru
Jungle Conservation Around Cusco – Peru
Conservation/Wildlife Project – Peru
North America
Bahamian Reef Survey – Bahamas
Materials Production Assistant – Costa Rica
Migratory and Resident Bird Monitoring Program – Costa Rica
Resident Bird Survey – Costa Rica
Costa Rica's Sustainable Coffee – Costa Rica
Safeguarding the Coral Reefs of Cayos Cochinos – Honduras
Costalegre Conservation and Sustainability Program – Mexico
Puerto Rico's Rainforest – Puerto Rico
Mapping Change in California's Mountains – United States
Asia
Marine Conservation – Cambodia
Kibbutz Lotan Eco Volunteer Program – Israel
Desert Wildlife Reserve – Israel
Unique Eco Tourism Project in South Nepal – Nepal
Southern Leyte Coral Reef Conservation Project – Philippines
Integrated Eco-Cultural Resource Management Project – Sri Lanka
Volunteer at a National Park in Thailand – Thailand
Europe
Natural Resources and Wildlife – Bulgaria
Cetacean Sanctuary Research – Italy
Faia Brava Fauna Monitoring Programme – Portugal
Faia Brava Woodlands Fire Surveillance & Conservation – Portugal
Mountain Ghosts: Snow Leopards and other Animals – Romania
Wolf Census Project – Slovakia
Africa
Survey Endangered Gorillas and Chimpanzees – Cameroon
Primate and Sea Turtle Census – Equatorial Guinea
Volunteer in a Rural Village – Madagascar

Shark Volunteer Experience – South Africa
Oceania
Dolphins of Western Australia – Australia
Marine Conservation Expedition – Fiji
Marine Conservation & Learn to Dive – Fiji

Wildlife Care & Rescue

South America
Eco Volunteering and Project Puma – Argentina
Black Howler Monkey Rehabilitation – Argentina
Animal Conservation – Argentina
Wild Animal Care and Rehabilitation Project – Bolivia
Animal Conservation in Santa Cruz – Bolivia
Wild Animal Rescue and Conservation – Ecuador
Animal Rescue Center – Ecuador
Amazon Rainforest Wildlife Rehab & Relocation – Peru
Conservation/Wildlife Project – Peru
North America
Habitat Evaluation for Wildlife Reintroduction – Canada
Wildlife Rescue Center Work – Cost Rica
Sanctuary Sloths, Smiles and More Sloths – Cost Rica
Eco-Reserve and Animal Rescue Center – Cost Rica
Guatemala Wildlife Rescue Center – Guatemala
Honduras Environment Iguana Project – Honduras
Sea Turtle, Crocodile and Iguana Conservation Project – Mexico
Community Outreach Project – Panama
Asia
Panda Keeper Assistant– China
Giant Panda Conservation – China
Urban Wildlife Rescue – India
VSPCA Sanctuary Shelter & Volunteer Office Work – India
Animal Shelter and Hospital – India
Wildlife Rescue Indonesia – Indonesia
Bird Rescue North Sulawesi – Indonesia
Sulawesi Macaque Rehabilitation – Indonesia
Desert Wildlife Reserve – Israel
Animal Shelter and Sanctuary Volunteers – Malaysia
Wild Animal Rescue Project – Singapore
Elephant Helpers, Veterinarians & Vet Students – Thailand
Elephant Camp in Chiang Mai – Thailand
Gibbon Rehabilitation Project – Thailand
Elephant Refuge and Education Centre – Thailand
WFFT Gibbon Rehabilitation Centre – Thailand
Sanctuary for Southeast Asia's Bears – Thailand
Thailand Animal Sanctuary Program – Thailand

Marine and Sea Turtle Conservation – Costa Rica
Olive Ridley & Leatherback Sea Turtle Programs – Costa Rica
Camaronal Sea Turtle Rescue – Costa Rica
Wildlife Rescue Center – Costa Rica
CCC's Research Programs in Tortuguero – Costa Rica
Sea Turtle Conservation for Teens– Costa Rica
Monitoring Nesting Leatherbacks & Hawksbills Turtles – Grenada
La Gloria Sea Turtle Conservation Program – Mexico
Leatherback Turtle Conservation – Panama
Asia
Mixed Projects for all Nature Lovers – India
Orangutan Research – Indonesia
Juara Turtle Project – Malaysia
Przewalski Wild Horse Repatriation – Mongolia
Unique Eco Tourism Project in South Nepal – Nepal
Integrated Eco-Cultural Resource Management Project – Sri Lanka
Sea Turtle Conservation Project – Thailand
Remote Island Sea Turtle Conservation Project – Thailand
Volunteer at a National Park in Thailand – Thailand
Marine Research and Rescue Unit – Thailand
Europe
Natural Resources and Wildlife – Bulgaria
Ionian Dolphin Project: Delphi's Dolphins – Greece
Zakynthos Island Sea Turtle Conservation – Greece
Sea Turtle Preservation & Education – Italy
Cetacean Sanctuary Research – Italy
Bottlenose Dolphins of Sardinia Island – Italy
Faia Brava Fauna Monitoring Programme – Portugal
Azores: Studying Whales, Dolphins and Turtles – Portugal (Azore Islands)
Mountain Ghosts: Snow Leopards and other Animals – Romania
Wolf Census Project – Slovakia
The BEARS Project – Slovakia
White Wilderness: Winter Wolf and Lynx Tracking – Slovakia
Whales and Dolphins of Moray Firth – United Kingdom
Africa
Research Assistant with Cheetah Conservation – Botswana
Survey Endangered Gorillas and Chimpanzees – Cameroon
Sea Turtles Protection Project – Cape Verde
Primate and Sea Turtle Census – Equatorial Guinea
Elephants of Tsavo – Kenya
Community Development and Conservation – Madagascar
Lemur Volunteer Venture – Madagascar
Mauritian Dolphin Volunteer Experience – Mauritius
Desert Elephant / Human Cohabitation Project – Namibia

Domestic Animal Care & Rescue: Dogs, Cats...

Animal Rescue and Care Tour Program with Yoga – India
Himalayan Animal Welfare: Dogs of Dharamsala – India (tour combo)
Bali Animal Clinic Helper – Indonesia
Bali Animals Business Management Consultant – Indonesia
Animal Shelter and Sanctuary Volunteers – Malaysia
Veterinary Spay/Neuter Field Clinic – Sri Lanka
Fun with Dogs: Shelter Help – Thailand
Providing Veterinary Care for Street Dogs – Thailand
Designers and Fundraisers for Dogs – Thailand
Island Animal Rescue: Clinic Assistant & Veterinary – Thailand
Europe
Animal Rescue for Volunteer Hearts – Bulgaria
Karpathos Island Animal Rescue – Greece
The Ark Rescue of Corfu – Greece
Animal Welfare: Ending the Tragedy for Greek Dogs – Greece
Africa
Abused Animal and Veterinary Assist Project – South Africa
Training Veterinary Nurses in Kamapala – Uganda
Hope for Dogs – Zambia
Oceania
Vet Treks & Animal Care ah la South Pacifica – Cook Islands

Domestic Animal Care & Rescue: Equine, Mixed Farm Animals

South America
Equine Aid to Underprivileged Working Animals – Peru
North America
Domestic Animal Rescue and Education – Costa Rica
Donkey Care and Rescue – Netherlands Antilles
Dogtown Doggie Duties – United States (UT)
Feline Friend Functions – United States (UT)
Farm Sanctuary Internship Programs – United States (CA & NY)
Asia
VSPCA Sanctuary Shelter & Volunteer Office Work – India
Indian Animal Welfare – India
Farm Animals and Beyond – India
Europe
Karpathos Island Animal Rescue – Greece
Africa
Kahama Donkey Welfare Project – Tanzania
Donkey Care, Health and Community Education – Zimbabwe

Veterinary and Animal Heath

South America
Small Animals Spay and Neuter Project – Peru
North America
Must Love Dogs: Veterinary, Socialization and Care – Mexico
M*A*S*H* Save Dogs and Cats - Fifty at a Time! – Panama
Asia
Mixed Projects for all Nature Lovers – India
Shelter Veterinarians and Rural Villages – India
Urban Wildlife Rescue – India
Animal Welfare and Public Health – India
Animal Shelter and Hospital – India
Indian Animal Welfare – India
Farm Animals and Beyond – India
Wildlife Rescue Indonesia – Indonesia
Bali Vetrinarian and Vetrinary Nursing – Indonesia
Bird Rescue North Sulawesi – Indonesia
Animal Shelter and Sanctuary Volunteers – Malaysia
Veterinary Spay/Neuter Field Clinic – Sri Lanka
Providing Veterinary Care for Street Dogs – Thailand
Island Animal Rescue: Clinic Assistant & Veterinary – Thailand
WFFT Wildlife Rescue Thailand – Thailand
Elephant Helpers, Veterinarians & Vet Students – Thailand
Africa
Vaccinations and Education on Farms in Abeokuta – Nigeria
Big 5 Wildlife and Conservation – South Africa
Abused Animal and Veterinary Assist Project – South Africa
Training Veterinary Nurses in Kamapala – Uganda
Donkey Care, Health and Community Education – Zimbabwe
Oceania
Vet Treks & Animal Care ah la South Pacifica – Cook Islands

Health: General, Mixed & Public Health Education

South America
Proyecto Horizonte:Uspha Uspha – Bolivia
Art to Heal for Burn Children - Bolivia
Health Care and Health Education – Brazil
Street Children Work – Ecuador
Summer Volunteer Program (rural health center) – Ecuador
Hospital in Ambato – Ecuador
Health Care Volunteer Vacation – Ecuador
Incawasi – Peru
Healthcare in Mountain Communities – Peru
Community Development-Helping Media Luna – Peru

Saving the Environment in the Sacred Valley of the Incas – Peru
Community Development-Helping Shismay – Peru
Peru Healthcare Project – Peru
Laughing Against All Odds – Uruguay

North America
Children's Health Education– Guatemala
Honduras Medical Project in Gracias - Honduras
Health Clinics and Education in Rural Villages – Mexico
Community Nutrition Program – Mexico

Asia
Integrated Orphanage Care, Teaching and Health – Cambodia
International Health Service Learning Program – Cambodia
Wheelchairs for Land Mine Victims – Cambodia
Aradhana Boys Children's Home – India
Street Children Work in India – India
Be a Miracle for Children – India
Remote Health Post Work in Nepal – Nepal
Provide Health Care and Education – Nepal
City Nutrition Office in the Philippines – Philippines
Street Children in Tacloban City – Philippines
Philippines Health Project – Philippines
Medical Health Projects – Philippines
Street Children Project – Philippines

Philippines Health Care in Tacloban City – Philippines

Europe
*Occupational Therapy, Applied Sciences, Youth Development and
    Education – Bulgaria*

Africa
Regional Hospital in Porto-Novo – Benin
Women and Children Center – Benin
*Speaking Out: Raising Awareness of HIV & AIDS – Cote d'Ivoire
    (Ivory Coast)*
Health Care and Health Education in Ghana – Ghana
Teach and Care for Orphans – Kenya (malnutrition)
Internally Displaced Persons (IDP) Camp Project – Kenya
Kenya's Maasailand Teaching &/or Medical Program – Kenya
Health Care and Medical Clinics – Kenya
Kenya Medical and Community Assistance – Kenya
Volunteer in a Rural Village – Madagascar
Health Programs Coordinator – Mail
*Rensida-Rede Nacional de Organizacoes de Pessoas vivendo com HIV
    – Mozambique*
Children in Christ Services School &/or Clinic Work – Sierra Leone
HIV/AIDS and TB Medical Project – South Africa
Rural Community Pre-school Volunteering – South Africa

Health Care and Medical Clinics– Kenya
Health Care Volunteering in Northern Madagascar – Madagascar
Volunteer in a Rural Village – Madagascar
Children in Christ Services School &/or Clinic Work – Sierra Leone
HIV/AIDS and TB Medical Project – South Africa
International Health Program – Tanzania
Physical Therapy Internship Program – Uganda
Global Health Volunteer – Uganda

Health Specialty Care Projects
(Dental, Vision, Prosthetics...)
North America
Health Clinics and Education in Rural Villages – Mexico
Asia
Free Dental Care for Underprivileged Children – Israel
Medical Health Projects – Philippines
Europe
Occupational Therapy, Applied Sciences, Youth Development and Education – Bulgaria (physical therapy...)
Regional Hospital in Porto-Novo – Benin (various specialties)
Medical Mission to Egypt – Egypt
AMURT Clinic Project – Akwakwaa – Ghana (midwives)
Africa
Health Care and Medical Clinics– Kenya (various specialties)
Health Care Volunteering in Northern Madagascar – Madagascar (dentistry)
Mental Health Matters – Nigeria (occupational therapists, physiotherapists)

HIV/AIDS Specific Health Care & Education
South America
Helping Hands – Argentina
HIV & AIDS Prevention – Brazil
North America
Family planning and HIV Education – Belize
Asia
Integrated Orphanage Care, Teaching and Health – Cambodia
HIV/AIDS Prevention Education Service Learning – Cambodia
International Health Service Learning Program – Cambodia
HIV Orphanage – Thailand
Africa
Speaking Out: Raising Awareness of HIV & AIDS – Cote d'Ivoire (Ivory Coast)
AMURT Clinic Project – Akwakwaa – Ghana

Woman's Health & Reproduction Education

Psychological Care & Social Work

South America
Social Work in Developing Communities – Peru
Home for Teenage Mothers – Peru
Laughing Against All Odds – Uruguay
Prevention of Child Abuse Program – Belize

North America
Center for Abused Children – Costa Rica
Nuevos Horizontes Home for Women and Children – Guatemala
Indigenous Women's Assistance – Guatemala
Work in a Children's Shelter – Mexico
Orphanage for Girls Run by Nuns – Nicaragua
Panama Children's Project – Panama

Asia
GVN India Women's & Children's Programs – India
Healthcare/Social Work: Women and Children – India
Women Empowerment Program in India – India
Street Children in Tacloban City – Philippines
Medical Health Projects – Philippines
Street Children Project – Philippines
Women's Assistance - Philippines
Vietnam Orphanage Program - Vietnam

Europe
*Occupational Therapy, Applied Sciences, Youth Development and
    Education – Bulgaria*
Romania Program with a Christian Mission – Romania
Work with Romania's Abandoned Children – Romania

Africa
Regional Hospital in Porto-Novo – Benin
Refuge for Trafficked Women and Girls – Cote d'Ivoire (Ivory Coast)
Health Care and Medical Clinics – Kenya
Health Care Volunteering in Northern Madagascar – Madagascar
Mental Health Matters – Nigeria
Gender-Based Violence Program – Rwanda
La No Che Projects – Tanzania
Village Outreach Worker – Uganda

Women's Shelters

North America
Casa de los Amigos Center for Peace – (Mexico)
Asia
Women Empowerment Program in India – India
Women's Assistance - Philippines
Single Mothers in Crisis & Childcare – Thailand

Teach English at Orphanages – Cambodia
Integrated Orphanage Care, Teaching and Health – Cambodia
Orphanage Care Service Learning Program – Cambodia
People with Disabilities and Orphanage Programs – China
Aradhana Boys Children's Home – India
Daya Orphanage – India
Jaipur Orphanage – India
Mother Theresa Society for the Handicapped – India
Bring Education to the Heart of India – India
Care for Rural Indian Children in Need – India
Be a Miracle for Children – India
Teach and Care for Orphans in Indonesia – Indonesia
Narayan Seva Childrens Home – Indonesia
Orphan Children's Summer Camp – Mongolia
Orphanage Volunteer Help – Mongolia
Compassion Orphanage – Nepal
Nandumaya Self-Sustaining Orphan Home – Nepal
Nepal Children's Home Project – Nepal
Orphanages in Nepal – Nepal
Pag-Amoma Childrens Place – Philippines
Field of Dreams – Philippines
Orphanage Assistance in the Philippines – Philippines
Teach and Care for Orphans in Chiang Rai – Thailand
HIV Orphanage – Thailand
Integrated Buddhist, Teaching English, & Orphanage Op – Thailand
Orphanage Care Service-Learning Program – Thailand
Vietnam Orphanage Program – Vietnam
Caring for Disabled Children in Vietnam – Vietnam
Victims of Agent Orange – Vietnam

Europe
Orphanage Home to 250 Babies and Children – Bulgaria
Occupational Therapy, Applied Sciences, Youth Development and
  Education – Bulgaria
Rasarit Kindergarten – Romania
Romania Program with a Christian Mission – Romania
Work with Romania's Abandoned Children – Romania
Orphanage Volunteering/English Teaching – Ukraine

Africa
Center for Troubled Youth –Benin
Women and Children Center – Benin
Our Children, Our Future – Cote d'Ivoire (Ivory Coast)
Triumph Care & Development Centre – Ghana
Orphanage and Child Care – Ghana
Children's Home/Orphanage – Ghana
Education and Youth Development – Ghana

At Risk Youth & Street Children Projects

Street Children Work in India – India
Healthcare/Social Work: Women and Children – India
Street Children in Tacloban City – Philippines
Philippines Childcare Project – Philippines
Street Children Assistance – Philippines
Youth House School and Disadvantaged Children – Vietnam
Europe
Summer School for Deprived Children in Rural Romania – Romania
Africa
School and Vocational Instruction – Cameroon
Children Are Not For Sale – Cote d'Ivoire (Ivory Coast)
Soweto Pre-School Volunteering– South Africa
Our Children, Our Future – Cote d'Ivoire (Ivory Coast)
Orphans and Vulnerable Kids Scholarship Project – Kenya
Good Community Good Work – Morocco
Fostering a Love of Learning – Morocco
Children in Christ Services School &/or Clinic Work – Sierra Leone
Fundraising/Office for Children in Christ Services – Sierra Leone
Bicycle Volunteer Project – South Africa
Orphan Care & Child-Headed Household Outreach – Uganda

Community or Youth Centers & After School Programs

South America
Child Minding Center – Bolivia
Working in a Favela (Squatter Community) in Rio – Brazil
Casa do Caminho – Brazil
Fostering Leadership in Street Youth – Columbia
Fighting Poverty with Education – Peru
Cusco Arts Haven – Peru
North America
Community Park Volunteer – Guatemala
GVN South Dakota Program – United States
Asia
Volunteer in Children's Art Center – Cambodia
Special Needs Children in India – India
Street Children Project – Philippines
Teaching Basic Computer or Advanced IT Skills – Thailand
Volunteer and Training Center in North Thailand – Thailand
Center for Disadvantaged Children – Vietnam
Europe
Rasarit Kindergarten – Romania
Africa
Kwahu Tafo: UVO – Ghana
Township Project in Capetown – South Africa
Life Skills Volunteering – South Africa

Women Empowerment & Village Banking – Uganda
Funding for Sustainable Development Projects – Uganda
Income Generation and Small Business Development – Uganda

Community/Rural Development & Poverty

South America
Stay Together – Argentina
Proyecto Horizonte: Uspha Uspha – Bolivia
Huancayo Community Education – Peru
Community Development-Helping Media Luna – Peru
Community Development-Helping Shismay – Peru
North America
Women's Empowerment and Development Project – Costa Rica
Community Development – Dominica (teens)
Helping Children through Community Development – Honduras
Rural Sustainable Development/Farm Life – Nicaragua
Asia
Teaching and Empowering – India
Integrated Eco-Cultural Resource Management Project – Sri Lanka
Island Community Eco Education – Thailand
Africa
Ghana Community Development Program – Ghana
Small Business Development – Ghana
Coral Reef Monitoring Project – Madagascar
Community Development and Conservation – Madagascar
Cape Town Teaching and Community Development – South Africa
Soweto Grassroots Volunteering – South Africa
Solar Cooker Volunteer Project – South Africa
Youth Empowerment & Community Service – Uganda
Funding for Sustainable Development Projects – Uganda
Care and Support to People Living with HIV/AIDS – Uganda
Income Generation and Small Business Development – Uganda
Oceania
Family Volunteers: Turtles & Community Development – Vanuatu

Habitat, Building, Construction & Maintenance

South America
Community Building Projects in Salvador – Brazil
Community Development in Piracicaba – Brazil
Rebuilding Homes in the Amazon Jungle – Ecuador
Galapagos: San Cristobal Reserve – Ecuador
Sustainable Building Projects – Ecuador
Global Village Trip to Paraguay – Paraguay
Reconstruction of Pisco – Peru

Nursery School Building for Orphaned/Vulnerable Kids – Kenya
Habitat Global Village Trip – Kenya
Community Development and Conservation – Madagascar
Taste of Morocco – Morocco (tour combo)
Pre-School and English Teaching – Mozambique
Primate Sanctuary Build, Garden, Cook & Video – South Africa
Township Project in Capetown – South Africa
Housing Initiative – South Africa
Cape Town Teaching and Community Development – South Africa
All Aspects of Running a School: Teach, Build, Fundraise – Tanzania
Community Building, Education and Health – Togo
Construction of Childrens' Lavatories at School – Uganda
Community Support, Awareness and Development – Uganda
Oceania
Habitat Global Village Trip – Papua New Guinea

Hostels, Kibbutzes Eco-Lodges & Hosts

South America
Hostal Volunteer in Beautiful Samaipata – Bolivia
Help Run an Award Winning Ecolodge – Ecuador
Work in a Hostel and a School – Ecuador
North America
Reception at The Children's Eternal Rainforest – Costa Rica
Asia
Kibbutz Lotan Eco Volunteer Program – Israel
Ecotourism Development in Nazareth – Israel

Nonprofit Fundraising, Grants, Marketing & Office Skills

South America
Non-Profit Tourism in the Bolivian Highlands – Bolivia
Wild Animal Rescue and Conservation – Ecuador
Island Conservation – Ecuador
Fighting Poverty with Education – Peru
Torre Torre – Peru
Supporting Artisans in the Sacred Valley – Peru
North America
Animal Shelter and Veterinary Clinic – Bahamas
Furry Felines for Fuzzy Feelings – Belize
Sanctuary Sloths, Smiles and More Sloths – Cost Rica
Energy Systems Technician – Cost Rica
Project Administration – Guatemala (families of city dump)
Deaf Education in Kingston – Jamaica
IT for the Dogs – Mexico
Agriculture and Eco-Tourism Project – Nicaragua

Interpretation/Guides, Education & Eco-Tourism Development

Reykjavík Photomarathon – Iceland
Volunteer in La Casita Verde – Spain
Africa
Ghana Community Development Program – Ghana
Everything Elephant-Work with Elephants – South Africa
Oceania
Dolphins of Western Australia – Australia

Art, Theater & Other Cultural Projects

South America
Art to Heal for Burn Children – Bolivia
Orphanage with Unique Arts Program – Bolivia
Street Kids' Music Project – Bolivia
Arts, Sports and Dance Projects in Favellas – Brazil
Sacred Valley Arts Orphanage – Peru
North America
Alternative Education Project in Mayan Village – Guatemala
Prespa Children, Prespa in Motion – Greece
Asia
Volunteer in Children's Art Center – Cambodia
Trek Program – Palestinian Territories
Wild Animal Rescue Project – Singapore
Africa
Raising Voices with Art and Creative Media – Cote d'Ivoire (Ivory Coast)
Life Skills Volunteering – South Africa

Museum Work

North America
Mammoth Graveyard Excavation – United States (SD)
Europe
Whales and Tourism – Iceland

Refugee and Work Camps

South America
Sustainable Agriculture & Community Projects – Brazil (Teens)
Africa
Internally Displaced Persons (IDP) Camp Project – Kenya
GVN Kenya Medical/Health Program – Kenya
Work Camps in Kenya – Kenya

Translators
North America
Health Clinics and Education in Rural Villages – Mexico (translators)
Asia
Teach or Interpret Onboard a Chartered Passenger Ship –
  Japan/Global

Projects for Age 15–17 (may/may not require an adult)
South America
Eco Volunteering and Project Puma – Argentina (16)
Arutam Rainforest Reserve – Ecuador (15)
Rebuilding Homes in the Amazon Jungle – Ecuador (16)
Orphanage & Development Center for Infants/Toddlers – Ecuador
(16)
Amazon Conservation – Ecuador (17)
Huancayo Community Education – Peru
Promoción de Derechos Humanos (human rights) – Uruguay (16)

North America
Marine Conservation & Learn to Dive – Bahamas (17)
Wild Dolphin Research – Bahamas (16)
Sea Turtle Conservation Program – Costa Rica
Bambu Indigenous Reserve – Costa Rica
Monitoring Nesting Leatherbacks & Hawksbills Turtles – Grenada
Guatemala Wildlife Rescue Center – Guatemala
Helping Children through Community Development – Honduras (16)
Asia
Sunderbans Smiles – India (16) (tour with volunteering)
Women's Empowerment with Greenforce– India (17)
Ultimate India: In Style – India (16)
Bali Bound – Indonesia (16) (tour with volunteering)
Juara Turtle Project – Malaysia
Teaching English in Ulaanbaatar – Mongolia (17)
Media TV Project in Mongolia – Mongolia (17)
Orphan Children's Summer Camp – Mongolia (17)
Orphanage Volunteer Help – Mongolia (17)
Community Development and Everest Trek – Nepal (17) (tour with
  volunteering)
Elephant Sanctuary – Thailand (17)
Thailand Hill Tribe Program – Thailand (17)
Europe
Avgusta Traiana-Beroia-Borui Excavation Project – Bulgaria
Restoration & Documentation of Ancient Pottery Workshop –
Bulgaria
Heraclea Lyncestis Excavation Project – Bulgaria

Fresco-Hunting Photo Expedition to Medieval Churches – Bulgaria
Reykjavík Photomarathon – Iceland
Conservation and Heritage in The Wild West of Iceland – Iceland
Conservation and Environment Between the Glaciers – Iceland
Nature and Heritage in the Reykjavík Area – Iceland
Videy Island, a Quiet Haven in Icelandic Capital – Iceland
Orphanage Volunteering/English Teaching – Ukraine

Africa
Teach, Empower and Impact – Ghana (16)
Marine Conservation Expedition – Madagascar
Customized Group Service Project in Mali – (15)
Marine Rescue of Penguins and other Seabirds – South Africa (17)
Abused Animal and Veterinary Assist Project – South Africa (17)
Great White Shark Conservation – South Africa (17)
Rural Community Pre-school Volunteering – South Africa (16)
Life Skills Volunteering – South Africa (16)
Bicycle Volunteer Project – South Africa (16)
Wildlife Volunteer Experience – South Africa (16)
Dolphin Volunteer Experience – South Africa (16)
Southern Hospitality: In Style – South Africa (16)

Oceania
Marine Conservation & Learn to Dive – Fiji (17)

Family Opportunities (Under 15 possible with an adult)

South America
Waterfalls and Wetland – Brazil (tour/volunteer combo)
Natural Natal – Brazil (tour/volunteer combo)
Teach, Learn-Organic Farming & Sustainable Living – Bolivia
Wild Patagonia - Future Patagonia National Park – Chile
   (adventure/volunteer combo)
Colors of Colombia – Columbia (tour/volunteer combo)
Garden, Reforestation and Environmental Education – Ecuador
Community Ecotourism and Conservation – Ecuador
Community Under-Fives Nursery – Ecuador
Customized Group Service Project in Ecuador – Ecuador
Incawasi – Peru
Incas & Amazons – Peru
Youth Care, Community and Conservation – Venezuela

North America
Wildlife Rescue Center Work – Costa Rica
Leatherback Turtle Conservation – Costa Rica
Sea Turtle Conservation – Costa Rica
Bambu Indigenous Reserve – Costa Rica
Camaronal Sea Turtle Rescue – Costa Rica
Wildlife Rescue Center – Costa Rica

Maasai Experience & Mt. Kilimanjaro – Tanzania
Orphan Care & Child-Headed Household Outreach – Uganda
Sustainable Agriculture for Rural Farmers – Uganda
Promo Video & Kids' Music/Dance Video Production – Uganda
Bula Children's Home – Uganda

Oceania
Quintessential Queensland: In Style – Australia (tour combo)
Fiji Explorer – Fiji (tour combo)
Taste of Fiji: In Style – Fiji (tour combo)
Southern Encounter – New Zealand (tour combo)
Natural New Zealand: In Style – New Zealand (tour combo)
Habitat Global Village Trip – Papua New Guinea (14+)
Family Volunteers: Turtles & Community Development – Vanuatu

Just for Teens, Tweens or Youth Groups!

(Some programs may be college accredited)

South America
Sustainable Agriculture & Community Projects – Brazil
VISIONS Ecuador & Galapagos for Teens or Groups – Ecuador
Work at the Maquipucuna Ecological Reserve for Teens – Ecuador
Service Work and Andean Discovery – Peru
Community Development Projects in Peru – Peru

North America
VISIONS Island Passages – British Virgin Islands (age 11-13)
VISIONS British Virgin Islands– British Virgin Islands
VISIONS Language Immersion Costa Rica – Costa Rica
Sea Turtle Conservation for Teens – Costa Rica
VISIONS Service Dominica – Dominica
Community Development – Dominica
VISIONS Dominican Republic – Dominican Republic
VISIONS French Language Immersion for Teens – Guadeloupe
Teen Project: Recreational Work at Oaxacan Orphanage – Mexico
Caribbean Marine Conservation – Netherlands Antilles
VISIONS Nicaragua for Teens – Nicaragua
Teen Recreational Work at an Orphanage in Ometepe – Nicaragua
VISIONS Alaska – United States
VISIONS Mississippi for Teens – United States
VISIONS Northern Passages for 11 to 13 year old – United States (MT)
VISIONS Service for Teens in Montana – United States (MT)

Asia
VISIONS Vietnam – Vietnam

Africa
African Wildlife Conservation for Teens – South Africa

Traditional Tours with Volunteerism & Service Adventures

South America
Waterfalls and Wetland – Brazil
Natural Natal – Brazil
Wild Patagonia – Future Patagonia National Park – Chile
Colors of Colombia – Columbia
VISIONS Ecuador & Galapagos for Teens or Groups – Ecuador
Service Work and Andean Discovery – Peru
Incas & Amazons – Peru

North America
VISIONS Language Immersion Costa Rica – Costa Rica (teens)
Solidarity Brigades - Cuba
VISIONS Service Dominica – Dominica (teens)
Mayan Stove Project – Guatemala

Asia
Animal Rescue and Care Tour Program with Yoga – India
Sunderbans Smiles– India
Himalayan Animal Welfare: Dogs of Dharamsala – India
Taste of India – India (tour combo)
Ultimate India: In Style – India
Bali Bound – Indonesia
Community Development and Everest Trek – Nepal
English Education Service-Learning Program – Thailand
Integrated Buddhist, Teaching English, & Orphanage Op – Thailand
Buddhist Immersion-EFL Service-Learning Program – Thailand
Village Vitality– Thailand
Tantalizing Thailand – Thailand
Thai Travels – Thailand
Taste of Thailand: In Style – Thailand
Northern Cycling – Vietnam
Hanoi & Hilltribes – Vietnam
Vietnamese Venture: Friendship Village – Vietnam

Europe
Service-Learning Experience on the French Mediterranean – France
Animal Welfare: Ending the Tragedy for Greek Dogs – Greece
Zakynthos Island Sea Turtle Conservation – Greece

Africa
Safari Explorer – Kenya (tour combo)
Captivating Kenya – Kenya (tour combo)
Taste of Morocco – Morocco
Zero to Hero Sports Adventure & Volunteering – South Africa
Southern Hospitality: In Style – South Africa
Maasai Experience & Mt. Kilimanjaro – Tanzania

Oceania

Quintessential Queensland: In Style – Australia
Fiji Explorer – Fiji
Taste of Fiji: In Style – Fiji
Natural New Zealand: In Style – New Zealand
Southern Encounter – New Zealand

Uncategorized Skills

North America
Health Clinics and Education in Rural Villages – Mexico (pilots)
Asia
Przewalski Wild Horse Repatriation – Mongolia (equestrians: experienced rider/campers to follow herd)
Transporting Instruction and Environmental Camp – Vietnam
Europe
Transnatura Mountain Bike Stage – Greece (events help & coordinators)
Faia Brava Woodlands Fire Surveillance & Conservation – Portugal (fire surveillance)
Africa
Business Development: Design and Merchandising – Ghana (apparel design & merchandising)
Health Care Volunteering in Northern Madagascar – Madagascar (technology, engineering)
Primate Sanctuary Build, Garden, Cook & Video – South Africa (cook)

✦ About the Author ✦

A columnist and author of eight books, Zoologist Nola Lee Kelsey is an animal addict, a serial volunteer and disturbingly obsessed with traveling the world. As a bonus, she becomes utterly nauseated by the notion of being a time-clock-punching employee. This delightful combination of personality quirks left her two options in life. She could be unemployed and broke, or be a writer and broke. Kelsey opted for the latter.

With few resources to travel on at the moment, Kelsey has channeled her infrequent flyer frustrations into what she hopes is a worthy outlet. From her home in Chiang Mai, Thailand, she has cultivated the fine art of compiling massive quantities of data and beating it mercilessly into book form, bringing her personal obsessions to the travelers of the world. Her books and articles on volunteer travel are the progeny of this singular focus.

It is Kelsey's sincerest hope to inspire other travelers to discover the joy of volunteering as an intelligent option for seeing the world. She believes travel must have a purpose in order to be its most enjoyable. In addition, one of her biggest thrills in her work now comes from providing the opportunity for small NGOs/non-profits around the globe to showcase their volunteer needs alongside the larger programs. Only in this way can she truly help to connect the right traveler to the right volunteer opportunity, being, in some small way, of service to them both.

Tenacity has had its rewards. All this interviewing and researching, along with the collecting, molding and refining data – over and over (and over) again – has resulted in making Nola Lee Kelsey a leading expert on the diverse world of volunteer programs - the who, what, when, where and why.

Her current titles: *700 Places to Volunteer Before You Die: A Travelers Guide, The V-List* eBook, *The Voluntary Traveler*, and now *The Animal Addict's Guide to Global Volunteer Travel* will be joined on bookshelves by another volunteer travel guide by the end of 2011.

What will the new book's focus be on?

✦ ✦ ✦

You are invited to connect with Nola here:

Author's Website: www.NolaKelsey.com (Includes forms to submit project information and reviews from travelers)

VolunTourist Column: www.voluntourism.org/newsletter.html

Facebook: www.facebook.com/#!/nolaleekelsey

The Voluntary Traveler Facebook Page: Connect with other volunteer travelers, find links to projects and articles, exchange ideas, ask questions, add photo...

www.facebook.com/#!/pages/The-Voluntary-Traveler/151304684939133

LinkedIn: www.linkedin.com/pub/nola-lee-kelsey/32/599/663

Twitter: @Nola_Lee_Kelsey

✦ ✦ ✦

By exchanging information travelers will work together to shape future editions of this book, bringing about improved and even more diverse project listings. Furthermore, networking creates a united voice. Through collaboration we have the power to tell the industry what we like and what needs improved. We have the power to learn, to educate, to exchange ideas and to encourage others along the road best traveled.